Second Printing
Copyright 2015 by Ganna Walska Lotusland

Published by Ganna Walska Lotusland
695 Ashley Road
Santa Barbara, CA 93108
www.lotusland.org

All rights reserved. No part of this book may be reproduced in any form without permission of the publisher.

ISBN 978-0-9645213-0-8
Printed in the United States

ACKNOWLEDGMENTS

We would like to thank and acknowledge a number of people who have worked very hard and dedicated their time to help produce the second edition of Ganna Walska's autobiography. These people provided assistance in research, editing, proofreading and fact checking: Sierra Butler, Bob Craig, Anne Dewey, Virginia Hayes, Kathy Hulick, Laurie Marx, Gwen Stauffer, Hania P. Tallmadge, Rose Thomas and Georgina Torez.

INTRODUCTION

Always Room At The Top is typically, but erroneously, known as Madame Ganna Walska's autobiography. Rather, in this book an earnest Ganna Walska recalls fragments of her life experiences that were deeply significant to her, without concern for chronology. She explains her thoughts and feelings about her passage through life to share the lessons she learned, revealing an incredible vulnerability that she describes as the ultra-sensitiveness of her Slavic nature.

So sincere and focused is her purpose in imparting her insights that she dedicates the book to anyone reading her words that they might find in those lines an inspiration for their own life's journey, and never give up.

Ganna Walska begins her story with a quote by Voltaire, "My life is a struggle." While her misery is a recurring theme, her story is truly the paradoxical mix of joy and suffering, optimism in the face of fear, scarcity in abundance, and paralyzing doubts while doggedly pursuing ambition.

For this second edition of *Always Room at The Top*, the text has not been edited but has been left in her exact words as first written. She eschewed the services of a literary collaborator in order to ensure authenticity. This book was, and still is, her story to tell and, in her words, only those whose souls are ready will be able to identify with it.

Ganna Walska succeeded in many selfless achievements in her lifetime that she briefly mentions with little explanation, or never mentions at all. Among those, she was the life-long benefactress of many Russian aristocrats who were exiled after the 1917 revolution. She was a facilitator of social diplomacy among European statesmen. She was a member of the League of Women Voters, testifying before American congressmen for a woman's right to own a property separate from her husband. She volunteered with the International Red Cross during World War II to assist refugees fleeing the Nazi invasion of her native Poland.

Perhaps none of these accomplishments could match her overwhelming devotion to her most intimate and personal expression of herself through her musical work. While the beautiful art of music brought her great pleasure, she describes her arduous practice of her art as constant torture. Her thorough study of operatic singing completely consumed her every day. So much so that she sought out a multitude of vocal and spiritual teachers over the years to help improve her ability, even dabbling in the occult for assistance. This pursuit of musical perfection eventually transformed into a simultaneous desire to acquire spiritual enlightenment. She became a seeker.

Born a Catholic, Ganna Walska claimed to be a Christian "in the real interpretation of the word," but admitted that she did not follow any specific religion, having adopted a spiritual philosophy she defines in the book as a mosaic of all philosophies. In addition to studying eastern and western philosophies, she experimented with palmistry, telepathy, hypnotism, séance, numerology, astrology and the Ouija board. She studied with seers, mediums and populist prophets, only to be disillusioned by their lack of authenticity and poorly disguised failure to transcend the material world.

Ultimately, Ganna Walska determined that if she desired to be distinguished, it was for something achieved through her own effort. Despite her constant labor and sufficient musical successes, many music critics maligned her efforts. Even while some praised her talents, the ruthless paparazzi of her time feasted on the details of her personal life, often fabricating stories that would cast her as a notorious diva.

Indeed, Ganna Walska was a Slavic beauty who debuted in the Russian Czar's court and became a Baroness at the young age of seventeen. She had been married to three famous American men and one prominent Englishman by the time she wrote this memoir. In these marriages, Ganna Walska felt a duty to help these men beyond physical being to find a higher vibration in deep, spiritual love. Her reason for marrying each of these men was publicly misconstrued. The popular attention she attracted was surely instigated by her personal tastes and charm. As the self-described "enemy of the average," with "a particular aversion to following the multitude in styles of any kind," Ganna Walska forged her own elegant and avant-garde persona. She was a true original, at risk of being labeled eccentric.

Consolation came from the words of Swift, who wrote, "Criticism is a tax which the public levies on prominent men." Ganna Walska realized that mediocrity escaped attention, and she occasionally found amusement in the more ridiculous accounts by the press. After a time, she was even grateful to all who had hurt her, for she viewed them as instruments in her spiritual welfare, which pushed her to a higher path.

Malgre' Tout - in spite of everything – was the motto she placed on her personal letterhead. Throughout the book, it is clear that Ganna Walska hopes to leave something of lasting value for the world, but she was seemingly vague. Perhaps she meant to leave a legacy through her contributions to the art of music, or perhaps through the messages she conveys in this book.

Even after all of her suffering, Ganna Walska finishes her story with certainty of her own happiness. She has moved to California, a "Babylon" on the west coast, where she is sure she will achieve spiritual attainment at her new home "Tibetland" in Santa Barbara. Little does she know that she is only glimpsing the nascent legacy she will build for the next 43 years, and then leave to the world – her incomparable garden, Lotusland.

Gwen Stauffer
Executive Director
Ganna Walska Lotusland
2015

G.W.'s Favorite Picture

ALWAYS ROOM AT THE TOP

BY
GANNA WALSKA

DEDICATED
TO ALL THOSE
WHO ARE SEEKING THEIR PLACE
IN THE SUN

*For constant dropping of water wears away stones.
By diligence and patience the mouse ate the
cable in two. And little strokes fell great oaks.*

— Benjamin Franklin

My life is a struggle.
— VOLTAIRE

I DID NOT want these memoirs to be written by a literary collaborator who might take the facts of my life and by romanticizing my personality through his interpretation of my character thus obscure the true psychological issue and not conform to reality. For it seems to me that most writers are too interested in reinterpreting a character through their own eyes to grasp exactly the expression of another's soul.

If my reader finds it difficult at times to follow all my experiences, it will be because his soul has not passed through the same labyrinth of thoughts and feelings as mine and therefore he will be unable to identify himself with the phases of life I have lived through.

My one regret is that I did not put down all my experiences at the time they happened so that my reader could share the exact state of my feelings at that moment rather than the reminiscence of a past sensation. Often I remember only vaguely the precise state of my mind in bygone days. The veil of time hinders me from recapturing the exact sensations I experienced years and years ago. However, I am glad that I did put down at least the first episodes of these reminiscences while I was still in what I call the destructive period of my life. For certainly now that I am in a new cycle of living I am a different being, and my reactions towards my past inner life are different. I would not now be able to mirror those thoughts in an absolutely precise way for fear of embellishing them too much by the reflection of my present bright outlook.

I do not remember what actually gave birth to these memoirs. I had few outer experiences and was entirely unaware of my inner existence. In my extreme loneliness I suppose my secretive nature desired a confidant and could think of no other possibility than the friendly white pages of a confessional. But I never even dreamed that one day I should share my deepest thoughts with the world.

During the years that passed the deformed skeleton of my experiences often filled the front pages of newspapers with sensational articles with no regard to my inner feelings. Bitterly I confessed the real side of the story, vaguely thinking that I might one day avenge myself and show how much I was misunderstood. It was pleasant to indulge in the feeling of being a martyr.

As more years passed I outgrew the desire of self-justification. I grew in wisdom and mind. I understood much. And finally I comprehended the extraordinary adventure of my soul. At the same time I saw that I could not keep such a great experience to myself alone. I felt I must share those revelations with those who really seek the truth.

Hence—this book!

Passion is good as an auxiliary, but worthless as a rule.

JULES SIMON

IN MY swiftly moving life I have met people of all classes: distinguished business men and women, humble and obscure individuals, the extremely rich and the painfully poor, artists who have arrived as well as hard-struggling students. My life has touched the lives of people in almost every country on the globe and my intuition has given me insight into many hidden tragedies and hopeless situations. In all these contacts I have never known any person so poorly equipped for the service of that self-sacrifice demanding art of singing as I was when I undertook to become a singer.

In America a girl of sixteen not only knows the names and reputation of every important prima donna but also can give you a fairly accurate story of their private lives even down to the name of their pet dogs, not to mention the number of their marriages, divorces, alimony and alienation of affection suits. At seventeen I was already married and did not even know the meaning of the word O-P-E-R-A.

In those days in Poland young girls were educated very strictly, and severity of morals was de rigueur. Before her marriage, a young girl (*panienka*) was not permitted to go to the opera or the theatre because the plot invariably pivoted on the theme of love. The circus alone was within her reach as the one form of entertainment not at all concerned with love. For this same reason we were not allowed to read newspapers, romances or novels. And the only music and singing I heard was in Church, unless it could be called music when we girls played the piano. For in my country in every family each girl was obliged to study the piano, no matter how slight her inclination toward or intense her hatred of music. As a rule poor piano-playing was a necessary attribute of a well-educated girl! If one played well, one might be suspected of doing something out of the ordinary. The rule was strict conformity.

A typical illustration occurred when a guest once hearing me sing in the garden said to my father: "She has a voice, you ought to make her study!"

"Study?" asked my father. "What for? She sings well…"

* * *

Speaking of my unpreparedness for the extremely difficult profession of a singer, a very important question enters my mind as to who is the greatest artist—the genius or one who acquires his ability through hard work, strong will power, perseverance and unshakable determinations. Different examples support both sides of the controversy. Patti was a supremely endowed *Wunderkind*, a born singer but in spite of the exceptional purity of her voice even her contemporaries reproached her coldness and her artificiality and blamed her limited repertoire. She was rebuked for singing the same operas over and over again. But when she attempted to sing Wagner in London, she did not meet with her usual triumphal success. I am sure that today in these times of terrific speed when people want to hear, see, be deeply touched and expect to find all these things combined in one person, Patti with her gifted voice alone could not have the same phenomenal success she had with our grandfathers.

On the other hand there is the example of Lilli Lehmann whose will power brought perfection to her art of singing. Mother Nature was not very generous to her. Her lack of sensitivity and natural beauty of voice would have handicapped any singer, yet Lehmann achieved a greater artistic perfection than did Patti and did so at a time when the demands on an artist were much greater.

During the first years of his career, the great Caruso was a wretched man. Demonstrations were so hostile against him in Italy every time he sang that he wanted to quit a thousand times. Through heroic perseverance, however, he became the idol of the world.

I believe that was due to the fact that the development of the subconscious through conscientious application is greater than the mere use of consciousness without any added development. Whatever we get through our subconscious cannot be taken away from us. We walk without thinking. We put one foot forward, then the other; and when we lose a foot in an accident, our subconscious does not realize it. Men who lost limbs in the last war experienced pain in those limbs long after the physical flesh had disintegrated. What we store away in the subconscious second by second, hour by hour, we can never lose as long as we live. If there is immortality, it must be in the subconscious which survives death. The quality of the content of the subconscious—therefore of survival—depends upon the kind of life we lead.

Personally I believe that the artist whose attainment is acquired chiefly through work reaches a greater perfection than the so-called natural talent, except when the latter type is driven by a colossal genius such as the force which inspired Beethoven or Leonardo da Vinci and led them—in spite of themselves—to such magnificent creation. They were already the personification of The Subconscious.

* * *

With those preliminary words I would like to tell the event which pushed me toward the career of singing. For had it not been for a romance, Ganna Walska would not have existed today. The name is fictitious anyhow and was born in an emergency. In those days a married woman could not have her name appear in print—she dared not even have her address on her visiting cards—so I was not able to use my husband's name at an occasion when I was to sing for charity. [1] At the eleventh hour I had to think up a

---

1 Virtue which makes much to-do is no longer virtue.
—Father des Grieux

substitute and, like all Poles, I loved to dance, especially to waltz. So suddenly I said: "Waltz, Valse, Walska… !"

* * *

I was not yet twenty. He was only slightly more. He seemed very handsome and wonderfully superior to all others. He looked foreign. To me he personified an American for he was clean-shaven. I mention this because a clean-shaven man was a great attraction to me, accustomed as I was to Polish and Russian men with mustaches and quite often with long beards.

Naturally, to my romantic mind, he possessed all the virtues but as subsequently developed his one handicap turned out to be his wealth. He was, in fact, the second richest man in Russia. If I am not mistaken, the richest people were the Youssoupoffs, the family of Prince Felix who killed the wicked monk Rasputin. Unlike the Youssoupoffs, however, his fortune (another similarity to an American) came from his father, or was it his grandfather?

Gossip went around that he had fallen in love with a French cabaret girl and had bestowed millions of rubles worth of jewels upon her. In Russia millionaires did not marry chorus girls or stenographers or anyone not of their class but made it the custom to give diamonds as large as eggs—a custom far more expensive than the American system of giving a wedding ring to a sweetheart, which could be followed in a few weeks or years by a divorce, the comparatively easy way of retaking your love and regaining your freedom.

But oh horror! The report also ran that one day he saw his mistress kissing his chauffeur. What an indiscretion! From that time on, he lost faith in women and also the faith in his own personality. Unlike other boys of his age, he found no joy in life, despite his exceptional position that provided him with many opportunities. He studied the piano intensively, though never wishing to play when anyone was present.

Such was his state of mind when first he saw me in St. Moritz. Later I met him in Russia. Apparently he was greatly interested in me, or should I say in love—as I so hoped at that time?

His unnatural shyness and abnormal reserve distinguished him from other men around me. I was completely fascinated. Unsophisticated as I was, it was easy for my heart to rule my mind.

He had a vague way of speaking of his feelings. Instead of saying outright that he loved me and asking whether I loved him in return, he would murmur some indefinite phrase, instantly adding: "I know I cannot be loved for myself. I have no more illusions about that, thank God!" Thus he referred to his vast riches and the lesson his latest sentimental affair had taught him.

But when he said those words looking straight into my eyes, the insult of them gave my heart a profound shock. Nevertheless I would not let him see it. I immediately changed the conversation to banalities, and I believe he never realized what a mark those words made on my sensitive soul.

He left that same evening for a three days' trip. Only after his departure, locked in my room did I allow myself to let go. I suffered the unbounded limitless agony that only Slavs are heir to and dawn brought little relief.

When daylight was bright enough I wrote him a letter —a volume that went on page after page! In my girlish romantic head I had only one thought. He had insinuated that he could not be loved except for his money. Very well! Not for the world would I let him know that I was in love with him. Proud and overcome with the fear that he might guess my feelings, I wrote him a thousand lies to confuse him.

My letter told him that he was right to suspect that he would not be loved for his own sake… That without his fortune no one would even look at him… That it was enough to know his *parvenu* background to realize that fundamentally he was a peasant in spite of his higher education… That his father would be allowed in my parents' home only by way of the service entrance… And that his sister had married a count thanks only to her dowry…

Only when I had put the letter in the postbox myself could I breathe freely and at last fall asleep.

On awakening I felt a bit disturbed without understanding the reason for it. Had that happened today I would have known it was a presentiment of what was to follow. The full force of it struck me three days later when he did not return as previously planned. In my panic an impulse prompted me to send a telegram asking him not to read the letter I had sent but instead to bring it back to me unopened. Or was that merely a dream? I cannot be sure…

In those days I was so wrapped up in my hidden romantic life that I could not always distinguish between reality and the fantasy of my exalted imagination. The fact remains—he did not come!

Every girl of deep emotional feeling will know how unbearable my life was for many months after the unfortunate incident of my impulsive cruel letter. As I write now, I find it impossible to recapture all the misery I went through at that time. The kind of misery that is engendered by love is as old as the world and can be read in every story of love.

* * *

When I was sure he would not come back, I left for the Crimea, where the Czar was to spend the summer at his newly rebuilt palace in Yalta. Everybody was to be there on that occasion and my hero had mentioned that he too expected to go there. But after an anguished week of waiting in vain, I abandoned that hope too and went to St. Petersburg where he lived.

Upon my arrival in the capital, I learned that he had been given the honorary appointment of attaché to the chairman of the Marynski Imperial Opera House. I went to the Opera every night expecting to meet him there. Deep in my heart, I felt that if only he were to see me once again he would resist no more and would fall at my feet...

During the first three weeks I did not even get a glimpse of him. Ah, those three weeks! I experienced genuine torture sitting there for hours, night after night, unable to appreciate, let alone understand, the operas. I could get through the first act and the first intermission fairly well —the hope of seeing him would buoy me up. During the next act, fear and then agony would overtake me. Anyone without a real background of music who is forced to sit through a tediously long opera will know how I felt.

At the end of the second act my hope of seeing him would vanish. At the same time my eyelids would grow heavier and heavier, almost as heavy as my enormous *à la Russe* diamond earrings. It took a superhuman effort not to fall asleep. However I would stay on to the end, hope reviving slightly that as I was leaving the theatre I might see him waiting outside for his carriage.

I could not even find distraction in watching the audience, for in those glorious days of St. Petersburg it was not the thing to go to the opera. It was fashionable only to attend the Ballet on Sunday nights, when the Czar came with his magnificent court and all the military men were in gala uniform. That was truly the most spectacular sight I ever saw.

* * *

At last one night my long watch ended. I met him at the entrance door. He bowed to me politely but extremely coldly. That was all. I returned the bow in such a way as to convey that I hardly remembered who he might be. But— but my heart—oh my heart! How fast it beat, and how my legs trembled as they carried me to my seat. I really do not know how I managed it.

I only remembered that he had spoken English to an

elderly lady. The next day I took my first lesson in English.

A few days later, I saw him for the second time when unexpectedly in the middle of an act he came in and sat two seats beyond me. However he disappeared before the intermission. I do not know why. Maybe he saw me. Maybe, as an official of the house, he did not want to be there when the lights came on.

As I was going home that night, what seemed like a brilliant idea illuminated my wretchedness. *I would sing* on the stage of the same house to which he had been appointed attaché. Surely such proximity would conquer him —he would no longer be able to resist me!

I must confess that it was rather humiliating for a person with an old-fashioned upbringing such as mine to contemplate going on the stage. In those days there was very little distinction made between a cabaret singer and an Imperial Opera prima donna—it was just as wicked to be on any stage. (To this day even here in New York the husband of my best friend often says to me: "How can such a nice girl as yourself sing?") And the only real career for Polish women at that time was marriage and, if possible, a marriage that would bring wealthier and higher social standing. A marriage into a lower social class than one's own family or circle was definitely a *mésalliance*.

Nothing existed however but my hero, and I was willing and glad to sacrifice my pride to him. Such a trifling idea as that it might not be so easy to get into the Imperial Opera never entered my mind. The only obstacle in the way was to overcome my aversion to going on the stage. It did occur to me that perhaps I ought to go to a teacher but I had no conception of the work that would have to precede my going on with a professional career. I soon learned that the baritone Tartakoff, stage director of the Marynski Opera, was giving lessons. To study with Tartakoff would enable me to be near someone who saw Him and had the same interests as His. I jumped at the opportunity and began the lessons.

I must admit that the lessons were very short ones. It seemed that I always arrived so late it was almost time for Tartakoff's next pupil. Like all those who are extremely busy doing nothing, I could not get there on time. Yes, in Russia those days it was terribly hard to be on time. Nobody ever was. And to tell the truth I really did not feel that I needed to take those singing lessons but I could not frankly say to my teacher: "Here are ten rubles, do not trouble yourself or bother me about the singing, just tell me if you saw Him today… What did He say… With what prima donna did He speak?"

So from time to time for a few dollars I was able to get that much desired news. It was never pleasant, however, as my teacher hated my idol and did not hide his feelings. I do not know whether it was envy of money's power or just the politics behind the scenes, but certainly they did not get along.

A few months later I learned that the current fashion in music circles was to study singing in Paris with my illustrious compatriot, Jean de Reszke. Desiring to impress my hero to the utmost, I left for Paris immediately and upon arriving went straight to de Reszke's studio and forthwith began my lessons. I took two lessons a week. Yes, two half-hour periods weekly seemed sufficient to me then.

But a few months later the great war was upon Europe. I took counsel with friends. They advised me to visit America for a few months in the belief that in the meantime the war would be over. It was not an uncommon belief at the beginning of the European conflict that three months at the maximum would mark the end.

* * *

It amuses me now to reflect on the early experiences of my first singing lessons. At that time I took them with the utmost casual lightness, whereas now that I know there is no royal road to a song I work harder than most other people around me and am lucky to be able to stand up under it. All my teachers agree that I am a phenomenon of will power, health and determination. For years now I have not stopped for Christmas, Easter or Sundays, nor have I even taken a summer holiday. I begin my day at eight o'clock in the morning and often work until eleven at night, and I keep that schedule the whole year round. My friends of today would hardly believe that the girl who took ten minute lessons in St. Petersburg merely as a pretext to speak about the man who occupied all her thoughts is the same hard-working woman I now am. Even to me it seems odd that the present Ganna Walska could be that same person. Work, especially the beneficial atmosphere of work, has chased from my romantic head those fanciful sentiments about a certain clean-shaven young man. Then too I saw so many of them in America.

* * *

I have told you the story of my youthful exaltation to point out how destiny shapes our lives. Sentimental people who choose operas for their librettos, or fans who only go to movies that have a love interest will doubtless find in my tale all the elements of the book of an opera or a movie scenario with plenty of material left over for good measure. For the same destiny that guided me so curiously also overtook the man who involuntarily set me on the hardest of all roads.

Czarism fell. The Russian revolution was born. My hero was chosen—only God knows why—as a member of the cabinet in the Kerensky government. I still cannot understand why they picked such a rich dilettante of a youngster for such a responsible position. Probably I never will know, and I cannot say that it interests me particularly any more as I am not writing a *curriculum vitae* of Kerensky's regime. However I would like to know and have tried in vain to ascertain the reason which made him take a position that subsequently ruined him financially and even jeopardized his life. For when the Bolshevist party came into power, they put my hero with his fellow statesmen in prison where he remained under the dreadful daily threat of being shot at dawn.

One day in New York I opened my morning paper only to be confronted with a dispatch which reported that He had been shot while trying to escape over the border into Finland. Oddly enough the next day's papers announced the arrival and displayed the photograph of Mr. Konovaloff who had been Secretary of State, if I am not mistaken, in the same Ministry of which my young man was a member. Immediately I telephoned the Plaza Hotel to ask Mr. Konovaloff if it were true that his colleague had been shot. In answer came a hearty laugh and the assurance that it was not true, that my friend was safe and living in Stockholm.

The next information I had was when a Russian general informed me that He was married to a pretty French woman and was then living in Paris. When I went to Paris in 1920, an American friend asked me to take part in arranging a charity concert. The chairwoman of the Russian branch of the charity subsequently came to thank me for my willingness to participate in that worthy cause. The lady, as I later learned, was his already divorced wife. Twice I saw him in the street but only at a distance as I was passing in a car.

Two years later, the celebrated tenor Dimitri Smirnoff informed me that my hero had begged him to ask permission to see me. Unfortunately I granted it. I say unfortunately for the reader's sake as much as for my own because there are many who would think it more romantic if I had not met him again. However, wishing to find out what he was really like, how much of him was real and how much was the work of my fantasy, I decided to see him. Naturally, I was anxious to know if he was worthy of all the thoughts and feelings I had expended on him all those years.

He was extremely reserved at our first luncheon. He gave the impression that his secretive character would not let him show his real nature. I tried to dismiss the feeling that perhaps he was not exactly a great man as he seemed to have nothing to say. Still Molière said: "A fool who says not a word and a learned man who remains silent are not distinguishable one from the other."

Perhaps he was just a mixture of snobbishness, vanity and pride—the pride of a small soul without the meekness which goes with goodness. Perhaps he had a certain amount of earthly qualities and defects. Or perhaps his apparent arrogance was only a ruse to hide his timidity. So ran my thoughts…

I do not want to abuse him or humiliate myself by supposing as I did at first—I regret to say—that he insisted on renewing our acquaintance because our financial situation was then reversed. I was rich—he was poor! But he insisted so much that we forget the past and become good friends that I must confess I suspected him. Declining the honor, I explained that friendship is not as easily given as a youthful heart since friendship is a voluntary gift, whereas love is forced on us by some mysterious power. Friendship gives assurance of an unselfish feeling. Love comes and goes of its own accord, like a fever. Nothing can stop it, nothing can prolong it either, for love positively refuses to obey the reason or its command. Perhaps this bit of French verse says it more clearly:

> "L'amour vient sans qu'on le veuille Comme
> à l'arbre vient la feuille,
> Et personne n'y peut rien,
> L'amour part comme il vient."

I explained to the involuntary creator of my operatic ambition that since I really did not know him I could not give him my friendship as easily I had given my juvenile love, because I had now begun to realize the value of that rare gift which—together with maternal love—is the only lasting and essentially good affection to my way of thinking.

His outward arrogance, which was so characteristic of him in earlier days and which I had hoped would be changed with the hard experiences of the intervening years, evidently was stronger than the bonds of prison or moral and physical miseries. For upon my refusal to accept his friendship at once, he never tried to see me again.

Were I ever to write scenarios, I would use the material of this story, especially the meeting in Paris, only I would make my hero pass *à son tour* through all the misery I suffered because of him. In a very effective final scene I would tell him that, now that I had money, it was I who could not trust him, as my mind would have been poisoned by the thought that he loved me not for myself but only for my riches. Accustomed to luxury he would not be able to go without them, not being rich enough in himself…

To reveal my intimate thoughts, I must confess that at the time I often entertained the romantic idea—later dismissed by my intelligence—that his pride had forced his heart to stay away from me so that I could not suspect him of coveting my fortune. Sometimes I was ashamed of those fancies so typical of a youthful provincial *Fräulein* but my thoughts were so used to turning toward him that the habit worked automatically. Yet it was pleasant for me to indulge in momentary illusions from time to time. The actual facts were probably less romantic and much more *terre-à-terre*…

Science has not yet solved the mystery of our sleeping dreams. There are those who even believe that our real life exists in a sleeping state. The fact is that in my case I was utterly absorbed with thoughts of my Russian for so long that even now as I write about him I find that I dream of him many, many nights a month…

At this point I would like to make a parallel between the Russian and American, as they are quite similar in many respects. Both have bigness of soul, largeness of spirit, childish naïveté and limitless confidence. Both are idealists, both are ready for any sacrifice. Yet there is one tremendous difference between them—Americans love to create, Russians must destroy. If misfortune overtakes a Russian, he will resort to heavy drinking while philosophizing over the glass from which he drinks... About the misery of the workers who made the glass... About their extreme hardships, etcetera... He will contemplate not only his own sorrow but that of the entire world and commit suicide, preferably to the sounds of sad gypsy music.

The American in parallel conditions of misfortune would forget his own and the world's misery in incessant hard work, even if it were unsuccessful. I believe that is why Russia has never produced such a great self-made man as Andrew Carnegie or Henry Ford.

"The mystery of cause is impenetrable."

Upon my arrival in New York I sang at the Century, which was then a French theatre owing its existence to the generosity of Mr. Otto H. Kahn. One day when I was hoarse, I told Mr. Kahn, who was present during a rehearsal, about the troubles I had had with my throat. Mr. Kahn advised me to see Dr. Joseph Fraenkel, whom he considered the only man able to help any difficult, hopeless or helpless case.

"He is not an ordinary practitioner. He is an artist, a poet, a great man, a genius!" Mr. Kahn added.

Impressed by such a recommendation, I immediately telephoned Dr. Fraenkel's office but since it was summer I was told the doctor was out of the city until the following month. I was disappointed and subsequently forgot all about it.

A month or two later when badly in need of help, someone suggested that I go see a certain well-known psychoanalyst. The name of Professor Freud, father of psychoanalysis, was then unfamiliar to me, as were very many other things indeed! For an hour I searched up and down West 56th Street but could not find the office of that doctor whose name now had slipped my memory.

Suddenly I remembered that Dr. Fraenkel should be back by that time from his vacation. I immediately went to East 66th Street. Yes, the doctor had just returned. His secretary escorted me up a mysterious spiral staircase, and I found myself in a beautiful if dark library full of bookcases with the effigies of wise thinkers everywhere I set my eyes.

A long-haired, extremely artistic-looking man, rather small in stature–as great men often are–rose from the desk. I tried to recall which of the famous musicians he resembled facially–or was it Lincoln? Taking off his enormous tortoise-shell glasses the "Genius" looked at me very strangely indeed and after a moment's embarrassing silence indicated a chair, saying in a deep voice: "What can I do for you my child?"

I started to explain my troubles but was interrupted by his saying that he was not curious to hear about them.

"You need help, my dear child but I am not interested in the whole *curriculum vitae* of your throat!"

"But how can you help me if you do not know all the circumstances?" I asked.

"Do you think I am a fool?" He said. "Do you think I have studied for fifty years to be laughed at now by an ignorant young lady like yourself?"

Without further ado he started to prescribe something. But that was too much for me.

"What" I shouted. "Without even seeing my throat?"

"Listen to me young lady, " he replied. "I am afraid you will go to some other doctor who through an operation might ruin your health forever.[2] Well, I pity you… I will look at your throat just to please you but I know what is the matter with you without seeing your throat. I knew the moment you came into the room!"

I began to be a little uneasy. I thought him rather queer. I was just wondering how to escape when I saw him open one of the drawers of his desk and take out a large picture of a woman, which he showed to me in perfect silence. Much surprised at such strange behavior, I glanced at the portrait of a handsome woman, but immediately and without a word he took it from my hands rather roughly, put it back in its place, and proceeded to continue writing the prescription.

Then he asked me my name. When I had told him, twice he repeated "Walska! Walska?" as though trying to remember something, which surprised me as I was totally unknown in those days. Again he opened a desk drawer

---

2 Later I learned that Dr. Fraenkel considered all operations criminal, not believing in surgery on the grounds that if Nature gave us certain organs it was not for the purpose of having them taken away.

and looked through a lot of old papers. Finally he found a yellow sheet, read it, and asked me if I knew Jim McVicker. Upon my indifferent and negative answer, he said: "Oh yes, you do. See this!"

With the angry irritation of one who reproaches a child for not telling the truth, he put the yellow paper before my bewildered eyes. There I saw written by some trembling hand the following words: "Don't you have anything to do with that Walska woman!"

On the other side of the paper a date had been noted in the doctor's handwriting. I was too flabbergasted to speak, and anyhow I felt quite panicky.

"Where were you January 3rd, 1915?" he said suddenly.

I told him I was coming for my first visit to America on the "Arabic," which later was torpedoed and sunk by a submarine.

Dr. Fraenkel took back the yellow paper and put it away without any further explanation. Much later he told me that Miss Olive Whiting, social secretary to Mrs. W. K. Vanderbilt's niece, whose life had been saved by Dr. Fraenkel, was subject to mediumistic influences and had written the message with Mr. McVicker pressing her hand as a bit of after-dinner entertainment. It seemed that Mr. McVicker had himself been very much surprised at seeing my name and had explained that it was uncanny, because "Walska" was the name of a Russian girl (as he then erroneously thought I was) whom he had seen in Paris and with whom he had unsuccessfully tried to dance. He further explained that he had never spoken to her beyond asking for a dance and had only received a negative shake of the head in response.

I did not learn his name until much later, but that afternoon Dr. Fraenkel was convinced that I was Jim McVicker's sweetheart and had come to the United States because of him. He reasoned that I must have been very close to him if Miss Whiting had caught my vibration. Now I see that she sensed—what neither Mr. McVicker nor Dr. Fraenkel knew then—that I would spend a few years of my life in the same library where the paper had been written. For indeed ten days later that house was my home! I had the privilege of marrying that wonderful man, who changed me from an undisciplined, rich Slavic nature into a person morally and intellectually worthy of being the companion of such an exceptionally-minded individual as was Dr. Fraenkel.

The picture the Doctor had shown me was that of Frau Gustav Mahler, widow of the famous Viennese composer who had directed the destiny of the New York Philharmonic Orchestra for so many years. After Gustav Mahler's death, Frau Mahler had accepted Dr. Fraenkel's proposal of marriage, but taking advantage of a woman's privilege had later changed her mind and married a Viennese architect.

By the end of the war, Frau Mahler had realized her mistake and had written to her former beloved—during the war communications between Austria and the United States were interrupted—but by the time her letters began to arrive at Dr. Fraenkel's house, he had been dead for several months.

Years later, while in Venice at the International Music Congress, a lady came to my box and said simply: "I am Alma Mahler!" (She was then Franz Werfel's wife.) We became friends. Now she calls me her sister. There was never any rivalry between us, but perhaps she never realized to what degree her passage in the Doctor's life was a tragedy to me, for unfortunately I realized only too late the reason for the trembling of the Doctor's hands when he first shook mine and his rather sudden proposal of marriage the next time I saw him—an act not easily comprehensible coming from a serious-minded European thinker of his stature. The explanation was simple, if cruel to me—I looked very much like Frau Mahler, and the resemblance made him believe he loved me. I realized that fact, alas, too late—when we were united…

*He will not go far who knows
beforehand where he wants to go.*
— NAPOLEON

IF I DO not succeed in doing something worthwhile during my stay on this earth at least I will have nothing with which to reproach myself, for I have not sat comfortably in an armchair with folded hands waiting for a roasted pigeon to fall directly into my mouth, as our Polish proverb says.

Whatever I have got I have got by hard work, unshakable tenacity and a very strong will. My effort may be considered still greater if I add that for each step I have taken I have paid with great effort—and often paid more than it was worth. Still I always have taken the initiative to get what I want without thought of sparing myself any discomfort, as for instance I could have done in the case of my meeting Harold McCormick.

* * *

The Chicago Opera Company came to the Lexington Theatre in New York as usual for its winter season. Sitting in my regular front row seat on opening night, I remarked that a gentleman in one of the proscenium boxes looked at me rather persistently during the whole performance.

The following day at the Tetrazzini Concert I heard Mrs. Howard Spaulding of Chicago—while talking about people at the previous night's performance—casually mention the name of Harold McCormick, thanks to whose generosity, she was saying, the Chicago Opera Company owed its existence and was enabled to visit New York City each winter. I also gathered from her conversation that Mr. McCormick had been seated in the proscenium box. From her description I thought I recognized in him the man who had looked at me so frequently the night before.

* * *

I desired to sing with the Chicago Opera Company as Campanini, who was then its director, had heard me sing in a studio audition and had told me that I was not only a perfect type of Fedora, the Slavic heroine of Giordano's opera, but also an ideal Thais. He had further said that when I was vocally prepared I should let him know…

* * *

One day I saw in the New York papers that Mr. Harold McCormick had arrived from Chicago and was stopping at the Plaza Hotel. I recalled that opening night of the Chicago Opera. Immediately I decided to telephone him.

"Hello," I said. "Madame Walska speaking. You do not know me. My name does not mean anything to you. I would like to speak to you…"

"I am sorry," came the answer. "Impossible! I am going back to Chicago today on the Twentieth Century. I already have an appointment at twelve and after that a quick lunch with my son and I'll have enough time to catch my train."

"Please, Mr. McCormick," I said, "just say you do not want to see me, for I simply refuse to believe that one cannot find five minutes when one really wants to."

"Oh, no!" he said. "I really mean I have no time. It is not merely an excuse. Could you write me?"

"I certainly could write," I replied, "but I will not. What is the use? If you cannot give me five minutes of your time it would really be useless to bother you. From a man who cannot find five minutes I can expect nothing…"

"Wait a moment," came the voice and then a moment's silence. "Could you be at the Plaza at twelve, exactly at twelve o'clock and only for five minutes?"

"Certainly! I will be there at twelve and only for five minutes. Thanks! Au revoir!"

* * *

At twelve precisely I announced myself.

"Which Mr. McCormick, junior or senior?" said the clerk.

After a moment of hesitation I said: "Senior."

A bit of telephoning ensued after which I was told that Mr. McCormick would be right down and was shown to an armchair in a corner of the sitting room.

A few seconds later Mr. McCormick came in. To my amazement he was not the man who had stared at me at the Lexington Opera House. However this man looked at me with such wonderful boyish blue eyes… We shook hands and sat down. In a very few words I told him of my desire to get an engagement with the Chicago Opera Company and the whole story of my meeting with Campanini. Now that I was prepared to sing "Zaza" I asked Mr. McCormick if he would let Maestro Campanini know about it, as a word from the opera's angel would surely have more value than any vague encouraging promises to a débutante…

"Do you think you can do it?" he asked and as he spoke his wonderful eyes—the reflection of his beautiful soul—looked straight into mine.

"Yes, I think so."

He promised to speak to the director…

One o'clock… It was I who reminded him about his train…

* * *

Several weeks passed. One day Mr. McCormick asked permission to call. In those days in America the average person thought that all pretty young foreign girls were French. And a French woman, thanks to a few unhappy examples and the legendary reputation of being *femme legère*, was almost invariably considered an adventuress. Mr. McCormick evidently was not so sure where he was going for he brought with him as a chaperon his son Fowler.

Instead of the proverbial French boudoir perfumed with

intoxicating incense, instead of the dazzling flowers and laces indispensable to the occasion, he was surprised to find himself in an extremely severe-looking library, facing Goethe to the East and Dante to the North… A great many books which were obviously not mere wall decoration… And the bust of Abraham Lincoln eyeing him rather reproachfully… In short, the atmosphere was not exactly what he had expected… Obviously he had troubled his son uselessly.

His embarrassment was still greater when I came in and introduced Dr. Fraenkel, whose reputation had also reached the West—in fact it turned out that the Doctor was Mr. McCormick's cousin's physician. His surprise was complete on discovering that Madame Walska was Mrs. Dr. Joseph Fraenkel.

However the unstaged background of the situation made a fine impression on Mr. McCormick, for thereafter he took the risk of coming to see us unescorted. We became friends and his sweet letters and telegrams were helpful during the great and fatal illness of Dr. Fraenkel.

Little did I think that this charming man, then married to John D. Rockefeller's daughter, would later play such a big part in my life!

The law of the mind does not differ from the law of the body, which can only maintain itself through continual nourishment.

— VAUVENARGUES

FIRST UNCONSCIOUSLY, then with utter awareness, my soul —more and more like that of Faust—has passed through its sinister Walpurgis Night and experienced not only the long night of my own tortured mind but also its share of the restless and diseased spirit of our century.

In America—especially since the First World War—more and more people have been examining the metaphysical world with utmost intensity, conscious of the fact that their forefathers' traditional inheritance has not sufficiently solved many of their soul's demands.

Just as the physically sick look for help from medical help, Carlsbad waters or new diet, so the spiritually ill, morally restless and disappointed in heart, seek in the occult sphere for some illumination of the until now unanswered question their lucid intelligence demanded.

Nor did I escape this search into the realm of mysticism, for I, too, sought for the explanation of my existence from outside sources.

* * *

My first experience was at a spiritualist seance conducted by the well known John Slater in the old Waldorf-Astoria.

My heart beat as rapidly as does that of a trapped wild animal. Always timid, I trembled throughout the seance lest the medium announce my thoughts to the audience of several thousand people, but I promised myself that if the diviner were good, I would see him alone—so anxious was I to learn my future. As Mr. Slater went on making what seemed to be many most successful demonstrations I became simply terrified that my turn might come.

The modern Nostradamus said to a round-faced man: "You told your wife on the way here 'If Slater tells me that I will sell my Bronx house and the prophecy materializes I shall believe in spiritualism.' Is that correct?" The owner of the house in the Bronx was assured he would sell the house and sell it to advantage.

Later Mr. Slater told the girl sitting next to me: "Before leaving your house you changed your gown twice and finally you decided to put on this pink one. Is that right?" My pretty neighbor admitted that the oracle was not mistaken.

The audience grew more and more excited, while my terror increased at every new demonstration until it reached the proportion of panic. Over the meeting hovered the fear that the police would stop the seance as they had already done in other cities. The atmosphere grew more and more tense as this fear increased. The medium in a thunderous voice challenged the authorities to come and stop his speaking God's truth. To my inexperienced mind Mr. Slater was simply a martyr who braved those in authority. In my candid ignorance I saw him as a Christian torn and devoured by Nero's lions.

* * *

I spent the next few months collecting the addresses of all mediums in and around New York. That was not easy, as the law forbids fortunetelling for money and those who practiced had to be careful not to be caught at it.

Naïvely I thought that a knowledge of tomorrow would help meet the demands of life today. Like an ostrich hiding its head in the sand, I tried to avoid life's responsibilities. It never occurred to me that I was wasting my time, energy and moral forces—not always harmlessly, either—on castles in the air.

Whenever I think of that period, I remember the story of the man with the unclean face who complained unceasingly that he could find no cure for his plight, in spite of the fact that he had spent a fortune on creams, lotions, doctors and all to no avail. One day a friend asked him if he had ever tried using soap and water. "Soap and water?" said the man, "Why, no!"

None of those omniscient persons among the spiritualists ever told me: "There is a force in you. Go and work!" Instead they fed me with vague prophecies that never came true. For instance, one clairvoyant told me that within the next fortnight a great prima donna would suddenly become ill and the manager would beg me to take her place to save the performance. The greatest operatic divas who were being starred that week were Geraldine Farrar at the Metropolitan Opera House and Mary Garden of the Chicago Opera Company at the Lexington Theatre. That was at a time when I was making only my first steps in vocal study… I had no repertoire… Then, no matter how much I believed in my omnipotent medium, could I imagine that Mr. Gatti-Casazza or Mr. Cleofonte Campanini—the respective directors of those two lyric houses—would consider such an outsider as myself even if I was adequately prepared, which was far from being the case!

However, eagerly anxious to believe the medium, I begged to be given the name of the unlucky woman whose shoes I was to fill—and I say "unlucky" because it was further predicted that she would not recover from her malady.

"Wait a moment," said the medium. "No. No, I do not see… I cannot tell you… No! It is not Anna Held… No, Anna Held is dead. No, it is not Eva Tanguay. No, I cannot see!"

My feelings can easily be imagined…

* * *

Apart from the so-called professional spiritualists who take remuneration, I also encountered socially some sincere if unbalanced seekers of the Unknown. At heart they were good people, albeit somewhat lacking in modesty, for they imagined themselves exceptionally gifted and specially protected by those departed to higher spheres.

One of those psychic individuals—introduced to me by my dear friend Rosemary Baruch—brought me a gardenia at my debut with Caruso at the then famous Biltmore Musicales.

"Jenny Lind sends you this flower," she said. "She is with you in this important event of your artistic life. You shall sing today as only she could do!!!"

During and after the concert I kept asking where Jenny Lind was seated and wanted to know if she really was such a great singer...

* * *

Fortunately my blind belief in mediums was finally shaken when in a street car with the medium who had just been giving us messages at a seance, she confidentially complained that she would never again give messages in the same church because jealous rivals were fighting her. That night she had taken the place of a sick colleague and although she was better known than the other person she had only received $3.00 for her services whereas the other medium would have received $9.00!!

Patatras!

* * *

Then the Ouija Board, my next experience, played a big part in my life. During several months the Ouija Board kept spelling what my heart desired most, and at that moment my unconscious wish was to be engaged by the Chicago Opera Company, I received—in answer to an anxious question of mine—the assurance that I would sign the much coveted contract within the next month.

Because Mr. Campanini, the maestro of the Windy City opera, had once told me what a wonderful Fedora I would make, "Fedora" was much in my mind. And when the Ouija Board advised me to study that opera I obeyed without hesitation.

"Fedora" was too dramatic then for my uncultivated lyric voice and as a result while studying it I forced my voice.

Thank you, Ouija Board!

Nothing further came out of that episode about singing in Chicago but a little later I found an Italian impresario —or rather he found me—who did not ask if I knew how to sing, if I knew "Fedora" or if I had ever sung with an orchestra. Oh, no! All he wanted was that I guarantee one performance in Cuba which after all offered no risk whatsoever—he assured me—for the great Anna Pavlova would be billed on the same program with me.

As I had never sung with an orchestra, I was promised at least one full rehearsal, but the mourning due to the death of Theodore Roosevelt prevented any music during the days scheduled for rehearsals and my opera debut was a disaster. The Italian gentleman (?) took all the money I had with me and I was obliged to pawn my jewels in Havana in order to leave for New York where I could cry my eyes out on Dr. Fraenkel's waistcoat.

Thank you, Ouija Board!

A year before my initial acquaintance with the Ouija Board I had lost a valuable pearl necklace while traveling on a Pullman. My all-knowing friend, the Ouija, informed me that the necklace had been stolen by a Negro porter who lived in Washington. The definite street and address was given. I was also told that the necklace had been divided in halves, one of which had been sold to a Frenchman living in Lyons, France (again a definite name and address was given) while the other half—more difficult to sell—was being worn by the porter's wife. How glad I was! I wanted to go to Washington at once. The practical side of my nature fortunately prompted me first to secure a map of the Capitol. No such street as the one indicated by the Ouija existed in Washington!

Thank you, Ouija Board!

* * *

One further step into the Unknown and I familiarized myself with the materialization of the departed soul. Frequently I saw the floating hands and felt the cooling breeze of luminous bodies passing by me. In the dark rooms I could see the long white forms, some of which would have been radiantly lovely to look at if anxiety was not so great in my heart from this unexplainable phenomena.

The most vivid impression I retain from that episode of my life was of seeing the materialization of President Lincoln who sat gently—on my lap! With great kindness Mr. Lincoln assured me that my singing teacher was a perfect choice. "Is His Excellency receiving a percentage?" was my cynical thought, for my healthy inborn intelligence would not allow me to be blinded to such an extent as to believe that a great mind like Lincoln's would materialize in order to emit such a platitude.

During those seances of materialization the spirits talked to their families as those present seemed most anxious to receive messages, but even the souls closest to them could but repeat: "God bless you, my dear."

There was only one experience beyond my comprehension. A well-known French medium, C. V. Miller—about whom Willy Reichel wrote at length in his book "An Occultist's Travels"—restored to a Cartier representative a gold pencil lost during a recent trip to Washington although the man was not even aware of his loss. The spirit brought the pencil from the Capitol to New York and presented it to its owner at that memorable seance! !

* * *

I next turned to the teachings of Yoga to help my singing. A soft-voiced Hindu advised me to practice the development of my breathing by holding my breath as long as possible. Later I learned that good singing consists in not holding one's breath but in letting it out slowly and smoothly.

A western Yogi—Dr. de Kerlor, the Polish ex-husband of famous fashion creator Schiaparelli—also promised to help my singing. I learned from him that the secret of good singing consisted in always having the fingers of both hands in contact so that your magnetism should not leave you and thus you could gain power over any audience. I shall never forget how in my simple-hearted way I desired to warn Caruso always to keep his hands together while on the stage. Luckily my natural timidity prevented me from exposing myself to ridicule by doing so.

During and immediately after the last war, such prominent and strikingly beautiful women as Margaret Mills and her sister Barbara Hatch, the daughters of Mrs. W. K. Vanderbilt, were faithful followers of Dr. Pierre Bernard at his Westhampton colony. Dr. Bernard, or the "Nyack Omnipotent Oom," as he was mockingly called by the press, advocated washing the stomach three times a day as well as standing on one's head for protracted lengths of time. I succeeded beautifully in standing on my head, although I did not continue it as a regular practice as does the extraordinary Elsie De Wolf, Lady Mendl, to this day. If Dr. Bernard knew how to apply Yogi wisdom I could not tell, for being just a plain doctor's wife I was never permitted to even approach the great man. I only looked with a little jealousy at the door behind which the Vanderbilt girls received enlightenment by the hours.

My first encounters with Yogi philosophy produced no more fruitful results. Still my admiration for the people of India was great and has remained so ever since. They were a fascinating race to me even if their theories of bodily control seemed to have little constructive value in this practical age. Of course one should not judge the race by Tahra-Bey who sticks pins into his cheeks and throat. But Western ignorance of Eastern civilization puts all Hindus in the same category and in speaking of *fakirs* easily includes such a great poet as Rabindranath Tagore.

* * *

My belief in help from the metaphysical world had now begun to wane. However I kept on and on, trusting that in each new discovery I would find the collaboration I was looking for—the assistance from outside.

With such an idea in mind I consulted the celebrated astrologer Evangeline Adams to have my horoscope established but being unable to give her either the approximate hour of my birth or even the exact year, I was prevented from knowing my future through that source. However she read my palm instead, not wanting to lose a fee for an appointment, and declared that I had the Napoleonic star on the Mount of Jupiter and therefore was in danger of a vertiginous fall. (My patronymic name is Napoleonovna, according to the Russian form of using the father's first name after our own. Thus in Russia I would be addressed as Ganna Napoleonovna instead of Madame Walska.)

Miss Adams also told me that I had a line of artistic success similar to Sarah Bernhardt's except that my achievement appeared much later in life than hers. You can imagine how willingly I accepted those extremely flattering comparisons to such an emperor as Napoleon and such a queen of the arts as Sarah Bernhardt!! Yes, the consultation certainly was worth the twenty dollars.

* * *

While it sounds as though I jumped from one experience to the next in record time, it actually took months and years of my life because I gave each method a fair trial before going to the next one.

Among my various branches of learning I came across the study of astrology under the guidance of a Polish woman of great culture who had herself been initiated by H. P. Blavatsky, the founder of Theosophy. This woman also wrote my hypothetical horoscope with full details as to what should happen to me almost hour by hour. If I remained passive things happened as they were predicted in the horoscope and therefore as I was expecting them to happen. On Wednesday morning for instance I was to feel badly depressed and I *did* feel badly depressed! ! Humiliated, I decided to counteract the indications of the horoscope—just to test it—and I succeeded in blasting all the predictions and proved to myself that will power is stronger than environment or fate. I began to believe that we can direct and shape our own destiny. Napoleon said that *he* would rule the stars… (Did he?)

* * *

No real help came from knowing about the Zodiac, however, and when my lady Theosoph admitted her inability to make me happy, she sent me to Dr. Mills, who was in her opinion the only person who could help me.

Dr. Mills was a meta physician. The title seemed imposing to me even if I did not understand the meaning of it. Or maybe because I did not! Early in life he had practiced medicine in Chicago but had given it up in favor of his own healing method which cured him from a great illness after he had been pronounced incurable by the diagnoses of medical authorities. At the age of eighty when I met him, he seemed young, alert and full of vigor. He claimed he could bring the dead back to life. But after giving two or three years of my life to his teaching, I saw that in spite of his most sincere efforts he could not even cure my dreadful migraine.

To jump ahead of my story a little, I want to say more about that affliction of mine. Ever since I could remember I had suffered from those terrific pains in the head. I presumed the malady was hereditary, for my mother suffered severely from the same thing. No medicine could cure it, no change of climate bring relief. Dr. Fraenkel used to say that he was able to cure many bad maladies but was helpless in the face of a woman's headache. Several years later I went to the American Church in Paris to attend a healing meeting being conducted by the Englishman Jones Hickson. Those wishing to be healed were asked to write their troubles on a piece of paper. Then each one knelt before the altar and the healer laid his hands on the person's forehead. I wrote the single word "headache." After receiving the healer's touch my headaches miraculously disappeared. The skeptics may well say that it was coincidence. Very well, then, but all the same, it was curious, wasn't it?

At my first meeting with Dr. Mills I explained my vocal troubles and my teacher's inability to help me. Dr. Mills asked me to sing. I did and very badly. But to my great surprise Dr. Mills pronounced it wonderful and perfect. Knowing that I was confronted by a layman in the field of music I reproached him bitterly for giving such extravagant praise although I suspected that perhaps his kindness would not allow him to give discouraging criticism. Without a word he took me into his tiny inner room and remained in there without saying a word for what seemed an endless length of time. Finally he broke the silence by advising me to leave my singing teacher and take instead… my own Divine Master within me—which was all Greek to me. But I had been taught as a child not to argue with older people!!

Then I did what I had never done before. I tried meditating in silence as he called it. The result was that when I left him that afternoon, I was sure my soul was in my eyes: I felt so exalted, exalted and persuaded that overnight I would be able to sing like Patti.

Filled with hope for years I faithfully followed his teaching not so much for the sake of my voice as for the sake of Dr. Fraenkel, who was critically ill at that time and whom Dr. Mills had promised to cure. However, my husband died shortly afterwards, and my voice was never helped in the slightest.

I still considered Dr. Mills a very good man even though

unable to perform miracles, and I would have continued as his follower forever had it not been that my critical and skeptical mind would not stand compromise. I suffered genuine shock when during the war Dr. Mills, forgetting that he was a priest, had his class pray for all the nations involved except Germany, the enemy nation, and again when he refused to hear "Parsifal" even though sung in English on the grounds that it was not right to hear Wagner's music during the war. Finally I was dumbfounded when he said that Negroes do not have the same soul as ours. I could not blind myself any longer.

Being very young in the search for Truth, I might have been able to forget all this if later on he had not taken a downright meddlesome part in a household matter. While in the country, my cook tried to coerce me financially. Dr. Mills with the best of intentions first advised, then insisted, that the best way to prevent a kitchen scandal was to pay her off. When I refused, without my knowledge he took the liberty through my house guest, Mr. McCormick, to pay her off. That was the last straw! I was beside myself with indignation and pointed out heatedly that his actions were in every way contrary to his teachings. From then on, I could meditate with him no more.

* * *

The following year in Paris I learned from Mrs. Philip Livermore, who had also been a member of Dr. Mills's class, that a Christian Scientist had helped her where our metaphysician had failed.

Immediately I sought him out. The first and only encounter was a hostile one. His conduct appeared monstrous to me. He assured me that Alec Cochran, whom I had lately married, could be cured of his mental and physical troubles but that he would not treat him because Mr. Cochran had not asked him personally to do so. It was the rule of the faith—he said—never to help people who do not ask for help. Indignantly I replied: "If a man is dying, knocked down on the street, is it then your Christian idea that a doctor should not help him because he has not personally made a previous appointment?"

That finished me with Christian Science. Still I continued to wonder and ponder. Did not Michelangelo believe more in prayers than all the medicine in the world? But I wondered so often… And never received the answer…

* * *

While in Paris I naturally ran to the meetings of the famous Coué, until one day we were told to press our hands together tightly. Then we were told that, even if we tried to pull them apart, we could not do so. But I did!

Adieu, Monsieur Coué!

* * *

Still later on when the press made me conscious of being a prey to stage fright I went to a hypnotist in Budapest. The only result I had from that experience was actual physical illness after seeing a dozen miserable beings lying asleep all over the place, victims of that modern Mesmer.

* * *

My last illusion—or shall I say the tremendous handicap for this period of my development—in the search for Truth came and went in the person of an English fanatic, Dr. Rawson, who preached more or less in the same manner as Dr. Mills, but promised to give quicker results than his colleague in the interpretation of God's teachings.

It was the month of July in Paris. I was leaving for Dieppe and then for the United States. I had closed my house on the Rue de Lübeck, discharging the household staff, not knowing if or when I would be back in France. The kitchen-maid came to me in tears saying that she would never be able to find another position so late in the summer and would thus be forced to go back to her village which she disliked so much.

Following the Englishman's theory, in order to help her I prayed for hours. Four days later, Mr. McCormick —then only a friend—told me that his daughter Mathilde was arriving in France in a few days and would need a maid. I jumped at that opportunity to recommend my girl, who could not possibly have been as happy about it as I was about such miraculous results of my meditation. What a wonderful future! Think of it—a few hours of meditation and I could have everything my heart desired…

A week later my protégé was arrested. She stole not only her mistress's linens and gowns, as it developed, but she had previously stolen mine and also the belongings of other people in the same hotel.

That disappointment was the only result I got from being Dr. Rawson's faithful disciple for years. That British prophet preached that there was no need to be ill, no need to sleep, no need to wear out our clothes. In fact Dr. Rawson even went to the extreme of trying to persuade us that he was the Messiah spoken of in the Bible. He believed in immortality on this earth. However, he committed one great error. After a short illness—he died. He did not intend it to be a lasting death for he predicted that —like Christ—he would return. The faithful prayed day and night and waited for the miracle that never happened, until the police broke up the meeting in order to disperse the blind followers and get on with the funeral.

* * *

Then, I was introduced to telepathy. A clever man gained my confidence by telling me the Christian name of my mother and the name of a scarcely remembered girlhood sweetheart that I had written on a piece of paper tightly held in my hand. This telepathist, Professor (?) Rees, burned some paper in my presence and while so doing murmured something in Yiddish. I was sure Dr. Fraenkel—then very ill—would get well, so convinced was I of the Professor's power on account of his ability to give me those names known to no one but me. However, the only outcome was that telepathist got the better of me to the tune of a few hundred dollars.

* * *

I also explored the theory of mathematics based on vibrations. I studied with Mrs. Cochran (no relation to Alec Smith Cochran), a woman of profound knowledge, a truly remarkable person who commanded the respect of many scientists and physicians. Her diagnoses were astonishingly correct, and their accuracy useful in the medical realm. Although she was often taken for a mind-reader, she had nothing whatsoever to do with the psychic field, for her teaching was purely based on the cosmic law of the ancient teaching. She was persuaded that she had rediscovered Pythagoras's lost theories of numbers in connection with vibrations, and as a result she was changing the names of all those that seemed to have inharmonious and negative vibration.

However, again I did not get any help even though I tried to follow Mrs. Cochran's teachings for some time. I even changed my name and used the one she baptized me with for years. Maybe the time was unpropitious, for the events in my life persistently turned out contrary to the logical predictions of Mrs. Cochran's teaching. So I gave up the science of numerology, too. Perhaps, if I had met her later on when I was more developed, I could have understood this philosophy better. Perhaps it was just as well that I gave no more time to unconstructive learning, for my pursuit was neither philosophical nor mystical—my pursuit was musical. The vital question for me was why I had strange difficulties with my singing. Why could I not make as normal progress as any other student?

* * *

The doctrine of reincarnation captivated my susceptible mind even if it perplexed me for a while when I was unable to grasp which of my two departed husbands would be my husband in Heaven!!! The misery of my life—especially the injustice that had visited me—was so unbearable that I was easily convinced I must be paying for sins I had committed in a previous life. Actually, that belief helped me greatly—it brought me much relief and most of all was a reasonable explanation of many difficult problems.

* * *

In the course of that time I made an examination—oh, very superficial—of the teachings of theosophy through the writings of the distinguished Annie Besant. Blavatsky's "Secret Doctrine" up to that point seemed to me but a succession of incomprehensible words.

* * *

I also had a glance at the Rosicrucian philosophy and frequented many classes in New Thought where I learned about the Akashic records, the Aquarian Age, the lost Atlantis, etc. Those lectures, however, were not spiritually helpful to me. They merely helped me to have an idea—a most vague idea—about the general knowledge of Great Wisdom but certainly not about the spiritual development of my own soul. And each instruction, because it was always connected with money matters, prevented me from getting any benefit to my inner being.

For there was always the question of money. For instance, the lady who expounded the Gospel had her husband at the door to collect the twenty-five cent fee and unless that fee was paid, you could not learn the road to Heaven. In order to augment her income still more, for the sum of ten dollars the lady would tell you about your previous lives. Naturally she proclaimed that I had been... Cleopatra! Later I discovered at least ten Cleopatras without going beyond the circle of my intimate friends. Somehow all the women were flattered to have been Cleopatra. It was something like the circus barker saying: "Here is the skull of Alexander the Great when he was twenty, and this is his skull when he was fifty." All women want to have been Cleopatra, just as every singer sooner or later wants to sing Carmen. Why... ?

* * *

After these last experiences, for the time being having nothing else, nothing new for me to investigate in the realm of mysticism, I finally closed my active search for help from the metaphysical world, help from unknown forces and from outside powers. And yet there was one more spectacular experience that should be recorded in concluding the story of the first period of my spiritual adventures. It was very picturesque and dramatic, though staged entirely for me, for I was not the main actress, I was only the audience, a deluded audience, as often happens. (If my friends, the reporters, could speak, they could not resist adding: "Especially if Walska sings!")

I was on friendly terms with the uncle of the Czar, the Grand Duke Alexander (whose daughter was married to Prince Felix Youssoupoff). The extremely handsome Grand Duke was a wonderful man. There was so much good in him that he could not see any evil in others and trusted everyone implicitly. Unfortunately he was an enthusiastic believer in spiritualism—spiritualism, that word so often confused with spirituality but having nothing in common with it. He introduced me to his medium, a lady who had enjoyed a distinguished position in Russia before Bolshevism, but who—like so many other exiles—had fallen into reduced circumstances since the revolution.

On account of my supposed knowledge of and experience with the occult world, the Grand Duke's family asked me to prove to His Imperial Highness that there was nothing constructive in the practice of illusionary happiness. Consequently, at the first opportunity, I pointed out to him that speaking to departed spirits was only the work of our own imagination and that too often the personality of the medium dominated us because of our desire to believe in the superhuman and our belief in miracles.

The result of that first attempt of mine was not very successful. The Grand Duke only pitied me for my lack of faith. Out of the kindness of his heart, he wanted to help me by bringing me also into his fold, and from time to time he sent me word that his guide from above spoke of me, sent her love and promised her help. Evidently that celestial adviser was a feminine one. This reminded me of a suffragette who finished her lecture with the words: "Girls, have courage! God will help us! *She* is with us!"

Constantly I was informed of the seances the Grand Duke arranged and of the progress made in putting the dead in touch with the living. Soon I heard reports that fresh flowers had fallen at the Imperial feet although the doors of his room had been locked and the windows hermetically sealed. And one day I even was shown a present my august friend had received from the spirit world. The Grand Duke had been told that centuries ago he was a great Pharaoh and an authentic bronze image of him as such had been presented to him by a spirit, appearing from nowhere directly on his desk. With pride and ecstasy he showed me the tiny statuette. To my horror I saw that underneath it was left a price tag bearing the mark of a well-known department store which manufactured millions of similar articles, something like our 5 & 10 cent stores. Those who gave it to him were so confident of his absolute faith in the power of spirits that they had not even taken the trouble to hide their deceit.

One day the Grand Duke asked me to lend him six hundred thousand francs as his guide Ela had told him that in three months Bolshevism would be over in Russia and His Imperial Highness The Grand Duke Alexander Mihailovitch Romanoff would again be in possession of his billions. It was extremely hard to refuse that loan. I certainly suffered more in not giving it to the Grand Duke than he did in not getting it, for, of course, he had been certain he would get the money from me—had not Ela said so?

Some time later and without warning, I was informed by the Grand Duke that I was bound to succeed with my singing because I was the reincarnation of Catalani, a celebrated singer of Napoleon's era. As a result I bought and read all the literature of that period I could put my hands on and soon knew the life of that vocal acrobat as well as if it had been my own. This was a great help to the antique dealers as it enabled them to sell some of their old prints and otherwise worthless and almost unsalable books. But it did not in the least help my voice.

The following month a message came to me, again via the spirit world, to the effect that I must possess something in my studio which had belonged to La Catalani in order to surround myself with the aura of her success. Immediately I sought out an Italian friend and asked him to ascertain who in Italy had inherited Catalani's belongings. In that way I procured the names and addresses of the descendants of that phenomenal singer and joyfully reported to the Grand Duke that I had all hopes for a good result.

I did not realize at the time that my enthusiasm was not shared at all by Alexander Mihailovitch, or rather by his spirit guides. But a few hours later I was informed that I was on the wrong track. Further orders came to leave everything to them and they would take care of everything.

"Do nothing until next week," was the spirit message relayed to me. "We shall have something definite to tell you then."

True to their word in a few days I was told that Catalani's portrait had been painted by a famous 18th century painter, Madame Vigée Lebrun. Immediately I instituted a search through the works of that artiste but all my inquiries were in vain. I reported my futile search to the Grand Duke. Again he rebuked me severely: "If Ela says so it must be so. Ela never makes a mistake!"

Evidently Ela was right, for the Grand Duke telephoned a day later to say that Catalani's portrait had been sold at public auction in 1906 at Mulhausen's sale to a Dresden art dealer for ten thousand francs. What had become of it thereafter no one knew. However, Ela would inform me later. But if I really desired to succeed in singing, I must get that portrait in order to be surrounded by her atmosphere. Furthermore I was not to breathe a word to anyone about this matter, for if I did, the portrait would disappear and I would never find it again.

I obeyed gladly that command as it seemed obvious that I could not go to Dresden and visit all the art dealers saying that Ela from the higher spheres had sent me to look for the diva's portrait. However, while I was still puzzling over a solution to the mystery, another message advised I should go at once to a certain number Avenue des Champs Élysées and ask for a certain man who might give me some valuable information.

I was surprised that Ela should have connections in such a smart quarter of Paris and even more when I discovered that a most palatial looking antique shop was located at the address given me.

It was Sunday. Very shyly not to make a fool of myself —I asked the concierge whether Mr. X. lived at the house.

"Certainly," came the answer. "He is the owner of the Antique Shop."

I went away slightly dizzy at the prospect of being so near the realization of achieving my life's desire.

Early the next morning I telephoned Mr. X. He had not yet arrived. I left my telephone number and waited impatiently for his call. By four o'clock that afternoon he still had not called. Unable to control my impatience any longer I went to see him. My heart beat rapidly when he appeared.

"I was told you could give me some information about a certain portrait of Catalani," I managed to say, expecting he would give me the name of a Dresden art dealer.

I was completely dumbfounded when, instead, he opened the door of the elevator and said: "Do you want to see it? Step in, please."

We went up one or two floors, then out and along three or four long halls, the walls of which were covered with pictures. We passed through another small door and finally found ourselves in a tiny room entirely draped in grey velvet. He pulled one of the curtains aside and there confronting my bewildered eyes was the portrait of Catalani.

How unattractive she was! How masculine! How utterly devoid of charm! I struggled with great and contradictory emotion, trying to conceal my feelings from the merchant. Finally I regained my self-control sufficiently to manage to ask the price in a quite indifferent voice.

"Eight hundred and fifty thousand francs," he replied.

"How much?" I said. I thought I had heard wrongly and there must have been a trace of incredulity in my voice. But no, I had heard correctly.

"You are joking," I said. "I know the value of this painter's work at that late period of her life."

"Oh, no," he answered, "that price is quite reasonable. I could easily ask a million francs. It is worth it."

"Then why don't you," I retorted. "Why should you make me a present of a hundred and fifty thousand francs?"

There was a pause and during the long silence I understood much. Sadly I went home…

Two years later the Grand Duke confessed that for the sake of justice and to prove how wrong I was he had sent someone to inquire about the price of the portrait. Triumphantly he announced to me that it was still the same price as I had been asked, one hundred thousand francs, forgetting completely that this amount was different from the one named to me. So, when his family begged me again to make him realize the danger he was in, knowing his affection for me, I told him the truth about my Catalani experience.

He listened guiltily, then began to cry. It was tragic to see that colossal, thoroughly blue-blooded man crying like a baby.

Before leaving he said: "Why, why, did you tell me all that? Even if there is only five per cent of truth in spiritualism, I was satisfied, for I could fool and blind myself. Now I cannot live any longer. I have no reason to continue my existence. Why, why, did you destroy my illusion?"

* * *

With this last experience in psychic phenomena came the end. No more spooks, palmistry, crystal-gazing, mind-reading, telepathy, astrology, numerology, theosophy, Coueism, seers of vision… After almost binding my liberty with Free Masonry, I abandoned the search for help from the metaphysical world.

Réculer pour mieux sauter…?
Maybe.

Everything comes to him who waits.

CONTRARY TO general opinion derived from a great deal of hearsay about my marriages and divorces, I never inspired quickly passing flirtations. Men whose lives I touched always professed rather a profound love for me. I was the woman of their whole life, the lady of their Destiny—the Only One.

Somehow I was urged to touch the mind of men in an exceptionally strong way. When their love for me filled their whole being, the great force in their hearts enabled them to elevate their souls to a higher summit and brought out the greatest qualities of their spiritual beings. Probably for that reason mentally small men were never attracted by me. That may also explain why I never cared much for the younger type, probably feeling that even a rich nature if immature was unready to grasp the Reality of life, mistaking a passing mood for the Essential.

Once in Paris I told Dr. Babinski, a celebrated nerve specialist already quite advanced in age, that he was too young for me and therefore could not help me. He blushed like a young girl—from pleasure probably, for he never sent me his bill.

I have always much preferred to know such a person as Einstein to any young and handsome Hollywood idol. In short, if I were told that a Wise Man lived at the ends of the earth, I would not hesitate to go there, if only to find disappointment.

First intuition and then experience taught me that the ordinary expression of man's love brought me only disappointment since it was not sufficiently high in spiritual quality. Still I consider that even those women who through the primitive element have power over great men—men who are achieving something—do good by instilling a sort of vivifying radium into the blood of the genius, as champagne increases the strength of the convalescent.

Sometimes I feel that the forces in me are too high merely to fortify others. Perhaps one day they may be sufficiently concentrated to crystallize in some individual creative manner. Somehow I sense that through my suffering this force, doubtless deposited by infallible Nature (who dictates that nothing shall be lost but merely transformed), will bear fruit sooner or later and manifest itself, if only in one single thought, a unique idea, or even by a failure—for I believe along with Carlyle that it is the effort and not the success of individuals that enriches human thought.

If Fate decides that my achievement here below consist solely in the effort I have made, then perhaps my trials will at least prepare the mental ground for some future person who—without my example—would lose time in searching through a virgin state of sensation instead of profiting by my discoveries and thus reaching the coveted goal much more rapidly. "It is not the desire to become famous, but the habit of being laborious that allows us to create," as someone so wisely said.

In moments of inspiration when my soul seems to touch the sublime, I realize that even if I give nothing at all to the present generation, nevertheless the sincerity of my efforts will remain as quintessential vibrations deposited in the air just as Nature, after accumulating the elements, discharges them through the burst of a storm. I would be sufficiently gratified if an effort like mine could one day contribute to the invisible but strong spiritual force around us that strives to abolish wars and illnesses and postpone that death for which we are not at all prepared and of which we are now afraid. None of us is reconciled to die because we have not achieved what we were sent here to do. We feel that intuitively and desire to have more time to fulfill our destiny, sensing that Death alone cannot exonerate or transfigure us…

"Father, if it be possible, let this cup pass from me…"

* * *

When I married Dr. Fraenkel, I lost my personality which had as yet only manifested itself on the exterior. Although, upon my arrival in America the well-known painter of outstandingly beautiful women, Coles Phillips, chose me as a type that seemed to him more individual than eight other beauties of various nationalities, still I had become just the wife of a celebrated man, the very young companion of a great Aesculapius. The most important New York and Newport homes were open to me, Mrs. George Henry Warren's, Mrs. Vincent Astor's, and those of the exclusive—if not social register—Jewish patriarchs, such as the late Jacob Schiff, the Warburg, Nathan, and Strauss families, the only representatives of bourgeoisie in America.

People seeing me at that period pointed out "the wife of Dr. Fraenkel." I was almost thirty years younger than the Doctor. To the stranger's eyes I was just a beautiful Polish girl, whom great wise Dr. Fraenkel called "Baby." However, the beautiful Polish girl wished by all means to participate with the full enthusiasm of her juvenile heart in the wonderfully instructive talks of that exceptionally illuminated man. He told his friends that he had been studying Goethe for forty years—Goethe was his *livre de chevet*—and still he could not entirely grasp certain ideas until one day he spoke about them to his "Baby Wife." It might be more correct to say that he was rather thinking aloud in her presence with no thought of her being able to understand. Therefore he was thunderstruck when, like a flash and without hesitation, his "Baby" explained to him what he had failed to solve in a lifetime of study. From that moment on, he preached that a woman's intuition is stronger than any knowledge acquired by long study—for it is infallible.

* * *

Though without the slightest degree of vanity, even then I did not feel quite in my right place, vaguely sensing that I could not always be known as the wife of a celebrity. Although I had no idea what the future held in reserve for me, already in a meditative mood, I thought I had probably been brought into the Doctor's life to soften his soul, hardened as it was by the thirty years' fight for a place in the aristocratic, autocratic Austrian sun where traditionally there was no room for a poor Jew eager for learning.

It is said that "great lights proceed from goodness." Dr. Fraenkel was lacking in goodness, owing in all probability to the hardships of his persecuted childhood and also to the fact that almost since birth he had suffered from a mysterious malady which embittered his noble character to a great degree.

I thought that destiny had sent me to him to relieve those 'mental and physical miseries, although I learned about his grave illness only after our marriage. During the three years of our life together he suffered pains in his stomach that were bad enough in the afternoon but terrific at night. He would lie on the floor by his bed groaning like a wounded lion. I always kept open the door which gave onto the narrow hall joining our rooms in order to be able to hear him. Every night—even if he closed his door tightly in his desire not to waken me—I could hear those groans that so cruelly tore my heart to pieces. Even years later when I was singing Tosca in the act where her beloved is tortured by the inquisitors, the memory of those unbearable nightly sufferings would revive in my heart and it became terribly hard for me to awake to the reality of dramatic pretense.

The instant his groans wakened me, flash-like I jumped up, plugged in an electric boiler especially ready for this purpose and gave him water to sip so boiling hot that it seemed scarcely possible anyone could have stood it. I could not have held the glass for a second unless I wrapped a towel around it. But he would swallow it instantaneously without feeling its excessive heat, his pains were so much greater than the burn of the water. Then he would beg me, actually crawling on his knees and clinging to my nightgown, to have mercy on him and to put an end to his misery—to kill him.[3]

Even in those early days of intuitive search for the Light I never doubted that Idea was stronger than Matter, that thought could materialize, act and even kill—as demonstrated in Dostoievski's "Brothers Karamazov." It seemed to me that the legends of black magic in the ancient time could probably be explained in the same way.

Our process of thinking depends on whether we consider everything in this world as accident or believe that everything is worked out by an invisible force incomprehensible to the majority.

When we are young, everything seems to us matter of fact and it does not surprise us that each morning God never fails to hang out the sun. That reminds me of the discussion between the man deifying the Sun and the man deifying the Moon. The first one, on being asked by the sun-worshipper, "Why do you adore the moon?" gave this candid explanation: "Because the moon at least gives some light whereas the sun is useless anyhow in the daylight."

Later life teaches us to think and perceive what to inexperienced youth and the eternally short-sighted is hidden by a *Niebelungen helmet*. Then we realize that in this great invisible world there is something that directs our destinies. Otherwise it would be incomprehensible that a violet is so full of scent or that an organ apparently so delicate as the

---

[3] My countrywoman, the actress Uminska, not so strong as I was, put an end to the hopeless sufferings of her cancerous husband. Her trial in Paris made history as it opened the question of mercy killings.

human eye is so protected through every moment of danger in our lives that it sometimes lasts a century and is more enduring than if it were made of steel, a longevity that most man-made machines cannot rival.

* * *

It will perhaps be easier to understand what I mean by superiority of mind over matter and its creative possibilities if I tell of such an experience in my own life. For I most certainly created something out of my thoughts, just as a woman feverishly desiring to bear a child will create the illusion of pregnancy with such realism that she often succeeds in fooling even the best doctors. But what a tragedy is hers when she discovers it was only the figment of her imagination! Such a tragedy was mine, although in a somewhat different manifestation!

One hot summer day in 1916 or 1917 at Islip, Long Island, there was a fashionable wedding in the Knapp family, if my memory is right. I was walking with Dr. Fraenkel in the garden with hundreds of other guests who were to attend the wedding breakfast when my eyes alighted on a man who probably looked quite ordinary to the others but who stood out from the crowd to me. I noticed that his arm was in a sling. I took him for a foreigner, a Pole possibly. Because I could penetrate him right away, he seemed closer to my Polish blood. Dr. Fraenkel did not know the identity of the man but thought that his face was familiar.

At the wedding breakfast he was seated behind me. While at my table the guests were busy gossiping about an eccentric man who had left his entire fortune as well as his eccentricity to his nephew, I was not listening to that extraordinary story but all my mental force was centered on the man who had made me so aware of himself. As the conversation continued, I could not help hearing a talkative lady say that this eccentric person had broken his arm while playing polo. In a flash it dawned upon me that they spoke about the man I was interested in. But I was too late either to catch his name or to learn anything else about him.

After the luncheon, Dr. Fraenkel, recalling now that he had known this man years ago, went to look for him—but to no avail. In all probability he had already left. So did I—taking with me the vision of that sickly and pathetic-looking figure.

From that moment on my thoughts kept dwelling on him. I often asked my friends if they knew him. The answer would invariably be: "The sick man? The eccentric? The rich one?" But no one seemed to know that timidly savage bear sufficiently well to arrange for me to meet him.

When leaving for the Metropolitan Opera which I attended almost daily, the Doctor, wishing me a pleasant evening, would compliment me on my appearance often adding: "If So-and-So sees you he certainly will be lost!" And on my return he would emerge from his deep studies of Paracelsus and greet me by saying: "How was it? And did you see HIM?"

One day while driving down Park Avenue I thought I recognized him walking very slowly, bent almost into the shape of a question mark, more than thin, a cigarette glued to his lips, a raincoat hanging negligently over his bony arm. I ordered my chauffeur to turn back a few blocks… This time I saw him better but my heart was not sure it recognized him… I wonder now if with my timidity I would have had enough strength to stop him even if I had been certain it was he… I wonder…

After many fruitless inquiries finally Anna McCullough, niece of Mrs. W. K. Vanderbilt, upon learning from Dr. Fraenkel that it would give me pleasure to meet the man, immediately invited him to dinner. Contrary to his habit, he accepted the invitation.

I was very excited as I entered Anna's parlour that night. However one look at her sweet but guilty expression and I understood without even hearing her apology that he had telephoned his regrets a few moments previously.

That is the way in which the chrysalis of my active thought was vitalized every few months by asking questions about him and still more by thinking about him. He existed for me in the same way as does some book already written but not yet possible to obtain and read. He certainly was very much alive in my thoughts. I had materialized him even if he was not consciously aware of it. I say consciously, for in spite of my impression that he had not seen me at all at that wedding or even looked at me, I later learned that he had asked his inseparable friend, Bob Perkins: "Who is that woman? I must meet her!" and asked with such conviction that his pal really thought he had met me that afternoon and could not believe later that such was not the case.

* * *

Three years later a terrific calamity crushed my mind, broke my heart and blackened my soul. Dr. Fraenkel died. The whole world which had been built on a reasonable and stable idea for me was shattered and its foundations torn to pieces. God himself proved to me the fictitiousness of his existence, in fact his non-existence. Only the circumstances and the unity of facts reigned powerfully. They had practically become the deity, for they and matter, execrable matter, alone cried victory. Morally unlawful death came and triumphed. God had sent to earth a man with a soul great enough to heal human misery and then—without any apparent reason—took him away. God endowed that man with a great mind, lined with Platonian knowledge, to enable him to adapt the soul's quality to twentieth century exigencies—and all that evidently to no purpose…

Had God overdosed while making him too great? And then, afraid that he could not stay long in this material world, did the All-Powerful decide to nail him to this earth with the terrific physical pains which began in infancy and which were to cut his wings unmercifully—since the higher he rose toward the great realization, the more severely he was clutched down by that physically unbearable agony? Or were the gods jealous of their creation that was stronger in spirit than they wanted him to be? And did they revenge themselves through matter, since mere bodily pain had been unable to overcome his spirit?

But, oh horror! Matter was victorious! The spirit was defeated, but the means by which the victory was won—the lack of a few morsels of food—gave evidence that his superior spirit would not fight such a base enemy, preferring to depart to its own sphere.

To me who witnessed that tragic fight, too upset by evident facts, the explanations of those ideas came only much later. At the moment indescribable despair was overwhelming me…

Many people lose those dear to their hearts, but they admit the existence of sickness. They are so sure that death is inevitable that each morning they prepare their mind to a great negative thought of catching cold when putting on a warm coat. Thus they look death in the face. But I was so sure that God could not be a failure, that He would not create such a superior mind for the sole purpose of curing the stomach trouble of Mrs. W. K. Vanderbilt or removing a pimple from Otto Kahn's cheek! And so to me Dr. Fraenkel's death was the end of everything that *was* and that could be. There was no God! Nothing but circumstances and the poorly developed science of medicine!

* * *

It was no wonder that after such a shock my mind was far from being in a normal state. In the Catskill Mountains where I went with my singing teacher my voice was dreadful. While I was being told to put the tone one place or another, my mind kept saying: "What for? What for? Nothing exists anyhow… Nothing."

* * *

Six years have passed from the time I first asked myself "What for?" And today like the first day, as it will be on the last day of my life, I still am and shall be without an answer.

* * *

Seeing me in such black despair and knowing that I had signed a contract with the Chicago Opera Company for the following winter, my guests in the country, Dr. and Mrs. Mills, were sure that I would be unable to fulfill my engagement. They were going to Europe in July and after lengthy persuasion they succeeded in getting me to agree at the last minute to go to Paris with them under the pretext that I could get my opera costumes there. Secretly they hoped that a new atmosphere and a different occupation would restore me to normality.

* * *

When I boarded the "Aquitania" that Saturday and found myself near the passenger list, there at my elbow stood the object of my mental creation those past years—the man of the wedding party—again looking at me as if he did not see me. And again I was not sure if it really was the same person. After all I had seen him only once. Three years ago... And our eyes had never met...

In order to verify his identity I searched for his name on the passenger list but it was not there. It could not be he... I must have made a mistake... Still my name was not on the list either, since I had only booked passage at the last minute.

Some friends were bidding us goodbye in a rather noisy way. He stood nearby—a cigarette in his mouth—looking apathetically at me, at us, at the space in front of him, for not a muscle of his face showed that he saw us, was looking at me, or even that his eyes were voluntarily fixed on anything. In spite of the fact that his cold expressionless eyes rested on me once or twice, I was sure that he was far from seeing me.

His cabin happened to be on the same hallway as mine. I often saw him pass by during the crossing but he never seemed even curious enough to glance through the door which was wide open to catch any draft because of the terrific heat.

One afternoon I saw him sleeping in a deck-chair. For the first time I was able to look at him closely and study his face without his being aware of it. He appeared very plain to me... That is to say his face had no soul, no life, and its lines were the kind one gets from the wind and not from the experiences of life when every wrinkle means suffering—tangible records of deep feeling. Instantly I classed him as a prototype of Joseph Conrad's sailor's face, dry and bitten by the elements. Again my heart doubted if he was really the man from Islip. And I wanted to meet him to find out for myself who he actually was...

Harold McCormick, who also happened to be on board (and perhaps not by chance), mentioned the man among the well-known people on the ship. He said he had known him years ago when playing tennis and proposed to reintroduce himself in order to present him to me. In spite of my strong wish to know the man, somehow I hesitated and decided to postpone the meeting until a later moment of our trip, if at all.

As I was walking the deck on the last day of the voyage on my usual round before luncheon, I acknowledged the greeting of a Chicago friend of Mr. McCormick, Mr. Richard Crane, who was standing with my mysterious man. The latter—a man with an obvious knowledge of manners but blasé with utter indifference—did not even bother to lift his cap but merely touched it with his two fingers.

"Just what one would expect of a man with such a face," I thought.

That same afternoon when I was sitting on deck with my usual entourage for the first time during the entire trip, I saw him walking back and forth. With him was a lady who looked toward me persistently. An hour later she stopped in front of my chair, hesitated a moment and then told me sweetly that she wanted to meet me, for she had been a friend of my husband.

"All friends of Dr. Fraenkel are welcome indeed."

She scarcely listened. In fact she interrupted me by turning round and making a sign to her companion.

"My I present Mr. Alexander Smith Cochran?" she said, and leaning nearer she whispered: "Please excuse me. He begged so much to be introduced I could not help it."

Naturally my surprise was great. Coolly master of the situation, he took the chair next to mine, from which Mr. McCormick had just arisen in order to greet the handsome Mrs. Frank Henderson—it was she who had just made the introduction. He started to talk to me with such an obvious disregard of any of the others present that they said: "See you later! —So long!" and left him to his monopoly.

Left alone, we talked about America, a country he disliked at that moment[4] but which I loved without restriction in those days before my glorious popularity with the newspapers. I mentioned religion… No! He did not believe in God and dismissed the subject with "Bosh!! !"

Twenty minutes later the first call for dinner sounded. As he told me later, while dressing he determined: "I will marry that woman if she will have me or I will never marry at all!"

After dinner we met at the pool room. Under the pretext that it was too smoky there, he led me to the top deck. There and immediately he asked me to marry him. I did not answer. He became insistent, requesting permission to come to Paris. He was going to London.

"Paris does not belong to me. Anyone can come," I said

---

[4] It seemed that he had just lost the race for the Lipton cup for the nth time and in a peevish fury had ordered his yacht to be sold immediately at any price while he hurriedly left the country swearing never to return.

stupidly.

Furious, he landed at Plymouth very early in the morning without even trying to communicate with me.

The next day no sooner was I settled in Paris than he telephoned from London to inquire whether I would dine with him that night if he flew over. I accepted. That night again he asked me to marry him. And again without words I shook my head in negative reply. Still more infuriated, he left again…

He went to Pau for hunting but at the end of the week he returned and forcibly placed a perfect oriental pearl ring on my finger, saying: "If by January you still do not want to marry me, send me back this ring. I will understand that Harold McCormick is too much on your mind."

We parted.

I was returning to America in a week. He had left for England and the ponies so dear to his heart. Two days before I was to sail he telephoned and pleaded with me to meet him at the Crillon Hotel the next morning at eleven. He must see me upon his arrival.

I went. He begged me to marry him. He said it was the only thing that could save his miserable life. Even if I did not care for him, I must marry him—it would be a work of charity.

"Save me. Save me!" was his plea.

He was pathetic.

We were married that same afternoon…

* * *

The gods punished me in a very cruel way for my rivalry with them. They permitted me to imitate them by creating but did not allow me to master my creation. When we love, we project our state of feeling to the one we would have feel as we do. I gave too much to my creation—he could not receive it. The creation I made of him in my inflamed imagination did not correspond to the very poor creature he was in himself. His rich man's arrogance, whose money had swept everything before it until now—was humiliated at being indebted to me, for he was unable to repay me in the same quality I gave him. His independence, tyrannically bought by dollars, and his extreme egotism made him desire to see me happy. He did not want to be troubled by remorse and so have such evident proof before him of his impotency to feel deeply—or to feel at all for that matter.

Actually he was the most miserable man I have ever met in my many contacts with every type of man. Even in the abstract he did not know what happiness was. He lived only to kill a day—a day so very short to us others and so long to him. Time that is so very precious to us was for him something to waste that it might pass as quickly as possible. For instance he disliked St. Moritz because there is nothing to do there after the sun sets.

He could not stand having the same people around him for any length of time. He realized that it was sometimes convenient to have a wife but he would have preferred to see her twice a week at the most and preferably after dinner—dinner after all being less boring at the club. As a matter of fact it would have been quite satisfactory if his wife did not care for him at all, for although he did not show any sign of having a soul, he was not without some charm, if only the charm of his ingenuous selfishness.[5]

Far from being stupid, he was filled with a mixture of childishness and snobbishness. He would dine out four or five times a week with persons of high social standing whom he despised for their low morals, and, even though

---

5 When we were furnishing the house in Paris on the Rue de Lübeck he found an antique leather wastebasket which was just what I desired for my desk but he did not dream of giving it to me. "Oh no, it's for my room," he said laughingly, to my great astonishment. Three days later he brought the basket to me. I was beginning to fell remorseful at having judged him so severely when candidly he confessed: "You can have my basket now. It does not go with my chintz."

he was aware that they put up with his bad temper because of his money, nevertheless he would seek their presence—so afraid was he of eating a dinner in his own precious company.

In his home he behaved like a Puritan. For example, he would not allow anyone to smoke until coffee was served in the drawing-room. Coldly he would even refuse his own brother Gifford—dear Gifford! —an invitation for dinner on that account.

"You cannot dine properly," he was telling him, "you must always smoke at table! I will not have it!" And he would get extremely embarrassed, to the point of blushing, if a friend's mistress spoke to him in my presence, for he would not dare—naturally—to introduce a mistress to his wife. On the other hand, if he were short of company, he would not hesitate to ask the owner of an antique shop where he had perhaps bought a table that morning to lunch with him, knowing perfectly well that the merchant would accept only to please an eccentric millionaire customer.

As much as he hated eating alone, he would not see the same people often, if he could help it. Twice a winter was the most he could associate with the same person without showing obvious boredom on his arrogant face. Machiavelli said that the worst thing in the world is neither trouble, poverty, suffering, sickness or even death but boredom, terrible boredom. And when Goethe wrote that a selfish heart cannot escape the torment of boredom, he described Alec Cochran to perfection.

He was extremely cruel, with the cruelty of those who do not have sensibility, who cannot feel. He also had that lack of tact which characterizes the insensible. How often I suffered because of that trait. For instance when I went to dine for the first time at the home of his sister, Elinor Stewart, suddenly Alec stopped eating and pointing to a magnificent Gainsborough portrait of a lady hanging in the dining-room said:

"Elinor, I gave you that picture as a present but now that I am married, I think I'll take it back and give it to my wife!" And he laughed heartily as if it were a good joke, without even seeing our embarrassment.

He was cruel in the unconscious (perhaps unrealized) way that children are. Today I can scarcely see a pussy catch a fly without fainting (if I were capable of fainting); whereas when I was around seven or eight years old like other children, I would laughingly chase lovely butterflies to pin them alive on a board and for days and days watch them die. Now my extreme sensitiveness does not allow me to dismiss my completely deaf chauffeur, knowing he might not find another job; whereas when I was a child, I was so nasty to my German governess that she was forced to leave, preferring to risk her livelihood rather than endure any more of my cruelty and I was proud when she had gone, already busying myself with preparations for the torture of my next victim.

* * *

I realized the dreadful tragedy that Alec Cochran was only a myth, the work of my fantastic mind, when, alas! it was already too late—a few hours after human law had stamped the seal uniting my highly exuberant nature to his heart so ignorant of elevated elan.

After the wedding dinner, Alec was in such a hurry to be alone with me that when the headwaiter proposed liqueurs and cigars with the coffee, he rudely dismissed him with: "*I do not want anything else.*"

Mr. Cochran hurried me to the Crillon where he was stopping. He disliked my hotel, the Ritz. Consequently it never occurred to him to move there or even to ask my preference. In fact, in the afternoon, while we were at the church, my maid had moved my trunks to the Crillon; and on the way to his hotel I remarked to my three-hour husband that I was not sure of finding my things in order. As if to remedy this, he informed me that he was accustomed to taking a walk before going to sleep. So he would leave me to follow his routine, while I could in the meantime attend to my clothes.

An hour later I heard him enter the enormous sitting room of our royal suite. As soon as he had closed the door behind him, I heard him laugh. He laughed and laughed quite joyfully. At every step he took toward my room his laughter became more hilarious. To me it seemed quite out of place on such a day, on such an important day in his life. When he finally stopped on the threshold of my room, I asked the reason for his extraordinary gaiety. He tried to tell me several times. But each time he started to speak, he had to laugh again—and each time his laughter became more uncontrolled.

At last between paroxysms of laughter he managed to describe to me how as he was walking along the Avenue des Champs-Élysées, the Ladies-of-the-Avenue who blossom on the street at that hour began inviting him to visit them; and how his silence seemed to discourage most of them. However as he was nearing the end of his promenade, one of the sirens who was particularly insistent would not leave him. So, turning toward her suddenly as if it were a huge joke, he had said: "Not tonight, my dear. Tonight I am married!"

"Ha-ha-ha-ha…"

I MARRIED Alec Cochran with the understanding that I was to continue my operatic career. I explained to him that I was not the kind of person who could be happy living as a decorative mannequin in this futile world; that I wished to pursue the vocation which called me so forcibly; that I had a feeling that I was strong enough to accomplish something by my own worth.

Even very early in life I had utterly disregarded flattering opinions about my looks and never took a personal merit that nature gave me a classical nose—although they say the course of history might have been changed if Cleopatra had had a different nose. I was ambitious—although unconsciously so—to leave a more useful record of my passage on this earth. If I desired to be distinguished, it was for something achieved through my own effort, independently of my husband's millions, my beauty, my Slavic charm or providential luck.

I even felt insulted when people insisted on always speaking about my looks. I often asked myself, "Do they think me so stupid as to imagine I could reap what I had never sown?" And it went on to such a degree that out of contrariness—paradoxical as it may seem—I was glad when some remarked that I looked pale and weary, since such an appearance was the result of overwork and forced people to see me in my true light and not merely as a doll on exhibition. Often the newspapers would write things about me that were insults to my intelligence, like this:

> I caught a glimpse of Ganna Walska at the Alsen recital. She was a radiant apparition in a costume of jade velvet with a hat of the same material and the whole speaking well of Parisian ateliers. Most women in this imperfect world would be more than content to look like that, and would gladly forswear any desire to sing…

* * *

Making our plans for the future, we had agreed that after our wedding Mr. Cochran would go to England to hunt—his favorite winter occupation, and I actually mean *occupation*—as he had planned; and I would return to America to fulfill my contract with the Chicago Opera Company. Later, either Alec would join me in New York and then take me back to Europe or—if for any reason the former plan could not be carried out—we would meet in March, in Monte Carlo, where I had been engaged to create the leading role in the new Chapuis opera, "Mademoiselles de Saint Cyr."

I had to sail two days after the wedding. At the last minute, however, my new companion insisted that he could not let me go alone and ordered his cabin. This decision surprised me greatly, for I do not change my mind unreasonably in a rush. Furthermore, I intuitively felt that this change of plans was not wise, knowing that the winter season in America, particularly in Chicago, never appeals to a man who yachts, plays polo and hunts. I feared he would find it more than dull without his sole distractions of ponies in the daytime and womanless clubs at night. Nor would I be able to do the social rounds with him, as my time would be fully occupied with rehearsals before my debut. In short, I knew that he would have to rely largely on himself for amusement—a very poor resource indeed!

On the other hand any woman would have been only too happily flattered that her husband did not want to leave her right after their wedding, in spite of any previous arrangements or promises. Forebodings and wisdom were therefore easily overcome by the unreasoning desire of the chosen one to be by my side, although the inner voice of warning was not entirely stilled.

I have often noticed that when an idea is wrong, the smallest of circumstances seems to prove it. My misgivings soon started to haunt me. On the boat my cabin was on one deck and Mr. Cochran's on another and his was a very small one, being the only one he could get at the last minute. So our honeymoon trip was spent on separate decks, which made Alec furious, especially when a terrific storm kept me in bed most of the journey (for I was not as good a sailor on a rough trip as he was), and this forced him to go to meals alone. My heart already sensed a warning…

* * *

We stayed in New York a month before going to Chicago. I did not find this very pleasant as I heartily disliked the social world and Dr. Fraenkel having accustomed me to seeing only a few people, such as Fritz Kreisler, for instance, whose talk benefited the soul or the intellect and taught something about real values, whereas in society—even such international elite as the home of James W. Gerard, war ambassador to Germany, or of such a beautiful hostess as Mrs. Norman Whitehouse, Alec's best woman friend—individuality disappeared, and general conversation at a dinner of twenty or thirty persons could not possibly be of vital interest, for tacit convention decreed that you address the neighbor on your right for a certain time and then your neighbor on the left for the rest of the duration of the meal, and the general topic could only be the weather and your preference for the mountains or the sea.

However, Mr. Cochran's numerous friends wanted to meet his wife and we dined out almost every night. If we did stay at home, it was only to receive in turn those to whose homes we had gone as guests-of-honor. At the first luncheon we gave, a characteristic incident occurred which explains the atmosphere in which I lived. We went to my studio for coffee, which I like to pour myself, as it is more *gemütlich*. I had just started to put sugar in the first cup when Alec came over, kissed my hand while thanking me for the charming lunch and (followed by his faithful Bob Perkins) departed—to the great surprise of all his friends and to my own astonishment, which I barely managed to conceal. So my heart was heavy when I finally found myself alone in my room... A short while later the telephone rang and I heard Alec's hearty laugh—it was destiny that his laugh should exasperate me.

"Guess what happened to me?" he said naïvely. "When I thanked you for lunch and left, you know I entirely forgot that I was married and that I was the host. I have just realized my mistake. Is it not funny? Ha-ha-ha. . . !"

Funny? Rather...

During that month in New York an ironical incident about my wardrobe amused me greatly. In Paris I had been too preoccupied with ordering my stage costumes to think about any other clothes and furthermore I was in mourning—or rather I should say in a mourning state of mind, for I am opposed in principle to wearing black and Dr. Fraenkel, whom I mourned, also disapproved of it. If I let the beautifully talented Lady Speyer choose from my *garderobe* a black cape to wear when sailing, it was only to show my appreciation of her interest in my reputation. Feeling far from coquettish, I just ordered one Callot black velvet evening gown called "Venus" which I wore at the wedding dinner.

I wore that gown to almost all the dinners we attended in New York. My husband's friends—to say nothing of his family—kept saying sarcastically that he certainly had an economical wife. Later they spoke about my extravagance with the same lack of knowledge of the actual situation. It just so happened that sixteen years later I was at a big dinner given by Mrs. Ogden L. Mills, one of the most uniquely beautiful women I ever met in America. The next day several of the smartest ladies who had been there begged an intimate friend of mine to find out where my gown had come from, but when I candidly confessed that it was the same sixteen-year-old Callot gown, they would not believe it. Some women will not divulge the addresses of their dressmakers so that no one may imitate their costumes.

They thought I was one of those.

Speaking about clothes, I have always been peculiar about dressing. I have defended my individualism against the standardized fashions of dressmakers. I was following the canvases of the great masters rather than the four seasonal, necessarily passing moods of the Parisian couturiers who are obliged to change the style as often as possible to force women to buy new clothes. Actually we never wear out our garments. Therefore the fashion dictators must make them look old and out of date so that we shall discard them and buy new ones.

Since I did not wear the same gowns or hats as other women—although I had more than dislike for eccentricity—I was looked upon as being an eccentric person.

Though not intentionally, it happened that I became a pioneer in the field of feminine embellishment. Fifteen years before the general fad, I was wearing turbans, having borrowed the inspiration from Rembrandt's pictures… Liking jewels and fortunate enough to get them of any existing size and color, twenty years before the actual fashion for big gems I designed for myself huge necklaces, bracelets and rings, and to make them I got the biggest stones I could find on the market, the largest generous Nature created. Had I not had the means to get expensive big jewels, I would have preferred to wear large garnets, coral, aquamarines or other semi-precious and much less costly stones rather than small sapphires, emeralds or rubies. I never would have thought of wearing tiny diamonds or an almost invisible string of pearls that cuts the line of the neck unbecomingly and contributes nothing to the beauty of the face.

Years before *la Dame Mode* discovered silver fox, before that noble fur was ever worn for breakfast, marketing, shopping, office as well as gala dinner, embassies and court, and every suitable but mostly unsuitable place, and before my cook wore it on her winter coat—I had in my possession a beautiful evening cape of this fur that touched the ground.

I remember that I shocked Molyneux by insisting that the skins be as white as could be found. White skins were not considered fashionable then. In the old days of Russia, no respectable lady would ever wear silver fox if it were not inky black. She never would venture such vulgarity even if the fur were to be used merely as a lining for warmth. But today the furriers force Nature to produce the platinum fox!

Years and years before the present Queen Elizabeth of England launched the hoop skirt, I wore one daily and when I did not wish to dance, I would use those balloons as an excellent excuse. And ten years in advance of other singers I gave my recital first in Europe, then in Chicago dressed a la *Empress Eugenie*. Those Second Empire gowns were so enormous that I could only come on the stage passing through a door sideways. Naturally this novelty produced a sensation, and during my singing I was inconvenienced by the constant clicking of cameras. The sensation was augmented by the fact that each change of gown was accompanied by a change of jewels. With my enormous white satin gown I wore enormous diamonds; my brown costume blended harmoniously with rubies; the rich gold one with deep emeralds, black velvet with Oriental pearls and so forth.

The unusual, the exotic, so appealed to me that during the Coronation I had Suzy from Paris copy for me all the turbans the Oriental potentates were wearing at this unique event. I embellished them still farther with the wonderful antique collection of Oriental jewelry in my possession.

I was never named as one of those so-called "best dressed women in the world." The press pinned on me the distinction of a rather eccentric, striking, original woman. In the beginning—to tell stories behind the scenes—the title of "best dressed woman" belonged to those who bought their gowns by quantity rather than by selectional choice. An American woman, perhaps the first who had that title in Paris, never wore the same gown twice. No matter how much she liked it, she was never seen again in that costume.

The dressmakers decided to capitalize this feminine weakness. Hence the birth of the well known title. To confirm this fact that was generally unknown to the public one had only to note that contenders for the crown of "best dressed" were always women of great fortune. No noted actress such as the admirably dressed Cecile Sorel—who sooner or later set the fashion for the greatest dressmakers, modistes, hairdressers and painters —was ever the possessor of that title in the early days. Still we have to be thankful for the origin of the then erroneous title because it led to the present procedure of having experts of beauty and artistes-painters decide the queen for each season. This custom did much to raise the standard of general taste in women's clothes.

A really smart woman cannot feel well dressed when wearing a new gown for the first time. There is always something about its initial trial that is not quite perfect. It is only by wearing it, by correcting the slightest line that is out of place, especially by accustoming the gown to the movement of the body, that finally we feel natural and can forget about the new garment and not feel *endimanché.*

I am sure that I was more individually dressed when I had less money but more time to spend, for then I gave more attention to choosing what I wanted, whereas later, counting every minute and often too absorbed with the miseries besetting me, I would order hats and coats indifferently without being quite sure they were just what I wanted. And the result of such thoughtlessness was that I could never wear those clothes.

For the sake of time, even when I did pick a gown at Alix's or any other passing fashion dictator's, I would have it changed to such an extent to suit my personality that anyone else ordering the same model could never have recognized it as a twin to mine.

I create my clothes to suit my type, of which I alone naturally have full knowledge. The dressmakers, with a few exceptions, are acquainted only with the coming style and are too bound by its special characteristics to see that some women of individual type cannot follow this or that particular fashion without great disadvantage. To frame my body I would rather collaborate with Mr. Gainsborough or Signor Botticelli than accept the help of our modernists who—for the sake of sex-appeal—would disharmonize our bodies by making us push our stomachs out and bend our backs at a sickly angle so that our lungs cave in and thus make us into unhealthy creatures deprived of the primary necessity—breath, spirit, life! Also, not being a slave to fashion, I have the advantage of being well dressed even if I am living far removed from the Rue de la Paix.

It has often happened that an American upon admiring an exceptionally beautiful hat of mine would inquire: "Suzy? Reboux? Surely a creation of Paris?" "Not at all" I would answer. "New York! John Frederick's!" Yes, and often it was a hat created for me by those truly great artists three years before, but its form and colors were so original, so individual that it could easily outshine any hat of the standardized one-for-all despotic Dame Mode.

Because I am not dressed as Number 2768 of Schiaparelli, Mainbocher's "Wally's Blue" or Molyneux's Spring Model 1938, people may call me an eccentric when I am only original in the true meaning of the word. Certainly I love to be very well dressed, and I can feel in perfect rhythm only if my clothes have real beauty in *tout ensemble*. So if I have real diamond buckles or antique ruby clasps on my Greek sandals, precious stones in my collection of dress belts, an opera cape of 16th-century velvet, bags of antique damask, antique Chantilly in my gowns, and lingerie made of real laces—it is because they fit in with the rest of my costume and the other jewels I am wearing. And, if I can afford to have those details—I who so love perfection—and if I have them at no harm to anyone else, why should I not thus augment its total beauty? But I think that one should wear such genuine jeweled accessories not because they are expensive but because they are very becoming and for this reason one really loves them and appreciates them the more for being beautified by the finest and best.

* * *

But let us return to my story. As the time approached for me to go to Chicago, diplomatically I tried to persuade Alec not to accompany me. Finally he agreed he would go to Aiken, South Carolina, to hunt. He insisted on coming to Chicago for my debut but finding he could not wait that long, he appeared in Chicago a few days after my arrival.

In the morning before I left for rehearsal, we made an appointment for luncheon at the Blackstone where I was taking my meals, usually at the same table. When Mr. Cochran asked for my table, the headwaiter told him there was no such reservation. Alec insisted, quite sure the table had been reserved. Later upon discovering that the table was reserved in the name of Madame Walska, whom the headwaiter—oh impudence!—did not know as Mrs. Cochran, my sweet-natured husband became so thoroughly enraged that he left immediately for New York—and without any luncheon.

From the train and again from New York he wired that he was leaving for Europe the following week and gave me stern warning—if not exactly an ultimatum—that I had better think over the situation and ascertain whether I was not ruining our happiness by continuing my singing.

Telegrams followed in quick succession. Finally he concluded a long distance call by saying: "… it may be too late!"

I passed a dreadful forty-eight .hours trying to see all the *pros* and *cons* of the situation. I knew I had to make a decision… I was standing at the crossroads… Which way should I turn? To Alec, whom I had taken for my husband? Indeed I could not change the destiny of my life every few months…

Having been born a Catholic, I considered marriage as a union "until death do us part" and not just a passing fancy. Alec? Yes, certainly Alec! ! But with him—and no resources of my own on which to fall back—it would be such an empty life. Snobbish traveling from one fashionable place to another, playing god to the *portiers* of the various palaces, with no hope for inner growth and no hope of contributing anything of real value to the world.

Or should I stay and continue my singing career? But by so doing I would not only put a cross on my happiness as a woman but also be obliged to carry disillusion in my heart forever.

In my terrible doubt, not seeing dearly in my own heart, I began to look for illumination from the outside world. First, I asked Tito Ruffo what he thought of the operatic career. His answer was that for some time he had been hoping to cut short his own career, but having sustained some heavy losses lately he had to continue his Calvary a few years longer. This possessor of a most glorious baritone voice never spoke of his art except to ask how to escape its burden.

In those days foreign singers were so often accused of coming to the United States merely to earn a luxurious dollar that I felt Mr. Ruffo's answer could not persuade me completely. Therefore I put the same question to the American tenor Edward Johnson, a charming man and a perfect gentleman.

"Madame Walska," was his answer, "I look at you and wonder why, why—having money—you should want to pursue the most ungrateful and hardest of all careers!"

Those words coming from a man of his high quality almost tipped the scales in favor of my leaving Chicago immediately. Nevertheless a few hours later hesitation and doubt again seized me. In despair I wired to New York to the only person in whose judgment I could have entire confidence, Mrs. Paul Warburg, who had been an intimate friend of Dr. Fraenkel, a woman of great culture and a real person. The next day I received the following telegram:

> "Why expose yourself to the critics' slander?
> Why with the restless stage wander?
> Why to the fickle public pander?
> Go home and belong to your nice Alexander!"

I was shocked beyond expression by that message. I decided to leave Chicago—not however to follow her advice but because, coming in such frivolous form, it paralyzed the best in me. I felt lonesome, small, useless…

"What for? What for?" I asked myself over and over again…

I left for New York without telling anyone the reason for my departure as it was of too personal a nature to explain publicly. I left before the stage rehearsals started, having only had a few hours of coaching in private. But because I did not give any reason for my departure, the newspapers made up such dreadful stories that their overtones have clung to me to this day and apart from personal anguish they made my artistic life practically impossible.

The story ran that I had left after the dress rehearsal, at which my voice broke—that the conductor Marinuzzi handed in his resignation, unable to bear my singing. A cartoon showed a man in the orchestra pit tearing his long hair and a foolish-looking woman dressed in nothing but pearls with her mouth wide open, while her partner (supposedly Tito Ruffo) stops his ears to avoid hearing her voice.

I must say right here and now that Mr. Ruffo was as kind to me as his voice was wonderful—which is saying a great deal as he was the greatest baritone of my generation. And if Maestro Marinuzzi thought little of my voice he was kind enough while coaching me never to discourage me, by keeping his opinion to himself.

One story went that Mr. Cochran objected to the tenor

Edward Johnson kissing me in that opera. Still another tale had it that my husband did not object to my singing in general, but when he saw my costumes for Zaza, they were too much for him.

Without any truthful foundation, these stories were like a thousand others about various people that are printed to assure sensational headlines featuring a name. They were the kind of stories that often, if not always, break the lives of those unfortunate enough to offer copy good enough for headline butchery.

* * *

I arrived from Chicago at my tiny New York house, which I had built for Dr. Fraenkel, only a few days before Christmas, and immediately I started preparations for celebrating it in my usual way.

I am very much of a traditionalist. Christ's birthday in Poland is an extremely elaborate holy function. In America Christmas is developed to the utmost—if not in a merely religious way. Having no children of my own, for many years I had dedicated this holiday to the daughter of my best friend, Rosemary Baruch. Only a few intimates were invited as in my mind Christmas should be only for the family, the servants, their children and those less fortunate than we should take an important part in those blessed festivities.

On Christmas Eve, dressed as Santa Claus, I stood on the window sill behind the curtain, with an enormous bag filled with presents on my shoulder, holding a piece of window glass that I would break with a hammer the moment I jumped, to sound as if I had actually come through the window. I wanted the illusion to be perfect on account of the skeptical minds of modern children. The first time I did this in Dr. Fraenkel's home, it was so realistic that he immediately left the library to call someone to come and replace the broken pane in the window, that winter being especially severe.

The distribution of presents followed under the vague light of the Christmas tree candles—such an innovation as electric lights was excluded, for they were not in keeping with the old-fashioned atmosphere.

When the first star appeared in the sky, we sat down to an early dinner consisting of twelve fish dishes. Meat was not allowed until the next day. There was fish soup, cold fish, boiled fish, roasted fish, fish with brown sauce and currants, fish with white sauce and grapes, and so on—an endless procession of fish served on a clothless table covered with hay to remind us that twenty centuries ago little Jesus was born in a stable. Above the table, under the table, all over the table, around the plates, under the napkins, in every possible and impossible place, there were tiny little presents that were distributed after each course.

Since my return from Chicago like a prodigal child, Alec was happier than I had ever seen him before. He was happy that I had left the Opera, happy that in a few days I was going with him to Europe, and especially happy at having his own way. He looked less bored than usual and smiled more often. He continuously asked me what I wanted for a Christmas present… I kept answering that I did not want anything.

"Would you not like some pearls? Cartier showed me some of exceptional beauty," he finally said.

I was annoyed at such a way of offering a present and purposely said I hated pearls for I could not help remembering a very ugly incident which had occurred prior to my departure for Chicago.

I had been at Cartier's looking at some bracelets. It was then the style to wear as many bracelets as you could on the same arm. (Gossip carries the story of a beautiful American woman in Paris who asked each of her flirts to give her a bracelet. As it was during the war, someone on looking at her arm loaded to the elbow with the bands of precious jewels maliciously said: "Service stripes?")

I had a few bracelets in my possession and I wanted to verify whether I would care to follow the trend of the fashion, which is a thing I rarely do as I have a particular aversion to following the multitude in styles of any kind. While I was trying seven or eight bracelets on one arm, I suddenly saw Alec in the mirror. He asked what I was doing. I explained.

I had already realized that I did not want to cover the natural beauty of my delicate wrists with the artificial beauty of rubies, diamonds and emeralds, encircled in rigid metal of platinum. Satisfied with the confirmation of my inner taste, the episode of those bracelets was promptly discarded from my mind.

A few days later Mr. Cochran knocked on my door around luncheon time and, showing his bored unsmiling face, forcibly threw a package on my desk, saying: "Here is the proof of my selfishness!"

If I had wanted to be witty, I might have asked him whether it was necessary to prove it—was it not plain enough? But in those days I was so crushed and so overcome by suffering that my sense of humor was buried deep within me.

I opened the ugly-looking package done up only with rubber bands, and to my great surprise eight or nine of those bracelets I had seen at Cartier's fell onto my desk. My heart stood still in disgust... But I controlled myself sufficiently to ask him for an explanation of the selfishness he had mentioned.

"Well, you see," he said, "when I met you at Cartier's the other day, it never occurred to me that by chance it might give you pleasure to have those bracelets. But today I was bored... I had almost half an hour to waste before luncheon... I did not know what to do with myself... I was passing Cartier's when an ingenious idea came into my head. I said to myself that Ganna had looked at those bracelets the other day... If I got them for her today it would kill a few minutes of my time... So I did, you see!"

I could not even thank him. I never spoke about it. He did not expect it anyhow. His purpose was achieved. He admitted if candidly. With a miserable joyless face and head bent low he left my room, feeling ashamed and humiliated…

* * *

That Christmas Eve as I stood in my room ready to go down and play Santa Claus with my snow-white beard and heavily loaded bag my devoted maid insisted on giving me a small package. Feeling too warm in my hood and mask and not being able to see clearly, I told her irritably to put it down some place as I had my hands full just then.

"It is Mr. Cochran's Christmas present," she mumbled. And only then did I notice the embarrassment on her sensitive face. Her noble heart understood that such a way of giving a Christmas present to a bride of a few months would mortify and crush my heart. With difficulty I opened a Cartier *écrin* and found in it a ring with the biggest heart-shaped diamond of magnificent water I had ever seen. I also saw—and how much more important—through tear-filled eyes my beautiful Christmas spoiled because my husband did not sense the difference between putting his present directly on my finger, hanging it on the Christmas tree for me to discover, or hiding it under my pillow rather than sending it through a servant.

My new life with him—and this time *for him*—started with this bad omen. Reality did not correspond at all with my imaginary vision! I could no longer blind myself!

A fortnight later in Paris I again had further confirmation. The house Alec had bought on the Rue de Lübeck in ten minutes' time before we sailed was to be rearranged and repainted to be ready for our return in March. When we arrived at the end of December, naturally nothing was ready. Therefore Alec decided to leave right away to hunt in England. I asked him if I could go along with him.

"Oh, no! Women are a nuisance when men hunt," he laughed contemptuously.

As soon as he had his own way, he forgot that I had abandoned my singing for his sake. In America, without his ponies, he desired my presence more than anything else but now riding to hounds reigned supreme and nothing else was more important.

As a compensation—he thought he owed it to me—he gave me a beautiful Rolls Royce; forced me to accept a sable coat worth a million francs and so big, so heavy that it made me look old and fat; reserved almost an entire floor at the Carlton Hotel in Cannes; and sent me there alone with half a dozen servants to enjoy the grand season on the Riviera.

I have never enjoyed the life in those luxurious hotels. Never having tasted a glass of wine or any alcoholic spirits in my life, not smoking, not dancing, not being fond of sports and not gambling, I have *always* felt out of place in all casinos. But in that moment of my life my presence there was rather dramatic!

I had been sent like a beautiful doll to obey my master's orders to enjoy myself. Naturally he wanted me to be happy so that his hunting season would not be the least bit spoiled by the thought that I preferred to be with him or that it was not by my own choice that I was in the south of France during the smartest month of the year!!... After five lengthy days in Cannes, I ran away from his idea of Eden for me and returned to Paris on the pretext that it was necessary for me to supervise the decorating of the house.

The inevitable had to come. Indeed! Spring found us reunited in our home on the Rue de Lübeck. In the daytime—separately though—we were busy visiting antique shops to complete the furnishings. But the evenings were dreadful.

Fortunately we rarely dined alone for Alec insisted on entertaining various friends night after night. If however we chanced to lunch by ourselves, he actually did not open his mouth unless it was to be rude to the excellent cook or to abuse the perfect butler we had, while with each morsel of food I swallowed my tears trying to conceal them from Alec and the servants—as if we can ever hide anything from those silent witnesses of our daily life!

Anyhow our house was more like a restaurant… It would often happen that in his inconsiderateness without consulting me he would telephone from the Travellers Club direct to the butler announcing that he was bringing four or six friends to lunch—friends of whose existence I had never even heard. On the other hand, for the sake of variety—as he considered it a bore to repeat himself—he would gallantly ask if he might invite certain socially prominent American friends to dinner; and then when everyone had arrived, not only was he not there to introduce them to me but the *maître d'hôtel* would suddenly announce dinner and seeing my surprise would inform me that Monsieur had just telephoned he was dining out.

Yes, the inevitable came. I can still wish that it might have come in a less ugly way than it did. Such things occurred as Mr. Cochran's having the furniture removed during my absence from my New York house which Dr. Fraenkel had left to me and even having spies set to try to get some evidence against me. All I can think is that he must have found some distraction from his boredom in such revengeful acknowledgment of his inability to accept the happiness my full juvenile heart desired to give him.

If he had only said he wanted a divorce, I would certainly have given it to him instantly. Actually we were divorced from the moment of our wedding—so such a thing as the legal papers did not mean much. Instead he left for a supposed two days' absence in London. His valet however the next day took all his clothes away without my knowledge. Returning that afternoon, I saw a huge "For Sale" sign in great evidence before our home. That is why I told his lawyer that I would fight the divorce to win one of my own and have right on my side.

I prefer not to remind you of the ugly details of that divorce. Suffice it to say that the newspapers had little trouble in trying to further their version of my scandalous career. To cap the story of my tragic disunion the press went so far as to cable from Paris that I had inaugurated a new fashion—two weeks of mourning after the final divorce decree! !

*Adversity is a severe climate in which the weak
succumb and the strong gather new vigor.*
— COMTE PELET DE LA LEZÈRE

HAVING LEFT Chicago without explaining the whys and wherefores of my departure, the resulting newspaper stories explain why I was never given a fair chance to be judged on my singing merits just like any other débutante. My divorce furthered my front-page newspaper career not as a beginner but as an already hierarchically established *vedette*. I was given headlines *hors concours* after marrying "the richest bachelor of America" and after the mysterious way I had left Chicago.

Curiously enough, when I first arrived in the United States and desired to give some concerts with the Russian Balalaika Orchestra, I was told it would be very difficult to get a chance as I was not known. Metro offered me a three year contract in motion pictures but refused to take me for only a few pictures, explaining that it would not be worth it as they would first have to spend a fortune to build up my name. As I did not want to forsake my singing for such a long period, I did not go to Hollywood. Now, because of the notoriety the newspapers have attached to my name, I have more difficulties than when I was a total stranger. That's the irony of fate!!!

A fantastic incident happened a few months after I arrived for the first time in America when a movie producer unexpectedly and urgently needed to find a substitute. Mr. Lee Shubert, who was most kind to me and wanted to be of service, sent his car to take me to the Fort Lee studio as quickly as possible. In order to make the best appearance I put on my Russian sable coat, my pearls, and the best things then in my possession. At Fort Lee I was shown to an almost empty ugly office with ordinary wooden chairs, one of which I disdainfully took.

Five minutes later a heavy man with an eternal cigar glued to his mouth burst into the room, looked around as though he did not even see me and shouted loudly:

"Where is that girl? Where is that girl?"

A boy ran in and simply pointed to me as I sat there in all my finery.

"What? That!" said the man with as much disgust and contempt as the mouthful of cigar would allow.

"Get me Shubert on the phone," he screamed in a thunderous voice.

"Hello! Lee? For God's sake, what do you mean? Making fun of me? I ask you for a Broadway girl and you send me Queen Mary of England!"

* * *

The stories of my divorce from Alec Cochran had hardly quieted down when those about my marriage to Harold McCormick began.

In those days all the members of the McCormick family were great favorites with the press. It started with the scandalous news about Harold's secret operation... (As if anything can be secret or sacred to the press! !) Then his children disputed the doubtful privilege of being in the limelight. The same news about Mr. Jones or Mrs. Smith would have been worthless to a newspaperman but the name of the rich McCormicks was like honeysuckle to a bee. Thousands of people are divorced and remarried, and nobody is dishonored by it. But because Mr. McCormick had divorced the daughter of John D. Rockefeller almost at the same time that I divorced "the richest bachelor in America"—the sensationalists could hint at a scandal. And if the storm broke over the head of Mathilde McCormick when she married a Swiss riding instructor, it was only because she was born a McCormick and a granddaughter of Rockefeller. Since she had no other claim to the public's attention, she was soon forgotten —but my public career made me the constant prey of reporters.

Even when I married Harold McCormick, the curiosity around my person did not diminish. At Salzburg, where we went after our wedding, many musicians and other artistically-minded personalities at the Mozart Festival followed the performance by reading the score. But the next day the cables had it that only I did such an extravagant thing. Somehow the press managed to make the news sensational!

And again in Carlsbad, where we stopped along with a great many other prominent Americans, it was our picture that was sent to all the papers, with the caption that after three weeks of marriage we were *still* together! !

* * *

In Paris I sang Beethoven's Ninth Symphony with great success. Nobody knew me then in France and to the critics I was just anybody who sang well. However the American reporters, unable to say anything bad about my performance, could not refrain from cabling that I was a success in —a chorus! !

Lest it be thought that I am suffering from a persecution mania, let me quote in this connection from an article by the revered critic A. J. Henderson, written on April 13th, 1923, about the performance of the Ninth Symphony given by the New York Philharmonic Orchestra under Mengelberg!

"The Ninth Symphony is not often performed because of the difficulty in securing *soloists* who can grapple with the formidable voice parts of the last movement, in which Beethoven's creative imagination soared into regions where singers cannot readily follow. The quartet passages have often been better sung here, but perhaps singers equal to such work are not easily found now."

The importance of singing that work can be demonstrated also by the fact that recently a soprano took a full page advertisement to state that Toscanini had chosen her to sing the Ninth Symphony.

Some of those who reported that Paris concert cabled that I had invented a new fashion by wearing a handkerchief attached to my wrist. Another reporter, more modest and unpretentious, contented himself with cabling about Mr. McCormick's presence at the concert and giving the names of the guests in his box.

* * *

Encouraged by the success of my French debut, I decided to go to America for a concert tour. Unfortunately I met with bad luck right from the beginning. Harold had to be operated on for appendicitis and that obliged me to postpone my already arranged tour for a month.

That made a very bad impression and many of the engagements booked before the delay were not renewed, for the local managers were afraid I might change my mind… *again*, as they put it!

The second reason for the canceled bookings was the threat of an American soprano, Luella Mellius, to get out an injunction against me to prevent me from giving concerts under my new impresario whom she claimed to be exclusively hers. She did not succeed in her suit. But many managers would not risk announcing my concert until the court had finally rejected her case. Nevertheless the harm was done so far as I was concerned, because with each such handicap I became more and more nervous and less and less sure of myself.

I opened my concert tour in Elmira. The next day's headlines were most generous, to the surprise of the local manager and some of the audience. They had not expected that I could sing, having been led to believe the contrary from the many newspaper reports, and went only to see the girl who married two great millionaires one after the other. In fact one woman even went so far as to telephone the box office to ask whether Mr. McCormick would be present at the concert as she would not get tickets otherwise...

The second concert was in Detroit. The same excellent house... The same reaction... One reporter made a special trip from Chicago to be there. After the performance several newspapermen enthusiastically rushed back to compliment me. My manager told me happily that he expected us to get some flattering notices and that the Chicago reporter had shown him a most favorable write-up, which he was wiring my husband's home town.

However I was awakened the next morning by persistent telephone calls from the press asking if they might announce that I was through with singing, that I was going to my hubby and would never sing again. I could not understand what they were driving at until I saw the morning papers. They all carried the story of my failure, printed not in small type on the fifth or sixth page under the signature of a dignified musical critic, but on the front page as if they were announcing an American Blue-beard.

After Detroit I went to Niagara Falls, where the unfavorable criticisms of the Detroit papers had already preceded me, while the good notices in Elmira never went any further than Elmira.

Here again I met with success. The next day one of the critics wrote:

"Perhaps I am only an ignorant provincial, perhaps I do not understand technique in the same way as my fellow critics in Detroit, but I cannot help admitting that I enjoyed her concert..."

God bless him for having the courage of his convictions. Who knows? Perhaps without his encouragement I might have weakened and given up then and there.

A Chicago critic, Herman Devries, wrote that I not only had a voice but knew how to use it. Not one paper in the country copied that. When I expressed my astonishment at such a strange attitude, it was explained to me that if Walska *could* sing it would not be a sensation at all.

* * *

After a short visit with Harold's dear old mother in San Diego, I planned my return to Paris in order to continue my studies as my teacher conducting our symphony orchestra was unable to come to America.

Prior to my departure that winter, Mr. Epstein, manager of the Chicago Summer Opera at Ravinia Park, kept insisting that I accept the engagement for the following summer. For two months he was after me, offering me a thousand dollars for each performance I would sing. However he expressed no curiosity in hearing me do those operas for which he wanted to engage me. I did not prize his offer as it made me suspect that he wanted me only for the Open-Sesame of the McCormick name.

Finally I accepted, wishing so much to spend a vacation with Harold at Lake Forest, a summer residence of Chicago and quite close to Ravinia Park. I was to sign the contract the day before my sailing, but at that point Mr. Epstein very mysteriously disappeared. Later I learned that Edith Rockefeller McCormick had promised him the necessary money for a much desired season of English Opera on one condition—that he would never have Ganna Walska in his company.

I understood. I did not blame him. Everybody has the right to take advantage of opportunities. And yet I cannot help but think that had I been in his place I would have frankly explained the situation. Unfortunately, as a rule people are afraid to tell the truth even when it is the simplest way out and the only way that might excuse anything, arrange everything. Somehow they always prefer even a transparent lie to the simple truth!!!

Failure is what makes the greatest success if you accept the defeat rightly.

Unlike America, jealousy and envy surpass all comprehension in the European theatrical world. Even before I knew the spiritual law, I felt that envious and jealous people ought to be considered as physically ill and therefore more to be pitied than condemned, for they actually suffer more than those they make suffer. Beaumarchais went so far as to say that jealousy is the malady of a lunatic.

A well known Metropolitan Opera singer in Gatti Casazza's time made herself miserable each day of her life because she was unable to bear the thought of anyone else having any good fortune. While reading the morning paper, she would suffer tortures at seeing that someone had got married and had a chance of happiness or that someone else had got money, even if it was an inheritance which meant the loss of a dear one…

I am happy to say I have never known what it means to be jealous or to envy. I am grateful to the Creator for sparing me such a handicap.

I envy—if it can be called envy—only those who have had a happy childhood, for they have been able to store up much of their strength and can draw on it later in life.

I envy those who lived in a century more favorable to vocal art, the century of Manuel Garcia—whereas I came in when Patti, Melba, Lilli Lehmann were gone already. Perhaps they were not greater artists than our contemporaries but Time plus legend has made them superbeings while our Chosen Ones are only human as ourselves. The artists working for the lyric drama are also gone. Bakst is gone! I would so have liked Bakst to do the *décor* for the Théâtre des Champs-Élysées! John Sargent is gone too! I would so have liked to be painted by John Sargent! Having seen his masterly portraits of women, I think he could have done justice to my very expressive face.

I envy those born into families who appreciate and cultivate music and who therefore have a natural background.

I envy the Germans for their knowledge of Goethe's language and a friend who has already read all of Dickens' works.

I envy those who saw Sarah Bernhardt in "Tosca."

I envy all those who were not handicapped by their beauty and rather served by their ugliness, for ugliness inspires sympathy while beauty inspires caution and doubt about morals and about serious intent and purpose.

I envy all those who have had good teachers from the beginning of their learning and thus have not lost precious time searching in vain and finally finding one has to spend several years to undo and forget what the others have taught.

I wish I had lived in Leonardo da Vinci's epoch when "The human planet never had been so rich, when a genius was a quite natural accident, an epoch when it was a rare case for artists to have only one talent," as Taine put it.

I am sorry I did not have Wagner's chance to visit daily the painters' studios, to attend performances of Shakespeare, Goethe and Schiller, to hear his sisters studying singing, and above all to have the privilege of listening to the world's best concerts at the Leipzig Gewandhaus.

Yes, those are my only envies.

It has always made me most unhappy to think that I should be the object of envy. That is why I felt ashamed of my money. Driving to my singing lessons in a luxurious Rolls Royce, I would feel sad when at the door I might meet a wet young girl tired from a long ride in a street car or the subway. It made me feel the acute injustice of this world, the lack of equal distribution of wealth; and it brought me the realization of my helplessness to remedy the situation. I was afraid that my expensive fur coat might hurt students in nothing but mackintoshes; and I dreaded the thought that they might envy my daily lessons when they could only afford two or three a week.

My sensitiveness was so acute that if on getting out of my car I should happen to confront a working girl carrying a box, I would always stop and let her pass by even if it were raining or I were in a hurry, for I feared that she might become embittered by comparing her poor life with what she might judge to be my successful and brilliant one.

For what is success? It is as relative as everything else. A chambermaid who marries a hairdresser and becomes the proprietress of her own establishment on the principal street of a small town with three employees to direct and counting among her clientele one movie star, a cousin of the mayor and an ex-sweetheart of a boxer would probably have the same line of achievement on the palm of her hand as Joan of Arc. A psychic medium in her presence would probably have the same impression of success as in the presence of Rudy Vallee or Henry Ford.

Beauty and morality have been said to be largely matters of geography. Likewise success is only a chain of circumstances and a question of time—Time the all-powerful. Napoleon had a pitiful end in spite of having achieved a name of the greatest historical renown of all time in both hemispheres.

One thing is certain. If you are a nobody, you will not inspire jealousy, envy or hate. "Only mediocrity is not exposed to envy," said Boccaccio. All those who give something to the world are martyrs to a certain degree but inevitably they are victims of their environment.

* * *

If only those who covet money could understand what slight value base metal has and how poor riches are in reality!

For what are riches? The greatest comforts in life are

derived from the most simple and inexpensive things. When you are really thirsty, only inexpensive water will quench your thirst. If you are hungry, what could be more delicious than a cup of coffee and a piece of bread even without butter? When you are tired or sick, what difference does it make if the linen on your bed is trimmed with lace? Often the miseries that money brings cause a person to toss sleeplessly on elaborately trimmed sheets and the sight of the embroidery only accentuates the suffering. But one does not pay to view the glorious sunset and one does not pay to hear the nightingale! ! !

Hans Ryner said it clearly in his words: "In the soul's region, the region of real treasure, nothing is worth buying of what is to be sold."

* * *

Naturally I would prefer to keep silent about all my fiascoes which are neither constructive, exciting or interesting to read about. However, I shall mention them to show how I gathered force to continue after every more or less great failure—to continue and to fail again and again…

* * *

As long as I was not known I was not envied. I sang in Paris and met with success in spite of the fact that in those days I knew nothing about singing in comparison to what I knew later, when criticism however was more and more severe. From the time I was engaged to sing in "Rigoletto" at the Paris National Opera some artists were jealous and could not stand the idea of someone with money wanting to take their places. Those singers whose careers were behind them and had no hope for an engagement in the future would not forgive me for getting a chance, wrongly imagining that this chance was bought. Those not blessed with a specially brilliant personality were persuaded I was engaged for my looks. Indulgent to themselves, they pretended to defend the Art by protesting such a commercialization of the Divine. They were to be the true Vestals! They would see that such things did not happen again! They would discourage such blasphemy and put a stop to such sacrilege!!

An article appeared in a very important newspaper saying I had paid a million and a half francs to the director of the Paris Opera for allowing me to sing. My lawyer forced the paper to retract this vicious statement. The newspaper apologized, but the harm was done—the suspicion was already implanted in the thoughts of the public. As I have proved, thoughts can materialize and doubts can flourish...

On the morning of my Paris Opera debut some Russians insisted on seeing me "for my own sake," warning me that I would be very sorry that night if I did not listen to them. I positively refused to see the blackmailers.

Just before the curtain went up that evening, after preliminary advice not to get nervous, I was told that the baritone with whom I had been rehearsing was prevented from singing. He was the second artist scheduled to sing with me. The first, Joseph Schwarz, who had been engaged a month or two before, had canceled his contract, owing to his illness. The Opera had had difficulty in finding another singer in Paris who could sing Rigoletto in Italian.

So for my Paris Grand Opera debut I saw my partner for the first time when we were already in action, without knowing anything about his acting. Still brave, I was almost calm when I threw myself into the arms of my stage father. The only thing I noticed was that he was taller than the one with whom I had been rehearsing. The duet went well, but at the end of it in spite of a high note that the audience always adored (and which I did well), the sincere part of the audience that applauded was stopped by the hissing of others. I knew then that the Russian visitors of that morning were keeping their word.

During the big aria, which I sang correctly, or if you prefer just as badly as others who had sung there the week before or might be singing the week after, twice I heard lone but persistent hisses. The finale of the third act was not repeated, contrary to the established tradition of the Paris Opera.

I try hard to remember now how I sang that performance. It is exceedingly difficult, for when we improve we cannot understand how we could ever have sung differently.

Judged by those who sang *Gilda* in France at that time, my performance was really not so bad as to warrant a protest in spite of many imperfections which I am the first to admit. The director of the Academie National himself admitted it was a conspiracy. "C'est une cabale! !" he said vehemently.

> *In spite of all discouragement a strong man pursues his object and does not give up except for impossibility.*[6]
> — THOMAS PAINE

If I seem to have dwelled at length on my description of my Paris Opera debut I have done so purposely in order to demonstrate that had it not been *un coup monté* in all its unfavorable circumstances my intelligence and critical lucidity would not have allowed me to believe in my voice any longer. For far from excusing myself, I demand more of myself than others do. Had I had striking and irrefutable proof of the futility of my pursuing my singing from that unfortunate debut, I would have quit right then. For contrary to general opinion, not only do I *not* like to sing but each sound I utter is a tremendous sacrifice to my well-being. It has been a continuous misery for me to go on vocalizing year after year for what is now the second long decade and my tenacity for working in such a frame of mind has been a parallel to Hamlet's "to be or not to be."

Once when I deprived myself of the joy of visiting Egypt for the first time or even going to Cannes for the three-day Mozart Festival because I was unwilling to miss any of my

---

6 Now the word "impossibility" does not exist in my vocabulary any more. Nothing is impossible!

lessons, a friend said to me:

"That is real love. You are the one and only person in the world who has faithfully and unchangingly loved for over twenty years. All celebrated *grandes amoureuses* are just babies before you. You are the only person I know of who knows how to love, really love."

But my answer perplexed him for I said: "All you say would be right if I loved singing but I do not—I DO NOT! I never did!"

"Then why in the world do you keep at it?"

To myself I said: "I do not know!"

To him: "Let's call it—duty."

*To strive, to seek... Not to find
and not to yield.*

IN JULY 1923 my mother-in-law Madam McCormick died, and instead of Harold's coming to Europe as we had previously planned, I immediately went to America.

I no sooner set foot in New York than the manager of the German Opera asked me to sing in some Mozart performances which they expected to include in their otherwise all-Wagnerian repertoire. I was agreeably surprised when they did not ask me to invest some money as had always previously been the case. The only thing they wanted was my name—not exactly a brilliant name in the operatic world—but they were probably thinking of the modern formula which Sarah Bernhardt had launched: "It is better to be spoken of badly than not at all."

I went directly to Harold's summer home at Lake Forest, a few miles from Ravinia Park, where I could attend the Opera nightly and from where I could easily be reached by Alexander Smallens, now a full-fledged American conductor to whom modern music owes well-deserved gratitude, who then was coaching me in "Nozze di Figaro."

A week before the opening of the German Opera Company in Washington, I was informed that the company could not be transferred from the boat to their destination owing to lack of money. I had not the heart to refuse them the initial $10,000 necessary for that journey. I had no personal interest in making that gesture for I was only scheduled to sing a few months later during the Mozart Festival. I gave the money with the understanding that it was only a loan until the company had reached Chicago, where I was assured all seats were already reserved for each of their performances.

It turned out that when Chicago was reached, they not only failed to give back the money which I had advanced but further informed me that if $4,000 could not be found by seven-thirty that evening they could not go on to Milwaukee where the next day's performance was announced.

That afternoon, as the Polish wife of such a prominent citizen as Harold McCormick, I was giving a reception for General Haller, Generalissimo of the Polish Army, and the Rush Street house was filled with people while the orchestra was playing lively music. However the gay atmosphere was obscured for me when at six I was informed that, with all hope gone, the German Opera Company, unable to raise the necessary money, could not take the evening train. While jesting with my guests that the brilliant, dashing Polish officers for the first time in their lives must drink lemonade or grapefruit juice owing to Prohibition, I kept constantly thinking about those poor artists far away from their country, family and friends and about to lose their livelihood. And again I gave…

From that day on the Opera sent the same appeal from every city they went to. From every town at the end of a week would come a long distance call to inform me that the musicians of the orchestra, union men, would wait no longer for their back pay and were refusing to take the train unless I telephone the orchestra manager my guarantee of payment.

It soon became an established precedent that on the evening of the performance either chorus or soloists of the company would not dress unless they were paid. And always a long distance telephone call worked the expected miracle —thanks to Harold's generosity.

Finally I was informed that if the company could only get to New York they would be safe, for they were to stay six weeks at the Manhattan Opera House and would not have the daily traveling expenses to paralyze their budget. They insisted that this would be their last demand. However they were no sooner in New York than the money received from the advance subscriptions was already used up. From conferences between their manager and my lawyer I learned that the situation was hopeless unless another $200,000 was forthcoming and that this was not a worthwhile investment as the empty house during the first week had already created a bad impression.

After arranging for those very interesting artists a Christmas tree set up on the stage of the Manhattan Opera House, where the chorus was singing the carols beautifully, I made my final bow and retired. Two days later the doors of the Wagnerian Opera were closed and the company left for Germany.

This philanthropic experience forced upon my easy response to any needy soul had a great consequence in my development as the contact with German Opera taught me discipline to the utmost, discipline without which nothing worth while could be achieved.

* * *

Up to this point I have explained only my part in the affair of the German Opera Company as money lender. (Harold did not want to figure personally.) Now I would like to tell why I did not sing with them otherwise than under an assumed name in the few attempts I made to take part in their Mozart Festival.

Having advanced the money, I did not want to sing and thus give the newspapers the chance to say I was singing because I had paid for the privilege. And yet from time to time rumor already had it that Mr. McCormick or I was the angel of the German Opera. I knew perfectly well that as soon as the rumor became public knowledge I would be unable to open my mouth from nervousness. And actually when I finally decided to start under the assumed name of Miss Brown in Pittsburgh—the town where my idol, the great Eleanora Duse, died—at rehearsal my voice did not come out at all, not a single note, not the tiniest sound! After trying a few minutes I gave up and postponed the rehearsal until a later date, pretending a sudden hoarseness and not wishing to admit my stage fright.

Later I was less nervous, but already longer and more frequent stories were appearing about my sponsoring the German opera, and I was more afraid somebody might know my real name so that at the next rehearsal with the orchestra I succeeded in using a very small part of my voice and this only in the high register; the lower, tightened in my throat, was absolutely unwilling to obey.

The same thing happened at the first performance in Buffalo, for already the reporters were running after me to interview Devah Navarre, one of many names Mrs. Cochran, the numerologist, had given me and the second name I had used now that the pseudonym of Miss Brown had been discovered.

After the performance I ran through the back of the theatre to an adjoining Negro restaurant with the help of my manager who tried to cover with his scarf the initials on my bag. What a comedy for what was then to me such a tragedy!

* * *

When the company came to New York, people were so sure that I would sing in spite of the fact that the name of another singer was announced that even my own friends would not accept my invitation thinking I was fooling them. Their surprise was great when they saw me in my proscenium box before the performance began.

* * *

Josef Stransky, the conductor of the Mozart cycle, whose State Symphony Orchestra played for the Wagnerian Company, asked me to sing at a February concert which was to take place in Brooklyn. I accepted just to show him my appreciation but I was not happy about it. That particular winter I did not want to sing in New York until I was certain of an opportunity to do it under the best conditions. And since Brooklyn was so close to New York, I was sure my friendly enemies would certainly not miss being present. The very thought of that made me nervous, not to mention the fact that the Brooklyn audience and critics are considered most demanding and most difficult to please. Besides I did not have even the repertoire ready for the symphonic concert. I proposed singing Elizabeth's entrance from "Tannhäuser." But this difficult piece was my first venture in Wagnerian music—with the exception of "Vogel" in Siegfried which I had sung behind the scenes without having to face the audience. I did not feel at ease with the style of the Bayreuth Master but as I had agreed upon that aria I studied it very attentively, as indeed I always do anything I undertake.

A week or two before the concert I received a letter from the Chairman of the Ladies' Committee of the State Orchestra Association asking me to contribute a thousand or fifteen hundred dollars to the association. Thinking that the Chairman was ignorant of the fact that it was thanks to my help that the orchestra had lived through the season (for without my last minute contributions it would have been stranded without work all winter), I explained the actual situation and referred her to Mr. Stransky himself for confirmation and further information.

A few days later I received a short and undignified letter stating that the Ladies' Committee had decided to invite another singer for that particular date, a singer willing to contribute money for the privilege of singing with the orchestra. My indignation was great. Instead of keeping a wise silence, I expressed my thoughts in a letter giving my opinion of the Ladies' Committee, its chairman, and their artistic association.

That was the last of several disappointments I experienced that difficult winter.

Ah! If that chairman had not been so obviously after my

money, if she had allowed me to make a fool of myself, it might have been the end of my struggle to sing.

Who knows?

* * *

I took the first boat for Paris where I myself was to give a Mozart Festival. However, my bad luck followed me. The Théâtre des Champs-Élysées was my property, but only the building as the lease was to run for another eleven years. Consequently I had nothing at all to do with the management. I was in the same position as anyone else—I could rent the theatre from the lessee for a day, a week or a month. The only difference was that as Mrs. Harold McCormick I had to pay much more than any other person.

Unfortunately that was not all. The business of the director of the theatre was not very brilliant. I was even informed that he was broke and on the verge of going bankrupt. However, he had decided to improve his affairs very cleverly through me or more correctly through the rich McCormick name: he proposed that I buy up the lease for many more millions of francs than the whole building with all that was in it was worth. When I indicated that I was not keen about doing this, he thought he could force my hand by creating so much difficulty for my projected festival that I would finally be obliged to accept his conditions. I turned a definitely deaf ear to his proposition, despite the difficulties it caused both me and the Festival, for we were unable to prepare sufficiently for the opening as the manager would not give us the stage for the necessary rehearsals although we had contracted and paid for such use. I became still more nervous when Mr. Straram, the musical director, was forced to take to his bed four or five days before the opening and was advised to undergo an immediate operation for appendicitis. Knowing that this would mean the end of the Mozart Festival, Mr. Straram positively refused to be operated on. When his terrific fever had abated, he returned to his post. But precious time had been lost and my nervous state was certainly worse by that time.

Such were the conditions under which I sang for the first time the part of the Countess in "Nozze di Figaro."

Even my enemies admitted it was a good performance, naïvely expressing their surprise. During the intermission the Director of the Paris Opera, Jacques Rouché, while congratulating my teacher insinuated that the latter had performed a miracle with my voice. The miracle seemed great to Mr. Rouché, for he had heard me only the one time I sang "Rigoletto" at his Opera House. It will be recalled that I could not do justice to myself in view of the unfavorable circumstances surrounding that performance.

The success of my debut stirred up my enemies. Having unwittingly given me a chance, they decided they must make up for their one lost opportunity. They were misled, however, for, knowing that some were working against me behind my back, I had asked Mr. Straram to engage a second singer for my part.

The first night the other singer took the part of the Countess. So my enemies did not think I would sing at all, especially since dispatches had gone to America saying I had quit after a quarrel with the tenor. The reporters were furious at having come to the opening night for nothing. Needless to say Mozart—especially "Don Juan"—was no great attraction to them.

Having missed the first opportunity to hurt me, my involuntary persecutors, the gentlemen of the press, came for my next performance, when some of my envious enemies tried again and again to create a disturbance during my singing. This time however I was encouraged by my previous success and was therefore more sure of myself. Furthermore the realization of the injustice that had been done me and the knowledge of my innocence gave me the necessary inspiration and strength.

There was a difficult spot for me in the second act where

I had to sing one phrase much too low for my voice at that time and which consequently I always sang carefully and timidly, lest I break on the notes. But this time in my newfound confidence, instead of remaining at the back of the stage as I should have, I advanced instinctively (or was it intuitively?) to the footlights and without realizing it myself sang the phrase in full voice as I had never been able to do before, even during the lessons in my studio. The audience probably felt this force in me, and no further disturbance occurred.

The day of the next performance of "Nozze di Figaro," mysterious telephone calls occurred early in the afternoon asking who was to sing that evening, Madame Walska or Madame Matzenauer. Several of those calls came from the Théâtre des Champs-Élysées and from six o'clock on the manager inquired every ten minutes of our *régisseur* which singer was scheduled for that night. But the latter had strict orders to say that he would not know until the first act was over. The Countess does not appear until the second act.

Accompanied by Mr. McCormick, I went to my box by the main entrance during the first act, instead of by the stage door as was my usual habit. I pulled up the collar of my cape and sat at the back of the anteroom to my box while Harold sat with our friends in the front.

During the first intermission my box was the object of much attention, for everybody stared at it. Not seeing me there, they concluded that I was scheduled to sing that night.

The curtain rose for the second act. Matzenauer opened the act with the short but very difficult aria "Porgi amor." A few measures had hardly passed when the whistling began and once the aria was over the applause was drowned out by the predominant if unflattering noise.

Then I was satisfied, not for the Festival, but for my personal vindication, since Matzenauer was one of the greatest singers of the time and there was not the slightest reason to protest against her singing. In the third act when it was clear that it was not Ganna Walska who was singing, she received much applause. Furthermore, a few days earlier at a concert Madame Matzenauer had been received with great and deserved enthusiasm, therefore it was evident that Matzenauer was at first mistaken for Walska.

Matzenauer's own explanation of the unique incident in her career—not *au courant* with the real situation—was that being German and one of the first *boches* to sing in Paris since the Armistice, her appearance had caused some French patriots to demonstrate against her nationality, for, as Saint-Saëns said, "If art has no *Patrie*, artists have."

Again I had direct proof to convince me that my voice was not the chief concern in that episode, therefore I had no legitimate excuse in my heart to give up my singing forever.

So I continued my struggle...

> *Neither disgust, nor discouragement. If thou hast failed, begin again.*
>
> — MARCUS AURELIUS

AFTER SUCH strenuous and heart-aching effort as the Mozart Festival, in which the singers with some exceptions put personal consideration and profit before their Art, I was so tired and so unhappy that I left immediately for Karlsbad.

There I underwent three rather exhausting weeks of Dr. Mayer's *Hungerkur*. Unfortunately my three weeks had nothing in common with Elinor Glyn's for they were twenty-one days of joyless monotony without the slightest diversity. From there I went on to Marienbad, not for the usual *Nachkur* but in order to study with my teacher, who had been ordered there by his doctor.

I had to hurry with my work to get my program ready for my concert tour in Germany, the opening of which took place the following month at Magdeburg with a success which may have been due to the fact that nobody knew me there and my incognito permitted me to do my best.[7]

My second concert at Hamburg went even smoother, encouraged as I was by the success of the first. My next destination was Berlin. On the afternoon of that concert I felt very queer. My vocal guide quietly remarked: "Probably stage fright…" I was doubtful, especially since I had sung better than ever those last days and was confident of doing well.

From four o'clock on I felt progressively worse. I had to admit to myself that I was definitely feverish. Inexperienced, I wondered what one does when one had to sing although physically unfit… By the time I reached the greenroom that

---

7 I was in such a negative state of mind at that time I needed to find a plausible explanation of such a satisfactory result.

night I was quite dizzy. I trembled all over and my teeth chattered so I was hardly able to speak. I became panicky… How I went on I could not tell. By the time I reached the latter part of the program I thought I would be forced to stop in the middle of a song… Still I managed to finish it bravely…

Now I am sorry I did not stop, for had I done so at least the people without prejudice (if there were any in the audience[8]) would have known that I was ill and hence unable to do my best, in spite of the fact that when we are not ill ourselves we cannot fully understand those who are. It is a fact and a cruel fact for artists on the stage.

Singing is by all means the most ungrateful expression of Art. Singers must always at all times be well and must give their best each time they appear—they will not be excused if they do not. An author may write a book during an illness, reread it later, and, if he is dissatisfied with it, he can destroy it. But we, the interpreters of Divine Music, cannot tear a bad impression out of the memory of our listeners.

The great Victor Maurel told me that he sang perfectly only twice in the course of his very long career: at the premiere of "Otello" and at the dress rehearsal of "Don Juan." If such an artist found himself at a disadvantage on the stage, how much worse could it be for an unfortunate singer making her debut, especially if that singer happened to be Ganna Walska, wife of the multimillionaire, about whose voice or non-voice so much ink had been spilled? It could be a tragedy—and it was such a tragedy I met in Berlin.

The exaggeration of my failure went on with the usual injustice. Yes, I say *injustice* and every time I say it I have a right to do so. I sought proof and only after getting it did I make this statement based on the thought that one falsehood entitles a person to distrust and suspect everything else as being just as untrue.

---

8 Again poisonous negative suspicion and lack of confidence!

Is that not fair?

Right after the concert the *Chicago Tribune* cabled the following lead: "Walska failed to charm the critics!" although the first criticism only appeared three days later. Then in a detailed description, it was related how the director of the *Staatsoper* Herr Max von Schillings left after the first number on my program. The actual fact was that he had promised to come to the concert if only for five minutes, as he had a director's meeting that same evening. So I knew that, whether my singing was good or bad, he could not have stayed long—and his short appearance was simply meant to be an extremely courteous gesture.

Also the cables to America were full of such falsehoods as that I was covered with diamonds and that one of my shoe buckles was worth a fortune—when the actual truth was that I did not wear a single jewel! I never travel with jewels anyhow. And naturally I do not wear them on the concert platform unless I am giving a costume recital; and upon such occasions I consider that nothing is too good to use that helps complete the picture. A Chicago critic wrote of one such affair: "From the buckle of her sandal to her emerald tiara she was a perfection!"

I feel that opera particularly justifies the use of anything to enhance the illusion. We must give an exact portrayal of the type we personify if we desire the audience to understand the motives of the protagonist. [For instance, as the toast of extravagant Paris, the fascinating Manon, whose desire for gowns and jewels was stronger than her love for Des Grieux, appears often dressed without the slightest folly about her, without shining baubles which at a distance could give the illusion of being precious diamonds and without which the public would not have the slightest indication of the craving-for-luxury character of Manon which the singer ought to paint.]

To go back to my Berlin fiasco, I dare say that in spite of my illness—which may well have been *Lampenfieber* for all the symptoms had miraculously disappeared by the next morning—my concert was neither so bad nor so important as to justify such a polemic. Indeed the Herr Intendant engaged me to sing "Butterfly" at the *Berlin Staatsoper* the following April because he heard me sing at that concert. This had the greatest significance for me, although, when the criticisms appeared against my engagement in the form of scandalous cables about my having bought my way into the opera, he wrote me a very charming letter—he was a *grand seigneur*—and canceled the engagement, afraid that people might suspect it was due to my rich name.

I do not blame him. Still in his place I would never have put myself in the position of being dependent upon criticism, nor would I have engaged an artist before hearing her sing the part for which she was being considered, for it often happens that an artist is splendid in some parts and quite inadequate in others, just as there are great opera singers who fail to charm on the concert platform and vice versa. I would confirm an engagement only if an artist were satisfactory to me, trusting entirely to my own knowledge regardless of the criticism or gossip.

I do not blame Herr Max von Schillings but his weakness hindered me from judging quite clearly once more my repeated failure.

Naturally the newspapers continued to invent sensational stories about the canceling of my Berlin engagement and my reputation as a voiceless singer grew immeasurably.

Even a failure is enviable because of the attempt made.
— GEORGE CLEMENCEAU

* * *

When I was ready to sing "Butterfly," I first tried it out in several small French towns under an assumed name —not, as the papers said, to hide my identity but because I had been engaged to sing in opera at Nice and the Director of that company thought it would not do for a star of his company to sing in cities of much less importance. To satisfy him and because I was anxious to have a trial before the greater performances on the Riviera, I changed my name to one which Mrs. Cochran had given me after finding that the two "n's" in Ganna stood for negation and were giving me the wrong vibrations.

As a result of this experience—instead of scandalous cables to the United States—I received quite good criticism and acquired the necessary practice I wanted in a normal and calm atmosphere. Furthermore those performances brought me an engagement to sing in the Puccini Memorial under the direction of the celebrated Czech conductor, Oscar Nedbal, at the *Staatsope*r in Bratislava, formerly called Presburg.

While singing there, "Butterfly" and also "Tosca" in the town of Linz, for once ("My father once played with Sousa!" as the saying goes) I felt like Farrar when the Gerry flappers demanded endless curtain calls before and after each act. Long after the performance the curtain rose again and again to make me acknowledge the audience's enthusiasm.

Full of confidence after such encouragement, I went to Nice. I do not intend to say I sang beautifully for it is all but impossible for a débutante to sing a new part and give as good a performance as an experienced singer doing it for the nth time in the same opera. Apart from that reservation, however, I must frankly admit that my performance was far superior to the average, for without false modesty (Goethe said, "Only idiots are modest!"), my interpretation was more interesting than the customary one, since I tried to portray a real yellow dancing girl, and I looked so different from a fat European, often a generously proportioned Walkuere, disguised at the most in a kimono, often wearing a Spanish flower in her seldom black but invariably curly and much ruffled hair.

* * *

The applause was rather anemic when the curtain fell after the first act of my "Butterfly" in Nice. Those smart cosmopolitan Casino visitors from Cannes, Monte Carlo and Mentone—all residents of the United States—had come only to see Ganna. They had been told so often by the prejudiced critics that Walska had no voice. Not being able to judge for themselves, they did not care to show their appreciation in the face of what they considered to be superior opinion. They should have listened to Molière's words: "Let us give way in good faith to the things which take hold of us by our innermost feelings, and let us not seek reasons for not enjoying the pleasure we derive from so doing."

During the second act someone in the gallery tried to create a disturbance. Later I was told that three men had been hired by the management to try to ruin the performance because I had refused to buy half the house, as an American girl who was to succeed me in "Butterfly" had agreed to do. I knew that the curiosity which my name always inspired would fill the house anyhow, even if it was not for the sake of art and music. And I was not mistaken.

When the men in the gallery began to hiss, the audience applauded, more out of annoyance at being hindered from hearing the opera than out of thought of justice toward me. Soon however they got afraid of being too individual and preferring to be *tutti quanti* stopped clapping until the third act, by which time the disturbers had been taken away.

The criticisms of that performance were splendid with the exception of the local manager of the *Chicago Tribune* who was doing publicity for the American girl mentioned above. He thought he would serve her interests better if he roasted me unmercifully.

As the *Chicago Tribune* belongs to the other branch of the McCormicks, it was entirely possible that the paper was afraid that they might be suspected of partiality toward a member of the family. At any rate, I was so sure of the facts that I wrote to Colonel McCormick explaining the case. As a result the man who had written the article was discharged, not for trying to ruin me artistically, of course, but for taking money from the American girl!

Some American papers carried flamboyant headlines such as "Walska's Triumph." Others reported: "Walska Failed Again." Those which spoke of triumph figured quite cleverly that it would be a far bigger sensation to carry "Walska Victorious" than "Walska Out," since repetition cannot be expected to attract readers.

The February 1925 issue of "Musical America" wrote:

> "Walska Wins Audience—Will Stick to Career" read the New York Tribune headlines over a two and a half inch dispatch.
>
> "Ganna Walska Fails as Butterfly" says the New York Times.
>
> The Tribune declares the wife of Harold F. McCormick "although nervous won the appreciation of the audience" but the Times devotes ten inches of type to a special cablegram telling of her alleged failure at Nice.
>
> In other words the story of Mme. Walska's supposed (I don't know which story is correct) failure at Nice wins a great deal more space than the report of her success.
>
> This abnormal condition of affairs in journalism is a natural outcome of the exigencies of newspaper practice.
>
> The story of negation or denial is almost always more important from the viewpoint of the newspaper writer. No journalist pays much attention to the distinguished astronomer who praises the theories of Einstein but let an obscure scientist pick a flaw in the relativity idea and your enterprising correspondent will keep the wires humming with stories: "Noted Savant Raps Einstein."
>
> Triumph or debacle, Ganna intends to return to these States within a couple of months.
>
> Then, maybe, we'll be given the chance of deciding which of the cablegrams from Nice was right."

Why, why, is there *always* some element outside the voice that determines my failure and prevents me from seeing clearly whether I should continue this Calvary?

* * *

After the Côte d'Azur, I was engaged to sing at the Vienna *Volksoper*, the management of which I begged not to say much about me to the reporters before the performance. All in vain! Vienna's second opera was poor, its attendance no richer. They needed to fill the house at any price, and in this instance the price was my wounded heart. Therefore three days before the performance the newspapers carried ridiculous stories about my millions and my Czarina's jewels (worn in "Butterfly"—imagine!) and so forth. Vienna had been in the throes of misery ever since the war! How were they to feel when reading about someone so privileged, who flaunted her impotent power of metal in the face of this cultured musical elite? One can easily imagine the atmosphere of that performance and its results…

Articles appeared saying: "All the millions in the world and the Czar's jewels cannot buy a voice," etc., etc.

As a débutante I did not expect to conquer instantaneously musically celebrated Austria—home of Mozart, Haydn and so many others—but I did want the same chance as any other young singer would have gotten.

I had expected the critics would rather like my performance but as soon as I saw those lengthy stories about my possessions and the manner in which I was presented, I knew I was done for. Naturally I got extremely nervous. Every new ludicrous article I read about my Croesus-like fortune augmented my fever and finally I was put to bed with two doctors in attendance, neither of whom could understand why my fever kept rising.

For the first time since I had sung "Butterfly" I did not do myself justice. By the end of the first act, with no experience in handling the situation and nervous and feverish, I was forcing my voice. I had still, as was usual with my public, generous applause and several curtain calls. Only in the finale when, instead of singing, I spoke a few low tones for the sake of the dramatic situation, I felt that the audience did not like this divergence from the traditional. But again I realized that their disapproval was caused by the prejudice against me personally, for a few days previous I had heard Lotte Lehmann at the Vienna *Staatsoper* speak a line for the sake of effect and this liberty she took was accepted with great applause.

* * *

In all my fiascoes I noticed unmistakably that always I had a marked success with the audience if not with the reporters. I purposely say "reporters" for not a single critic in both hemispheres ever wrote that my voice was devoid of beauty and sweetness of timbre, style, musical knowledge or interpretative talent, not to mention personality and showmanship. This fact contributed in the main to my stubborn—as the uninitiated would call it—endeavor to achieve the heights.

Here are a few opinions from American critics known all over the musical world for their impartiality as well as their severity:

Dean of music critics, W. J. Henderson of the New York *Sun*: "The voice heard yesterday afternoon was sufficiently large for any musical purpose, and it was quite as good at the end of the list as at the beginning."

Leonard Liebling of the New York *American*: "The Walska voice is of excellent quality. She put sense and style into her interpretations; she shows musical feeling, and her repertoire is confined only to the best examples of the song literature."

Pitts Sanborn of the New York *Telegram*: "Mme. Walska disclosed a soprano voice of professional calibre and range, uncommonly sweet and appealing in its native quality. Moreover, her production of tone was conspicuously free and unconstricted."

Francis D. Perkins of the New York *Herald Tribune:* "There is much more vocal volume than we had been inclined to expect..."

Olin Downes of the New York *Times*: "She showed inherent musicality..."

Harold A. Strickland of the Brooklyn *Times*: "They came to deride and went away dazed and surprised. The familiar 'Caro mio ben', warhorse of all singers followed, and this was sung as well as any singer has ever offered it. Ganna became a singer... and showed a lyric voice that had many moments of beauty."

K. Carleton Hackett of the Chicago *Post*: "Ganna Walska at her best in song recital. The voice, however, was much stronger than we had been led to expect..."

Maurice Rosenfeld of the Chicago *News*: "Her voice is wide in range, it has considerable power..."

H. Devries of the Chicago *Evening American*: "Her first song dispelled any further doubt. Mme. Walska can and does sing. Moreover, she sings artistically..."

Glenn Dillard Gunn in the Chicago *Herald and Examiner*: "For this woman has something more potent than voice and the fine art of song. She has something more potent than beauty, though of that her dower is justly famed. She is a personality. Her profile seen against any background is a perfect cameo. The harshest critic could not look on it unkindly. Her eager friendliness, her unaffected charm, the genuine kindliness of her smile and the unmistakable sincerity of her lyric address won her public. She sang a difficult program of German *Lieder*."

Ruth Howell of the Washington, D. C. *News*: "The voice is there, a voice of nice timbre with some power."

* * *

I knew I was not deluding myself when I presumed that the public liked me and was always interested in all my stage work, probably because I tried to give the complete illusion of the role I personified. For instance for years before I considered singing the part of Cio-Cio-San in

"Butterfly" I was giving much thought to this interpretation. I was reading much about Japan with its lilliputian gardens, bridges and houses. I even had a little Japanese garden on my windowsill in my New York home until I was obliged to take it away as the children from all the neighborhood were gathering about my window. I studied the habits of Japanese men and women, their manners, the way they walk, the way they live every day while Claude Farrère and Pierre Loti provided me with the atmosphere of their homes and Racinet instructed me on the correct dress; and viewing the Japanese collections in the museums—especially the Museé Guimet in Paris with its rich and rare specimens—enlarged my vision in true surroundings.

Tamaki Miura, daughter of the Land of the Rising Sun, taught me the dances she did herself in the second act of "Butterfly." However not to imitate her, I later changed those steps while studying in New York under the well-known Japanese dancer Ito and kept up my dancing in Paris with Kimora. I also learned to play the Japanese samisen, a kind of three stringed guitar, to the accompaniment of which I danced in the second act.

The result of those studious researches was so productive that some critics on seeing my "Butterfly" informed their readers that I must have learned the part in Japan with an authentic stage director. As a matter of strict fact, it was only after I had sung the part for some time and had already received those flattering criticisms that I took my dancing lessons. I had studied everything else entirely by myself: the wigs, costumes, walk, hand movements, finger placing and such. The well-known Russian artist Erté designed the costumes for me. He did wonders, but I had great difficulty to manipulate those voluminous kimonos. My wedding gown, for instance, consisted of five superimposed dresses each one longer than the other and each of a different color. In order to put on that nuptial gown at the finale of the first act I had the tremendously complicated task of taking off the four kimonos while singing on the stage! The great Antoine created for me the most fantastic wigs, thanks to his limitless imagination. My antiquaire furnished me with authentic accessories such as mirror, comb, pillow, doll; also knife for my *hara-kiri*, and a medical authority informed me of the reaction on a dying person from such a self-inflicted wound. So one can easily see that I did not miss anything which would contribute towards the perfect ensemble.

AFTER GIVING many performances of "Butterfly" all over Europe[9] in both French and Italian, assured that I was a definite success in that part, having never paid a dollar to sing it or to advertise, and having been reengaged to make a return appearance at the same opera houses—the best proof of achievement—*now* I thought it was time to face America.

The Manager of the San Carlo Opera, Fortuno Gallo, for many years, uninterruptedly directed a traveling company all over the States, thus giving many lesser cities the opportunity to hear the opera. He certainly succeeded brilliantly, considering that his enterprise was self-supporting and run solely on the merit of the performances without any sponsorship and especially—contrary to the almost established tradition of the small companies—without accepting a substantial check in exchange for a debut. That fact prompted me to ask Mr. Gallo to let me sing "Butterfly" with his company in New York that coming October, knowing that with his well-known reputation for integrity there could be no insinuation that McCormick's millions had paid my way. I insisted however that he should not let anyone know about the plan beforehand.

I arrived on the sixth of October, and we agreed on the thirteenth for my American opera debut. Again I begged Mr. Gallo not to make any announcement officially until after the stage rehearsal, thus also giving him the opportunity to cancel my engagement if he found me unsatisfac-

---

9 The most beautiful theatre I happened to sing in was the one in Bayreuth built from the plans of an Italian architect and still lighted today by kerosene lamps. Wagner's son Siegfried came to the performance and kept asking Harold what becomes of Butterfly in the last act. During my stay in the Wagnerian city I gave a dinner for Siegfried and his wife. It seemed that this wonderful musician Walther Straram did not especially admire the younger Wagner's compositions and so not wishing to discuss them with him refused to be present unless I would introduce him as an automobile manufacturer! But the joke was on him, not Siegfried; for the minute Wagner shook hands with Mr. Straram he said: "It is useless to ask if you are a musician. You certainly look like one."

tory. Evidently that was too much to ask of an impresario for, though he did not mention my name to the press, he did say that the singer who would do Cio-Cio-San would be announced later which naturally aroused the reporters' curiosity more than the announcement of the actual name would have done.

Suddenly, just before the first rehearsal, in distress Mr. Gallo told me that he had not got permission from George Maxwell,[10] Ricordi's representative in America, for me to take this part. He further confessed that three months before Maxwell had told him he would not allow me to sing "Butterfly". Mr. Gallo however had not cabled me that news, hoping that Mr. Maxwell would reverse his decision.

I had no sooner landed than the papers had it that I might sing "Butterfly" with the San Carlo Company. Thereupon Mr. Maxwell reiterated his decision that he would never consent to my singing Ricordi's music. I proposed that Mr. Maxwell should hear me sing at rehearsal, but to no avail. Without giving any reason, obstinately persisting in his cruel antagonism, he positively refused even to hear about me.

In the meantime the papers got busy. To them it was quite clearly a case of my again changing my mind at the last minute, evidently because I was afraid to face the critical New York audience. But they had to invent some kind of story. A clever singer from Gallo's company took this opportunity to attract attention by giving out the statement (or allowing it to be given out) that we had a fight. Again the newspapers blossomed with such headlines as "Walska Quits Again," "Ganna Cannot Sing," "Walska's Engagement Broken," and so on. I was helpless to do anything about it, especially since I was unable to make my American debut in any of Puccini's operas, as I also sang "Tosca" and "Bohème" all over Central Europe.

---

10 The same Maxwell who a few years previously had been mixed up in the scandal of the poison letters.

* * *

In the meantime I had several propositions to sing with minor opera companies. One manager, Mr. de Feo, mentioned that Mr. Maxwell was his personal friend and that he could get him to do anything for him as his company was going to Canada and Mr. Maxwell, an Englishman, was desirous of being knighted and was therefore anxious to please Lady Byng, wife of the Governor General of Canada, who was sponsoring that opera company. Mr. Maxwell believed that he could achieve his heart's desire through Mr. de Feo and so the impresario spoke to him about me.

My implacable enemy confidentially admitted that he would get into trouble with a very important person whom he had promised that he would not allow Ganna Walska to sing Puccini's music. The desire to be knighted evidently was stronger than his promise, however, for a week later he said that de Feo could give "Butterfly" with Walska provided that he (Maxwell) was not supposed to know about it.

"Afterwards," he said, "if I am asked why I allowed it, I will pretend I did not know about it. Naturally if it were New York I could not be unaware of what was going on but Canada…"

Mr. Maxwell wanted to have his cake and eat it too. Sure of authorization, now Mr. de Feo confessed that he had failed to get certain subsidies which had been promised, and I had given myself most solemn word never to sing in a company financed by myself. So that was that!

Unable to make my operatic debut under the best possible circumstances, I preferred not to make it at all. As I had no more time to study a concert program—my teacher being obliged to return to Paris to conduct our symphony orchestra—I decided to leave for Europe.

Once more the newspapers leaped at the chance to build up the false reputation about my voice and my fickle character. This was enough to justify the managers later in refusing to take me on for fear that as a spoiled rich woman I might change my mind any moment.

Again I had the opportunity to learn that it was definitely not my voice that prevented me from interpreting "Butterfly," for the "very important person" Mr. Maxwell had mentioned turned out to be Edith Rockefeller McCormick, Harold's first wife, then the sole sponsor of the Chicago Opera. It was a very clever move, for to prevent a soprano from singing Puccini was equivalent to cutting her wings...

* * *

I am only writing a few of the incidents of my artistic career and chiefly those which, had they happened differently, might have changed my entire way of thinking. But that does not mean that other cases were less painful and humiliating. They all were characteristic of the atmosphere I always breathed.

Actually some of my experiences were quite funny if only I had not taken them so seriously at the time. There were too many to tell them all, but I want to write about one that happened in Washington.

One morning while entering the stage door of a concert hall where I was to give a recital the following afternoon I heard an unusual sound. I went up the narrow staircase followed by my accompanist, behind whom walked my manager. I was almost at the top of the stairs when I heard a roaring like the lion that introduces the Metro-Golwyn-Mayer pictures. Startled I stopped thinking that perhaps my stage fright was making me hear voices like Jeanne d'Arc. I pulled myself together, took the last few steps, opened the door, and was met by a terrific roar.

I stood paralyzed on the door-sill while my companions ran downstairs. Looking around I saw nothing but a stage prepared like any other stage for rehearsal, with the piano in the center. There must be a circus or a zoo next door, I thought.

Soon my companions timidly reappeared. The accompanist started to play a Schumann song with slightly trembling hands. I had just begun to sing when a sound like thunder suddenly drowned out my sotto voice.

Panic... Screaming... The superintendent appeared trying to calm us. He explained that there actually was a lion on the stage but being in his cage he could do no harm. It seemed that a variety show performed each evening when the King of the Animal World danced a bit. As the tamer could not take the cage away, he just left it there during the daytime. But I need not be at all anxious as during my concert the lion's dwelling would be kept tightly covered and seeing no light he would sleep tranquilly.

We continued the rehearsal—and so did the lion. It was a curious duo in which the voice of the jungle, easily able to cover any Wagnerian fortissimo, from time to time accompanied lace-like delicate Mozart music. It might even be said that Mr. Lion was a bit of a critic, for when my interpretation was not right—and His Majesty often considered it was not right—he would start to roar stronger than ever.

One can imagine the front page stories that afternoon! "Lion Outsings Beauty," "Ganna Loses In Voice Duet With Roaring Lion," "Ganna Walska Bested By A Lion," "Ganna Walska Forced To Quit When Lion Sings," "Singing Beauty Faces Beast At Washington Theatre And Former Flees," "Beauty Routed By Bass-Singing Leo the Lion."...

The hotel management had plenty to do to handle the photographers who wanted pictures of me since my escape from—death! But the funniest part was yet to come. The day after my concert I read in the paper that the lion's owner intended to sue me for damaging publicity prejudicial to his profession in connection with my... voice! !

* * *

My meeting with Leo was not the only incident worth noting from that Washington visit. After the concert I was resting before attending a dinner at the Polish Embassy. To my amazement the telephone rang although I had given special orders never and under no pretext to call my room. All calls were to be directed to my manager, secretary, accompanist or my maid, but never to my room. Orders were repeated especially since the lion episode. However the bell continued to ring so persistently that I finally answered.

"This is the White House calling," I heard a voice say.

And before I could protest at the disturbance the voice went on:

"The President and Mrs. Coolidge will be happy to have you join them at luncheon tomorrow."

I was so puzzled I could not think fast enough. I had not met Mrs. Coolidge personally but as an American citizen I had paid my respects to the President only the day before. Being constantly prepared for unpleasant surprises, I did not know what to answer. Still thinking about the lion story, I feared lest some persistent reporter was trying to get a story at any cost. But already the pressing voice was repeating:

"Hello! hello! Is this Madame Walska? This is the President's secretary calling from the White House…"

Again he issued the invitation, as though he was not sure he was talking to me a moment ago. While he spoke my mind flashed to a similar call in the story of Charlie Chaplin's first visit to London after winning fame as the greatest tragicomedian of the screen: he was then feted by everybody of importance including the Prime Minister, given a police squadron to keep him from being molested by the curious mob and admirers and had many many other honors showered on him. To cap the climax early one morning whilst in bed he received a telephone call inviting him to lunch with the Prince of Wales. Great! It certainly was the culmination of achievement for a poor foundling to be at the table with the future King of the British Empire! When the hour arrived, however, Charlie discovered that someone was playing a practical joke on him…

"Can you hear me, Madame Walska?"

"Yes, I do." I certainly heard him but I refused to be as naïve as Charlie Chaplin, yet how could I be sure the call really was from the White House? I tried to gain time and not to compromise myself entirely…

"Yes, Madame Walska speaking. I am very honored; still I am at a loss what to say, for tomorrow I was to lunch at the French Embassy."

"Do you not know that an invitation from the President of the United States automatically cancels all other invitations?"

"Yes, yes, I know. Only I wonder. You see this luncheon is in my honor and to meet me Monsieur Claudel has sent out many invitations…"

"Just a moment, please. I will speak to the President."

What shall I do? How shall I discover whether it was really the White House calling? If I could only jump to another phone… But already I heard:

"As a courtesy to the French Ambassador the President bids me say that he does not wish to deprive him of your company and asks you to luncheon the day after tomorrow instead."

"I am most regretful," I answered, "but tomorrow, right after luncheon, directly from the French Embassy I am leaving for Chicago, where I have a concert scheduled the following day.…"

Again the voice begged me to hold the wire… Again silence… And while I was wishing I had a bell direct to my secretary's room, I was informed that the President had already gone to the dining room and asked if I could be reached at eight.

But there was no call for me at eight o'clock… So I was right to be cautious!… A few minutes later as I passed through the lobby of the hotel I complained to the manager quite casually that I had left instructions no calls were to go to my room.

"I am awfully sorry but as it was from the White House…" he said.

What? So it was White House after all!

"You can reach me at the Polish Embassy if the White House calls again," I said, still confused by the mystery.

I had no sooner entered the Polish Embassy than I heard the Ambassador speaking with Mr. Coolidge's private secretary, whom he knew personally:

"Here is Madame Walska. She has just arrived…" he said giving me the receiver.

Again I heard the by now familiar voice telling me that the President and Mrs. Coolidge regretted being unable to entertain me this time but hoped that I would stop on my way back from the West.

Next day after the luncheon at the French Embassy Mr. Paul Claudel presented me with a superb bouquet of American Beauty roses sent from the White House in care of the great French poet-ambassador. It bore the President and Mrs. Coolidge's card wishing me "Bon Voyage."

The mind once in effervescence always remains thus, and whosoever begins to think will continue to do so all his life.

— J.J. ROUSSEAU

As I LOOK back over the record of my singing experience, I do not wish to give the impression that pure stubbornness played any part in my determination to continue my course. Such an assumption would be far from the truth, for my extremely critical and demanding mind would not allow me to be obstinate.

I would analyze my case thoroughly and if with each daily lesson I would give myself another chance and another chance, still with all the lucidity at my disposal I knew it was useless, it was hopeless... Coolly I would speak to myself as an elderly person would speak to a child:

"Do not be obstinate! ! You cannot do it! Wherefore then continue this suffering? Wherefore these ceaseless agonies?"

"Very well," my alter ego would answer, "I *cannot* sing— but then how can I exist? Life without work is unthinkable to me!"

And immediately I started to envisage what else I could do. What? Naturally it would have to be something connected with the stage, preferably the dramatic stage, for each time I sang whether in opera or concert the critics unanimously praised my dramatic talent. (One Chicago critic even went so far as to say: "Madame Walska made more of a fascinating drama out of her appearance than any singer has been able to do with a song recital in a number of years.")

But being a foreigner, my accent would allow me to play only those rare parts where the heroine is a stranger to any country but Poland. With my voracious capacity for work I feel sure that if I had studied for the speaking stage I would surely have overcome this handicap but then I felt it was too late, too late…[11]

Still with the knowledge of my seemingly hopeless handicap I never lost any opportunity to try anything that came my way and when I was asked to take part in the celebrated French comedy "L'Habit Vert" for the Dowager Duchess d'Uzès's charity, I gladly accepted. The result was so encouraging that later when Parisians discovered my resemblance to the Divine Countess de Castiglione, I ordered a play to be written around that noted beauty and acted it in Paris with an ease that is generally lacking in débutantes.

After that, each time my discouragement in singing was too great to bear more stoically, I would search for another play. A year or two after "Castiglione" I decided to personify in French Lady Hamilton, but I had no sooner made that decision than I saw an announcement of the opening of a play based on the life of this English beauty—so that was that! ! My usual bad luck, I told myself.

Those were dark moments. I felt useless. I could not sing. I could not act. I was not even a good enough horsewoman to apply as a circus-rider!

The only artistic field still to be tried was pantomime, with which I made annual acquaintance each June at the Grand Prix Ball organized for charity by Princess Murat at the Paris Opera. There, gorgeously dressed I would go as Napoleon's sister, the extravagant Pauline Borghese, or as the Polish legendary Queen Barbara or as the huntress Diana on a white horse whose mane and tail were plumed with pink feathers…

As a result of those galas, in one of my many disheartened moments I made up my mind to venture the speechless drama in Max Reinhardt's famous "Miracle." But as poor Rosamund Pinchot, who was then playing with me and

---

11 Although I once remarked to Manly Hall, the philosopher, that the best years of my life were behind me and his answer still rings in my ears: "Mary Baker Eddy started her life mission only when she was 66 years of age."

who later committed suicide—said: "There is no future in a pantomime, and one cannot do 'Miracle' one's whole life."

* * *

Naturally in each period of despair my thoughts would turn to the movies but I got no offer from any serious company. The only propositions that came my way were from those gambling businessmen always ready to make a Greta Garbo out of any one if she will finance the production. But I had promised myself never to buy my way to any place in the sun of sacred Art. I had no desire for a successful career. I wanted to express my inner being and I knew from earlier experiences that with the help of money this cannot be achieved.

Furthermore, I was not sure that I was good for the movies. To be photogenic it is not enough to have a beautiful face—the failure of many so-called professional beauties in the movies has proved that. I knew that I had a very expressive face. Anyone looking at twelve photographs of me with differently arranged hair would never think they were of the same person and looking at my favorite portrait—a sketch of me at seventeen by a Polish artist—people invariably would say: "Oh! Sarah Bernhardt!" But I also felt sure that Hollywood would never consider starring me in an Ibsen play or a Dostoievski drama but in all probability would want to use my press notoriety to type me as a "Merry Widow"—although I must say it was always my dream to sing that beautiful Franz Lehar operetta.

As irony would have it, when I first went to America and was asked to make a picture as a trial before signing a contract, although I was barely twenty I was given the part of a mother, the mother of Irene Fenwick who was and looked older than myself.

At that period, however, motion pictures had not reached their present standard, and such a trifle did not disturb anybody. Nowadays movies have become actually a great art. I am afraid people do not consciously realize the educational value of this mind-developing medium and merely consider it an agreeable pastime, often even as a way of killing a few hours of the time that is so precious to some others like myself.

My education in history and geography has been greatly augmented by pictures dealing with those subjects, but the strongest spiritual impression I have received in these last few years was upon seeing that mystical picture "Lost Horizon." Such pictures as "Thomas Edison," "Pasteur" and "Abraham Lincoln" inspire our perseverance in highest achievements and enlarge our vision.

Being a lover of beauty naturally, I could not help being deeply impressed and my emotions almost ran away with me when I saw Norma Shearer in "Marie Antoinette."

Moving pictures certainly remove the barriers of space and open our eyes in an unbelievable degree to wider vistas!

* * *

Once upon my arrival in New York after five years of residence in Paris the Customs authorities insisted that I pay duty on everything I brought over, including an old automobile robe which I had brought from Russia in pre-war days and had used all those years I had been in America but could not prove that it had been a long time in my possession. I positively refused to accept the application of such an unjust duty without fighting for my rights. It was on that occasion that I learned of the law that a husband's residence not only determined the wife's resident status but that it carried over for voting purposes. An American woman, who is considered to have the greatest freedom and the most rights of any women in the world, could not vote in one state or city if her husband's residence was in another.

Such laws did not seem to me to be compatible with the great freedom this country stands for. Having mingled widely in European political circles, I was naturally prepared for its manifestation. Therefore I decided to fight for truly equal rights for women as sponsored by the National Women's Party, whose life member I have now been for years. I made many radio propaganda speeches previous to the presentation of the new bill in Albany where on the floor of the Senate I was surprised to see how young the senior representatives of America were, accustomed as I had been to the greybeards of the French legislative bodies.

Luckily the bill passed, first in the state of New York where it was signed by Governor Franklin D. Roosevelt and a few months later in Washington. American women won the right to have independent residence from their husbands.

Later, in Paris, remembering my first political success while totally unsuccessful in singing, I turned my energy toward furthering the Pan-Europe movement which was headed by the extraordinary Count Coudenhove-Kalergi, a league of nations in himself. However, the feminine element of that would-be United States of Europe did not welcome me with open arms, thinking more about saving their husbands from my seductive wiles than about the humanitarian cause. So one day when I happened to sing better, I gave up internationalism…

* * *

Invited to lecture at the Polish Consulate in New York, I chose as my subject "The Polish Woman" but my audience, mostly feminine, was obviously disappointed, with the exception of a Catholic priest who asked me to repeat the lecture at Columbia University, expecting to hear how my country-women obtained the reputation of being irresistible rather than learn about the profound part they have played in history.

Friends of mine in the audience told me that they heard such remarks being passed as: "How many servants do you suppose she keeps to run her house?" and "Do you think she is wearing a corset?" Paradoxically, more seriousminded people did not come on the presumption that I would talk about jewelry or husbands. Such an attitude discouraged my earnest endeavor and I refused to lecture again.

* * *

Then there was the time I decided to drop my singing in favor of accepting the Warsaw Opera's invitation to portray the Potiphar in Richard Strauss's "The Legend of St. Joseph." It was because of my graceful movements that I was asked to play that part but my friends, the gentlemen of the press, spoiled my fun forgetting that the celebrated Russian opera singer Maria Kouznezoff had played it at the height of her glory and merely reported that "Walska, unable to be prima donna, is engaged in Warsaw Opera as a prima ballerina…"

* * *

Thus it can be clearly seen that I tried to touch all branches of life expression: love, art, politics, philosophy, perhaps everything except sports. And if I went so far as to consider aviation, I who do not like anything mechanical, it was only in a dramatic moment of wanting to commit suicide. But even then I did not want to die unless my miserable exit could contribute something to the welfare of humanity, unless I could serve as a human target in hopeless cases when one is sure never to come back from a dangerous experiment.

On the one occasion when I happened to ride horseback, it was to please Alec Cochran, not knowing then that he liked women only after dark when he could not indulge in riding or hunting. In fact I was so utterly inept in my knowledge of things *sportif* that once, when persuaded to attend the Davis Cup tournament in Paris, at the end of a most exciting match I candidly asked my escort which side had won…

> *Art does not reach the height of its dignity when it charms without simultaneously arousing enthusiasm for all that goes to make the grandeur of life.*
>
> — J. REYNAUD

My upbringing left an extremely strong imprint on my life for, even in America—the only country where all who work are equal—I was inwardly ashamed of having any connection with the stage, although I never admitted it to anybody. Sometimes I was punished for thinking without justification *que je sortais de la cuisse de Jupiter*. For instance when I was singing at the rehearsal in Havana, the stage manager suddenly shouted: "Walska, now for you!" Deeply offended by this *lèse majesté*, with a look cold enough to freeze Niagara Falls, I corrected him by saying: "*Madame* Walska, please!" The Queen of England might have envied my attitude of dignity at that moment but the man looking straight into my eyes said: "Oh, no! One calls Caruso not Mr. Caruso." If an earthquake could have swallowed me up at that moment, I would have been happy.

After my marriage to Dr. Fraenkel, who found my throat in perfect condition and advised me only to change my vocal teacher, one day while speaking about my new teacher the Doctor expressed his admiration of my desire to achieve something by my own effort. In his naïve simplicity and bigness of his soul, he could not even for a moment conceive that I was not profoundly pushed toward the thorny road and discarded a lazy life of comfort.

I was deeply humiliated by his considering me better than I actually was. Instead of confessing this to him, however, I felt that the proof of my redemption would be of the greatest value if I tried to become what the Doctor thought I already was or ought to be. Miraculously enough, from that moment on, my shameful disdain of the stage disappeared and the desire for instruction became stronger each day.

In the years that followed I became a constant attendant of the Metropolitan Opera House. At first I went only when Caruso or Farrar sang, but later on I could be found in my usual front row seat, number fourteen, five times a week. Wagner still made me suffer a bit and I used to think it would never end although I no longer fell asleep as I had done in Russia.

Dr. Fraenkel—a great friend of Gustav Mahler, musical director of the New York Philharmonic Orchestra in pre-war days—once asked me why I did not hear symphonic orchestras but went only to hear singing. From that moment on I attended every more or less important concert in town. It got so that—my car waiting at the door—often in one afternoon or evening I would go to two or three concerts, wishing to hear, for instance, an overture conducted by Mengelberg at one place, the New York Philharmonic at another, some vocal soloist at Aeolian Hall. Besides sometimes I went at five o'clock to the concert given by "Friends of Music" or a private musical reception.

Naturally (*cela va sans dire*) I was, like all other women, waiting impatiently for Stokowski's concerts!!

I became music-mad, sound-intoxicated. I would practice my singing from nine to eleven and then rush to the Biltmore or Waldorf Musicale. A quick lunch between one and two—then the Metropolitan Opera till five-thirty. More practicing until seven and after a quick dinner or none at all off I would go to a concert or another opera.

Never tired, I was always seeking, always trying to learn more and more. And I never minded any inconveniences that this desire for instruction was occasioning. Just as readily I went to Philadelphia to hear a new Stravinsky composition under Stokowski's leadership, journeyed from Chicago to New York to see Duse, flew from Paris to the Belgian town of Angers to hear a singer who no longer sang at the Opera Comique in Paris but who was considered the best Manon of past years. And flying in those days was a rare enterprise, for every time I left for Le Bourget airport my household would bid me a very solemn good-bye, and if Mr. McCormick went along he would make a new will each time before leaving.

I would motor a whole day from Marienbad to Bayreuth to hear "Parsifal" and immediately after the performance drive back again the whole night. And when I married Harold McCormick, I did not hesitate to ask him to go to the Salzburg Festival for our honeymoon. As a matter of fact all those years I traveled only with the purpose of learning—never for pleasure, never for a very much needed vacation. Thus I deprived my mind, so curious to see everything, of the spectacular pageants of the fabulous Hindu potentates to whose jubilees or coronations I was invited. Also I missed the opportunity of visiting the sovereigns of Morocco and Algiers as well as courts of Egypt, Annam, Siam or similar ancient capitals of civilization, exotic and full of the great mystical past. In many of these countries I could have stayed at the embassies, where I should have had the best possibility of seeing everything—from the front row, so to say. Invariably, however, the idea of losing a singing lesson upset these fascinating excursions into the almost unreal world of the Orient.

As a result of seeing, hearing and absorbing such a lot of music I became a pretty good critic. One American paper after interviewing me about music proposed to me that I write their European musical news. To tempt me they flattered me by saying I would be paid the same price they paid the foremost European historian, Guglielmo Ferrero.

* * *

My first artistic inspiration I received from hearing Farrar sing the second act of "Butterfly" with her superbly human touch. How I cried after that performance! My heart was deeply moved and almost broke with emotion when I later heard the glamorous Geraldine do *"Zaza."* Then only I understood that one can sing the conventional form which is opera and still give much of one's soul.

Eleanora Duse was to me always the Ideal, the sublime emblem of Art although in the abstract, as I saw her act only a few months before her death. Were I able to choose I would desire to possess her type of beauty. What a poem her hands were!

From Mary Garden I learned what wonders pause and line can do.

Cecile Sorel's ability to project the quintessence of feminine coquetry demonstrated to me the terrific power we women possess if we know how to use it.

After seeing Tamake Miura, the Japanese soprano, I realized the shortcomings of all other Butterflies in comparison to her real Nipponese manners and charm, the charm of an exotic flower in which vulgarity is unthinkable.

Chaliapine's genius was so great that, in spite of the fact that his was a basso—ungrateful voice for song interpretation—he was an emperor amongst concert artists and as great an attraction as any famous coloratura soprano, if not greater. In those last years he was past his prime and his voice had diminished in power but he was still able to create a song by a mere lift of an eyebrow, a gesture of a finger and the layman would swear he had heard the most exquisite sound.

Battistini—Titan of the old school of singing—charmed us at almost seventy years of age. The extreme nobility of his bearing revealed the real grandeur on the stage. When he played the part of a king, he was a king and not a Mr. Smith or Durand masquerading in king's clothes. What a *seigneur* he was in "Hernani"! Also his diction was marvelous, no word escaped the listener's ear.

Vanni Marcoux's personality saved many operas. In "Monna Vanna" he was magnificent! I learned the part with the sole hope that one day I might be able to sing to his Guido. What a joy it is when your partner gives you the necessary illusion to express the sentiment the author intended!

The greatest of all Scarpias, Jean Perrier, proved to me what a real artist can do when he refuses to be limited to the actions indicated on the score. Since his voice has become too weak for opera he plays drama, comedy and motion pictures with deserved success. I am forever grateful to him for his instructions in "Tosca," "Louise," "Manon," and other operas I studied with him.

But it was Anna Pavlova who convinced me that perfection in Art actually can exist. She also taught me that by interpreting Beauty one incarnates it as she did. Those last years she seemed so beautiful that one did not know what to look at—her feet, arms, hands or radiantly inspired face.

Yehudi Menuhin was eleven years old when I first heard him. Tears bathed my face, tears of profound gratefulness to the Creator for allowing us to perceive such divine sounds. If I needed proof of the immortality of inexhaustible spirit, I would have gotten it upon seeing that child play.

* * *

Those and many other artists contributed to my development. But my musical initiation actually dates from the day I met my teacher Walther Straram, to whom I owe everything I am today artistically, musically and literally speaking. He certainly was one of the greatest musicians and men of highest intellectual attainment I have ever encountered until then. Furthermore he was acquainted with the voice—an exceptional thing for the average musician, just as the average singing teacher is rarely a musician.

Through my association with this great artist, I learned to love music with a quasi-religious reverence that I have carried like a relic inside myself ever since as a purification of my soul. The love of music to such a high degree betters us in every way and transforms our hearts through communion with the Divine, making us spiritually kneel before the greatness incarnated in the creators of Bayreuth and Salzburg, before a Beethoven symphony or before the purity of Bach and Haydn. Contact with such a musician as Walther Straram made my soul richer and bigger.

It was Straram who made me appreciate the most important part of an opera—the orchestra. Until then, like the majority of an audience, I thought almost as Dr. Fraenkel did when he was a boy, wondering why there was a conductor for an orchestra since the musicians could play without him…

The public acclaims and worships the soprano, the tenor and to a lesser degree the other singers. But it does not even suspect the abnegation of the hundred real artists, each a musician in himself, who never knows recognition but still is willing to contribute his God-given talent on the altar of Divine Sounds, often enduring the hardship of hearing flat singing of the over-and-over-repeated aria and still unembittered loves music till his last breath. If the audience would only realize the greatness of this collective soul and the richness they can receive from it, they would hold their applause for the singers until the orchestra has finished the last few bars that are so generally drowned out by the noisy curtain calls.

Privileged to having my own symphonic orchestra in Paris, one of the greatest of either hemisphere, I certainly could appreciate the real value of those artists. In all those long years of my association with them, not one failed in the trust I put in them and my respect grew bigger and bigger for the musician and the man! !

*Passionate illusion that made me
see Art as an idol and monarch.*
— MICHELANGELO

SINGING IS AN ART with a capital A and not a more or less successful profession, as it is considered nowadays. Unfortunately, this divine Art is steadily declining into a profession easily learned, without sacrifice, with little or no study, without long preparation. A singing teacher does not need any kind of a diploma or any certificate and can go about indiscriminately ruining the inner lives of those desiring to express themselves through the voice.

It is small wonder that this difficult art is slowly disappearing and that today it is possible to list the great singers on our ten fingers. The places of Jenny Lind, Malibran, Pauline Viardot, Ternina, Materna, Patti, Sembrich, Faure and Maurel—to name but a few of the last generation—are being taken by a new order of twentieth-century cultureless singers, without *feu sacré* but with the assurance that they are super-beings to whom God has given a sixth sense and put a four-dimensional wonder in their throats. How fine to be so distinguished by our capricious Mother Nature, is it not?

A dressmaker or a stenographer must work years to learn her profession, and at best her hard work day in and year out brings her only the bare means of existence. If a cobbler does not know how to make shoes, he cannot earn his livelihood. In Paris where the poorest classes do their business on the streets they provide their own advertisement by singing as they pass along: *"Chand d'habits!"* or *"Marchand d'chiffons ferraile a vendr'!"* as the opera "Louise" characterizes so well. These merchants have trained their voices to carry and to last a lifetime.

The singers of today evidently do not consider it vital to

express their soul in their singing, all they want is a successful career that is easily attainable through publicity, especially in America where advertising has become so potent. It makes me understand what Rousseau meant when he said: "Riches are progress and progress is worthless."

People in America, curious to see and hear everything, encourage this advertising system, for there is always an audience, especially in New York, for anyone who wants to give a concert. American kind hearts patronize them and have a pity psychology, saying "Poor thing! She is so young!" or "Poor woman! She is so old!" They applaud a singer who is ugly out of pity or forgive her because "she is such a peach!" In their great goodness they always find indulgence and some excuse, some justification.

In his autobiography Leo Slezak writes that when still young and ignorant he was engaged by the Vienna Opera. He made many musical errors during his first rehearsal. Finally the conductor stopped the orchestra and turned to Slezak:

"At least take the score and follow it!"

Candidly Slezak answered: "If I knew how to read music, I would not even speak to you!"

That a singer is not necessarily a musician is suggested by a story Mischa Elman tells. He had a pianist friend with whom he used to give concerts. For a long time they did not see each other and then Mr. Elman accidentally bumped into his old friend.

"How are you? And what are you doing these days? How goes the music?" Elman joyfully asked.

"Oh! I am no longer a musician." "No? What are you now?" "Now I sing. I am a tenor!"

* * *

Modern singers study a little here, a little there. Their teachers encourage them to believe they are half-gods. Most of them would make fun of the letter Lilli Lehmann wrote at fifty-eight to the baritone Victor Maurel, confessing her discouragement at realizing how much she still had to learn and how little she knew. A story goes that after having studied a certain difficult aria for twenty-six years she finally decided she could sing it in public.

A few years ago at Salzburg the same Lilli Lehmann complained about those who were trying to follow in her footsteps. As she put it, they came from all over the world and wanted to sing Wagner at once, the most difficult music in German, without knowing the language, without knowing its style, with voices trained only for Broadway musical comedy…

* * *

We live in an age when everything goes faster and faster and everybody wants to arrive quicker than is normally possible. Singers, equally contaminated by this fever, want to get immediate success and a "job." They cannot be bothered or waste their valuable time; they would just attend to some other "business."

Is it a blessing that recognition comes more easily and quickly today? I do not think it matters much except as a personal comfort to the alter ego. Misery never stopped genius in its evolution. Mozart and Michelangelo were obliged to create their masterpieces under the whip of the need for daily bread. But that did not handicap them in their achievement and who knows but without compulsion they might have left much less in quantity to posterity, not to mention the quality which was heightened by their acute suffering.

Malibran, one of the greatest singers of the nineteenth century, left an immortal name as a vocalist at the age of twenty-seven, the year of her death. She achieved her perfection because of the terrible beatings she got from her illustrious father, Garcia, the greatest singing teacher of all time. Had she not been afraid of physical punishment, she would never have become La Malibran and contemporaries would have lost such an example of perfection to emulate.

Money is poor. It will not buy talent for you, instill a sincere look in the eyes, make old marble like Venice's San Marco, acquire health, create a hundred-year-old tree, stop lightning, bring a cool breeze in the midst of torrid heat, or make hair or nails grow back by evening if they have been cut in the morning. Poverty never harmed any talent, because talent is within us and is developed by our inner life while the outer life has little meaning. Those who blame lack of money and opportunity for their spiritual, mental or artistic stagnation only prove that the divine fire of inspiration was so weak in them that a passing wind from an unheated room could have extinguished it. As Madame de Lambert rightly said: "If you are wise, wealth will neither lessen nor increase your happiness."

Judging from my own experience, I would say that money can help art but not the artist. The only satisfaction my much coveted bank account ever gave me was the opportunity to create a center of music in Paris at the beautiful Théâtre des Champs-Élysées. In that glorious setting, I was able to give music lovers a great symphony orchestra chosen from the elite of traditionally great French instrumentalists which, thanks to the possibility of daily rehearsals, was to attain near perfection in music.

It is a well-known fact that the Théâtre des Champs-Élysées is the most beautiful theatre in Paris. It consists of three auditoriums completely independent of each other with separate entrances for each: first, the Théâtre des Champs-Élysées, where only concert, opera and the greatest musical performances are given; secondly, the Théâtre de Comédie des Champs-Élysées, where drama and comedy are performed, the so-called Théâtre Jouvet, named after the talented producer who there for years gave Paris the best in theatre, and where was first presented every new work of Girardoux; and thirdly, the small hall called the Studio des

Champs-Élysées where important *avant-garde* productions such as "Maya" were seen.

This marvelous temple of culture presents a facade entirely covered with marble and crowned by the majestic frieze "Apollo and the Muses," executed by the sculptor Bourdelle.

In the opera hall the borders of the luminous crystal-arched dome are the setting for four decorative panels admirably done in fresco by Maurice Denis, depicting the entire history of music: the Origins, the Symphony, the Opera, the Lyric Drama; the Muses and the Graces, dominated by Apollo, stand opposite Parsifal amidst the Flower Girls. The entire hall is enriched with marble and gold and its walls are so spacious that they can be used as a gallery for exhibitions of painting or other works of art.

Foyer des Artistes, an exceptionally large greenroom, is decorated by Marvel and fitted out with every conceivable convenience for the comfort and well-being of the artists.

While the Théâtre de Comédie des Champs-Élysées can be equally proud of its walls covered with paintings by Villiard and other famous men, the stage boasts an entire curtain painted by the great artist K. X. Roussel.

In short, from the moment of its conception, nothing was overlooked that could make the Théâtre des Champs-Élysées a monument to the Arts.

* * *

We become what struggle makes of us. How often do we hear of a musician or painter who has talent but like so many people with money does nothing really worthwhile after showing brilliant promise? The phrase is: "His misfortune was his money, for, not being obliged to work, he became a dilettante." Most of the great minds of all time had to struggle for their livelihood while carrying inside themselves the greatest of riches, those that do not come through earthly possessions.

Speaking for myself, I know that life was never so hard

for me before I had money or the reputation of having it. Money and beauty harmed me far more than my defects and insufficiencies. Being rich, people would never believe that I was earnest in my endeavors. And it would be erroneous to imagine that beauty played a favorable part in my seemingly successful, and full of wonders life! Just the contrary! It would be a mistake to think that the Harvester King fell in love with me and divorced the Rockefeller daughter because my beauty fascinated him! Because every time people were telling Mr. McCormick about my looks he would answer "Oh! But her soul is much more beautiful" and years after our marriage he sadly conveyed to me "You know, Ganna, I did not know you were so beautiful, I just thought you were nice looking but since we are married everyone speaks about your physique… If only I had known it before I never would have dared to ask you to marry me!"—"Why?"—"Oh, but what a responsibility to have such a wife! What chance have I with you when the whole world admires you… Who am I to be privileged to have you all to myself?"

I recognized Freud's hand. I knew Harold was being analytical following Dr. Jung's instruction…

He experienced once the same disagreeable feeling when we were leaving for Europe and seeing my passport he discovered that I was at least ten years younger than he thought me to be. He felt quite miserable about it. Answering my question: "Why should it make you unhappy?" he again repeated "But what chance have I with your reputation (mind you *reputation* for he actually did not feel my beauty and once told a friend: 'If only Ganna had larger ankles, hands and feet she would be quite handsome') of beauty and being much younger than me what chance have I?…"

Even the fact that I had a voice was against me, for, if I had had none, I would never have attempted the hard path I chose. To have a voice is the least of the struggle. In spite of

Rossini's dictum of "Voice first, voice second, voice third," experience showed me that Jenny Lind's maestro had better judgment when he said: "Firstly character, secondly character, and thirdly character."

Actually I believe it would be more true to use a compromise: Primo—the voice, especially if one wants to become an opera singer; Secundo—the character to be persevering, studious, undiscouraged and always willing to improve; and Tertio—an inborn intelligence or at least the willingness to acquire, develop and cultivate one.

Given a voice, the important question is then to learn to use it. To learn to sing, one must be lucky enough to find a teacher who knows something about voice—a rare person to be found these days—who is honest and who can help each individual case. It often happens that a good teacher cannot help a particular voice while on the contrary a bad teacher can accidentally produce one wonderful pupil although ruining the voices of many others who have come to him on the basis of the one success. As W. J. Henderson, dean of critics, wrote after the debut of a potentially great singer at the Metropolitan Opera House: "Even her teacher could not spoil the natural beauty of her voice."

A teacher who knows voice but is not honest can easily handicap your aspiration by allowing you to attempt public singing too soon or by permitting you to sing pieces not suitable for a particular voice, rather than risk losing the pupil.

Personally I prefer an honest if poor teacher, for a clean and uncalculating atmosphere at least gives the individual the chance to find his own way out.

Singers who have naturally placed voices must study particularly hard if they want to retain their voices for any length of time. Granted that a natural voice is a greater asset than a good teacher, nevertheless Nature did not intend any throat to sing Wagner or Verdi three times a week.

If you possess a voice and are lucky enough to have it

well trained, it will only give you the opportunity to become a good singer with a more or less good voice. But is that enough these days? No! How often, hearing good singers doing their best but preoccupied with our own thoughts, we wonder about fixing that tile in the bathroom! That is because only one of our senses—the hearing—was occupied while this good artist sang. But our mind, perpetually in effervescence, had nothing to grasp and ran ahead of time and space.

The chief requirement for our study is perseverance. We must never be discouraged because we do not see daily improvement; it comes suddenly, like spring flowers blooming overnight.

Though the old-fashioned opinion prevails that a singer needs only to have a nightingale in her throat, still a certain amount of culture is needed by the singer who wants to create her song or her role. With the nowadays swift moving through the world—a knowledge of languages is indispensable to the opera singer. Singers can easily render a most dramatic moment ridiculous by bad pronunciation or a funny accent. Italians and Americans are especially guilty of this when singing in French. America's great exception was Farrar who sang all languages beautifully.

* * *

In order to sing opera, it is not sufficient merely to cultivate the voice, for the opera stage today demands much more than beautiful singing. In the good old days—perhaps not so good after all to our eyes—there were only one or two sets for ten operas and the prima donna rarely had two different costumes. All that has changed now. Since the Ballet Russe called upon the modern painters such as Picasso to collaborate in every creation, each new production demands from a singer as her contribution to the ensemble an art combined with the voice.

When I was preparing the part of the Countess in "Nozze

di Figaro," I first worked at it mentally for two years and only then did I concentrate on it musically, vocally and scenically. I heard as much Mozart as I could to get the proper musical style. I never missed a Mozart performance in Paris, London or New York. And, of course, I frequently went direct to the source, to the Salzburg Festivals.

When I learned that the Vienna Opera still kept the ancient traditions, I went there to hear the true conception and the *tempi* established by departed masters from conductors such as Gustav Mahler. Incidentally I never spared myself any poor performances, for one can learn a lot by listening to bad execution provided it is not at the beginning of one's studies. It is good to see the mistakes one should avoid, for by comparison of the good and bad one can choose what to take and what to reject. As Pascal put it: "Sometimes one can correct oneself better by the sight of what is bad than by the example of what is good."

It seems to me that the best way to develop creativeness is to learn the technique of the great artists and to imitate them. First, do as well as they do; then try to surpass them in order finally to surpass yourself. To put it in the language of sports, always try to beat your own established record for in Art as in everything else, if we do not advance, we retrograde.

Then comes the most difficult period: to forget about technique and to be yourself, your best self, the best that is in you and it is deep in every being. Try to forget all you have learned, for "work alone wipes away the traces of work," according to Whistler. Michelangelo spent eight months in the Carrara mountains doing nothing but choosing the perfect piece of marble for his monument of Pope Julius. If such a genius, such a mental colossus, saw fit to do it, a little chrysalis of a débutante might well do as much.

The book of "Nozze di Figaro" was written by Beaumarchais and therefore I acquainted myself with the works of that author by seeing all his plays beautifully given by the Comédie Française at the Théâtre Molière. I especially admired Cecile Sorel in the part of the Countess in "Mariage de Figaro." When played as comedy without music, the part could easily be made ridiculous if it was not admirably played. With her remarkable *abatage* and dynamic personality Sorel made of that constantly weeping, wishy-washy female the most important and fascinating character of the play.

When the Comédie Française went to the Castle of the Duc de Choiseul to produce "Mariage de Figaro" in the place of its origin, where the actual prototypes were supposed to have lived, I followed them with excitement, happy to get more atmosphere and bathe myself in the environment that had inspired the genial author. When the Countess made her entrance in an authentic *chaise à porteurs,* I was easily transported to that decorative century for *ambiance* was perfect and illusion complete. Having studied this opera so thoroughly, no wonder the role of the Countess is one of my favorites!

* * *

I applied the same thoroughness to my preparation for concerts as I did to my studies for the opera and whenever I was learning old songs which date back to the time when there was no piano, I studied those antique melodies to the accompaniment of their contemporary musical instrument, the harpsichord. The queen of *clavecin* players, the great Wanda Landowska, initiated me into its tradition.

If I was contemplating a new creation, my all-observing eye and my exceedingly receptive mind became immediately aware of all things surrounding me, every tiniest impression, every manifestation of beauty. I was hearing all available lectures about music. I was looking for old prints and visited the museums more frequently. When I was preparing to play in Max Rheinhardt's "Miracle," I frequented churches and cathedrals all over Europe from quatrocento to baroque—in order to get the feeling of altitude into my soul.

If ever I take a little care of my health, it is only so that I may be strong enough to enable myself to achieve the masterpiece that I may be carrying in me. And so without coquetry—unless it is natural inborn Polish femininity—I am grateful to my Creator for the beauty of my hands because hands are the first thing that strike one on the stage, as our lovely Lucrezia Bori proves.

When several painters after seeing me in "Nozze di Figaro" said how strangely I resembled the portraits of the famous Castiglione, "*La Divine Comtesse,*" who reigned as Queen of Hearts over the Tuilleries and its romantic emperor, Napoleon III, immediately I began to read and learn everything about that legendary beauty and to collect her portraits, of which about nine hundred are now in my possession. And in 1929 the French dramatist Régis Gignoux wrote a play around her in which I impersonated the heroine. From that time I fixed my hair in the style of the Second Empire with long curls down each side of my head, while my contemporaries at the moment were cutting their hair and even shaving the nape of the neck so that you could hardly tell whether you were behind a man or a woman.

In learning a new opera or a song I always looked up all the gramophone recordings to compare the various singers' executions of the same aria. Recorded music is a tremendous educational help, especially to those who cannot go to opera and concerts frequently.

When I studied Massenet's "Manon," I saw that opera so many times and knew not only my own part but the whole score so well that when the opera was given at Salzburg for the first time I did the stage direction myself—and quite successfully, too.

I never missed any opportunity to learn anything that might contribute to my musical or artistic knowledge. Even when I went to London for the Coronation, I arranged to work those ten days with Elena Gerhard, that wonderful exponent of *Lieder*.

* * *

Perhaps my life might seem monotonous to a stranger, for I have done the same thing at the same hour for years. Usually I awaken just after five o'clock—in the country even earlier. I meditate, read and write until seven, when finally I can ask for my coffee: There were a few years when I was living in the country in France and had an Arab cook who was up at four and in the winter at four-thirty I always found a hot water bottle at my door and also a warming coffee upon ringing the bell. After glancing over my mail and the morning papers—American, Polish, English, Italian, French and Russian—I am ready to start my singing at nine. With very few interruptions I continue my singing until my luncheon: one piece of meat with a vegetable and fruit without any drink. Then reading for an hour to rest my voice and again I practice singing until four o'clock with a few short interruptions. From four to six I go out. I always drive in an open car—winter and summer, sun or snow—for only heavy rain forces me to put the top up. In that way I get fresh air while rushing about. At six I sing again until dinner which I usually avoid unless my private life forces me to join my husband in the dining-room.

When I feel that my program is not progressing fast enough, I go on working after dinner as, for instance, was the case before I sang "Rigoletto" at the Paris Opera when I often studied until eleven at night.

You might contend that no voice can stand such strenuous work, but I am not giving advice on the correct way to study. I am merely confessing my ardor to learn more and more.

After such a day's work it is small wonder that I want to go to bed as early as possible unless I have to go to the opera or a concert, again for educational purposes.

Only the ideal can bring humans to unity.
And the Ideal has as its foundation—knowledge.
— SCHILLER

Knowledge is the greatest thing we possess. Nothing and nobody can take it away from us, neither illness nor death. If anything is left after our bodily death, it is this undying quality of knowledge. The vibration of knowledge—true knowledge not just intellectuality—is Goodness, is Love. It is knowledge that distinguishes us from the animals. A humiliation so degrading to civilization as war could not happen if knowledge were greater in the world.

* * *

Art is immortal. In wonderful bygone days we find that only those rulers who protected the artists are known to us, perhaps because they realized that the great geniuses were the true sovereigns chosen by Divine Power.

What does it matter which king is present when Fritz Kreisler plays? Statesmen realized the mediocrity of their circumstantial power when their colleague, the Prime Minister of Poland, Paderewski played the piano while President Millerand of France sat in his box probably feeling—to speak vernacularly but descriptively—"like five cents."

And where would the French kings have been historically speaking without the architects like Mansard and Le Nôtre to build their Versailles or a Pierre Lescot to build their Louvre? Surely, if the name of Francois I is engraved in our memory it is because he called Leonardo da Vinci to his court to glorify his reputation as a great patron of the arts.

As Catulle Mendès says in his interesting book on Richard Wagner when writing about the first Bayreuth performance of "Das Rheingold": "The Emperor of Brazil, the Emperor of Germany, the Grand Duke of Mecklenburg, the Grand Duke of Baden, the Grand Duke of Weimar were amongst the audience; and not wearing their uniforms those Princes, half-hidden in their imperial boxes, were feeling that the Empire and Glory did not belong to them that night."

* * *

An old proverb says that music softens manners. It is true. Music is the only league and bond of union between nations or political parties. It has no nationality—only its servants, the musicians, have one. It is not limited by any frontier. It vibrates everywhere. It is free as the waves are free, and no one has power over it. Man can forbid listening to the universal waves but it is not in man's power to stop the waves themselves. Man has been able to unveil part of the mystery of universal sound but man is impotent when it comes to monopolizing it for his own limited purposes.

Musicians throughout the world feel a universal brotherhood more truly than any other men. They understand each other better than the average people do. They speak the same language—the language of sound.

Such a man as Arturo Toscanini is simply a musician of the highest magnitude in the hierarchy of divine sound who does not choose to bring music down to earthly levels. Instead he raises the multitude to the higher sphere where worldly considerations melt into one nameless, undivided sound.

All humanity desires peace. Musicians, sharing the higher sphere, desire that peace unrestrictedly. It takes a great character such as Toscanini to live up to his ideals. It requires great courage like his to make the world face this truth. It means total abnegation of selfish consideration in applying those high principles when the need arises.

* * *

My personal experience proves that music of superior

substance can change the human heart and enlarge the mental horizon. When I took complete possession of the Théâtre des Champs-Élysées and sought some glorious music for the opening, I brought Bayreuth to Paris. It was an extraordinary event as until then Bayreuth had never moved from Bayreuth.

Parisians were quite mystified at hearing the trumpets sound the traditional Bayreuth "Siegfried-call" from the roof of our beautiful temple of divine sound. Uninitiated in the Wagner tradition, people on the street would stop and look up as though they were hearing sounds direct from heaven. To supervise that part and give the signal at the right moment I sat on the roof for hours with a bottle of milk and some hard-boiled eggs for breakfast and lunch. As the performance started at five, during the intermission dinner was served in the lobby of the theatre. A horseshoe table was placed in my studio for my forty guests, amongst whom the German Ambassador was seated at my right and on my left sat the great music-lover, then Vice-Premier and Minister of Justice Louis Barthou, later assassinated with King Alexander of Yugoslavia when as Minister of Foreign Affairs he went to Marseilles to meet that unfortunate royal guest of France. He adored music and was considered one of France's greatest Wagnerists. Opposite me was seated Paul Painlèvé, Minister of War, about whom the rival political parties had said, "He is not a great politician (Good for him!) but he certainly is a great music-lover."

Then came M. Lescouvé the President of the French Supreme Court and just below him in the judicial hierarchy the Attorney General, M. Donat-Guigue. They and their wives—great friends of mine—were constant guests in my box at all musical events. After them followed many other great men in political and governmental circles of France.

Herr von Hoesch, German Ambassador, an extremely distinguished and handsome man of charming manners, was very much liked by Paris society. Although it was more than ten years after the Armistice, still he was unable to receive any French government officials at his Embassy. Therefore he asked me if I could use my friendship to sound out the Ministers of War and Justice about accepting his invitation to a dinner in honor of the Bayreuth artists, not wishing to receive their regrets if he himself should ask.

I approached M. Barthou first and brusque as he always was he shouted furiously: "Who does he think I am? Certainly I will come!"

M. Painlèvé quietly informed me: "Of course I will accept the invitation, but as a worshiper of Wagner and not as a War Minister!"

So, thanks to "Der Ring des Nibelungen," eleven years after the Armistice, French government officials again crossed the threshold of the German Embassy.

* * *

In the period of great tension between France and Italy when Mussolini was becoming the iron master of his country, during one of my elaborate luncheons I entertained the Italian Ambassador at the same time as Philippe Berthelot, in whose hands rested the destiny of the Quai d'Orsay—the French Foreign Ministry. Everybody was surprised at my daring gesture as all knew that M. Berthelot was not friendly to the Fascist Dictator.

At the end of the dinner there was placed before each of the guests an exquisite Chinese *bleu de chine* finger bowl. In each was a gardenia, flown from London by plane that day. Usually a gentleman presents such a flower to one of the ladies next to him. To the great amazement of all, M. Berthelot, Ambassador of France, took his gardenia, rose ostentatiously, reached way across the large table and presented his gardenia to the Italian Ambassador, Count Manzoni, with a few friendly words about the whiteness of that flower being a symbol of peace… For days and days Paris spoke of nothing but that incident.

* * *

Only a brotherhood of mankind can unite the people of all countries. Music could be helpful in bringing such a union to our hearts. I am not sure that people realize quite fully how great a gift God sent when he put radio at our service to promulgate all-consoling, all-healing music for millions of hearts to inspire them in their endeavors.

Though the mind make headway, it will never go as far as the heart.

— CONFUCIUS

THE SENSITIVENESS OF my Slavic nature was so great that I was never able to feel happy. The excessiveness of my character did not allow me even to feel indifferent, which would have been some small alleviation for me since I suffered so acutely at the slightest disharmony, at the most minute expression of ugliness.

Usually the emotional capacity of the feelings diminishes with age but my powers of feeling have remained unrestrained. There have been only a few fleeting moments when my soul sang gloriously, dilating my eyes to such an extent that I could no longer see well, my visual sense being too small to contain the greatness of my inner self. I floated above the earth, elevated to great heights and remained suspended there by a Spirit stronger than my environment. Nevertheless, even in those rare moments, the singing of my soul was in a minor key.

At the very tragic moment of my life when Dr. Fraenkel was having a hemorrhage and his assistants concluded (too rapidly and wrongly) that it was cancer, locked in my room I could only sing in a half-voice the last act of "Butterfly," that heartrending scene where the tiny mother bids goodbye to her baby before committing hara-kiri. Not understanding the depths of my emotion, the Doctor's family—his heirs before he married me—accused me of being so frivolous as to sing while the Doctor lay dangerously ill.

The acuteness of those momentary sensations of exaltation seemed particularly great on account of the rarity of the occasions, for each day of my life was full of unspeakable sadness and darkness. However, when able to lose myself, as in those rare seconds, I could have moved the whole world as easily as I pass the landscape on the road without its resistance.

But those were only lightning flashes… Immediately my brain returned to normal and the world, which a moment ago had been under my feet, began to oppress me with the heavy weight of all the forces of its vulgar matter. At the same time inferior intellect showed clearly that I lacked the actual physical time to achieve anything which would leave behind me for those to come any tangible trace that might enable them in turn to advance and prepare the means by which to conquer that hereditary enemy, Matter—as coal lays the foundations over the course of centuries for the diamond of perfect water.

> "What did you say?… It is useless… I know it.
> But one does not fight in the hope of succeeding. No,
> No! It is far more beautiful when it is useless…"

Even the consolation of a hopeful future was not granted to me. I perceived darkness still deeper ahead of me and felt that even under the best possible circumstances mental misery awaited me. For I had not the auxiliary faith to help as have those whose Faith charitably deceives them until the unexpected fatal end comes; those who finish their function of living without realizing that their passage on earth was meaningless and that they have made no preparation for their future spiritual life.

A destructive idea *à la Dostoievski* obsessed my heart that generation after generation would do exactly the same thing, with no thinker or philosopher to find the solution of life, while those who tried would succeed only in filling their lives with their own ideas without contributing anything to the development of the others. When we reason, we inevitably conclude that nothing is helpful and everything useless. Any peasant working in the field seems happier in the daily routine of his life than those who have the leisure to analyze. Montaigne considered the peasants fortunate in not being educated enough to reason—incorrectly.

People suffer less intensely when they lack the creative mind. Present-day civilization is the prime enemy of our happiness. It stands as a smoky screen before our eyes and prevents us from living-without-thinking—and that is the only way to live in the illusion of happiness, the illusion so essential for straight and honest living. For it is misery that turns us into criminals. It is misery that makes us selfish as we become so preoccupied with our own mental state that we cannot participate in or feel the unhappiness of others, just as a sick person cannot conceive that anyone else can be as sick as he is. Usually we think a person exaggerates when he claims to be the most unhappy person in the whole world, but for that person the whole world consists in his own feelings and it is hard for him to project himself outside. As Jules Sandeau said: "A suffering heart believes it is the center of the world and will not admit that there can be underneath the sun as great a sorrow as its own."

When a friend of mine lost her daughter under tragic circumstances, I had to remind myself of the condition I was in myself a few years previously when I lost someone very dear to me. It was only then that I fully understood her state of mind and felt frightened for her.

Civilization satisfies only our intellect. But intellect is the evolution of the brain, not of the soul.

Civilization has brought much cruelty to mankind, if only to judge from the progress in war. Its artificial light, its material evolution has not enlightened anyone as to how to live happily in the world—and that is the only thing that should be considered. Lack of happiness in us is the best proof that our civilization is retrogressing—in fact that it is an absolute failure.

The only real progress lies not in a tremendous effort to develop fallible matter but in the development of our inner moral forces.

People should be ashamed of being unhappy, whereas

they actually boast of this deficiency. They should hide themselves as animals do when they are ill. Birds are mortal, but you never see their lifeless corpses unless they have been shot or caught by a cat or bird of prey.

> *Riches are progress and progress is worthless.*
> — J.J.ROUSSEAU

IF WE THINK that civilization has progressed, why then, why is there not less misery in the world?

People, especially in Europe, are inclined to think that a scholarly education means civilization and the lack of it denotes barbarism. But what difference will it make in a hundred years if Mr. This-or-That finished school and had a degree? None! But if Mr. So-and-So had a happy life and consequently made other people around him happier and his grandchildren later reflect the same happiness, *then* Mr. So-and-So will have done something for the world simply because he was happy and did not fill his life with suffering. He was able to think of giving others contentment.

The question might be raised: "If Mr. So-and-So did not go to school, where would we find our great men whose achievements would set an example for us to follow?" The answer is as simple as the fact that formal education never was an essential to real greatness!

There are many who think with me that it would have been a great calamity if Goethe, Mozart or Michelangelo had not lived. And yet had they not left a trace of their existence to inspire others, I for one would not be thinking as I am now so destructively and so contradictorily as all seekers of happiness via the intellect do.

I am not trying to propound the theory that darkness of mind is the only issue for happiness. I only want to show how unhappy my life has been because of my ultra-sensitive and beautifully profound but non-constructive Slavic nature.

The largest part of my life is behind me—the best years as people say—and my memory can recollect only one day when I awoke happy. Just feeling happy without any reason whatsoever. On my way to the Caucasus, I was passing through Moscow, where I stopped for a day or two. While breakfasting at eight o'clock I was already singing, singing like a happy bird for those days I did not know what vocal study meant. I felt so exuberantly happy that I went out on the street where the shops were only opening and the sidewalks just washed. I could not walk, I simply danced along without feeling the pavement under my feet!

That is the only time I can remember feeling happy. The only one! The others were already mixed with thoughts, with doubts and fears for the future. Every morning when I opened my eyes—always very early so I would have more time to suffer—all was despair, darkness and hopelessness. I felt the weight of the whole world on my shoulders. Life with its thousand clutches penetrated all my nerves and cruelly sucked my blood…

My maid was instructed never to wish me good-morning as I could not speak for the first hour or two after awakening from sad dreams to sad reality. Within that first endless hour, I tried to read about other people's lives to stimulate my own. Only after nine when at work did I actually begin to live. But then came the real miseries of awakening more profound than ever as my sensibilities were fully aware and consequently could stand more and feel more deeply.

Then the doubts would crawl into my heart cruelly torturing my inner self. Only those who have counted minutes, hours, days and years of destructive, paralyzing doubts can understand that state of mind. Fate filled my being with doubts. I will have doubts while there is life in me unless age can lessen my sensitivity—but without ever succeeding in making me compromise.

If to those venomous doubts one adds my extreme timidity, it is no wonder that under those handicaps my life was not particularly pleasant. My bashfulness was such that even when sitting in the waiting room of a dentist's office where every person who enters is most naturally looked at by those already there—I would suffer intensely. And if that person glancing at me was a woman and I saw jealousy and envy in her eyes and on top of it if I anticipated the suffering my nerves would soon undergo with the treatment, no wonder I had an irresistible desire to steal some deadly poison behind the dentist's back and finish forever my misery which every step into brutal reality augmented. With those destructive thoughts of my mind (a mind so abnormally developed for suffering) and with such sensitiveness, obviously I could not enjoy life, for each step I took gave me an opportunity to feel miserable, afraid of hurting or being hurt.

I often forced myself to go out, not to forget or distract myself but only to strengthen my forces and to overcome my timidity. For the same reason I drove a car before I knew even how to back up. I remember once while studying with Eugène Ysaye, I motored to Scarsdale and on the way back I had to take a small hill during a heavy rain. I had no chains and did not know how to go into reverse, so the car would not climb the hill but kept slipping back. But I refused any help in order to discipline and train my nerves.

While out, dressed up and bejeweled, in a smoky reception hall, sometimes with noisy jazz tearing at my ears, I would smile and look as if I were actually enjoying myself. But this again was only in attempt to overcome my timidity. At the bottom of my heart I was passionately craving the solitude of my room, to cry by myself, if my eyes wanted to release the tears…

Friends are surprised because I never touch wine—I even dislike a black coffee—I never smoke, I never dance, I never flirt… They call me strong because I do not have their small weaknesses. For me a more difficult problem was reserved. Destiny enjoyed putting me in circumstances where a Napoleonic force was needed—but I am only a woman. Napoleon's power consisted in his lack of sensitivity, whereas I am full of it down to my smallest nerve and tiniest muscle. My heart is so soaked with sensitivity that life's minutest emotion, even inaudible sound, vibrates in me. Like an enormous sponge that swallows every drop of moisture in the atmosphere, I absorb everything, for nothing escapes my eye, my ear, my heart and my brain. The only difference between the sponge and myself is that I have never met a hand strong enough to free me at one grasp from the strange bodies that live like parasites in me.

It is a well known fact that we all are born alone and we die alone. But with my inexhaustible capacity of feeling so much and so profoundly, I always live alone. Even when we have ideas like those for whom we care and whom we understand thoroughly and two of us feel as one, nevertheless ultimately we are alone, alone, always alone! ! At least I always feel that I am alone. Alone…

It is sad to think that no other person can feel inwardly as we do, no one! The human ego is so big that none can realize its magnificence and so small that it makes us feel lonesome and fearful.

Inclined to dramatize everything, for me almost any pretext was good for desolation. That is why I was so exasperated and sad when first I wrote my will. After looking up the names of persons I wanted to leave money or souvenirs, after searching my memory to remember some dear person who in thought, if not in fact, actually was good to me, my mind remained blank, blank like the paper in front of me…

My reason kept encouraging me to try again, to keep on remembering. Having seen and known so many people in my exciting life I must certainly have met at least ten, five, even three or two persons who were kind to me. But no! I could not think of anyone. What a tragedy! No one of whom I could have happily thought as a successor for my earthly possessions. I did not believe in collective charity, just as

I do not believe in schools that kill individuality. A great mind will always find itself without benefit of schooling and I am an enemy of the average. My mind is either too destructive or too natural, for I prefer nothing at all rather than mediocrity and the ordinary schools are the cradle of such minds.

Extreme sensitiveness, paralyzing any effort, doubts together with ambition on the top of it all—were the gifts my Slavic nature found in the luggage during my travels on this earth!

* * *

I was told by astrologers that I am a Jupiterian type, and Jupiter stands for ambition. However, my ambition is of a moral sort, as are all spiritual experiences in this material world. I also was informed that on the mount of Jupiter I have Napoleon's star—the sign of tremendous uplift but also the indication of vertiginous fall. I should not be afraid to pay the price of being Jupiterian as I paid in advance for the privilege of being chosen and am paying, daily paying, with constant struggle, for which ambition supplies me with inexhaustible strength. Also Life has different ways and issues for every individual, for we are all different. There are no two alike in nature either among animals, minerals, plants or human beings. Moreover, unlike Napoleon, I cannot be hurt by any vertiginous fall: the small falls I experience every moment of my life have accustomed me to those sensations and they no longer make me dizzy to the extent that I lose my head. Although my sensibilities have suffered so cruelly, I have at the same time been so hardened against physical pain that now I can ever bear the heat, whereas only two years ago I could be totally prostrated by the forceful power of the sun.

No matter how little I achieve in this world, it will be comparatively great if it is remembered that I got it in spite of all the things against me and in spite of every possible discouragement. "*Malgrè Tout*" is the motto on my writing paper. In spite of everything...

* * *

Once we fall into a destructive way of thinking and into a negative attitude everything is colored by the dark shades of our mood. Under such circumstances even my qualities become unfriendly to me. My looks, the straightness of my character, my indomitable nature, my voice—all turn against me—and above all my ambition, which reaches so high a degree that it paralyzes all my possibilities. It becomes like a balloon so overfilled with gas that sooner or later it must burst in a catastrophic way.

> *Excessiveness of desire handicaps achievement.*
> — PETRARCH

Everything I have, everything I am, mentally and spiritually, I owe to myself and only to myself. Nature gave me much but at the same time put me into such contrary conditions of life that I really needed nothing less than the Napoleonic star to overcome in a single lifetime what would require centuries to accomplish if you take for comparison the process of the formation of a precious stone.

Fate placed me for the first fifteen years of my life in an atmosphere from which I have had to tear myself painfully ever since. It was hard to dissociate myself from the influences which had evolved from my early environment, since one is supposed to be fully formed by the age of seven. It is like expecting a person to have healthy second teeth when the first have been neglected. Only science and painful operations can do the work that nature could have done if properly assisted. Just as it is easy for children to learn foreign languages, while adults rarely master another tongue and when they do scarcely get free from an accent, so it took infinite force for me to break away from the ideas formed in my early childhood.

> *Criticism never killed anything which was meant to live and praise certainly never kept alive anything which was meant to die.*
>
> — CHATEAUBRIAND

SOMETIMES I FELT that I had been too egocentric, too narrow-minded particularly in my belief that I was being persecuted by my imaginary enemies such as the newspaperman—very real people indeed! I could not appreciate until later how hard was their struggle, how exacting was their profession and how limited was their reward... At times I had almost felt myself to be a martyred heroine *à la Leonardo da Vinci*. Only now am I able to realize that instability must be expected if it is based on human deduction; that gratitude is something we ought never look for; and that we should never do anything with the thought of doing something for others. We are the first and the direct beneficiaries of our good action by feeling light and happy, so by expecting gratitude we automatically annihilate the good we do ourselves. Therefore we should be governed only by the consideration of doing what we believe is right to do.

I suffered too much misery when the newspapers said that not even the McCormick millions could force people to hear me sing. Then, jumping to another extreme, I almost became proud when I read the following about Wagner's music:

"Gendarmes are required to push people forward to make them go to the Opera so that 'Rienzi' may not be performed in front of empty seats. A scheme is already formed to take Polish prisoners there... In this manner 'Rienzi' would at least be of some use..."

Yes, those small stings the press had bestowed on such a comparatively unimportant person as myself seemed a selfish comfort when I thought of what had been done to Wagner.

Later I reconciled myself a bit, suffering much less from adverse publicity when I witnessed how the greatest members of the French Chamber of Deputies were dragged in the dirt by their political rivals, and how an honest and respectable man, a minister governing the country, was openly described as hypocritical, conceited, pedantic, stupid, lacking in education, class or generosity—all because he had a responsible public position and consequently enemies in the opposition.

> *The bigger the man, the more easily can the arrow*
> *of jeering hit him. Dwarfs are more difficult to strike.*
> — HEINRICH HEINE

It certainly helped me to remember what Swift had written: "Criticism is a tax which the public levies on prominent men."

When I realized that only mediocrity escapes attention, I was further consoled for being attacked by the press. And I was almost able to smile when they kept on reporting wrong things about me. As an example at random, I was only amused when it was written up in the papers that I had sold my famous emeralds for a fabulous sum to Barbara Hutton-Reventlow, another victim of the press. I am not personally acquainted with her, although I was at her wedding to Prince Mdivani in the Russian Church of Paris when she looked most beautiful—but less so than she is now, for her girlish figure was a little too fat for a young bride. The gossip about the sale of my emeralds originated in the fact that she considered purchasing or bought the enormous emeralds that the Edith Rockefeller McCormick estate deposited with Cartier's for sale. And whenever the McCormick name was given to the press without it being made clear which McCormick it was, the newspapers always took it for granted that it was Walska-McCormick.

Mary McCormick had some differences with photographers or reporters, I do not remember which, and having lost control over her better self she slapped someone in the face. Because Miss McCormick was an opera singer, naturally the report went around that it was Ganna Walska McCormick who was involved in this scandal. The Polish newspapers immediately copied the story and printed it with my picture. This was tremendously shocking in my native country, which is rather reserved and where people could not conceive that a lady might display publicly such an excess of temperament. My poor brother, who adores me, kept making excuses for me, never suspecting that what is black on white may be utterly false. And when the same Mary McCormick married Prince Serge Mdivani I received endless letters of congratulation and... condemnation!

* * *

Our mental world goes round and round like our physical one—unless some day someone proves something to the contrary! Then we will believe in the new theory just as we trusted other physicists until Mr. Einstein came along and proved that we had been fooled for so many centuries.

The fact is that there is no stability on human judgment or time as both are fallible.

Darwin had a hard time getting accepted by the world as a serious thinker. Many people did not even know *au fond* who he was or what he did but even they accepted him as someone who gave something to the world and consequently he became sacred to those who value knowledge. Then came a day when in the great free and liberal country of America a Mr. Scopes, who had read Darwin and wanted to transmit his teaching to others, was persecuted for his pains.

Leonardo da Vinci was very nearly burned alive for witchcraft because he wanted—oh blasphemy!—to construct a flying machine.

Jeanne d'Arc was acclaimed at first, later burned at the stake, and subsequently canonized.

Tolstoi's "Power of Darkness" was censored by Czardom for its revolutionary ideas. Then the Bolshevists forbade his works to be printed, considering his ideas much too bourgeois and harmful for the new generation. Now however all that has changed again and Russia has prepared the centennial celebration of that great author.

And in that same Russia, the world's most wonderful theatre—Stanislawski's Moscow Art Theatre is now regarded as decadent, old and destructive to the individuality of artists.

While Madame Curie's name is still pronounced with veneration, there are doctors in Europe who are already whispering that, if cancer patients do not die from the disease, they certainly do from the radium cure.

Contemporary success really does not matter, neither does fame or glory. What matters is what lives on. Does it really make any difference whether Bacon was Shakespeare or whether Shakespeare was a man of any other name? Does it matter whether we owe the discovery of America to Americus Vespucius, to Columbus or to his teacher, instructor and encourager Toscanelli?

Since man lacks the stability, he is always in a waiting state—waiting for next spring, next summer, next month, next year—waiting with impatience, thinking nothing comes fast enough. He never realizes that he is precipitating his end, not because he dies but because he had stored up nothing inside himself he can take away with him or leave behind.

"It is a general mania with mankind," said Kotzebue, "always to look into the future and not to enjoy the present."

> *Great men are the real men, the human successes. They are not peculiar, they are in the order of things. It is the others who are not what they should be.*
>
> — AMIEL

ONLY NOW that I am able to discern the different motivations in my being do I consciously realize that my soul always craved an absolute devotion, a limitless devotion without any compromise. My heart yearned to be motherly although I was thirty years younger than the person to whom my heart went, for example, Dr. Fraenkel. My soul desired unrestrictedly to give great happiness, even if my inexperienced mind did not always clearly see the way to do so. My loving but selfishly loving heart often misguided me. My young tears blinded my judgment and any impotency to help a given situation threw me into an abyss from which no helping hand reached down to lead me out into the sun again.

Dr. Fraenkel's great old soul had to struggle every morning to resurrect itself from the physical suffering of the previous night, only to be knocked down again every afternoon. His colossal mind had enough strength only for a partial resuscitation from the night's bitterness that veiled his Goethean wisdom.

When free from his physical tortures in rare moments of complete moral lucidity, this thinker was paying the Karma of his race unless the divine qualities of his soul were overshadowed by his excess of intellectuality.

So, in my life with him there was no day, no hour of simple happiness, of beneficial, carefree joy.

My womanly intuition had even then taught me some truth. So that I could have shared with him a particle of newly perceived Immortal Beauty but the great difference in our ages and my extreme timidity closed my mouth. And unfortunate family conditions—Dr. Fraenkel married me unexpectedly so late in his life that it was a heavy blow to his heirs—gave me a decided inferiority complex. Weakened as he was by physical suffering and still loving the woman I resembled, he allowed his soul to be darkened by evil suggestion. Once I even found his room empty. His family had suddenly persuaded him to leave his own home by telling him that I intended to—to poison him!

The Doctor fully understood my real self only on his death-bed. While holding my hand in an ultimate adieu, with the last spark of human consciousness, he asked my pardon. He intended to raise my hand to his lips but the silver thread of his soul was already detached from his body and with the last flicker of his life he could only lift his own hand to his lips and kiss it, thus symbolically kissing mine…

* * *

If I never found so much expected happiness in my marriages, at least I can now see the purpose of the mental agonies through which I passed. That was my school of learning. Those men were instrumental to my development. They allowed me to see clearly who I was and where I stood. I only regret profoundly that I met Alec Cochran at such an early stage in the study of my inner being. Desperate in this early period of hard trials and indulging in my tragedy without limit, I was unable to help his excessively miserable nature. He certainly deserved more pity than any other being I have come across in my contact with individuals. But then I was not a healer… I was neither a reformer nor a salvationist… I wanted love. I wanted beauty. I was too young to think of sacrificing myself. Love *is* selfish. Youth *is* selfish. In those days I could not perceive why I should not have a right to the usual complement of feminine happiness. I craved understanding and loveliness. I had just been through an exhausting three year's trial in which I had sacrificed my soul to Dr. Fraenkel's intellectuality. I had just finished the stage of a night nurse, the stage of mothering a person a quarter of a century older than myself. I wanted to inhale freedom in my craving for breath. Instead, I suffocated under the weight of brutal actuality. Instead of exquisite beauty, I received the epitome of ugliness. Instead of a loving heart, I met egoism in its most infinite degree and limitless extent.

My dreams were confronted with the most prosaic platitudes. My mind—already open to knowledge and curiosity—was fed with the statistics on the best available ponies of the world market. From the very first day of my marriage to Alec Cochran, I was so crushed by cruel reality that I was unable to even put up a fight to defend the image my illusion had created.

My whole being gave way under despair. Alec's insane selfishness was doubled by a morbid desire to hurt, coupled with a sadistic need to see others suffer as he himself suffered, suffered from the incurable malady of being bored, mortally bored. He never deprived himself of the rare pleasure of hurting, and an unaccustomed and easy victim like myself gave him a machiavellian opportunity to enjoy his cruelty still more keenly by seeing my deep sorrow. Only much later did I learn that my tears augmented the morbid state of his mind a hundred per cent. He hated tears. They disturbed his ego. He wanted distraction in order to forget himself and not be reminded of his mental agony.

More lonesome than ever—for we feel emptiness more when we are not alone—I was sorry for the first time in my life that I had no child to whom I could have transferred all my affection. I did not have my music since I had given up my singing and did not want even a piano in my Rue de Lübeck salon to remind me of my first love.

Unlike Harold McCormick, Alec Cochran did not cherish his health, for life brought him only boredom and misery. He never even admitted that he actually was ill. If I had not learned from my devoted maid after our divorce that there were evidences that he had suffered a hemorrhage I would never have known that he was not only mentally but also organically a very sick man.

Had I known it, perhaps I would have been able to be more tolerant and less exacting. Perhaps I could have forgotten about my idiosyncrasy of the Absolute Ideal and would have seen only a man in mental misery and low physical condition. Perhaps I could have attributed everything ugly in him to his illness, just as I stood much from Dr. Fraenkel knowing that his atrocious pains diminished the greatness of his soul.

Once I remember that, thinking that Alec might not be well, uninvited I went to his room. I half opened the door but my heart froze at the sight of his steely gaze. Paralyzed, I stayed at the door unable to move. I never repeated that visit…

* * *

Years later when I understood that the tragedy of my meeting Alec Cochran was a constructive lesson to teach me that continuous thought has the power to materialize and actually create the situation desired, even though it be in the subconscious, I knew the answer when someone once asked me naïvely why I had married him if I did not love him. I hardly think it is necessary to state again the psychological explanation that I did not love Alec Cochran but the ideal which I had created myself, only to discover too late that he was not the one who should receive the richness and glory that my soul was unable to put into his soul. Hence the drama.

The shock of having made a mistake by pouring the essence of my being into the wrong vessel was certainly great without mentioning the pain of such surrounding conditions as the divorce, for instance, as I considered divorce, a shame. I thought I could not go out on the street without my cheeks burning. Divorce meant to me a public admission of my failure, of my mistake, the mistake of giving my heart to the wrong man. It is a disgrace such as men used to wash away in blood through duels in the olden days.

* * *

Some may think that the story of my giving Life to Alec is a great fancy invented by my fertile imagination. But is not our whole life a story of fancy? A love story, a war story, a story of being young, celebrated, rich? Sometimes an embellished story with imaginary pictures, but always a living story, constructive and creative…

> *One must make of Life a dream*
> *and of a dream, Reality.*
> — PIERRE CURIE

It is through the stories we weave in our minds that all great things happen in the world. In order to create, we first have to work out the story in our imagination. If our dream does not come true and in spite of the brilliant outlook to the outsider we are still unhappy, while people are astonished or indignant that we have so much and still are not satisfied, it is because we have much but we did not want that much—we wanted only the materialization of our desire, of our dream, no more.

> *The ideal of existence is the realization at a ripe*
> *age of youth's dream.*
> — GOETHE

As someone quoted after Marshal Pilsudski's death: "Fortunate is he whom a dream hath possessed Twice fortunate is he whose dream is worth the dreaming. And thrice fortunate is he who, within the span of allotted years, sees his dreams realized—a gift denied most men."

There was a great dream in me too, yet I was unable to give life to my thoughts, unable to materialize my inner desire which was buried so deep by my timidity. During the first half of my life I had constant dreams during my sleeping hours, and for a period of at least ten years I had dreams of flying almost every night. No matter where I was or what I did in my dream, as soon as someone made me unhappy, I would make a tiny but painful effort and fly up to the ceiling out of reach of human hands if I were in a room, or towards the Infinite when I was in the open spaces...

As we all know, dreams and electricity are still unsolved mysteries to even the greatest scientists. The more I learned, the thinner the veil of the Unknown became in my inner being and simultaneously I dreamt less.

Luther Burbank, the American plant wizard, told the wonderful story of how he succeeded in raising a spikeless cactus. First he imagined that centuries ago the cactus had no spikes. Then came a drought. The camels on the desert filled their stomachs with the juicy cactus. In order to protect themselves, the poor plants put out arms of defense, the spikes. Then Burbank reasoned that if he gave the cactus plant the feeling of safety, it would not need to provide itself with protection. He built four walls around the cactus shoot. The following spring a young cactus grew which bore only a few spikes. He repeated this process, using the seed from the first enclosed cactus, but each time building a higher wall until he succeeded in obtaining a spikeless cactus and a knowledge of the intelligence of the plant.

Such a poetical interpretation of nature's mind is not only beautiful. It also has a great and deep meaning. An idea is born, just as the idea about the cactus was born in Burbank's mind. Then with our sincere untiring effort we have to build the proper conditions for our desire to flourish in order to materialize it and in turn give life to it. That, I believe, is how the world was created. If the motive is good, if sincerity is absolute and perseverance is unbounded, we cannot meet with failure, for daring frightens away danger.

> *Only fiction does not lie: it leaves a hidden door half open on the life of a man, through which his unknown soul slips beyond all control.*
>
> — FRANÇOIS MAURIC

I am happy that my episode with Alec Cochran, instructive as it was, though hard to bear, finished in beauty. Upon learning from the newspapers that he was dangerously ill at the Savoy Plaza under the care of several doctors and nurses, each day I sent him anonymously a bunch of sweetheart roses, the flowers with which he had bombarded me while courting me in Paris—if the word *courting* could be used in connection with Alec. Afraid that I might be recognized by the florists, I changed shops each time, using all the Sixth and Lexington Avenue ones, avoiding the Fifth Avenue florists where his name might have aroused curiosity. Still when I said there would be no card my heart fluttered lest I be recognized.

Alec Cochran never recovered from that sickness. Shortly afterwards when I was by then in Paris, he left the world which had been so miserable for him.

The newspapers erroneously reported that he had willed me three million dollars. I did not believe it. It would not have been like him, for it would have been an indication of human feeling. Knowing that I needed money to give great music to the world, he would have been doing a consciously normal act. But, if he had been capable of such a gesture, he would not have died away from me so quickly in life, and I would have mourned him only upon his death instead of having done so years before.

Nevertheless, destiny decided that, in spite of him, his money would help art after all. Just as he had been the favorite nephew and beneficiary of his eccentric uncle Smith, carpet manufacturer of Yonkers, he left his fortune to his favorite nephew, Thomas Ewing, who followed him to the grave shortly afterwards. But Thomas Ewing's artistically minded widow, a lover of Terpsichore and herself a dancer, used that money to promote a ballet in America in all its beauty.

And that is all that matters. It makes no difference whose money it is if it is used to give inspiration which, in turn, develops the soul. That it was done by Ganna Walska or Lucia Chase is immaterial. Still a man like John D. Rockefeller is a privileged child whom God entrusted with the mission of such a great vision as Radio City!!

* * *

As I review my life now I realize that at no point did it ever occur to me that it could have been different. There was never the slightest doubt about the purpose of my life. Although this fact was entirely unknown to my young soul.

After I had married Mr. Cochran in Paris I was much too preoccupied during the next two days in helping Mr. McCormick to recover from the shock he received when he learned of the wedding, to indulge in any personal feelings.

When I became a widow, Harold McCormick asked me if I would consider marrying him if he became free. Feeling that joy had left me forever after Dr. Fraenkel's death, I said "No." Still, when he learned that I am going to Paris he decided to follow me under the pretext of visiting his wife who had lived in Switzerland for years under Dr. Jung's psychoanalytical care. Later he told me that he had hoped, once he was divorced, I would change my mind and marry him.

His wife, however, refused to divorce him. But, Harold, with obstinate persistence even in this difficult case, finally found the way to persuade Edith Rockefeller that, for her own benefit, they ought to separate. When she finally agreed, boyishly happy, he left Bauer-au-lac Hotel whistling as only he knew how to, and hastened to telegraph what he thought would be the good news to me. On the way to the telegraph office he met the messenger boy and he called to him gaily: "Hello, little friend! I have a wire for you!"

"So have I, Mr. McCormick" the boy replied, and Harold read the following: "Just married Alexander Smith Cochran. Hope you will understand and that we will always be good friends." (Mr. McCormick had almost introduced to me Mr. Cochrane only a few weeks before.)

The smile died from his face, and instead of the intended wire I received one announcing his immediate arrival in Paris. He stopped at the Crillon Hotel where we, newly wed, had come the night before, and excitedly, almost incoherently, he telephoned at seven o'clock in the morning to insist that he must see me immediately, *immediately*. Afraid something would happen to him, I accepted his proposal to breakfast with me at seven-thirty.

The scene which followed was worthy of the best theatrical pen and would have been quite comical had tragedy not been visible in Harold's eyes. While Mr. Cochran was still sleeping in the next room in his first day of married life, I was pouring the coffee for Mr. McCormick. In a businesslike way, quite naturally, and just as if he would say "No sugar, please," he said to me: "You see, Edith finally consented to give me a divorce. Now you must divorce Mr. Cochran and we will be married as soon as possible. I am sailing with you!"

As simple as that! But because he did not realize the enormity of what he was saying, the place where he was sitting, the circumstances in which he was speaking and the almost maddening look of anxiety in his eyes, I could only mumble something—to gain time—that what he asks is quite impossible just now, that I am sailing the next day, that he can not sail with me on account of the terrible scandal in which the Chairman of Harvester International would involve himself, when the press discovers that the young widow has married "the richest bachelor of America," but has sailed for her honeymoon with a man married to Rockefeller's daughter, a man with grown children. As he was always afraid of publicity, I succeeded in calming his excitement by suggesting that he should take the next boat.

Those last two days in Paris—first days of my married life—were sadly comical as we spent all of the time *en trois*, lunching together, dining, going to the theatre. The three of us even went together to my dressmaker. And when I had to go to the coiffeur Mr. Cochran stayed with Mr. McCormick to keep him company. When we were sailing Mr. McCormick accompanied us to the boat, threw rice at us, brought by a friend of mine who, I had arranged, was to take Harold back to his hotel and stay with him until he left by the next boat. (My "friend" took advantage of Mr. McCormick's sentimental state of mind and extorted from him twenty thousand dollars for an expensive radium cancer cure. Fortunately he was not afflicted with cancer, but Harold was so happy to do anything for a friend—as he thought—of his beloved that he did not doubt the words of this very healthy looking man. I do not mention the name of this papal count because he is dead now, but he died a natural death twenty years after this incident.)

I am telling this story only to explain how after my sudden marriage I was rather more preoccupied with Mr. McCormick's helpless state than with my own thoughts. And it never even occurred to me that my new marital situation might change in any way the outlook of my life. And if Mr. Cochran intentionally was trying to tempt me into involution of my being, frankly I did not realize that I was even tempted. And I did not react at all when, at breakfast, Alec announced that he had bought me a house on the rue de Lübeck—the house of Gordon Bennett, editor of the *New York Herald*—as his house on the rue de l'Elysées was far too small for two people! ! ! ". . . there are not enough closets even for a comfortable bachelor!" he added. I did not react either when, after luncheon at *Cafe de Paris* the most beautiful Rolls Royce, already monogrammed with my initials, was awaiting me and the very stylish chauffeur—excuse me, I should say mecanicien (smart chauffeurs are called *mecaniciens* in Paris and every Rolls Royce chauffeur is a smart chauffeur).

A million francs worth of sable coat that I found in my room that afternoon, Alec's invitation to go with carte blanche to Cartier and choose anything I desired as a wedding present and his business-like announcement that my bank would receive a hundred thousand dollars yearly for my "pin money"—all that went by me without actually touching my inner being.

> *Jealousy comes from our fear of being inferior.*
> — MME. DE PRESSENSÉ

ONE OF THE most beautiful souls I ever encountered in this valley of tears, as the Slavs like to call our earthly planet, was the delicately perfumed soul of Harold McCormick. It was most exquisite, indeed, but unfortunately thickly veiled by the hypocrisy of wrongly applied goodness and by that modern discovery, the inferiority complex. I say *modern*, for previous generations never knew about this disease, just as people did not know they had an appendix until doctors found it necessary to operate on them.

Harold's mind was especially confused by an abnormal sense of what he thought were his responsibilities, almost a mental complex of his duties, and an entirely misguided idea of what his part should be as an important citizen of his beloved city, Chicago.

He felt all this to the prejudice of his happiness, and it acted like a boomerang on the happiness of those nearest him, those like myself who could find happiness only in the harmony of a common life and in the happiness of the companion.

When still very young, Harold's pockets were already filled with pills of every kind. In later years his blind submission to the disciples of Aesculapius became absolute to the point of hypochondria. His obstinacy, the obstinacy of a weak person, did not allow him to take any sage and loving advice if it contradicted his idiosyncrasy.

Unfortunately that same idiosyncrasy led him to idolize the physical expression of love and he became insatiable in his search for the realization of the physical demands—insatiable because they were unattainable for him any more. Nature, in her wisdom, having fulfilled him by giving him four children, had chosen for his second wife an idealist who was able to put so much value on the richness of his soul that she could not even imagine the possibility of his preferring to seek further for a gross and limited pleasure rather than being satisfied with the divine companionship of the spiritual love she was willing to share with him.

Perhaps I could have made Harold happy, but it would have been to the prejudice of my own soul's development which could accept only those sacrifices that pass through the fires of purification.

If we are privileged to realize consciously the divine law that governs us, we should not indulge and accept that which encourages our lower nature just for the sake of selfish well-being, especially when Nature has dictated that it is no longer to be.

This misconception of love, this wrong application of charity—often the charity of his own health when dollars would have been more welcome—those self-imposed, rarely wise duties overbalanced his lovely soul and covered it with this ungrateful substance of reasoning, which was ungrateful because unstable as everything perishable is and when all misunderstanding has its origin in a false foundation. The result was that even Harold's best resolutions fell like a house of cards and his human mind—under the influence of the villain world—got the best of him.

Naïve, he could not see the bad. Weak, he could not rise above his environment and judged people's hearts by the limitations of the narrow atmosphere around him. His youthful azure-blue eyes sought the truth intently in the darkness, but the window of his soul was closed, for inborn obstinacy would not permit him to change his mind in order to see and feel differently and judge only by the dictates of his heart.

Constant reasoning on the wrong basis and the absolute necessity for analyzing every feeling, ever since he had become acquainted with Freudism through Dr. Jung whom he met when the latter was in attendance on his first wife,

Edith Rockefeller, masked his heart with the technique of analyzing—the study of negative matter. He was not, however, successful in understanding those studies, being too much of an idealist in the depths of his fresh soul.

Professor Freud dealt with beings only since their coming to this earthly existence. His destructive theory attributing the origin of all our ills to insufficiency of sex expression has done more harm to our century than all the horrors of war, for his doctrine encourages us to live only according to the dictates of our lower instincts. This theory augmented Harold's trouble.

He was unable to acquire entirely the system of psycho-analytical thinking, succeeding only in belittling the potentialities of his mind. He even became ashamed of his boyish dreamy nature and like most Americans began to consider it undignified and unmanly.

Moreover, he deprived himself of the only escape from and the only remedy for this sadly twisted situation by never wanting to speak about his motives, thoughts or reactions for fear it would hurt or aggravate the situation. By keeping everything to himself, he automatically condemned frankness in others around him and reduced even me to silence. My sincerity would not have been understood by his complicated process of analyzing everything and making a colossal problem out of the most simple statement such as saying, "Today is Wednesday."

To him it became a question. Why had I said it was Wednesday? No, my birthday was in June. Had we planned something for Wednesday that he had forgotten? So it went and he would brood for days if the thought of Wednesday came to his mind.

When he was still a child, he had not been allowed to be natural. All his boyish flights of imagination had been smothered just as his body had always been covered with socks, mufflers, sweaters, snow-boots, scarves and gloves. When he was allowed to go out he was so hermetically

G.W. at the Period of Meeting Prince Felix Youssoupoff

Prince Felix Youssoupoff

G.W. studio photograph circa 1916

G.W. studio photograph circa 1916

G.W. photograph by Underwood & Underwood, N.Y.C. 1919

G.W. photo from 1925

Dr. Joseph Fraenkel

G.W. at the Time of Meeting Dr. Joseph Fraenkel

G.W. in Hoop Skirt

G.W. with Her Favorite Kitten

G.W. When She First Arrived in America

G.W. When She First Arrived in America

G.W. at the Time of Her Debut with Caruso

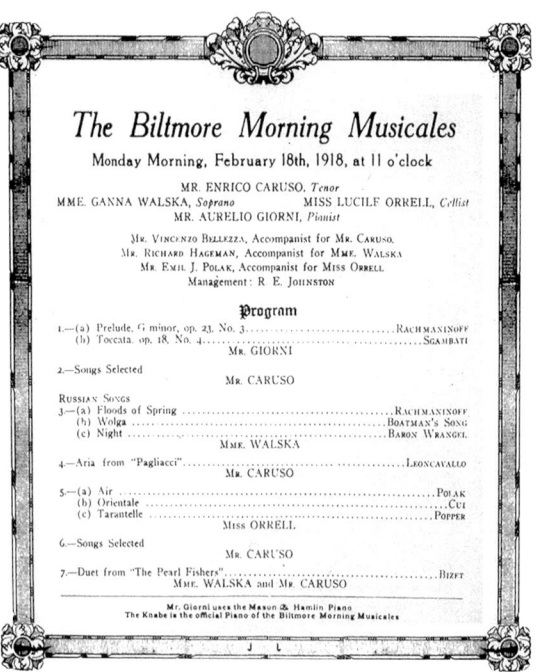

The Biltmore Morning Musicales with Caruso and G.W.

H.I.H. The Grand Duke Alexander, G.W. and Her Sister-in-Law, Baroness Alexandra Frederiks

Portrait of G.W. by Coles Phillips

Alexander Smith Cochran on his Polo Pony

Alexander Smith Cochran

Fritz Kreisler

G.W. in "Venus" Gown in 1932 - photo: Nickolas Muray

G.W. in "Venus" Gown

G.W. in Gown of the Second Empire

Carricatures of G.W.

G.W. Photograph by Arnold Genthe

G.W. in Turban

G.W. in "Tosca"

G.W. in "Butterfly" and "Manon"

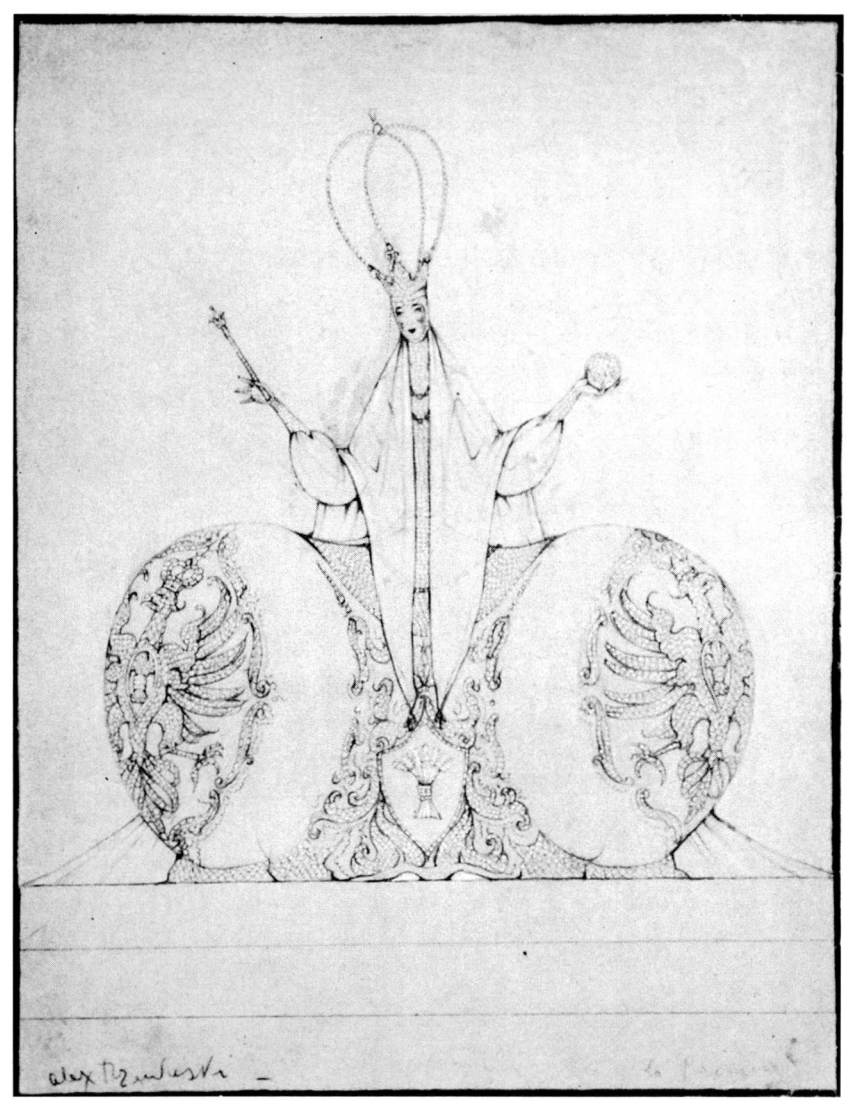

G.W. as Queen Barbara of Poland

G.W. as Pauline Borghese

G.W. as Diana

G.W. holding a bottle of "Divorcons" perfume

G.W. at the Rue de la Paix perfume shop, Paris, 1927

Siegfried Wagner with His Family

G.W. with Franklin D. Roosevelt

Leopold Stokowski

Walter Straram

G.W. with Walter Straram in Rome and Venice

Théâtre des Champs-Élysées

Proscenium

Painting by Denis

Sculpture by Bourdelle

Countess Castiglione

G.W. as the Countess

GW and Michael Detroyat at the Beaux Arts Ball, Astoria, N.Y., 1934

GW entertaining guests on the stage of Théâtre des Champs-Élysées, 1934

Arthur Toscanini

G.W. Photograph by Grand Duchess Marie

Ambassador and Madame Philippe Berthelot

Ambassador Count Manzoni

Eugène Ysaye

Fedor Chaliapine

Harold McCormick

Harold McCormick with His Children

G.W. with Harold McCormick, 1929

G.W. at home on the Rue de Lübeck, Paris

G.W. Father and Mother

G.W. in Mourning with Her Father

G.W. in Polish Costume

G.W. Singing the Marseillaise

Maharishe

Dr. Alexander Cannon

Paul Brunton

Mrs. Paul Brunton

Richard Strauss

Marquise Casati

Arcadie

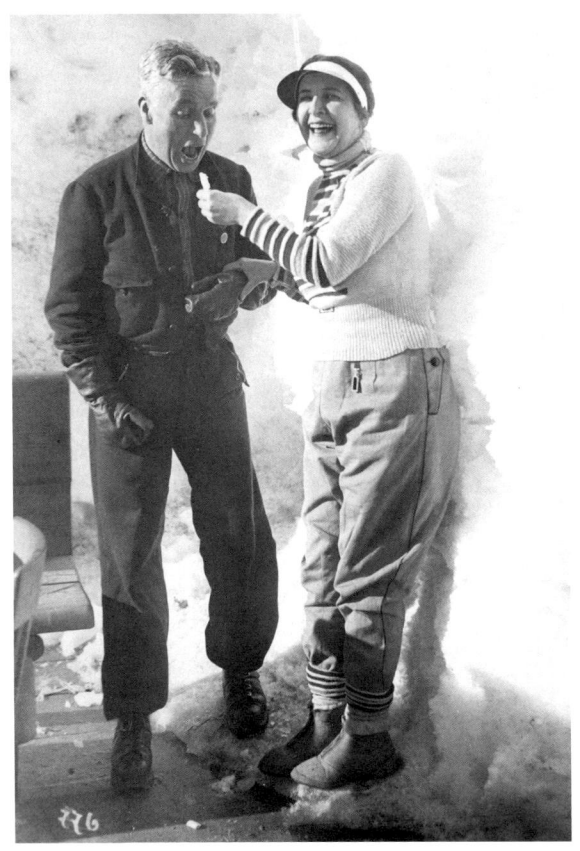

G.W. at St. Moritz with Charlie Chaplin

G.W. at St. Moritz with Friends

Meher Baba

Meher Baba at Galluis

Très Saint Père

Hanna Walska McCormick humblement prosterné aux pieds de Votre Sainteté implore la Bénédiction Apostolique et l'Indulgence Plénière "in articulo mortis", lorsque repentant, mais ne pouvant se confesser ni recevoir la Sainte Communion, invoquer de bouche ou au moins de cœur le Saint Nom de Jésus + +

Pope Pius XI

G.W. Photos by Baron de Meyer

Home on Rue de Lübeck

G.W. Portrait by J.G. Domergue

G.W. Portrait by Driant

G.W. Portrait by Count Rzewouski

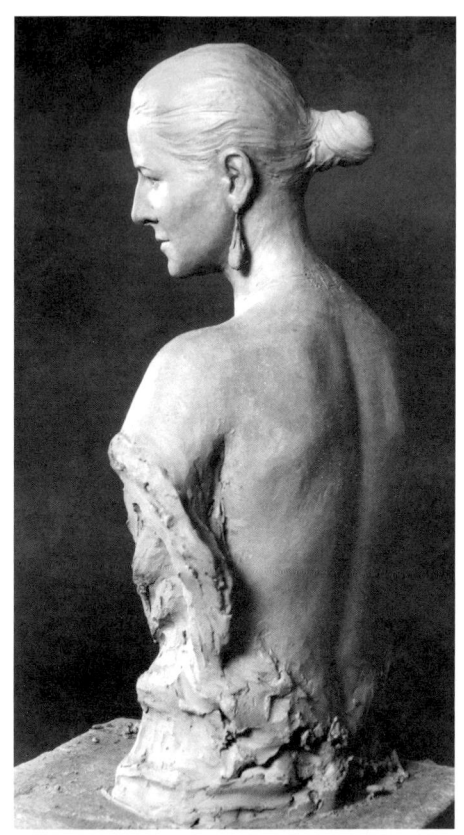

Sculptures of G.W.

Mussolini and G.W. During Her Visit

Grindell Matthews Before and After Eye Operation

Portrait of G.W. Made in Russia

Château de Galluis. Pond. Guest House

Dinner in Honor of Prince and Princess Nicholas of Greece

G.W. with Pet Peacock

G.W. with Isadora Duncan's Dancers

Tibetland in Santa Barbara

covered that he could not possibly have any contact through the great quantities of woolen garments with the fresh air, nature's most vivifying elixir.

Once, when I was leaving San Diego with Harold, his Mother, then very old and dangerously ill, begged me theatrically and in great secrecy to promise her as a great favor that I would take good care of her boy by never allowing him to go out in the rain without his rubbers!

The result of this pampering was that now he could not sleep with the window open without instantly catching cold or sneezing for many hours.

The extremely exaggerated and abnormal way his otherwise athletic constitution was taken care of in his childhood left such a strong imprint on his mind that he built an altar to his body and became preoccupied with his health to such an extent that with age it developed into a mania, an obsession, an idiosyncrasy. And finally—poor Harold—it became a second nature stronger than his own fresh soul, stronger than his beautiful loving qualities!

I lost him, if that phrase can be used to explain separation and divorce, but not in the real meaning of the word.

While we were married I wanted him to give me the same quality of feeling that I gave him. Now, being above personal feminine vanity and selfish desires for my own happiness, I can touch his beautiful self and overlook completely those differences that separated us in an earthly way. I can love him now in a much nobler sense.

I had always hoped that I could help him to find himself. I tried several times but it was too early. He was not yet ready to follow the stable but invisible path newly discovered by me.

Who knows the way of Destiny? And to grasp the Eternal Idea one does not need any time…

It is not so much the passions which are great but the weaknesses of men.

EACH TIME MY over-generous heart beat anew with womanly love I was certain that that particular time it was real love, love of the first magnitude, the love I, was waiting for so intensely.

My reputation of being an unfeeling woman was entirely my own creation for self-defense. Not for the world did I want anyone—particularly the one who had all my thoughts—to know the accelerated rhythm of my heart and the deep intimacy of my soul. As a consequence of this natural desire for secrecy, my friends began to judge me, quite casually at first, as an essentially practical-minded woman incapable of committing an unreasonable act.

This private opinion of a few later grew to such a degree that frequently I was considered to be an exceptionally level-headed woman, a thousand-headed monster, a hard working machine; while my executive ability and quick judgment often made my friends call me "Leader in skirts!"

French women, unlike Americans, jealously hold on to their past, present and future flirts. One Parisienne once informed an admirer, in her fear of losing him, not to pay any attention to me because, as she informed him, ninety-five per cent of my time was taken up by work. Even if I were to see him during the remaining five per cent, it would probably only be to let him escort me to a theatre or concert, where even during the intermission I would not leave my seat, as I did not smoke and I much preferred the latest screen news to a commonplace conversation in a smoky lobby.[12] The gentleman passed this report on to me in the hope that I would deny its veracity.

---

12 The Parisian theatres had luminous screens to give the latest news during the intermissions which in France are eternal.

"She is entirely mistaken," I told the man.

"Just as I thought," he said.

"Yes," I said. "She told you that only ninety-five per cent of my time is devoted to work but she should have said a hundred per cent…"

I have an idiosyncrasy for wanting to know and absorb everything. My capacity for learning is immeasurable. If I had more free time I would be a walking encyclopaedia, thanks to my excellent memory for everything except very technical matter or exact dates.

I once told a charming diplomat who was attentive to me that work was the only thing I was interested in. Years later the fiery Italian reproached me with the fact that his undivided devotion to me had made him the sentimental joke of all Paris. I then reminded him how I had warned him at the beginning of our acquaintance that he was wasting his time and that he had better devote himself to a certain French lady who had no desire to be cruel to him. Naïvely he answered:

"But I did not believe you then!"

The great Maestro Toscanini calls me *femme fatale* and obstinately refuses to believe that I am the victim of my highly emotional nature rather than a sort of pre-war Hollywood vamp. Funny as it may seem even to those who think they know me well, I am one of those women who helps herself to the worst piece of chicken at dinner in order to leave the best for her husband!

Far from protesting against the reputation of such insensibility, I found that such an interpretation of my outer personality was an extremely easy way to escape the indelicate indiscretions of the people who are always trying to penetrate into our most private thoughts with their galoshes on, as the Russians put it.

The myth began at the time I was in great sorrow over my tragic disillusionment about Alex Cochran. I jumped at the opportunity of not only confirming it but amplifying it with all the exaggeration my character could muster. Soon the legend was widespread that I was nearer to the North Pole than to the natural qualities of a loving woman, in spite of my extreme femininity, from which I never parted, leading the life of olden days when women only smoked exceptionally, when they cut their hair only after typhoid fever, considered black coffee as a drug or something rather vicious and forbidden, when they preferred early retiring to a smoky restaurant, night club and dance-hall. Those were the days of such operas as "The Secret of Suzanne," where the heroine was suspected of having a lover because it was incomprehensible otherwise that there could be the smell of cigarette smoke in her room.

While speaking about dancing, let me mention that I never understood how women can find pleasure in the arms of all their dancing partners. I suppose that the majority of the *sexe faible* dances without thinking. Otherwise they would realize that there is very little difference between abandoning oneself in the arms of the beloved or in the arms of a casual dancing partner. In the former case we are close to one man, *mon homme*, as the feminine apaches say in Montmarte. In the latter, if a girl is especially attractive—and the American girls always are—she may find herself nestling in startling physical closeness in ten to twenty pairs of men's arms during a single evening.

I presume that those girls must be so blasé about leaning on a man's breast that when—without jazz—they are close to their beloved they must consider it an unimportant event in their life. The poor sisters!!

There are however two sides to every medal. For myself, I know that, when I once made an exception after not having danced for ten or fifteen years, I found myself almost unable to waltz owing to the new emotion of being so close to a complete stranger, whom I had met only that evening and on whom I had made a very strong impression. He lost his head—it was a case of love at first sight. But as nothing can be permanent or really beautiful when built on the wrong foundation so this flame was no exception, did not last and died out in a rather ugly atmosphere... A pity!

* * *

However in spite of the reputation of being a monster of coldness, I actually loved or thought I loved, in the abstract if my soul was not objective every day of my life—loved to the utmost. And each time my heart was pitifully crushed.

Ever since I can remember I loved and ever suffered through love. When I was only eleven years old, I adored a boy whose eyes met mine in the silence of the church where we children prayed for successful schoolwork. Later the same boy corrected my spelling, and anew my suffering started. It was unthinkable for me to look him again in the eyes after such shame, and death seemed the only recourse left me.[13]

My heart was broken for the first time. Ever since bad luck has persisted in each of my romances as well as in every one of my marriages, although I can see now that this bad luck was actually my benefactor, for it forced me to break off a romance before it culminated in engaging my entire life.

We European women, being Catholics for the most part, cannot easily sever our marriages. Most certainly we do not enter into wedlock with the advance consideration of divorce as it was reported about a famous international marriage, the husband, that true Catholic justified his demand for a Vatican annulment by explaining that his wife had said while on the way to the altar that if the marriage did not work she would ask for a divorce. But because he bore one of the great names of France, the Vatican did not choose to set a demoralizing record for *la Vieille France* and gave the annulment with much difficulty and delay.

---

13 Thirty years later when will power dominated my emotions I saw him again while visiting Warsaw. His feelings were then so uncontrolled that he was unable to light his cigarette.

In a recent magazine I saw a characteristic cartoon of the American attitude. It showed a woman saying to her lawyer: "Well, if it's going to be so much trouble divorcing him, I guess I won't marry him after all!"

In Europe, even nowadays, people do not marry in haste. The law is such that it does not encourage elopements; by requiring a minimum delay of two weeks for a marriage license and a month of registered domicile in the same city, it forces people to think matters over.

As an exception, perhaps to confirm the rule, I did marry Alec Cochran in Paris with a few hours' notice. When at lunch time Mr. Cochran, who had arrived at noon from London, told the distinguished Franco-American lawyer to prepare marriage papers before three-thirty as the American Consulate closes at four and we had to be there a little before, Mr. Loeb informed him that if he were the President of the French Republic he could not be married that day.

"Never mind. You prepare those papers, and I will bring the authorization at three-thirty," Alec replied with his habitual arrogance.

At twenty minutes to four I had the authorization and took the "Open-Sesame" to the lawyer while Alec went to the American Consulate to keep it open in case I arrived with the papers after four o'clock. I never knew, I never asked how he got that exceptional authorization. When the lawyer saw it I thought his eyes would pop out of his head. Choked with surprise, he mumbled between his teeth: "He must have bribed everybody from the Prime Minister down to the last bailiff!"

The reminder that one marries for a lifetime makes one think twice before rushing to the nearest judge for an after-supper marriage. I was happy to read that lately those cocktail weddings have been abolished.

* * *

The intensity of my feelings every time I loved—or

thought I loved—was so great that it always seemed as if it were happening to me for the first and only time in my life. I felt I loved "for better or for worse, for richer or poorer," for life, for eternity. If I could have thought for a second that it might not be forever, I could not have loved, I could not have married. Such a thought would have made me see that it was not love if there were a possibility of it ceasing one day. And I was never able to compromise with my feelings or bargain for a partial extension.

Unfortunately, Destiny—as I thought then—did not sponsor my desires, for as soon as my heart cherished someone I felt profoundly miserable. My devotion always met with disaster, due to the physical, moral or mental conditions (and sometimes all three together) of the one I had chosen. Blind fatality or a cruel curse followed me to such an extent that in spite of all my feminine advantages I never had what my heart desired most and what I thought ought to be my destiny, my life—to be the adored wife of an adored husband!

After each crucial development, I was so tired from my unlimited debauch of feeling, so exhausted from the excesses of my rich emotion that I felt certain that this was the last time I would ever be able to feel, to love, to adore…

When I became sober again, there was no life left in me; my heart was closed, hermetically closed, closed forever; my head was empty, my blood ran thin while my mind desired only peace, beneficial peace. The excessive vitality was gone, I had nothing to give nor did I wish to ever receive anything again.

I desired above everything to feel free, free… And to be free meant to me not to feel at all. I wanted to live finally in the enjoyment of Nature's generosity which I had never known, never felt, since I was continually absorbed in one fixed idea, in one desire: to give happiness as my happiness depended utterly on the happiness of my twin soul, the other half of my being—the one I loved.

When those moments actually came and I was able not to feel, not to feel at all, I was so happy about my newly gained freedom that I wished I could have stopped Time. My intuition sensed that such perfect bliss could not last forever. Soon, too soon perhaps, I would have to fulfill my destiny, for in those years I believed that all that happens in life, the smallest detail of daily existence was either accidental or premeditated by Fate, Destiny, or shall I call it God?

> *What we call an accident is not and cannot be but an unknown cause of a known effect.*
> — VOLTAIRE

How foolish I was not to take advantage of the armistice so generously granted me. The premonition of future tragedies already haunted my well-deserved peace and I felt the steps of those tragedies at the door ready to enter…

* * *

It has been said that the more the heart gives itself, the richer it becomes. Already I thought what an ugly state to be indifferent. What a selfish attitude to feel content without any special reason! What a small character to enjoy the happiness that comes without a struggle! What a beastly existence! Functioning only to eat, to sleep, to dress, but not actually to live.

I had always preferred the tragic expressions of life, perhaps even then I unconsciously felt that there is no royal road to Nirvana—to Heaven—to God.

* * *

I waited and waited years and years, time after time, for absolute happiness. Oh, how ready I was for that state and how I prepared myself for it, never neglecting a single effort, never escaping a sorrowful experience or humiliation, never avoiding seemingly unbearable difficulties, never shrinking from self-imposed duty, philosophically accepting the constant downfalls, solving almost pyramidal problems with an undying devotion, with infinite patience, with unshakable faith in final success, with sacrifices which would have made a weaker person than myself permanently lose equilibrium, always hoping in spite of many missteps and mistaken judgment, blinded so often by adversity!

It was all of no use. Destiny was irrevocable! I had to bow to it. The only consolation I had was the realization that if I lost the battle, it was not before I had turned every stone on the road of my ungenerous path.

To make it still harder and almost unbearable, I had to realize that, simultaneously with and parallel to my inner discouragement, my work in singing gave me the same quantity of torture and the same anguish as did my womanly wounded heart.

I was forced to see that, as long as my heart desired something, it could not have it. When through will-power, determination and persistence I still pursued the thing I wanted, I only prolonged my misery by years, postponing that painful but salutary operation which could deliver me from that feeling of nightmare and sever me from harmful illusions.

My constant misery, day in and day out, year after year was so unbearable that my thoughts turned more and more towards my ultimate deliverance. If I did not voluntarily end my all but unenviable existence, it was only because deep in the bottom of my heart I could not feel I had failed, I could not give up. Actually I had made several previous attempts to do away with myself but had succeeded only in landing in bed for a few days. No! In my heart I could not admit failure!

> *Great passions like great masterpieces are rare.*
> — BALZAC

Unable to command the stillness of my heart and wishing to protect myself against too much sorrowful disillusion, I finally decided to choose a way by which this poor heart of mine could be wounded less brutally and if it had to love with its every beat at least it would love someone I did not know personally. Thus I would run less risk of enduring one shock after another. Also in that way I would be able to give without any restriction. I had so much to give but in the past I never had the opportunity of giving myself to the utmost, of emptying my soul and so unburdening myself entirely because those I loved were unworthy, not ready to receive such a great amount, or unable to accept a given quality, or quite content to get less, much less.

As a rule, a man is humiliated when he gives less than he receives—less heart, less brain, less effort, less money. This applies especially to the American man, who despises weakness and has an instinctive desire to protect a woman.

I never even had the sweet consolation of feeling I could blame those lords of creation, the objects of my affections. No, they were themselves and in their proper place. It was I who was out of place, who was in the wrong century, not in sympathy with progress and removed from earthly considerations.

I was abnormally sensitive. I could not face any sort of compromise. Half beauty was not beauty at all to me. I believed that even trying to arrange something in the sphere of feelings constituted a lie. And I could not lie to myself. When I loved, I could not be anything but sincere and simple. If necessary I could admit an ugliness but an ugliness without deception, without hypocrisy, giving all, let it be bad, but let it be everything, no matter how little or how much one's heart and mind contained.

I could overlook anything but a false word, the slightest untruth, even when done or said for my benefit, even if it were for the sake of my happiness. For I felt I could not be happy if that happiness were based on the wrong foundation. To lie about love seemed to me unnatural, monstrous, "chemically" impossible. There could be no love where there was even a partial lie. I could not admit the physical possibility of lying when one carried the feeling of love—any love—in one's heart.

* * *

Often I became deeply interested—never could I do anything comfortably or half way—in men whom I had never met, but whose books, for instance, inflamed my imagination; whose music attuned my soul to the highest vibrations; the severity of whose forceful sculpture I admired immensely; whose dictatorial and uncompromising tendencies approached my taste and ideas; whose musical instruments helped me to create an illusion that I could carry for years; whose humanitarian lectures permitted me to imagine that the masses are good and that it is encouraging to work for them through any channel we may be capable of; whose powerful and luminous pictures or notable intelligence gave energy to my active intellect; whose interpretation of a noble part by the masterly delivery made me attribute to the interpreter the qualities put in the character's mouth by Shakespeare…

Slowly but surely, one after the other, my idols fell. Some after a day or a week, others after months or years but always inevitably and irrevocable, they crumbled.

Often my deep adulation was instantaneously sobered and my intuition sadly humiliated at the first contact with my idol, sometimes at the moment of shaking hands for the first time. I wondered how I could have been so blind. It was so obvious that the individual was entirely different from the person I had imagined him to be. How could I have given my intimate thoughts to the stranger before me who could have nothing in common with me? How could I have given the best of me to a man who shook my hand so weakly and meekly? Brrr... I felt cold... The contact made me shiver... What a *Katzenjammer* of mental indigestion!

How could I have filled all my being with the thoughts of a man who paid me a cheap compliment on seeing me for the first time and then could not comprehend why I should not wish to see him again? I could have given him so much, and he obviously wanted so little!

How could I have been so thick-skinned as to have let my thoughts be occupied even for a single evening with that famous poet who, lacking inspiration for his writing, published letters received from girls in love with him in order to increase his popularity? And that illustrious violinist, who while his soul rendered divinely the beauty of a Brahms Concerto was actually counting the empty seats to know how many dollars he did not take in?

And that well-known painter who pretended that his adoration of me would inspire him to paint the masterpiece of his life, but as I later discovered—and I always did find out such things—who really desired above all to exhibit my portrait for publicity's sake. And that aristocrat whose snobbishness shocked me to the utmost. For, like lying, snobbishness to my way of thinking is the worst defect in a human being and the furthest step from simplicity—and simplicity is my idiosyncrasy.

George Sand said: "Simplicity is the most difficult thing in the world to attain; it is the last term of experience and the last effort of genius." Paradoxically, the most difficult attainments were always in every way the most easy and natural for me.

Among my illusory idols also was that celebrated politician whose fight for peace, justice and humanity could deceive only such a willingly blinded person as myself.

Then there was the handsome ambassador, whose love for me was so great that at any diplomatic or political function he would jealously keep me to himself during the entire evening so that the next day all Paris would say "Did you see how Ambassador X monopolized Madame Walska?" But it was all because my spectacular personality could easily persuade public opinion that he really was interested in ladies!

And to cap the climax, that saintly mystic, that man of God, the apostle who pretended an immeasurable love for the Lord in order to see more of me...

In all honesty I must admit I did everything in my power—and my power was great—to fool myself in order to prolong such a ravishing state of beatitude and renew at any cost the lease of my imaginary life of beauty.

> *The religion of Beauty is the source of moral elevation and of the progress of the human spirit.*
> — RUSKIN

For I loved Beauty, Beauty with a capital "B." I was blind to everything that meant ugliness. It was physically unbearable for me to accept even the natural functions of life. My Polish education helped even more to build such a shrine to beauty, for to this day I cannot, unless forced to it, pronounce the words "leg" or "trousers" without stuttering. It is a tragedy to me to think that if I did not masticate my food, my spirit would be less strong in me.

When very young, already living in a dreamland untouched by worldly prose, my romantic imagination made me see in an ordinary Egyptian Bey the possibilities of a wonderful romance *à la* Antony and Cleopatra and once when we were in a restaurant and he disappeared for a while I—upon his return—asked where he had been but hearing that he was washing his hands, I almost collapsed. I wanted to die for shame. I could scarcely face the brutal world again and I certainly never saw my poor Pharoah after that.

I remember also an episode when I went to Montmarte for the first time. My husband presented to me a very handsome young man with whom I danced all evening. I was extremely flattered that such a smart Parisian was so attentive to such a young provincial girl as myself. But I was literally confused when as I was leaving the place he asked if I would give him something. Not yet seventeen, just married and not daring to give him my handkerchief or a flower from my bouquet, I just bashfully pointed to him my husband, to whom he went immediately. My heart stopped—certainly a duel was imminent, for my frightened eyes saw with horror that Arcadie's right hand was reaching in his pocket for his revolver. I almost fainted. But, no! He took out some gold louis and paid the professional dancer for his services. Needless to relate my feelings…

If my sympathies were in favor of monarchies, they were not inspired by any political considerations but because in tradition there was much beauty. Certainly the greatest spectacle of beauty, *le plus beau théâtre* I saw in my life —and I have seen many—was the coronation of George VI. I was so impressed by its oriental touch that I had my Parisian modiste Suzy copy for me the turbans of all the Maharajas present at this magnificent event and with my collection of Hindu jewels I had exact replicas of something outstandingly beautiful.

If I have never believed in free love, it was not on account of puritanism but only because that expression of love necessarily brings out untruths, lies and ugliness, my dislike for which is stronger in me than any other sentiment. I will not face the realities of life—its ugliness! I will not! ! I cannot! ! !

If I have loved culture—as far back as I can remember I have always wanted to learn something; languages, astronomy, antiques, guitar—it is because culture meant primarily beauty. For the sake of beauty, when just married and newly arrived in St. Petersburg, I became the pupil of Michel Fokine, the great choreographer.

What glory in beauty! Not even the sky was my limit for there could be no limit to my ecstasy. I wanted bigger, higher, limitless altitudes. You can touch the sky with your eyes, you can admit its immensity and try to count its stars. But the state of my mind reached where Beauty blinds, where only four-dimensional power reigns, where the physical eye cannot see or touch, where only the possibilities of eternal wandering exist, where ugliness is powerless to stop one's inspiration, where the conceptions of the body are lost, and we melt into one with the universal immensity...

> *We can have but little because we want much, and we reach the good only because we have the idea of what is better.*
>
> — SAINT MARC GIRARDIN

THE HIGHER MY spirit soared, the harder—Icarus-like—I fell at a stupendous speed and crashed into earthliness. Each succeeding inspiration and crash made it more difficult for me to rise as high as previously and finally I realized that I could not, I would not take any more knocks on my sensitive solar plexus. I simply *would not*—WOULD NOT! I would find the strength to still the slightest movement of my heart.

While in that state of mind, the mysterious name of the greatest adventurer of our epoch, the man who continually disputed the title of "Mystery Man" with Sir Basil Zaharoff in the press, commanded again and again my attention.

I read the all-but-impassive descriptions of his tumultuous life by the various reviewers who gave him contradictory titles: one making him a hero of the first constellation, another considering him a vulgar spy, while a third raised him to the throneless kingdom of Arabia.

Arabia—so far away, so *ballet russe*, so unreal a land to my highly imaginative but geographically poorly-informed earthly mind. Arabia and its heat burning all solid proof of his existence, burning under a sky of torrential fire!

This was for me the unique opportunity. I would send my fluid thoughts to that mysterious man. How reassuring for my easily shocked sensibilities to have him so far away! I certainly did not risk meeting him, even if he actually existed and was not a mere legend invented at the eleventh hour by a hungry journalist in need of a sensational article. In the event of his disappearance, I would not know about it and I would still have the compensation of thinking that his death—like his life—was a legend.

Positive and quickly decisive in character, I no sooner thought than I did it. From that moment on, I was passively happy for a few years. Nothing could interfere with the ascension of my soul to the burning desert, and the slightest news about the man greatly stirred my imagination that was always so easily inflammable.

I kept sending him concentrated thoughts with my dynamic power, which was still reinforced by unhampered possibilities of limitless development of my feelings and by the complete absorption of all my romantic urges that filled every cell of my being.

Free from the killing of my vitality emotions, I was able now to put stronger vibrations into my singing, my other and more positive field of expression. That gave me more courage to fight the visible and invisible worlds. I was relatively happy.

Having wasted less energy during that period, I actually made a big step forward in my vocal studies. All my being was now absorbed in my work, but as usual the excessiveness of my qualities now handicapped my progress. Or, as Louis XIV put it, "Often on account of too much fervor, our impatience holds back the things it wishes to bring forth."

But the day came when I read in the paper that my mysterious Colonel Lawrence (I suppose everyone already recognized him from my description) was living in England in a cottage near Moreton under the name of Mr. Shaw. However, even that commonplace announcement was so full of doubts and contradictions that neither the correspondent nor myself was sure how much truth there was in that news.

Word came still later that Mr. Shaw, whom everybody suspected of being the adventurer Lawrence, had met with an accident and what an accident for an uncrowned ruler but definitely crowned adventurer who had risked a thousand deaths! To avoid a boy on a bicycle while himself going at top speed on a motorcycle he put on the brakes…

Unconscious he was taken to the hospital…

The radio announced that George V had sent his personal surgeon to try to save the hero…

The King? So he was Colonel Lawrence after all! He was that solitary pilgrim! He was a hero and not a vulgar spy if the King of the British Empire was anxious to save his life!

New vistas opened to my heart. Before I had loved him only to fill the emptiness of necessary desire to love at any cost, to worship an ideal but not for his actual value! Now the great realization had come! I had chosen him intuitively and he was a reality, my Reality. Now I must know him… I can love him now without danger… He was the one I had waited for all my life! I must see him… I must go to England at once, I must, I must! !

At last! At last!

* * *

"Colonel Lawrence died last night without recovering consciousness" the radio announced next day…

* * *

The foundations of my tranquility, made solid and firm during those years, tumbled and crashed. Emptiness entered my heart again.

Solitude… Eternal solitude…

> *Art does not attain its full height when it just charms men without at the same time calling forth their enthusiasm for all that goes to make the grandeur of life.*
>
> — J. REYNAUD

THE LAST DESIRE to sacrifice myself in serving someone came when I read that Madame Paderewska had died. At that time, I did not yet consciously realize that there is in me a creative spirit of perhaps higher vibrations than is possessed by those whose servant I have been or wanted to become. Bitten, scoffed at, trampled on, I was certainly far, far away from the idea that I would be called to play a Parsifal rather than a service-begging Kundry.

When my faithful Mary brought the evening paper which related Madame Paderewska's death, I said:

"Mary, now I will marry Mr. Paderewski!"

"What, my young girl marry that old man? God forbid!" said Mary, for to her I was always "my young girl" and when she put twenty-one candles on my cake for my fortieth birthday and I asked her in surprise why twenty-one, frightened she answered:

"Oh, Madame, did I put on too many?"

Old man? But that is the point. He is almost double my age and is sick, spoiled and moneyless. (I had just been asked by his friends, without his knowledge though, for help to pay his tax arrearages on his California property.) He needs help and strength.

The enormous fortunes he had made by his art he had generously given away. In Europe, since the war, he played only for the worthy causes, for the needy institutions, paying out of his own pocket the necessary sums for his own expenses.

Yes, he is old and lonesome of late, for his wife in ill health for several years has not been a companion to him... He cannot play much longer... Even now his undying spirit is more powerful than the elasticity of his mortal fingers. I will take care of him! The strength of my soul will raise his vibrations higher than ever. When he becomes unable to play the piano at all, or chooses not to play so he may take a great role in the politics of Poland as a great patriot that he is, then I will make him feel that he can be even greater upon discovery of his real, undying immortality, unperishable immortality that will provide him with the source of eternal *youth*. And when he is broken in human mind and body, he shall not need to give in to the powers of destruction and death, for I will pass on to him the parcel of spiritual knowledge which I am already fortunate enough to have received.

* * *

Through Mr. Paderewski's friend Ernest Schelling, who was soon to see the Polish titan in Switzerland, I made this proposition of our union naturally in the spirit of renunciation and without any gain. But while the words were coming directly from the profundity of my heart and were still forming themselves on my lips, I could read total misapprehension in Mr. Schelling's eyes. Hardly could I finish speaking, much less explain my motives. Unwanted, unwelcome words remained in my throat... Already I was sorry I had begun...

I am sure our national hero never even knew about my bold presumption. Mr. Schelling is too correct to pass on such—to say the least—vague ideas! Naturally I would prefer that my great countryman never knew of such heresy!

After all I merely desired to give to that great soul, to that imposing personality, to that man already old, broken in health, and without future, my years of remaining youth, the unrestricted richness of my generous nature as well as my earthly possessions for his service.

That was what I wanted to give in exchange for what a cynical mind might see as arthritic fingers, bygone glory, bygone sentiments, weary in soul, by trying to make his countrymen happy in the way he thought they ought to be happy. To the man who *was* — I wanted to present the precious gift of what I *am*. I wanted to bury my real self in the shadow of his past victories, perhaps his embittered mind and his mortgaged Swiss estate…

My audacious thought was to allow that worn-out, thin, yet majestic body of a featherless eagle to have the illusion of still being, being always, to assure him that, in spite of age and ills, the world needed him more than ever, that without him Music, Art, *Patrie* would tumble down like a house of cards!

No, it is not Paderewski's wisdom that saved me from willingly seeking again a slavery for as I have already mentioned I do not think my hero ever knew about my desire for that self-sacrifice. It was my Guiding Spirit that protected my seeking soul, not yet on a stable foundation, from wanting to give itself to a soul that already found expression in a self-created personality. "When we act in all sincerity, without any apprehension of the mind, in general we act well," as Boutain wrote. So I do not regret the flight of my exalted imagination. It is one more experience…

Through repeated falling down we learn to walk.
— E. BASTIAT

And again after a long period of solitude my heart started its search...

Sometimes, when at a reception and surrounded by the most brilliant admirers, I would discover an unassuming man in a dark corner, too modest to come nearer to the light, afraid perhaps of burning his wings. Cleverly I would manoeuvre to get near him, to speak to him. In his bashfulness, he would not understand such generosity and would try to diminish his value by telling me he was just a poor devil, he would belittle himself, assuring me he was not good enough for such a great personality as the glamorous Ganna Walska, he would refuse to accept my exceptional attention...

And so my search continued...

At the Colony Restaurant while lunching with the Grand Duchess Marie, I completely ignored a handsome young man sitting opposite me, who carried on a conversation across the table with my imperial guest. But an hour later, when I realized that the brilliant creature left the room in a wheel chair, my heart went out to him instantaneously.

Such a tragedy for one so young. What suffering must be his! Those thoughts automatically inflamed my mind. Upon learning his name and discovering that I passed by his ancestral dwelling place daily, I put all my life in those red bricks, hoping against hope that I would see him emerge from the door one day.

In vain. Ultimately I got up enough courage to telephone him but was not successful in reaching him. Often I sent him anonymous flowers or short notes...

At that time I was about to sail for Europe. The day before leaving I lost all control. I simply had to speak to him. But again I had no luck over the phone. Unable to still my longing to hear his voice, I sent a wire asking him to call me at eleven o'clock at my private number knowing he could not find out whose number it was.

While waiting for the phone to ring, I was blinded by a positive fever of excitement and my heart beat so loudly it deafened my ears and made my hands tremble.

He called... Those few words he spoke were so banal... It hardly seemed possible I could have built such a world around him... It was the end...

I sailed... And he never knew...

PART TWO

THE ADVANCE TOWARD MY STAR
1934

One loves the more for having by degrees given more.

UNABLE IN THE past to scrutinize objectively my mental self with absolute lucidity, I am now looking back over my sorrow-impregnated life in such a detached way that it would seem as if it were the experience of someone else, whose most intimate movements of heart and most secretive thoughts I knew to perfection.

That we do not remember our previous coming to this earth is not sufficient reason for not .believing in its existence, although the most intelligent minds do not take the lack of evidence as proof.

Often I cannot imagine that it was I who felt so negatively during all my past life, that it was I who had such cowardly reactions to great sorrow ten years ago, or that it was I who desired to end life when unable to endure final separation from my beloved.

How can we remember our previous lives if we can hardly recollect our childhood, early youth, the joys of a few years ago, last month's grievance, the taste of yesterday's meal or even the warmth of this morning's bath? We cannot remember all those sensations because everything we feel through the senses is changeable, unstable, unfixed and unreliable.

Now that my inner self has changed and, with the change, the reasons for my agony have disappeared, I am actually surprised to recall that previously I took this or that condition so tragically to heart. Then the sleepless nights increased more acutely the exasperation of my mental state while today sleep restores my wasted physical energy, and my mind—inexhaustible source of profusion —does not require renewal of its endless power.

* * *

Today I analyze my heart just as a bacteriologist would analyze the development, the progress or the retrogression of certain germs, analyzing it in a dispassionate way. And now I see clearly that all the good and bad in my life came from the unusual sensitiveness so generously donated by Mother Nature perhaps to test my character, to test the unlimited forces of my inner being for a purpose which I could not perceive at the beginning but the existence of which I now feel with absolute certainty. Yes, I am convinced of it and when the time comes for me to express it, I shall be ready and soldier-like will answer: "Present!" I am also sure that I shall know the actual moment. Till then "Thy will, not mine, be done!"

Just as it is impossible to see the city from the street, so with my soul aching I could not picture myself in the proper perspective. But today I can trace my quasi-*maladive* sensitivity to my earliest childhood. In going back I can recognize myself in this frail girl dressed in deep mourning after her mother's death. Curiously enough the only picture in my possession of me as a child is one taken in that symbol of sorrow. To see my face, the photographer made me take off and put by my side the hat veiled with a long practically non-transparent crepe that hung over my eyes.

I can visualize myself skating one day in the Baltic University town of Dorpat where a little girl three or four years old timidly smiled at me… I smiled back… Later, when passing by, she came toward me as though wanting to tell me something and almost fell. I rushed to help steady her but at that point a young woman, whom I had not noticed before, tore the tiny hand from mine, hysterically screaming: "What do you want of my daughter? Leave her alone! If you like children, why do you not have your own? Never dare to speak to my baby again… !"

I was just then married and not quite seventeen but since that day every tragic moment of my dramatic life has been accompanied by the memory of this infuriatedly jealous mother. At each sorrow I have had in life I have wanted to disappear, to die or have the earth swallow me up, just as I felt after that painful scene. I felt I could not accept life after seeing such ugliness and so much malevolence.

Such an ultra-sensitive soul with such extreme receptiveness as mine has its maximum sensibility already developed in childhood. Our character—already formed by the age of seven as authoritative observers claim—remains super-sensitive for years and years afterwards; but the hypocritical conditions of our lives teach us consciously to hide our real selves from the outside world. In America man, in self-protection, hides even from himself this quality of sensitiveness, disdaining it as being rather feminine and unwilling to admit the slightest weakness.

> *The man who has lived most is not the man who has lived most years, it is he who has most felt Life passing by.*
>
> — J.J. ROUSSEAU

* * *

Though grown-up, if at a very tender age, now I see that my sensitiveness did not diminish with years, for while in Paris during the first few months of World War I, being entirely free, having no family, no obligations, sensitive to suffering and brave as only romantic youth can be, idolizing with all other women *Le Roy Chevalier* of Belgium to the extent of keeping his picture under my pillow, still I could not have gone to the front, because the merest drop of blood almost made me faint, and so I knew I would only be a nuisance to the doctors and a hindrance to the sick. Later, in America, I sang in the Polish camps but in France I sewed sheets for the soldiers in hospital. No, I did not sew them well, for I cannot sew.[14]

Some say that one can get used to the sight of blood. Not I. With all the self-control I have today, the one thing I do not even try to overcome is my reaction at the sight or even the mention of a wound.

In Spain, at the bullfights, I disgraced myself in front of the King and Queen by emitting such a piercing scream that it made Alfonso XIII turn his head to find me deathly pale and leaving the stand at the most exciting moment.

I was told that the first bullfight often makes such an impression and that if I went a second time I would surely love it for, in the opinion of my friends, I was too much of an artist not to appreciate such beauty. Other great admirers of tauromachy suggested that I see some of the great *toreros* such as Belmonte and then I would most certainly be converted. However, my second experience at the bullring even with Belmonte performing was still more horrible than the first!

No, I am decidedly not a great artist!

* * *

It is said that as a rule exceptionally deep emotion diminishes in intensity with years. But my capacity to feel rather increased with time and my suffering became unrestricted. After so many years of an extraordinary eventful life, filled with an unusual amount of variety, meeting the greatest personalities of our time, visiting courts and embassies all over the world, entertaining prime ministers, presidents of republics and royalty, even now when I enter a drawing-room, no matter how unimportant a gathering it may be, I still am uneasy, nervous and extremely uncomfortable,

---

14 Unfortunately I can neither cook nor sew, and when Madame Alda, whose excellent cooking I have enjoyed so much, presumed to advise me to take up cooking instead of singing, she flattered me by judging me by herself.

because I have never outgrown my innate timidity or my permanent shyness.

In America, people are never satisfied until they have put a name to things. In my case they would call it an inferiority complex and speak about it quite simply, stating the fact as if it were self-explanatory, as if I were left-handed or had flat feet. But as Dr. Fraenkel once told the family of a patient, "What benefit would it be to a patient if I diagnosed his malady and pinned a name to it if I could not cure him?"

* * *

Unable to stop this plague of self-consciousness, while my soul passionately desired to live its interior life, I finally made a decision to try and preserve by wise care at least its exquisite delicacy by protecting its existence from a violent death by profane hands.

Already at seventeen I had the unconscious tendency to jump over my life and be rather sixty, an age in those days considered for a woman as biblical if not Methuselan.

Intuitively I wished to escape the Calvary which, as I now see, was so necessary to my spiritual development, to growth of my soul.

Fortunately the gods were generous to me, for they neither punished my cowardice nor accepted my fear of life as definitive. They gave me a second chance to improve and rehabilitate myself.

Around forty I understood with a touching sadness that my dreams, those constant reveries conceived in the abstract, had not materialized. I realized that youth was already behind me and that the only joy—if I may profane the sacred word *joy*, a thing unknown to my heart since it ignored me all my life and was ever my benefactor and therefore I owe it no gratitude—the only joy I had while I was still young and was envied, as people in the public eye usually are, was my morning coffee! And such an admission from a person whose only limit was the sky is a tragic admission. "*C'est tout un programme*" as the politicians say.

I admit that fact with sadness, heightened by the realization that this prosaic joy will still be left when I will have definitively parted with all my illusions, when I will have buried forever all my castles built in air, when I will willingly have surrendered my arms, when ultimately all my dream phantoms will be destroyed one after the other.

If my innocent ambition in attempting to raise the consciousness of the world's most illustrious inhabitants who crossed my path, those who direct the moral pulse of the universe—if that ambition can somehow mark my passage here below, because I lighted in those people the creative spark so essential to the chosen, so indispensable to the apostleship of a life dedicated like mine to inner beauty profoundly implanted in the soul—if I have been allowed to be an inspiration to few or even to one, I will be satisfied. Confucius said: "He who planted a tree did not pass on this earth in vain."

* * *

Soon and slowly, but every day more clearly, I began to realize—though still in a veiled way as a half dream only just piercing my consciousness—that what I always called Bad Luck might be something else, something directed from above and for a purpose—perhaps even for a Great Purpose.

Also I began to realize that I was accepting my cruel trials with a great deal of vanity, feeling extremely superior to my environment and to those who were put to a lesser test than myself. Often I even felt conceited at being chosen to suffer, not yet realizing whether I was chosen because I was sensitive or was sensitive because I was chosen. I think that sometimes I almost enjoyed my misery as one enjoys a very tragic but beautiful performance. I certainly indulged in suffering...

Gradually I started to sense something new in me. "Dreary

misfortune has its good" and after each knockout blow—as if recuperating from an operation—I vaguely felt, without understanding yet, that it was preparation for something still bigger to come. I distinctly could see that each comeback after the depths of suffering was accompanied by some kind of inner release. The more intense the storm, the quicker the return of the rainbow and the glorious sunshine.

When the last person dependent on me had been taken away from me and I was left quite alone for the first time in my existence, my mind began to sense a new light. And when I say *alone* I mean it—not even a cat! I mention cats because I have loved them dearly all my life. When I was a child I adored a homely little pussy to such an extent that when it was taken away from me I went down to the river to drown myself. However the water only came up to my knees, while a terrifying looking black crustacean caught my little toe. Unable to shake it off, I screamed in such an unearthly way that someone came and saved me from suicide and black crayfish, the Polish crab, an animal I had only met previously in its red state on the luncheon table.

After years of constant unspeakable emotional loneliness and vain calling out into the desert wilderness, I perceived the coming of new color into my life.

Lonesome at heart as I had been, I had nevertheless succeeded in hiding this fathomless depth of my soul in order that I might perform my various duties. I am grateful for the urge that led to that self-imposed obligation, for in order to sweeten the life of those entirely dependent upon me—until the present there was always someone to whom I meant everything and who could not envisage life without me—I was constantly forced to smile. Like a boomerang that saved me from the complete blackness of my thoughts, from suicide or other emotional extravagance.

* * *

During ten years of so-called materialistic life, if one can call a life wholly dedicated to all branches of the arts materialistic, with many people in my care to whom I was indispensable for their very life—I had no heart, no atmosphere and no actual time for the mystical experiences which had sobered me so thoroughly early in my search by turning out to be complete disillusion.

Throughout that period, I had never questioned myself about the mysteries of life until the passing away of my teacher, Walther Straram, who was not only my vocal instructor but also the conductor of the celebrated orchestra which bore his name and the director of the Théâtre des Champs-Élysées. His Voltairean mind was hermetically closed to everything but visible acts and tangible facts—except the divine sounds of music. He passed away after my difficult attempts to prolong for years longer his life, so valuable to music, to prolong it by terrific operations which he underwent only thanks to my beneficial influence over him. He consented to the dreadful cure because he loved me as he loved only his music. And this allowed me to persuade him to live for the sake of the sublime tones he could recreate. To this purpose I had put at his disposal an orchestra the members of which caught the divine spark from their leader and raised music in Paris to new heights of perfection.

Only when Walther Straram had departed from my life, did I begin to think in the abstract rather than in terms of the next lesson, next concert or next dreadful cauterization of an ill throat. Not until I became absolutely isolated, absolutely free for the first time in my life from anyone dependent for my help, my sympathy, my pity, and when I was no longer obliged to sacrifice my taste, my point of view, my sensibility, my preferences—only then could I again think about myself and wonder if those years of misery did not mean something more than merely Bad Luck, this Bad Luck that had persecuted me to such a great extent during all my life. And because of its extraordinary persistence my mind began suspecting it might have been after all my Karma as well as it might have been some Black Magic...

...Bad Luck... the name by which I called all those dreadful trials, great misfortunes and petty disappointments, for I took it for granted that everything unfavorable that happened to me was Bad Luck!

When my misery was too great to stand it more stoically, I wanted to know whether it was not something else than unluckiness. I wondered if there were enough grounds to justify me in thinking that some curse was upon me because everything I started almost automatically turned against me. Everything!

And almost joyfully I would cry "Aha! Again Bad Luck!" just to give myself a reasonable explanation of my unhappiness. At the same time I took for granted any happiness that came my way, for I knew some unthinkable moments—if only abstract moments—of that godly nectar, when for instance I was allowed to love. In those great moments when I was not yet disillusioned—although ultimately I always was—my soul was in ecstatic touch with another soul in an ecstasy of a divine quality like Beatrice and Dante.

Mentally free, with a great sense of independence born of the unlimited spirit rooted deep in my nature and what people took for eccentricity because I would not follow the mass in fashion and paid no attention to what my neighbor thought, I went back to the state I was in during a previous decade and soon found myself in a more or less profound search of the Truth.

The first push towards this new epoch in my life came through my casual meeting with my country neighbor, Grace Gassette, an elderly American dwelling a few miles away from Galluis in an 11th-century priory. I was led to her somewhat providentially, as I believed at the time. At our very first meeting Miss Gassette gave me to read the works of two Englishmen, Alexander Erskin and Dr. Cannon. The latter's "The Invisible Influence" had caused a most unusual stir in the circle of the followers of mysticism.

Those books again awoke in me—stronger than ever—all my natural inclinations toward the mystery surrounding us. Mr. Erskin scientifically asserted in his book that any mental or unorthodox illness such as deafness or blindness could be cured by hypnotism or its milder brother—suggestion, a cure *à la* Freud, a spiritualized Freud, not merely going back only to the supposed psychological childhood source of the trouble but thousands years into the past, everything being relative to our mind.[15]

I also learned from Mr. Erskin's book that under hypnotism one will divulge the reason of one's mental trouble. And at that time I was very anxious to know whether my enemy was Black Magic in the form of a curse, some psychic condition, or just my Karma.

To me even the knowledge of the worst was not as bad as uncertainty, that invisible opponent acting in the dark. At least half the battle is won when we know the true situation. In my case, for instance, if I had known there was some curse on me I would have tried to annihilate it if I had the means, or I would simply have stopped singing, realizing clearly that under the best conditions I still could not succeed.

The contents of Erskin's book gave me new hope, a new interest. I wrote to the author but I never received any answer. Small wonder, for I soon learned that Mr. Erskin had died a few months before I happened to read his book. Naturally, I said to myself: "Again my Bad Luck!"

However, undaunted in my endeavor, I reasoned that as Dr. Cannon fully endorsed and quoted Erskin's theories and also wrote about hypnotism himself I might try to meet

---

15 Speaking about relativity of time, I once visited a famous Chinese antique dealer. While still bowing reverently in exquisite courtesy, he asked if I wished to see the modern galleries first or on the contrary to finish my inspection with them. The friend who accompanied me on seeing my surprise and being acquainted with my lack of sympathy for modern furniture, later informed me that those sons of the Orient, those lovers of antiques, consider the 18th century a modern era.

him instead. Moreover this was easy to arrange, for Miss Gassette was already in correspondence with Dr. Cannon, having requested his authorization to translate his sensational book into French. When she next wrote him, she asked if he would see a friend in need of help, suggesting that it would also give her the opportunity of personally discussing the translation of his work.

Dr. Cannon afterwards informed us that out of the hundreds of letters received daily since the publication of his book he instantly chose ours, following the instructions of his spiritual guide, an Egyptian, who was also our guide as we later learned. Therefore we quickly received an appointment for an early date, in fact so soon that I was unable to manage the time and begged that our meeting in London be postponed for two days.

* * *

At Grosvenor Street we found ourselves in a Dr. Jensen's office. Dr. Cannon, being physician of the Kent Mental Hospital and therefore in the service of the state, could not practice for himself.

As we crossed the entrance hall I laughingly said. "Dr. Cannon has not arrived although there is someone here with a silk top hat. Certainly Dr. Cannon does not wear such a hat!"

I was mistaken. Dr. Cannon wore a top hat as well as white spats and a cutaway morning coat just as though he were dressed for a fashionable wedding or an important funeral ceremony.

I certainly did not expect that a man who had crossed oriental rivers without the usual help of a bridge would be dressed in traditional Harley Street fashion. This man, who in Tibet had sent messages hundreds of miles away in the wink of an eye without the aid of any apparatus, also surprised me greatly by using glasses like any uninitiated office clerk. For the past five years I had felt ashamed of being unable to read without a vulgar pair of glasses in the intimacy of my room or an eccentric looking monocle when out! However Dr. Cannon explained the use of his spectacles as a protection against the evil eye or something similar. His explanation did not wholly convince me. I felt that if Dr. Cannon were strong enough to overcome the mortal bites of cobras and to brave other deaths in his dangerous Himalayan expedition, he should be able to face the gaze of his Brook Street compatriots, unconscious of their destructive possibilities.

On first looking at Dr. Cannon, I was surprised to find that the soul of such a great mystic could be contained in that jolly man, much too opulent for my ideal of a superior omnipotent mind. A greater surprise awaited me however when Dr. Cannon took me to an office, where a girl medium was seated, and asked her to let him know what was wrong with my health, informing me with pride that she was the finest diagnostician in England.

The medium, fat and sympathetic—as plump girls generally are—pronounced me full of illnesses, the existence and even the names of which I was not aware. Dr. Jensen, according to procedure, wrote down the medium's statements, automatically adding the prescriptions for the cure of each of my multiple diseases.

When this new type of Aesculapius could detect no more ailments in me, I was dismissed but not before receiving orders to see Dr. Jensen the next morning for a more detailed medical examination, a thing I had not undergone in all the years of my life.

Apparently I—the widow of a great medical man who was an enemy of stereotyped medicine—had made the journey to London to learn about my blood pressure, my pulse beat, and all the regular physician's paraphernalia.

The evening of the second day, I made the acquaintance of another medium, who Dr. Cannon hypnotised instantaneously and then asked her about my various troubles. The situation was even more ridiculous than on the previous day and the medium—not fat this time—was less sympathetic. But Dr. Cannon took it all very seriously and repeated everything she said with conviction. When finally he authorized me to question her for the sake of verification, I asked where I was born.

"In Paris," was the prompt answer.

This amused me greatly and I informed Dr. Cannon that I was born in Poland. Smiling at me in a condescending way as if I were a naughty child he said:

"I am certain she is right. She is always right.[16] Once someone was told by her he was born in America. The gentleman was very positive that he had been born in England. A year later, however, he wrote an apology, saying that he had just discovered that his mother had been visiting America at the time of his birth, a fact he had never known until that moment."

The seance continued. When I was invited to put another question to the medium, I asked,, if there was a curse upon me, hoping that I could thus find the confirmation of my suspicion or be reassured to the contrary. I explained to Dr. Cannon that, as even my smallest wish never was granted to me and anything I planned about my singing or any of my heart's desires always ended in tragedy to my soul, it seemed reasonable to suspect that everything I touched turned against me.

"All great artists have their tragedies!" came the flattering answer from the philosophical medium. "When you go to New York call on Mr. John Frazier in the Manhattan Building. He will certainly help you. He was the teacher of Caruso."

I knew Caruso well. I made my debut with him but I had never heard of such a teacher or even that the possessor of the voice of the century had a teacher in those last years

---

16 However, a few months later Dr. Cannon admitted that his infallible medium had proved unsatisfactory.

of his prematurely finished life. Later on when back in the United States I looked in vain—for my conscience's sake—for John Frazier in the Manhattan Building.

When the medium finally awoke from her forced sleep, Dr. Cannon not in the least perturbed by my skeptical attitude, announced that it was now my turn to be hypnotised and cured of all my ills. However he never was able to put me to sleep. Later he explained that this was not extraordinary, for—as he had written in his book—some persons cannot be hypnotised at all, and some succumb to the hypnotic influence only after the sixth or seventh seance.

A year later "The Mysterious Cobbler" told me that he was able to hypnotise only about fifty per cent of the subjects he tried. And out of that percentage only a part could be healed.

But Dr. Cannon did not warn me of such possibilities at the time. When he failed in his task, he even tried to persuade me that I actually was asleep although I knew I was not. For justice's sake, while the modern Mesmer continued telling me I felt nothing, nothing at all, not even the touch of my hand or feet or anything I imagined I felt —I pinched myself to see whether it hurt. It did—and how! I most certainly felt all those sensations in spite of his suggestions to the contrary. Finally, I could endure no longer the hypocritical comedy. I leaped from the couch screaming: "I have not slept, I have not slept!"

I could hardly keep back my tears of irritation and disillusionment but at that moment Dr. Cannon turned to Miss Gassette triumphantly and said: "Great reaction, wonderful reaction!"

If I managed to control myself at that moment and give him only a cold look, I am certain I shall always be able to do so in the future.

After a second and final unsuccessful seance, instead of telling me honestly that I was one of those subjects with a strong personality who cannot be hypnotised or asking me to remain in London much longer to try and try again, Dr. Cannon (in order to gain one more seance) suggested that we should not fly back the next day but instead should take a boat the day after as there would be a terrible catastrophe in the air in which we would be not drowned, since we were protected. Still he did not want us to get uncomfortably wet!! (Dr. Cannon also predicted that the Prince of Wales would soon be reigning as David I.)

My confidence in Dr. Cannon began to diminish greatly… Before leaving, wishing to assure myself of doing no injustice to Dr. Cannon's diagnostic medium; I went to her but she told me in a private seance nonsense that was too ridiculous for words.

The morning we departed I received a bill from Dr. Jensen, as Dr. Cannon could make no charge being on government pay and therefore had to divide his fees with the colleague whose office he shared. The bill was for such a large amount that I doubted whether I would be able to leave London without cabling to my Paris bank for help.

That shocked me all the more because—all the teachings impress this on us—any spiritual manifestations can be helpful only when given without expectation of recompense. Naïvely I also imagined that miracles could not be catalogued…

To add a funny note to my London visit, I might say that during one of our dinners with Dr. Cannon he casually confided that in one of his previous incarnations he had been that "bad boy" Julius Caesar. On hearing that, I could not help thinking that Mrs. James Corrigan, who entertains royalty and seldom anyone even a little below those listed in the Almanac de Gotha, certainly would be jealous should she have learned that while at Claridge's I entertained no less a personage than Julius Caesar and, mind you, Confucius! Yes! Dr. Cannon told Miss Gassette with great authority that ages ago she had been that great Chinese philosopher. I certainly felt low plebeian and only good enough to be permitted to pay the dinner bills—a great and appreciated honor indeed as Mrs. Corrigan knows...

Speaking about the privileges of paying reminds me that during the reception I gave at the Théâtre des Champs-Élysées on the occasion of taking possession of that beautiful temple of art, the founder of that masterpiece made a speech glorifying me for what until then had merely been an act of notary business on my part, flattering me to such an extent that I finally revolted at so much insincerity. I stopped the general applause by saying:

"I thank you, very much dear Mr. Gabriel Astruc for your kindness but I cannot accept all your compliments as they do not belong to me. It was you who were illuminated with the vision to create such grandeur while Mr. Peret's genius allowed him to materialize such a conception that twenty years later it is still up-to-date and had he built it at present time he could not have improved so high was his inspiration. All music lovers, we thank you, Mr. Peret. And if we will be privileged to hear divine sounds in this frame of beauty in an atmosphere of sublimeness, we will owe it to such a perfect musician as is present with us here, Mr. Walther Straram!! So what is there left for me? The vulgar gesture of signing the checks. I am sure you all agree with me that this is neither an especially flattering nor heroic action."

* * *

Returning to Dr. Cannon, it seems that the elite of America belongs to the Four Hundred and in Europe those with royal blood must be found in the Almanac of Gotha, but Dr. Cannon on his visiting cards included something more. Among his other titles of K.C.A., M.D., Ph.D., D.P.M., M.A., Ch.B., F.R.G.S., F.R.G.M., F.R.S., TROP. M. & H., was printed: *Master the Fifth of the Great White Lodge of the Himalayas!*

And although considered as one of the most secret organizations of the Spiritual Universe, Dr. Cannon nevertheless was gracious enough to give me the whereabouts of the other Masters with their exact names, addresses and telephone numbers, which fact made it easy for me to meet Master-the-Fourth living in America.

I was informed that there are five masters altogether but I could never discover whether Number Four was superior to Number Five or vice versa. To this day I do not know if Dr. Cannon is the Benjamin of this celestial constellation of five or the highest in their hierarchy. When I was at school the best mark given was five. In France however it is considered the poor one. How about the Himalayas?

* * *

A few months after my visit to Dr. Cannon, I went to the United States where I met Master Number Four.[17] Following Dr. Cannon's instructions, I addressed him as "Master" and gave the sign inscribed on my triangle, which I was constantly wearing since Dr. Cannon taught me to do so, the triangle by which he was to know that I belonged to the same school of initiation, only in the infantile degree of the order as in the French Legion of Honor one begins by being a Chevalier.

During that winter in America I saw much of co-religionist Master Number Four. Still my preference went to Dr. Cannon, whose company I found interesting, whose conversation was fascinating as was the description of his extraordinary experiences during his far-off travels and whose English naïvete was really enchanting to me, for I am ready to admire any theatre, even the caricature of an English one. It was the same kind of admiration as I had for

---

17 And two years later Master Number Three—a half-English half-Italian living in England—blessed my golden triangular symbol on a gold chain. To be sure that the magic would work constantly, I was informed that I should send him an exact replica of my chain and triangle to enable the Master to protect me at distance. I am sure that magic worked under those conditions especially for the goldsmiths, as I have already twice lost my chain with its triangle.

Mussolini's attitude when I visited him for the first time at the Palazzo Chigi.

Anatole France said that "Hope and desire are often much better in themselves than that for which one hopes and that which one desires." Unfortunately that proved true in the case of Master Four of the Great White Lodge for he was the most tedious provincial person in the whole state of New Jersey where he lived in a small bourgeois house of characterless facade and insignificant color. Great souls do not treasure earthly possessions. But Master Four found huge satisfaction in the ownership of his home and in boasting—with no indication of being an especially highly advanced spiritual person but rather like any ordinary human—that: "The house has two floors, you see... Oh, yes!"

Mr. D., as we shall call Master Number Four, invited the neighbors in to meet Ganna Walska. A curious couple frankly admitted they had little interest in or knowledge of anything that happened beyond the confines of their small village—excuse me, their small town—but they did confess they were happy to meet—Ganna—Ganna McCormick, wife of the Harvester King, think of it, to see her in the flesh! The higher spheres had no attraction for them. But they could appreciate a good meal and good beer... And certainly they did justice to the supper!

If my host had any knowledge of the Great Beyond, he made much mystery about it. In fact he never spoke about anything that was worth while. On the other hand he had many annoying idiosyncrasies. "Small considerations are the tomb of big things," Voltaire said and everything about Mr. D. was small, small and un-American. Provincialism, that plague which has overrun Europe, dominated everything else in him.

If I asked him to join me at dinner or accompany me to the theatre, he would ask how much he owed me for the ticket or the meal. Whenever he wrote a letter he always sent a stamp for the answer. That may have been inspired by an almost religious sense of honesty or it may have been on account of that spiritual law which prevents the use of other people's money unless taking their Karma (Destiny) with it.

He carried this feature so far that whenever he asked me to cable him from France he begged me to write how much I had paid and when I ignored this demand he just sent the money anyhow and always more than covered the expenses. As a co-religionist of Dr. Cannon, he certainly differed in his interpretation of their prerogatives. But no matter what his motives were, it was an awful nuisance and did not show any of the grandeur of soul one expects from a Master.

Mr. D. was extremely devoted to his young daughter, a wonderful qualification for a father but not what one would expect to find in a Great Master who is presumed to be detached from personal feeling. He was also unmasterful in the extreme attention he paid to his reputation, the reputation of a real estate dealer with offices near the ferry, where everyone knew him as a very respectable citizen. Even the policeman at the crossroad saluted him in a friendly way.

He cared so much about his neighbors' opinion of him and protected his good name to such a degree that when he—a mystic—asked a medium to come to his house, he met him at the corner of a certain street whence he accompanied the stranger to his home. He could not have made more mystery of it if he had belonged to the court of England. The medium himself and each of us was given a fictitious name so that no one could trace or be traced. Our Master's brother for instance was Mr. Smith for the sake of originality. I became Madame Something-or-other, sounding Polish.

Though an omnipotent Master of the White Lodge he was dependent on his neighbors' approval of his spiritual opinion!

* * *

My meeting with Mr. D. was without importance to the

development of my soul and gave me no new knowledge. My association with this Master, following my disillusionment with the English wizard again brought disappointment into my heart—newly reopened to great mysteries. And for many months after my connection with them I did not wish to hear anything more about masters or about any occultism whatsoever.

However only a few weeks later my curiosity was aroused again by a countryman of mine, possessor of a great historical name, who was a follower of Zoroaster, the founder of the Parsee faith, worshipers of the Sun and Fire. But the exercises I was told to do and the way in which one had to get in touch with the cosmic element seemed to me too definitely impregnated with human magnetism to satisfy for long my search for the Divine. Furthermore, the character of the man himself did not say much for the doctrine he practiced—he drank madly...

* * *

During that winter I also came in contact and studied with a Brahmin, who more than anybody else personified Goodness, Peace and Serenity. He certainly would never have dreamed of criticizing, of judging anyone, or of distorting the truth. On several occasions he confessed he knew the manifestation of divine protection: he had walked through the Indian jungle and his flesh was held in respect by the wild animals—by wild animals, yes but not by those of the poultry yard for one day he complained that—being so good he could not refuse anyone anything—he had eaten a tiny piece of chicken, although in general he was not carnivorous. The result was that it had not agreed with him, he did not feel his usual self—the piece of chicken gave him a stomachache!

> *When a book elevates your mind and inspires you with noble and courageous sentiments, seek no other rule for judging the work: for it is a good one and has known the touch of a craftsman.*
> — LA BRUYÈRE

To show perhaps that everything has its reason, even though my meeting with Master the Fourth seemed to have no purpose, it was through his recommendation that a few months later I read "A Search in Secret India" by Paul Brunton, the reading of which again and definitively put my mind in the searching attitude.

When I finished the last page of that book, I was transformed and more deeply than ever interested in the mystery of our being. I felt a higher desire to learn more and more about the Unknown…

While reading Brunton's interesting book I mentally traveled with him all over India, meeting the most interesting sages—some real and sincere, if fanatic—others just professional fakirs. The author reported so clearly his reaction that I felt I had experienced it all myself. And at the end of the volume I went with Mr. Brunton to Maharishee, whom he accepted as his master and with whom he remained until an equatorial fever, combined with the economic depression in Europe, compelled him to leave the beloved teacher and go back to London.

* * *

All that winter I kept asking those around me who Paul Brunton was and his whereabouts. I was eager to know why, oh, why—if he had found the One for whom he searched, to whom he manifested such a devotion—he had permitted a business consideration to take him from the goal he had attained. And then if he had found a divine path, how could sickness creep into his mind and overcome the divine and omnipotent? How? Oh, how?!

If he was so near the Source of Real Truth, Real Knowledge and had found the True Initiation, why should the financial crash in Europe be able to take him from the only reality that exists? And why could he not learn the law that could heal him of any disease? And how could he contract the illness when so near to God, in such a saintly place, with such a saintly man?

Those were the questions I wished to put to him. They troubled me greatly. In one way his book raised the quality of my vibrations to heights then unknown to me, yet at the same time I was stung by cruel doubts. Why should there be limitations to the Infinite? Infinite means without end. Then why? Why? Always unanswered questions!!

A few months later I was greatly excited to discover that Brunton's second book had just appeared. I did everything I possibly could to get it from London immediately. How I regretted that there was not yet any airmail over the Atlantic!

In that book, "The Secret Path," the author confessed in the first few pages his intention of renewing his wanderings across Egypt, across Asia. But on the eve of his departure his master had appeared to him and told him that he had no right to accumulate more knowledge without first communicating to those in the West what he already knew from his experiences in the East.

I was greatly inspired by the fact that Mr. Brunton was guided by his *guru* (teacher). In a moment of exultation I wrote to him in care of his London publisher expressing my deep thanks for his soul-elevating books…

In the meantime Sir Francis Younghusband came to New York to prepare for the next London Congress of the World Fellowship of Faiths. Remembering that Sir Francis had written a preface to Brunton's first book I immediately asked him what had become of his protégé. His face darkened as he told me that Brunton had recently been in Egypt and planned to go back to India against his advice.

"By now he has probably gone. He is a sick man. A very sick man. He will be unable to stand that climate. I am awfully sorry." Those were Sir Francis's words.

My heart grew heavy. So he must die! He might be dead now! But how could it be possible Who then has the Ultimate Power? Could it be Matter? Matter again? Always Matter, Matter triumphant?

I never went further than Chapter II of "The Secret Path". What was the use?

What was the use of anything? ? ?

* * *

A month later in Paris a letter fell out of my hands because of the emotion which overwhelmed me. It was from Egypt and signed by Paul Brunton who announced a flying visit to Paris the following week.

The greatest moments of my life were either through artistic manifestations or steps toward higher spiritual progress. One of my never-to-be-forgotten steps in the latter direction was upon my receipt of that letter. It was beyond all description! Like all stupendous things. . .

* * *

A few days later Mr. Brunton telephoned. We made an appointment to meet at Cook's. We did not know each other. He told me he would wear a grey suit.

While listening to him, I visualized a tall distinguished old gentleman, grey-bearded like Rabindranath Tagore with the mysterious atmosphere of the East about him.

I was aroused from that train of thought by hearing him inquire if he could bring his fiancée along. I managed to answer naturally although for a second I was speechless. My imagination pictured an old spinster, very English, of course, even though she had probably spent all her life in India where they had undoubtedly met, highly spiritual, the twin ray of Mr. Brunton—hence the betrothal of those two old souls...

Again Mr. Brunton's voice interrupted my wandering thoughts by saying: "She will be happy to meet you for she also is Polish..."

My picture of his fiancée was suddenly replaced by one of the typically Polish female well known for her racial charm. "No one can resist the charm of a Polish woman," flashed through my mind. "By her the wisest of men sin..." And I saw "my" Brunton suddenly as a sinner, as a Flaubertian Athanael.

When I finally met him, I was not yet at the end of my surprises, for he was half an hour late for our appointment and when he apologized he peevishly blamed his fiancée for the delay. Alas, I knew that punctuality is the spiritual law as well as royal prerogative.

My astonishment was complete on finding a young man already quite bald, extremely short in stature and of a very pronounced Semitic type, followed by a robust decoloree blonde nearly twice his height, tempting enough for any wise, ignorant or saintly man—even St. Anthony himself probably would have had difficulty in resisting such a test. No, there was not the slightest hint of spirituality about her. Certainly no one would ever have accused her of that! Under the circumstances I took them for tea... to the Ritz.

Thinking Mr. Brunton a very sick man, after what Sir Francis Younghusband had told me, I had concluded that his visit to Paris was to consult specialists about an operation or to rest in some nursing home. Consequently I had previous to his arrival sent him a cordial invitation to be my guest at the chateau. I did not want to mention his convalescence, wishing to ignore the fact that he was a sick man. I just asked him to come to rest in a quiet country place during the great heat of July in Paris. But Mr. Brunton informed me that he had come to Paris for the sole reason of joining his fiancée and marrying her as quickly as possible. Politely I asked if she would visit Galluis, too. He immediately accepted my invitation on her behalf as though it were quite natural!

In extending my invitation I had felt that the visit of such a holy man to Galluis would automatically bring divine blessings to the place and much knowledge of its chatelaine, God's faithful servant.

For several weeks (during which time Mr. Brunton wrote his "Secret Search of Egypt") those two extremely different people stayed with me. However, being unable to get married in Paris owing to some legal complications, they left for London where as a Britisher he might have less difficulty in uniting his life to hers for ever and ever after.

> *To realize itself an idea takes hold of fervent minds and makes of them its servants; henceforth they belong to it and see nothing ahead of them but the goal to be attained, this goal which recedes as one advances.*
>
> — MARIE CURIE

SINCE I WAS reading everything that appeared in the field of metaphysical literature, no wonder that my eye fell on "The Mysterious Cobbler," an autobiography of Mr. Spray, the shoemaker of Bexhill-on-Sea, Sussex, England. The author described many healings he had performed in a rather miraculous way without his being consciously aware of how or why he did them.

As soon as I arrived in France from the United States, I wrote him asking if he would be good enough to receive me during my visit to London in the near future.

At that same period Dr. Cannon, after admitting that the medium of the previous year had proved unsatisfactory, wrote me that *now* he positively could help my singing through the medium of a certain Madame X. However in a long exchange of correspondence which lasted the whole summer he never enlightened me as to whether the lady was a medium replacing the previous one, or a singing teacher, as her Italian name suggested. He also mentioned the institute of a certain Dr. Radwan and guaranteed that in three weeks' time for a comparatively modest sum I could be made into something a little short of a nightingale. The modest price turned out to be the trifling sum of fifty thousand francs!

Fortunately my recent experiences had taught me, if nothing else, that the true and noble things one gets in life are those for which one does not pay. The added fact that

Dr. Cannon demanded that the money be paid in advance seemed proof that my doubts were right.

It reminded me of an incident I had during the war with a fashionable shoemaker in Paris. He was an Italian—as fashionable shoemakers always are—who considered he greatly honored his customers by making their shoes and demanded as a minimum the price of three dozen pairs in advance. He simply would not bother making just one pair. I declined the extreme honor, but not before having the satisfaction of telling him that his condition certainly was the surest way to get orders. Otherwise his patrons might never voluntarily order a second pair after seeing how badly the pair was done.

* * *

Given Dr. Cannon's knowledge of spiritual laws, I could hardly understand his real motive. The idea that a Master of the White Brotherhood should ask a comparative fortune in advance for a proposition not even explained very clearly seemed monstrous to me.

When I recovered my balance, I wrote to him the same answer I had given the Italian shoemaker. However, Dr. Cannon persisted in tempting me with guarantees that this time he could cure my voice of all its troubles. But had I troubles? I was not sure and neither was he!

By then the situation had shaped up so that my visit to London looked as though it would accomplish a lot. First, the Bruntons were in London; second, the Mysterious Cobbler was awaiting my arrival; and third, my critical mind was curious to investigate what were the guarantees Dr. Cannon could give me about healing my voice and healing it from what? For, until then, no one had ever told me there was anything wrong with it. I hesitated no longer. I left for London.

* * *

I motored down to Mr. Spray's and two hours later my car stopped before a tiny shoe repairing shop. When I found myself in the garret, his reception room, I asked my host if he could tell me what was the matter with my voice and also if he could enable me to read again without glasses.

Mr. Spray's technique, as I was informed afterwards by Paul Brunton, who had learned about it himself the previous winter in Cairo, was the ancient Egyptian method of healing which the Cobbler subconsciously remembered from his previous life in the days of the Pharoahs when he presumably had been a priest.

Though I found Mr. Spray an extremely honest and thoroughly sincere man he could not tell me what was the trouble with my voice and his efforts to help my eyes were not successful.

Strangely enough, I did not feel disappointed that time either because Mr. Spray was a genuine person or because by then I was so accustomed to disillusionment that one more or less no longer mattered. Perhaps I had begun to sense that the real help could only come from within myself...

* * *

While Paul Brunton had still been at my country place, I had had the courage one day to let him know of my surprise at his prospective marriage, basing my remarks on the premise that he surely knew that at a certain stage of spiritual development such as he professed to have, due to his initiation in India, one no longer needs the physical expression of love, as one can also no longer feel lonesome. And surely his fiancée did not look much like a spiritual sister...

His answer was that of course he did not need to satisfy his lower instincts any longer nor did he care especially for his fiancée. But he considered it more selfish not to marry, for—after his final initiation— he could live in India without any earthly care whatsoever in a state of complete beatitude like his Master. Still he voluntarily chose the harder way: instead of seeking egotistic happiness he would give to the West what he had learned in the East. Marriage would compel him to return to Europe and teach those who could not journey to India for their spiritual studies. He would settle in Egypt. To have a home he would need a wife, not of course for sensual reasons, but to help him in his work by attending to the meetings, lectures, in a word by taking care of everything. Being fully occupied with his spiritual work, he could not attend to the odd jobs himself. Anyhow it was woman's work. However, seeing a certain incredulity in my eyes, he added as a supreme excuse, knowing my great admiration for that California philosopher, "Manly Hall is married!"

He did not know, on the other hand, that unwilling to accept the explanation given by the philosopher's friend, I could not as yet exactly understand the motives behind Manly Hall's marriage.

* * *

It is easy to imagine the sickening of my heart when, during my visit to London, Mrs. Brunton (being my countrywoman and not knowing the English language) felt the irresistible need to confide in me—much against my wishes—about her spiritually-minded husband. During their courtship he had vowed that if she became his wife there would be no consummation of their marriage but now he seemed to have no intentions of foregoing his privileges as a husband. She went on to say that when she asked him for an explanation of his metamorphosis and chided him with what his Master would think of him and how he would be unable to face the holy man in India, her hundred-per-cent husband replied that the "moment he reached Maharishee he would become chaste and live in purity, for once in contact with the saintly man he would no longer be troubled by any lower instinct. Meanwhile in the short time that remained for him to be an ordinary person he felt he should not deprive himself of a normal existence!

Mrs. Brunton also complained that her position was not one of a helping wife but rather of a cook, to whom shopping was no small matter with the tiny amount of money she received and with no knowledge of London and the English language. She did everything about the house herself from marketing for food to preparing for the lecture hours, while her intimate life did not help her do such hard work light-heartedly…

Having seen both sides of the situation I could not, in spite of my ardent wish, sympathize with Mr. Brunton when he complained that he had made a mistake in marrying Jan, because she did not even know how to buy good tea much less cook his vegetarian food.

In the atmosphere of those two-sided confidences, it was impossible to profit from Mr. Brunton's talk and no longer could I meditate in his presence. Furthermore the crude description of their intimate life made a shocking impression upon my imagination and did not enable me to concentrate upon sacred things in a state where the senses reigned fully.

Taking the risk of being considered a fickle student, I daily found a new excuse to absent myself from evening meditations: nerves, cold, weariness—anything would suffice to keep me from the presence of that mystic. But unable to pretend much longer I shortened my visit and left London. And who should insist upon accompanying me to Paris but Mrs. Brunton who declared that if she remained longer with her husband she would have no strength left to sail to India, whence escape would not be so easy. She felt it imperative that previous to her departure she should have a well-deserved vacation from her bridegroom of a few weeks. She put it as an ultimatum to her spouse, who accepted when he was informed that I was paying the expenses of her flying trip to Paris.

* * *

During the last few weeks in London, as I was seeing less of the Bruntons, I took the opportunity finally to meet the Madame X who was to help Dr. Cannon make me into a Patti. First of all she informed me that she was writing a scientific book on the voice. The greatest professors of the greatest universities found her ideas great. Indeed, there was too much academic greatness for my taste.

The Junoesque lady expressed the usual opinion about my singing that all teachers utter to their new pupils: "Your professor was absolutely wrong!" ,

(Where did I hear that formula before? A rather familiar, if not especially agreeable *Leitmotif* !)

This new Marchesi was more original than her predecessors, however, for she was teaching not to breathe while singing but scarcely to inhale through the nose as if merely smelling delicately the odor of an intoxicating flower or an exquisite perfume.

With my usual faithful perseverance and sense of justice about giving everybody a chance, including myself, I found myself holding a gardenia in front of my nose during those days in London. It was wonderful—for I love gardenias for their exotic aroma and pure whiteness.

Not sufficiently satisfied with the results of this new experiment, I begged the lady to follow me to Galluis in order to continue smelling Chanel's "Ivoire" the next three weeks, it being very difficult to get gardenias in Paris.

Having sung all those weeks without support, not permitting myself to take just a vulgar deep breath like any common human being, by the end of the first month I was quasi-paralyzed, so little relaxed I was during my lessons.

* * *

Before my disillusioning visit with the Bruntons, I had

planned to accompany them to India. So eager was I to meet the holy Maharishee! But now the bitter disappointment in my heart made the projected pilgrimage out of the question. Again, and for the umpteenth time, everything was dark and gloomy. There was nothing to look ahead to but desperate loneliness, exasperating incertitude and doubts, killing doubts…

Just then Mrs. Chauncey Blair of Chicago happened to bring me "Unveiled Mysteries" by Godfrey Ray King.

That book made such a strong impression on me that, when I learned that the author and his wife were lecturing in New York under the name of Ballards, I decided to go at once to America and meet those messengers of St. Germain, that great initiate who always had inspired me immensely.

Again I was saved. Again I was full of energy, full of hope and the desire to know, to study, to find out, to trust… To trust!

Upon landing in New York I discovered that the Ballards, who by opening new vistas to my searching heart had interested me sufficiently to bring me to America so *subito*, were lecturing in Washington. The friend who told me of their whereabouts informed me that a certain Mrs. Fisher, who directed a Center of Truth at the Roosevelt Hotel, could give me all the information I desired.

That was at a period when I no longer accepted any more invitations to parties, dinners or receptions unless they were diplomatic or similar functions which I was compelled to attend. Nevertheless the day I arrived I spontaneously accepted the invitation to a Thanksgiving dinner at the home of a charming couple, who were until then mere acquaintances. Upon entering their house, the first person I met was the Mrs. Fisher, about whom I had heard a few hours previously, and who informed me that the Ballards were giving their last two lectures in Washington the next day and the day after prior to their departure to California for the winter.

I left for Washington the next morning.

* * *

... at the end of the lecture Mrs. Ballard played the harp most beautifully. What soft music! What is it? I seemed to know so well that melody... I could almost place the words... Oh I actually found myself putting Polish words to this music. But what is it? My commotion was unimaginable when I finally recognized a piece which was composed by none other than myself when quite a young girl and which I had never played since!

Warm tears were falling down my cheeks. Grateful tears! This was certainly proof of the Divine Guidance which had taken me here...

In the hotel room I fell on my knees and gave humble thanks for the light that my soul had received. I was purified and felt an exaltation I had not felt since my first communion in my very girlish years!

The next day I visited the Ballards. I was received with heartfelt love and learned that they were Chicagoans, had followed with deepest interest my struggle for my art ever since my marriage to Harold McCormick and were positive I would win in the end. They also informed me that artists more and more are discovering God in themselves, giving the example of Mary Pickford and Galli-Curci. That can be explained by the fact that as artists must deal with something that is of three dimensions. For years the Ballards had awaited me and because their writings had fallen into my hands at the critical moment of my helplessness and discouragement, they were certain I had been guided by St. Germain himself. I was happy to be reassured that I was guided.

All that winter I followed St. Germain's teachings and was so certain of being on the right path that I could close my eyes to the theatricalities of the Ballards' interpretation of Truth by getting only the Truth. If my analytical mind sometimes behaved like a doubting Thomas, it was only temporarily. After such a crisis—each of which diminished in intensity—I came back every time with a greater certitude of following the Divine Course.

For the first time in my life I had found the *Truth!* At last! For the first time I had an answer to all of my troubles. For the first time I could remedy any of my many mental problems.

Simultaneously with my spiritual advancement, I also progressed in my singing until one day I allowed a very insincere man to discourage me utterly, never suspecting him of having personal reasons for his act. Later I discovered that he had tried to induce me to give up singing concerts under the pretext that my personality required a much greater outlet than any concert or opera stage could give me; that he did this in the hope that he could persuade me to give up my voice study and direct all my efforts and (what was more important) my money to motion pictures, thus giving him the chance of playing the role of a great producer!

From that moment on, my inner tears started to flow again and sadness blinded my judgment. I did not progress… Rather I went backwards. Those melodies I had been able to sing pretty well in January, I was unable to sing at all three or four months later.

Frank LaForge insisted that improvement would come if I studied long enough. As he spent week ends in Connecticut I begged him to let me drive there each Sunday morning in order to study two hours more. After singing with my throat choked by unswallowed tears, frozen morally and physically, morally from despair, physically from driving two hours in terrific snow, singing two hours, then the two hours' drive back—I was quite a pathetic figure. I so despaired about the darkness of my situation that had it not been for my following the teaching of Jacob Böhme, I would certainly have quit. (Quit what? Life?) But that simple German

Initiate taught me through the medium of his books to sing with the running water. Any time black doubts surrounded me I would go to my bathroom, open the tap and sing to the accompaniment of the falling cascade. As I sang I could hear my voice vibrating beautifully; it was like the time some ten years before when, completely discouraged, I had sung in the tunnel in Central Park in order to hear the echo of my voice multiplied a thousand times and thus I regained a little confidence in myself.

To be certain I was not fooling myself, I once asked someone to listen to me singing first from the adjoining room and then from the bathroom. That friend never believed that the almost voiceless person of a few minutes before was almost able to make the walls of her bathroom tremble.

* * *

Along with attending all musical manifestations in those days I could also have been seen at all lectures connected with the teachings of Ancient Wisdom. That was how I happened to hear a Dutch woman tell about colors and their use for healing purposes, by artificially replacing the color deficiencies in our aura.

I met that mannish Hollander and learned that she was a disciple of a mystic Mr. L. of Chicago and was spreading his gospel in a great European capital. She heard me sing and in diagnosing my case contended that two or three colors were lacking in my aura. In her opinion, that deficiency handicapped the normal development of my voice. She assured me she could easily remedy that shortage when we should both be back in Europe, if I would come to her place equipped with the color machineries. In the meantime, to confirm her opinion, she suggested that I see her Master. When I agreed to go to Chicago with her to meet him, she immediately wired asking permission to bring a friend in trouble.

Having received a favorable answer, we left for Chicago.

There we registered, I under a fictitious name, at the Pearson Hotel, East Pearson Street, a section of Chicago unknown to me till then.

* * *

My meeting with that Master and what it meant afterwards to my soul is too sacred to put down on paper.

* * *

During the course of a general conversation about well known teachers of philosophy and religion on the last of my four days in Chicago, I asked Mr. L.'s opinion of the Ballards knowing that many people were definitely against them. Instantly my heart became icy upon learning that the Ballards in the opinion of that saintly man were simply making a luxurious living through their lectures and books —a pure business. It seemed that two years ago Mr. Ballard had been a promoter. The word *promoter* was pronounced as if it meant he was a shrewd banker, and the inflection of the voice gave depreciatory meaning to the title. My heart was frozen, not because I was disappointed about the Ballards, but because I had not expected words of judgment of condemnation or criticism to come from the mouth of that man.

No matter how unjust it may have been to condemn someone for having failed, having been poor and subsequently living in abundance, still from that moment on I could no longer blindly follow the teachings of Godfrey Ray King. No, I did not lose faith in them because faith was in me! In my heart I liked them. I was grateful to them for having been instrumental in bringing me the help I had received during the past few months when something tremendous entered my being and replaced everything else, leaving no space for other sensations.

As to the presumptive teachings of St. Germain, even previous to the severe opinion expressed by such a great soul, my intelligence had been unable to accept those cinematographic stories of St. Germain who produced his visiting card on a golden plate—but who took it back every little while and never left it as a tangible proof of his existence. Also it was hard to comprehend why—as one of Mr. Ballard's books related—St. Germain protected a young girl who as yet had no personal merits and was too young to have had a chance to do anything worth while. Apparently St. Germain, ever gallant, did it because a few centuries ago he had known—her mother!

* * *

As had happened so often before, the moment I would lose one *raison d'être*—in this case the Ballards—almost instantly and startlingly I found another, usually greater than the lost one. Both in the path of my spiritual and vocal searches, each time I felt that surely I was at the end of my endeavour and that now I had found the right Master, now I had discovered the right singing method.

To each of those teachers, vocal or spiritual, I gave all my heart and all my newly born enthusiasm, as rich as if it were for the first time. And in each case I felt I had found a method and a knowledge new to me and usually I forgot the misery of the last experience, automatically severing myself from all ugliness, all disheartening past disappointments as though they had never existed and as if I were again sweet sixteen and my life just beginning. I felt entirely purified. I felt new…

* * *

Of all my spiritual experiences and religious researches (and how many I did have!), Mr. L., the Chicagoan, was the first person who appeared to my soul as the personification of Goodness in its highest form. I had finally found the Ideal I had been searching for so long, so long—oh, so very long! All my life!

Mr. L. was not only a man teaching Goodness, Purity and Love. He was Goodness, Purity and Love! He *was* Goodness. He *was* Purity! He *was* Love!

* * *

Even as a tiny girl my imagination was so full of love that I built castles in my heart and created imaginary persons not corresponding to those in my earthly life. Now it is easy for me to recognize that even then I was obliged to tune myself down—unconsciously of course—to the people and environment surrounding me in order to make myself understood. Always I was forced to come down to their level, never up—always down.

The more people I met, the lower I had to descend in order to be able to speak their language and give them the impression that we felt on equal terms. From the difference of vibration between me and others originated my excessive love of solitude, my craving for air, craving for an open car from which I could look way up, up, up where there is no limit to my sight!

 I always wanted to escape from the state of pretending. I wanted to unite myself with that limitless world where I could lift my tune up, u-p, UP! Oh, the joy of being able to better myself, to fly freely with those higher than I am. What stimulation! And what joy not to run alone in those heights, in a special class, so to say! What ecstasy to be myself without lowering my inner being! What joy—unmeasured, four-dimensional, elevated joy! Unexplainable joy that cannot be understood by anyone who has not experienced it, just as colors cannot be explained to the blind nor the sweetness of sugar to one who has never eaten it.

But such joy lasts as lasts the smell of a flower, the taste of cool water… Ordinary mortals only get that feeling on this lower planet when they are in love and their inner being touches the sublime. To enable us to compare this sensation with our usual feelings we express it as "being crazy about someone." "Being crazy" means not feeling normal.

Oh, when we are in love—when our vibrations fuse with other vibrations and bodily sensation disappears... fades away... melts into eternity... becomes one with the universal pulse... where there is no time... where space is limitless... when—as the poets express it—we touch the stars—what a bliss!!

Once having been allowed to live through such a divine moment and taste the eternity of it, we can never feel as we did previously, we are unable to readjust ourselves and descend to a *terre-à-terre* environment—we can only live on this earth of matter and facts as emotional corpses, definitely divorced from the atmosphere in which we lived before.

The divine possibility of unthinkable heights and un-graspable capacity of feeling makes us realize that Love with a capital L, human love, primitive love or divine love rules the world. It is in its name that humanity commits crimes, exterminates nations, crusades until fratricide results. All this in order to get Love, the unbounded almighty feeling of L-O-V-E or its imitation, its illusion, its caricature, its distorted vision. It is Love that inspires the poet. It is Love that makes of a man a mystic. It is Love that creates heroes and their opposite—criminals. Love around which revolves the whole world...

* * *

When I arrived from Chicago, I felt more than ever the essence of Love. Divine Love in me and around me. I knew perfectly well that I had shed one more veil from my personality. But was I a personality? Certainly not! I was a bodiless super-conscious being, floating high in the space reserved only for heaven, absolutely detached from the material incarnation of this low world.

My joy, my bliss, was marred only when a friend who met me at the station questioned me:

"And how was it, darling?"

As if I could answer! As if I could put into words the most extraordinary experience of my life, which the human mind could hardly understand, an experience prepared for me by Destiny for centuries and centuries!

No, I could not speak. But unwilling to be unkind to a friend who had risen at five in the morning to meet me, also unwilling merely to gossip about the Pittsburgh flood, though not wishing to divide the most wonderful page of my new life which seemed too secret and too sacred to share with anyone and more personal than anything that had ever happened to my soul until then—I simply informed her that I had no right to say anything about my Chicago visit... I knew she would understand as she had associated for years all over the entire world with many great mystics such as Nicolas Roerich, and the descendants of Baha-ula, and as her father was a great Mason and she herself through her initiation was bound to absolute secrecy.

Only when she asked me about my voice, did I suddenly realize what an extraordinarily important place my new experience had taken in my life—for during those four days I had not given a single thought to the essential reason for my going to the Windy City—the only thing that had mattered for years and years and that had now grown pale beside the new inner light which inflamed everything in me and about me.

* * *

The routine events of life however must take their rightful place and I had to come down to earth to consider the demands of the moment. There were only two weeks left before my scheduled sailing for Europe, and I had to attend to the trivial but indispensable occupations of our civilization, such as readying my passport, getting a sailing permit, attending to income tax, packing and so forth.

I never can remember how I did it. Somehow it was done., I suppose habitual gestures did it automatically for me. Absent-mindedly I could think of nothing else except that this time, at last, no one and nothing could awaken me from my blissful state—this time nothing could take away my eternal peace!

I realized I could never be happier than in those days. For the first time in my life I was not looking forward anxiously to the morrow. I was not looking for such and such an event to occur, usually pivoted around singing, music, theatre…

I was living, just living! Probably I was not even doing any thinking. I was in a perfect state of beatitude where the external world somehow did not exist, where the brain fused with the mind to form one substance. Certainly I would have been infinitely surprised if someone had suddenly asked me what were my desires. I had none! For myself I had a whole world and that whole world was mine! What more could I wish for? I did not need anything…

* * *

Ah, if one could stop Time!

* * *

It was small wonder that in such a state of beautitude I was unable to even feel greater happiness when I learned that Mr. L. planned to come to New York before my sailing in order to give me additional instructions to help the work of bettering myself while I was alone that summer. Just as one feels physically restless and mentally tired when hearing too long most perfect music and just as the smell of a rose is wonderful if it lasts only a second, so it is with happiness. We can receive only so much and no more, if we do not want it to turn into unhealthy hysteria. As Flaubert said: "Man is made to taste every day but a little nourishment, a few colors or sounds, sentiments or ideas. When his measure is overfilled he becomes tired or drunk."

The wisdom of my heart was unable to receive anything more at that point and the four-dimensional state being immeasurable I could not consequently want more. I could not absorb anything more now. I just could not! Was my subconscious afraid of being awakened?

Anyhow, I did not welcome immediately Mr. L.'s generous proposal to come to New York, primarily on his account. A few days before our meeting he had had a serious automobile accident which resulted in a deep wound in his throat. Naturally, under the circumstances, I did not want him to travel, to miss the dressings of his wound by his surgeon, to handicap the normal course of the healing by the discomfort of the journey. With an angelic devotion, however, my newly discovered but old friend still insisted on coming. We agreed finally that if his physician would give him permission to leave in four days' time, I would certainly be most happy to receive him.

I had not wanted to interrupt the happy state of my non-existence even by increasing its intensity, yet already my heart commenced to jubilate to a still greater degree while awaiting the arrival of that great soul. There was no room for skepticism in my mind those days and yet I began to prepare many questions which my heart was sure would receive satisfactory answers from his wisdom and judgment. I particularly needed to be enlightened about a point which had arisen at the eleventh hour. Mr. L.'s Dutch apostle just before taking her boat for Europe had spoken to me about her love for me. At any other time it would have been a natural shock but coming at that time from a woman in God's service, L.'s disciple, from the head of his movement in Europe, it was beyond my conception. But this woman had not the slightest comprehension of wrong, seemed to have forgotten what she was teaching and what she was living. I had to find out from L. how it was possible that his pupil could be so far from the Truth. I must…

Mind you, I do not condemn those unfortunates whose last male incarnation (to my way of thinking) has left such a strong impression that involuntarily they continue to be themselves. I have always been sorry for those freaks of Nature, as contrary to general opinion they just follow their instincts and do not go against them. But here was not a question of abnormality. It was something far more important to me as my soul wanted to know how, instead of feeling unhappy because destiny had sent her such a cruel trial, she spoke about it so naturally, almost boasting about it.

* * *

While awaiting the medical authorization for L. to travel, I decided in the meantime, apart from my concern about his health, that I would still prefer even with the doctor's permission not to let him go to the expense of traveling, knowing that he would never allow me to reimburse him and also knowing that his modest income must be used to help those less fortunate spiritually than himself.

Therefore I telephoned him and on learning that he persisted in his decision to come *if only for one hour* or *only to take me to the boat*, I begged him to let me do the flying and do it by night to save the time. He agreed but not before repeating again how happy he would be to come to New York, how much he wanted to do that for me, as his only joy was to give, to be of service to his brothers and sisters.

The next Monday morning after consulting my lawyer and my secretary I discovered I could not possibly leave without the risk of missing my sailing as it was essential to me to sign certain important legal documents.

Accordingly I wired my regrets to L. In the meantime each day the mail brought me beautiful ethereal letters from my new Master, Master not because he had accepted me as his disciple or that I demanded that privilege but in the sense of his being a great soul in comparison to my little self. Only a poet of the first magnitude could have written such letters—letters that raised the beauty of one's soul to the highest vibration. Only a dreamer could have filled four pages in exceedingly small handwriting without actually speaking about anything but the beauty of the roses I had sent him, about the exceptional position of those roses in the world consciousness, about the place the writer chose for them near the picture of his Lord, or about the impression they gave him in the twilight to the accompaniment of an old tune...

Wednesday morning before I telephoned to find out about the surgeon's final decision, I got L.'s morning letter and while reading its first page a chill went through my being. Yet there were the same words, the same subject or rather the same lack of subject, the same detachment from earthly ugliness, the same complete lack of consciousness of commonly-accepted reality. With every page my heart sank deeper and deeper until the frost covered my whole being, and I read the last phrase without any surprise, without the slightest shock, for my heart had already prepared my mind for the eventuality.

The letter ended: "Being God's soldier, *ever doing a soldier's work*, I must on my Master's command be in New York in two months' time, so I will not come now... Be sure, however, that my blessing goes with you, with you always."

Life stopped in me... Later in the day, after recuperating enough energy to write, I sent him a letter confessing my feeling of extreme disappointment, of terrific shock...

If my attorney or my manager had acted with such inconsistency it would have been most surprising. But such behaviour from the sainted Master was unbelievable! While writing the letter—with death in my heart—I still hoped, perhaps without admitting it to myself, that his answer would clear up the situation, that the reason for his change of mind was of such great importance, of such an unearthly quality that it would raise him still higher on the pedestal on which I had put him, and that it would be of such spiritual significance and of such divine substance as to make me feel ashamed of my smallness, suspicion and lack of faith. I would gladly have felt that way about myself if I could only attribute all Goodness to him.

His answer, first by a wire and later by a lengthy letter, assured me how sorry he was that I could think him knowingly capable of hurting any human soul, a thing that had never happened in his entire life…

It was the last straw. The miracle had not happened. I knew it! I knew it!

* * *

When the Dutch woman and I had been at L.'s home in Chicago, we were greatly taken by the serenity of his Master's very rare picture. We certainly never even dreamed we might have a similar portrait for ourselves but L. with Christlike kindness told us that some day he might be permitted to send us a copy of it.

Forty-eight hours before my sailing I received by mail the vaguely promised picture of his beloved Lord, his own original picture and not a copy, the coming of which had been announced in that crushing letter. Feeling dark—dark to such an extent that it was impossible for me to adjust myself now to the useless, hopeless and gloomy aspect of life—when the wooden packing case was brought to my room I simply said:

"Please put it anywhere."

And when Mary asked if she should unpack it, I answered almost irritably:

"No, no, I will take it to Paris unpacked!"

But I began to wonder whether I should accept the picture at all… It could no longer mean to me what it had before. Should I not send it back to its owner? Extreme bitterness took possession of my heart… I closed my eyes… The depressing darkness continued… I could not control my despair… My soul was falling deeper and deeper into the abyss…

While I was indulging my ceaselessly acute agony to the

utmost, suddenly like a flash the idea took possession of my mind that I must open the case and see the picture. Yet my logic protested that it was so well packed that if I wanted to send it back I would never be able to repack it as well. But would I send it back or take it with me? After a painful inner fight and a few minutes' hesitation I was soon prying up the edge of the box with my penknife not wishing Mary to know I was acting contradictorily to what I had told her. It had been wrapped with good protective cardboard and enveloped in a great quantity of tissue paper with extreme care—no, one should rather say with loving hands. Finally the picture emerged. I placed it on the mantelpiece. I lay down… I looked at it… Instantaneously peace came to my soul… The sun from the picture lighted the room which had been so gloomy until then…

* * *

Up until the last minute before leaving the house I kept the picture in front of me. And in spite of the cumbersome size of the cardboard I insisted on carrying the box myself and was only satisfied when I had personally put it in my cabin. When the visitors had gone and the steward had taken away the empty flower-boxes, I made an altar on the east wall of my room. I lit a seven-day candle—L.'s present too—and arranged the magnificent garden of mixed flowers sent by many charming friends and as usual by dear Harold in spite of our divorce.

Thanks to the picture not only was my crossing marvelous from the first to the last hour—the smoothness of the water could only be compared to that of a lake—but my mental state if not yet completely healed had at least become partially anesthetized.

* * *

I have never parted with that picture… I never will…

SUMMER OF 1936—GALLUIS

Like the bird, the higher the soul rises, the happier it is.

— CHANNING

My inner life, felt more consciously during the last ten years, consisted of three particular lines of interest, each different but fundamentally all based on the same search for Perfection: perfection in love, perfection in singing, perfection in Inner Life.

The first and earliest expression was the womanly desire for egoistic love. I call any extreme devotion egoistic, for when we love, we love our own feelings much more than we actually do the other person. As Proust said: "When one loves, one loves no one."

My second *raison d'être* was my complete engrossment in the study of singing and all its attendant branches of art.

The third urge, which had a gradual period of growth until it reached my present state of realization, consisted in seeking for the spiritual explanation of my Being.

Of those interests, the dominating one—which parallelly and simultaneously absorbed my soul and mind—the search for inner peace, left the strongest imprint on the Calvary of my suffering.

It was through the spiritual intangible bridge connecting the inner and outer life that I acquired my solid feeling of the soul's immortality and its immeasurable deductions—the essential reason for our coming to this earth.

The tremendous knowledge this gave me opened wide the door to the present and future state of my mind and much later, when unhappy in love, it also gave me the possibility of realizing that the abstract feeling of love gives us far more satisfaction and benefit than the application of it to one specific subject. Being impersonal, such unselfish affection does not risk meeting with disastrous suffering through lack of reciprocity, comprehension and in the majority of cases the lack of the same quality of vibrations.

Mind you, if I am able today to stand outside my own small selfish ego and look back with quasi-motherly pity on all my past *bobos*—self-understandingly, it is not without the realization that only through hardship, clear determination, the lucid consciousness of having left nothing undone by human—often superhuman—effort, through the unbending will to advance, to know, to learn, to persevere, to fall and rise again, that I made it possible for myself to enjoy now my well-deserved and much appreciated peace and little bit of serenity!

To know oneself is the key to all that is. The problem all thinkers, scientists and initiates have been and are trying to solve is that of unveiling the secret of the ultimate Reality.

* * *

Now there are no doubts within me! Yes, no more doubts! And yet even today I cannot see how the technicality of earthly conditions can help or hinder our communion with the Infinite. And why it is that there can exist as many different paths leading to heavenly feeling and the comprehension of the world's criterion of Truth as there are different methods of singing.

No! There is no longer any room for doubt in my heart. No doubts! Sometimes my intellect, so accustomed to work ("Bring every day a basket of earth and you will raise a mountain," said Confucius) still registers certain contradictory impressions through this changeable matter—as our mind is—and the problems that directly are not mine but the experiences of other people raise a disturbing element in my mental food.

Still judging by external appearances, the case of

Galli-Curci for instance, made me very perplexed. This great diva was—if I am not mistaken—a faithful follower of Christian Science. For that reason she would not submit to the surgeon's knife to rid herself of a goitre that kept growing and tightening her throat to the point of handicapping her wonderful singing. However, she finally had the operation performed and by so doing forsook the Christian Science dogma for what evidently was to her a higher expression. Thanks to the favorable results of the operation, she announced her come-back and proclaimed before her second Chicago debut that she expected to sing better than ever, for now she had discovered a soul in her voice. I suffered at the thought of her making advertisement and propaganda out of the inner and sacred movement of her being, just as in another field I was shocked when the marvelous dancer Argentina heralded herself as a wearer of the Legion of Honor for publicity.

Apparently Galli-Curci's debut did not meet with the success she had prophesied. That raised the most troublesome question in my mind whether a soul can meet with a fiasco. I did not believe so and had to decide that her statement about her soul had merely been a press agent's work. That seemed a pity to me and in order to exonerate her I hoped that perhaps she could not help it, or that she might not even have been aware that such a thing had been said in her name, unless the story of her having found a soul in her voice was used like the story at the beginning of her sensationally started American career when she confessed that the birds had been her only singing teachers...

I was even more confused when I recently discovered that the foreword of Hindu Swami Yogananda's "Whispers of Eternity" was written by no less a person than Galli-Curci. So she did know! So she had spoken of her soul-voice! And yet, and yet she could not sing...

No! There was no more room for doubt in me. Still I asked myself if it were possible that Truth could be accommodated to any sauce, to any selfish interpretation. Like the story about the Sunday sermon against drinking given by the priest who thought to make it more convincing by demonstrating how happily a worm wriggled about in a glass full of pure water, whereas the same worm when put in a glass of whiskey curled up and died immediately.

"Do you see now what alcohol does to your health?" said the priest holding up the glass.

A red-nosed man stood up and asked: "What kind of whiskey did you pour in?"

"Any kind would do the same dreadful harm," said the priest.

"Oh, I see! Then the trouble is with the worm not the whiskey!"

* * *

Everything is confusing and changeable. And where to find the right explanation? The only unchangeable and consequently immortal book in this perishable world, the Bible, is much too hard to understand. It is too symbolical to be easily applied by the average mind. If our Testament were written without symbols, if our Bible were adapted into modern simple everyday language, I am certain people—especially Americans with their inborn facility for suggestion—would no longer fall heavily asleep over a detective story or a newspaper's lustful description of a scandalous divorce case—either of which might induce a nightmare and disturb their peaceful rest—but would realize instead that constructive words and healthy feelings would help their sleep and their day's work would be smoother after having read a few lines of the Gospel upon awakening.

An important Paris paper put the following question to a group of serious-minded authors, poets and scientists: "If all books had to be destroyed but one, which one would you keep?" The answer was unanimously: "The Bible."

So we find that the human brain has not improved upon that old-fashioned book we find on the night-table of the American hotel room, that Bible which the *avant-garde* finds so easy to ridicule but which it cannot outdo.

* * *

When I went to a singing teacher, I never allowed myself to argue, no matter how fantastic his demands were and so long as I could utter a sound. Blindly I accepted everything that was told me, reasoning that if I needed a teacher I must submit to his demands or leave him.

It reminds me of the story I heard about old Pierpont Morgan in connection with his art mentor, Jacques Seligman, against whose advice the multimillionaire never bought a picture for his marvelous collection. Once a party of the Italian Mafia, the Black Hand, warned the art dealer that unless he gave a favorable opinion about a copy of a masterpiece they wanted to sell Mr. Morgan as an original, he would bid a supreme adieu to this earth. Naturally Mr. Seligman was tormented to the utmost, afraid of their revenge but also unwilling to ruin his reputation of an honest connoisseur. Finally, sick at heart with anxiety, he went to his wealthy patron and confessed the whole story, dramatically adding:

"My life is in your hands, Mr. Morgan!"

The latter silently wrote out the check required by the gangsters for the value of the supposedly original picture and handed it to his cicerone. When Mr. Seligman thanked him profusely for saving his life, Mr. Morgan in true American spirit said:

"No, Seligman, I am not doing this for you. If I am such an ignoramus that the whole world knows I am not capable of having a judgment of my own, I must pay for my lack of knowledge. It serves me right!"

* * *

It is pretty confusing to have to deal with what is

considered the material knowledge of singing, which is not material after all except insofar as it is connected with material-minded teachers who try to enslave the Divine in tangible form in order to make it comprehensible to themselves. But when spiritual leaders not only praise their own exclusive method of disclosing the Truth but also assure us that theirs is the only way for us to reach God, then it is time to cry halt. I ultimately reached that conclusion but not without much suffering.

In my early days of seeking the Truth I met with every step I took the contradiction of its application. For instance where one Truth-giver taught that it was better to care for a dog or a cat than to have a closed heart to any affection—another almost sent malediction to those who replaced children (even if you have none) in their hearts by dogs or cats.

While one school of teaching said that without constant meditation one could achieve nothing, another proclaimed that meditation is useless unless followed by action, and when one monitor tried to persuade that the only way to meditate was the Buddha's posture commonly used in India, another insisted that the *only* good service to the Infinite could be achieved by sitting erect in a chair. Naturally my intuition as well as my common sense revealed to me that such claims were nonsensical, almost an insult to my intelligence, still reflection on those subjects had a snakelike way of letting doubts slip into my heart and made me wonder whether, if these apostles could make such mistakes in small details, the essential doctrines also were not erroneous. Unfortunately, we often judge by the small events and by the multiple happenings in our daily life more than by an important idea that is difficult to grasp.

From every lecture I attended I always got something. Often it was more than worth while but just as often it was marred by small contradictory detail such as being told by one teacher that I, for instance, should wear a sapphire for good vibrations, while another would recommend emeralds and a third might affirm that only my birthstone would be beneficial to me. Poor scrubwoman—if her birthstone happened to be a ruby!

While one color-lecturer would say that the stones themselves have no influence over us and that only the color of the stones mattered—red, for instance, would augment our vitality—another of God's messengers would not advise anyone to wear red in the belief that it symbolized the lower instinct and had fewer spiritual vibrations than any other color!

I recall that when listening to this last theory I had a bouquet of red roses pinned to my belt. I unfastened it and threw it cunningly under my chair so that my neighbors should not know how low my vibrations were. Poor flowers! Also during one whole winter I made myself forgo wearing red which—together with jade green—was my favorite color for brightening the dark winter furs.

One woman, speaking about the miraculous cures made by the application of color, was of the opinion that under no circumstance should we wear black as it had an extremely depressing influence. While initiating us in that absolute truth, the speaker herself wore a black dress without a touch of color anywhere.

Some Hindus use black to absorb their flickering thoughts in order to improve their meditations. To me black is the most distinguished and the smartest of colors for clothes, especially for evening wear. For the past few years I had felt perfectly dressed in the evening only when wearing black which harmonized with the beauty of my pearls to form the quintessence of art and simplicity.

Preference apart, I now realize that one should be able to overcome not only mild dislike but even organic aversion for any particular color as well as for anything at all. And yet, before such realization comes, how many doubts fill our heart and how important such petty questions seem to us!

* * *

All the seemingly unimportant daily happenings of our lives look too ridiculous to give even a thought to them but, alas, at the time they take on the proportions of the Himalayan Mountains!

For a long time I had imagined that pure accident had directed me toward the most difficult path of my self-expression—the path of singing. Now as I look back with infinitely better judgment, fully developed womanly intuition, no longer blinded by the ceaseless suffering that upsets the mind and renders us unable to control the emotions, I see clearly that even if it had not been for that petty romantic, otherwise insignificant episode of my youth, the desire to express myself through the medium of singing would most certainly have come, perhaps in a different way. But it must inevitably have come. Sooner or later I was bound to sing, it could not have been otherwise. My nature could no more have been stopped from its life than a sunbeam can be imprisoned or a river turned from its course. Given the generous nature incorporated in my emotionally rich body, it *had* to happen!

Having been brought up as a child in a very orthodox family, had it not been for my inner urge I would certainly not have lighted a concealed candle, after my bedtime devotional prayer and my Mother's goodnight kiss, in order to recite in a whisper, for fear of being heard, some tragic poetry taken without authorization from Father's library.

Curiously enough, youngsters are attracted much more by the dramatic expression of suffering and pathos than by happiness, freshness and beauty. Naturally, the further we go in life, the more we are forced to see misery. For the sake of contrast, we want to forget our daily disturbing happenings. We seek as compensation the carefree joy that cruel destiny often withholds from us, while children without any experience, in order to feel strongly, seek to borrow new sensations from books.

* * *

After a visit to a candy shop as a tiny bit of a girl, whenever a grownup would ask me what I would like to become, I would answer: "Saleswoman in a candy shop!"—much to my Mother's shock. That was the height of my dreams, until one day someone cruelly told me that those saleswomen were not allowed to eat the candies. For months I pondered that difficult problem. Finally some charitable person explained the actual situation to me by saying: "You could eat as much chocolate as you desired but a few days later you would no longer want to eat any. You would be sick even at the sight of candy."

That was too much for me. Such absurdity, and from an elderly person, too! Fancy being able to eat as many sweets as your heart desired and not wanting them! Oh no, that was unthinkable!

But a few years later, on coming out of the church one Sunday morning, I saw a strange picture. A young woman in a waist-less skirt, one breast naked and wounded, blood falling on her torn white shirt, her blonde hair hanging Ophelia-like, was walking down the middle of the street. Her beautiful eyes were wide open. She mumbled something to herself, unaware of the mocking crowd following her…

I looked on quite fascinated for I had never seen anything to equal that scene. Unfortunately I was forbidden to watch her any longer. I asked who she was but the only answer I got was not to look at her because she was crazy.

Crazy? Crazy! What was that? How fascinating! What a wonderful thing it must be to be crazy…

Metamorphosis. My dreams about the candy shop paled. How could I think about candy? My thoughts had changed. I wanted to be crazy! Crazy at any price. I would be crazy or I would be nothing at all…

Yes, I can see now it was the theatre that attracted me

even then. The staging, the escape from ugly reality... Yes... I wanted the theatre and the unattainable, for I never visualize myself playing with dolls as a child. But I can see, as if it were today, a little girl of six or seven seated on the floor and trying for hours to catch with her tiny fingers the mercury taken from the broken window thermometer in a moment of no supervision. That happened so often that scarcely was a new thermometer put up than it was down again. With unbelievable patience for such an age, the tiny fingers always pressed on emptiness, the quicksilver ever escaping rebelliously but already her will power directed another finger trying to catch the mercury, the unreachable on the floor. Severely punished for breaking something that was not for a nice girl to touch, she was undaunted and did not hesitate to take the first opportunity to repeat the experiment, knowing the consequences of disobeying again but sure at heart that the next time she could imprison the rebellious matter. Each time it resulted in the same fiasco and brought bigger punishment but she was undiscouraged and soon tried again...

The perseverance of that little girl was a symbol of my whole life...

* * *

At fourteen I heard a neighbor who returned from Italy sing the tenor's adieu from "Tosca" and also the heartbreaking aria from "Pagliacci." The tragic sadness of the music found a faithful echo in the emotional stirrings of my heart, and I thought there could be no higher glory than to sing and sing while crying out your soul.

Since childhood, my impressionable nature desired—though unconsciously—to become a server of Beauty, a Vestal of the Secret and Sacred Flame, supreme guardian of the Mystery of Immortal Inspiration.

Little did I suspect how dear Dame Nature would make me pay for having chosen the way of uplifting service to

God, for even unknown to myself I was always "God-hungry," although the Catholic religion into which I was born did not permit me to discern that until much later.

Now, that my partly unconscious life is over, bringing the end to my suffering, I can state that if I had to start life all over I would willingly relive all my miseries, because it was my ceaseless struggle which made me spiritually what I am today. And, if my conception of art is nearer to Infinite Perfection, if I shall be fortunate enough to help a few through my example of perseverance and courage—it is only because my attainments were nourished by an unceasing stream of tears, by constant sacrifices, by the scornful persecution of the press—which made me the laughing-stock of both hemispheres—as well as by the antagonistic attitude of my own people who never had the slightest belief in me—never—none!

The natural jealousy of a husband sincerely prevents him from wishing his wife the fulfillment of even the highest of aspirations, since, contrary to reality, he imagines that the materialization of her hopes might separate him from his beloved and force him to share her loving heart with the only rival utterly unbearable to a man's vanity—a career, if mighty elevated art can be called a career!

Had I ever met anyone who might have told me "Ritorna, Vincitor!" had I met with a little success at the beginning of my struggles, with the least encouragement or the slightest sympathy as so many debutantes are fortunate enough to get, I would today probably be just where I started—nowhere!

My contemporaries, my colleagues upon whom the Bountiful Lady once smiled, are now gone, long since passed by, artistically forgotten, spiritually diminished, having left no imprint whatsoever of their passage upon the shrine of Art.

But I exist more fully than ever before. Yes, I do exist! I am alive, full of energy, full of inner beauty, full of passionate love for my work, my sacred work. I am full of desire to learn everything that is accessible and what is usually considered quite inaccessible! I am full of desire to recreate on this earth what I see in the immensity of the Infinite, to catch the Shadow and unveil It, to express all the accumulated wealth of my soul, previously handicapped by my enslavement to the work of vocal technique when each lesson was used as a barometer for the day's hope or despair.

How naïve I was to think that it was possible to use painstaking will-power to deal with such a mysteriously elusive and subtle force as the human voice, which does not come from our body but merely passes through it!

Goethe said: "A limitless activity, whatever its nature, is bound to end bankrupt." And I see now that the semi-lethargic state of mind is far more propitious than the dictatorily concentrated thoughts. To approach this difficult, unexplainable Art of singing, one should bring a tender adoration arising from deep profundity rather than a passionate fervor. One should come to it with a relaxed and passive mind, with clairvoyant inspiration, unlimited vision of solitary stillness and ecstatic absorption—but never with the domination of the brain.

I had allowed myself to be persuaded that so many more miles of exercising my vocal chords, so many more thousand hours of hard and conscientious work and I should be able to chisel to perfection the God-given divine, immaterial instrument...

* * *

Only a short while ago I was permitted to visualize the voice in the four-dimensional dominion where singing can be good only when it is perfect and it is perfect only when the spirit of music does the singing for us. Now I could see that we are much nearer to Reality when we do not allow our physical being to interfere. And if we want to take advantage of our passage on this earth, we must acknowledge the Divinity in us whose spark inflames our inspiration.

But how many deceptive moments we must endure before that knowledge comes to us! How many hurts and discouragements! How many venomous doubts demoralize our mental health! And this atrociously monotonous, ceaseless waiting! And those perpetually vanquished revolts when our inner resources are unable to destroy incertitude, when gloom and desolation easily conquer hope, when the skeptic intelligence constantly analyses the despairing lack of progress and when retrogression is so evident that it blinds the critical mind! ! !

We are bound to pass through all those mental peregrinations until, finally, the resurrection gloriously illuminates our mental horizon and Faith—reinforced by clearly visible proofs and obviously simple thoughts—brings the reward in the Healing Power that puts light in our hearts, joy in our work and the ultimate transfiguration that ennobles our way of acting, thinking and being!

Until that time many tragic experiences and persistent researches must be undergone to reach what—in the majority of cases—is the unattainable. "Many are called but few are chosen!"

Women especially, traditionally not being called into the professions as men automatically are, have ruined their lives by being unable to express their heart's desire in the abstract; downhearted—often with a soul full of bitter revenge—they marry but their early disillusionment does not allow them to enjoy contentment. When they are old, often grandmothers, they will whisper in melancholy tones as if speaking about a dead one that they, too, studied singing, music, painting, acting, social reforms, but… Their inner sorrow never lets them finish the sad phrase.

Through intuition they felt that the unsatisfied soul-call —which received no echo—was somehow different from any other big event in their lives, perhaps because it eluded them. They could not grasp the Unknown, could not get nearer to the Nameless and so could not have the tangible beauty in their hearts that gives peace of mind for the rest of our earthly life.

* * *

Those students of voice whose limited income has not allowed them a variety of research and a quantity of experience at least have the sweet consolation of later stating that they started to study but could not afford to continue— a familiar phrase so often heard. While those, like myself, whose difficulties were not of a financial nature but who had ample opportunity to receive colossal blows and endured inexpressibly painful trials, those who went from one teacher to another only to find each less satisfactory than the previous one and more tenacious about criticizing the ignorance of his predecessor—those were not to be envied.

The most level-headed students lose even the semblance of intelligence when they allow their professor to do such things as, for example, putting a broken match stick between the upper and lower teeth in order to force them to sing with their mouth open or when they reduce their dignity to the extent of lying flat on the floor and permitting their inquisitor to pile several telephone directories on them for the purpose of quickening the work of the diaphragm.

One such teacher told me to sing higher and higher and keep my eye at the fortieth floor windows of an opposite building. I reversed my head to such an extent that it was impossible for me to utter a sound and when I complained I was sent to a doctor to be cured of… chronic laryngitis! The sad part of that story is that I did go to a doctor and not only to one but to each well-known, well-recommended throat specialist in the whole of New York City.

Another maestro made me move the piano around the studio while singing, presumably to strengthen my muscles.

One condemned my vocal cords to silence for a whole month. I was then living at the now defunct Knickerbocker Hotel where I had at luncheon Enrico Caruso on my left and Antonio Scotti on my right—both, alas now dead. I had flirted with the great tenor by correspondence. Once

I sent him five dollars requesting his caricature which he did immediately keeping my money. I ordered my meals by signs like a dumb person. A month later, however, my voice was in exactly the same condition as before. I visited every doctor, chiropractor, osteopath, healer, simple instructor of elocution of whom I happened to hear and each time put the hope of my heart in their hands. I even went to a sanatorium for stutterers. Why not? Demosthenes chewed stones to improve his articulation!

* * *

Speaking about singing, I finally understood that there is no such thing as the "placing" of the voice. "Good" singing by any standard is a very controversial qualification, for while one teacher says "higher," another hears the voice "lower" and vice versa. I verified this myself a hundred times when putting my tone higher and higher but still not sounding high enough to satisfy my teacher. Then at the point of desperation I did just the opposite. Enchanted, my instructor joyfully exclaimed: "Now it is placed high enough—now it is perfect! You see, you can do it if you want to!"

I know now that good singing consists actually not in having your voice set in any particular place or touching any special organ but only in pouring it out into space, to return from whence it came.

That is the reason why it is quicker and easier to teach young beginners without any previous training whatsoever than singers with some experience already behind them. That is why, with so many years of hard work, different methods and contradictory systems behind me, I could not easily free myself from that self-imposed yoke and begin to perceive the Truth except through great tragedy.

But it was this tragedy that brought me nearer to the Light, because mental deduction showed me that in the summer while in my country place in France when I sang with only an accompanist and no teacher I actually sang better and made much more rapid progress, for then—in so far as my exaggerated consciousness allowed me—I almost succeeded in forgetting the many instructions which had been hammered into my head. And in winter while studying under a teacher, I invariably sang better in the beginning of the season than at the end. Contrary to what one might think on account of my misjudgments—my vain attempts, I was always able to perceive the slightest progress or retrogression in my voice. When, still knowing little about singing, I followed blindly my teacher, it was because I was aware of my ignorance and being afraid to make a mistake I preferred to continue my study with the same maestro until I received concrete proof of his inability to help me.

* * *

Of all the battles I won in my life full of struggles, the greatest was the battle won despite the prediction that it was of no use, that I never could sing. But still I continued my work, I even increased my efforts.

When doubts encompassed me, leaving no room for hope or sunshine, when there seemed to be no way out, when a selfishly jealous husband prayed that I might fail in order to have more of me for himself, when friends warned me that teachers were fooling me for the sake of selling me more lessons, when those that really cared seeing my misery advised me to quit—in spite of all these difficulties I still had hope in the future.

But I needed inner force stronger than steel to ignore the same advice to quit my study when it came from my favorite Californian philosopher, Manly Hall, because he had no personal reason whatsoever to discourage me.

Stoically I ignored his warning but it was hard! I needed superhuman strength still to go on and forget his words constantly ringing in my ears:

"You cannot succeed, the stars are against you. Jupiter

will not allow you to sing and even if you attain your goal, something will prevent your stupendous efforts to bear constructive fruit because Jupiter—terrible but generous Jupiter—will prevent your succeeding in things, small to his conception, in order to prepare you for the bigger things later... later... maybe even not in this life..."

Yes, ignoring Manly Hall's words was my most glorious victory!

SALZBURG-1936

It is not sufficient to take steps which will one day lead to the goal; each step should be in itself a goal at the same time as it carries us forward.

— GOETHE

AGAIN SALZBURG...

From the moment I arrived I automatically became reminiscent of past suffering. My heart recognized all the pains it had experienced while struggling years ago in that beautiful spot. At that time it had been comparatively easy to bear the heavy burden of my destiny as all my life was in front of me and the mightiest of all friends, Hope, unlimited Hope, prophetic Hope encircled my whole being. Now—emptiness, the pitch-black darkness of my soul took Hope's place and set itself out in victorious relief.

How excited is Madeleine on her first visit to Salzburg! What an event in her musical life!

So was I when just after my marriage to Harold McCormick I went on our honeymoon trip to the Salzburg *Festspiel* for the first time. Eager to know everything, to miss nothing—I felt like a happy trout wriggling in fresh water—*in einem Bachlein helle*...

I was thrilled to the utmost in meeting the greatest musical and literary lights of our time. I was thrilled to know the Austrian poet Hugo von Hofmannsthal, author of "Der Rosencavalier" and other librettos to Richard Strauss' operas as well as author of the plays that Max Reinhardt was producing at Mozart's birthplace.

What words shall I use to faithfully express my feelings when I met the composer of "Rosencavalier" and of "Till

Eulenspiegel"—Richard Strauss at Mr. Reinhardt's wonder castle, Leopoldkrönen Schloss? Of all private houses I have ever visited anywhere in the world, that baroque one as a home, as a dwelling place was to my taste the quintessence of beauty.

How interested I was to know the admirable Moisi, one of the greatest German-speaking actors of our time! How enchanted I was to speak to the spiritually beautiful Helen Timig, the present Mrs. Max Reinhardt!

I have never been blasée, nor am I now. The tiniest expression of beauty, of grandeur thrills me to the utmost now as in those days in Salzburg. But now I know much more, I have seen much more and, alas, I also know that only too often it is a cruel disappointment to meet the greatest Muses of this world!

We imagine that because a man is great as an artist he must be great as a man but the contrary is so often the case. It is as if Nature by giving him so much in one line had deprived him of all other supplementary qualities and opened to him only one spiritual window to the prejudice of all others.

Cabanes tell us: "It would seem that sensitiveness, like a determined quantity of fluid when it pours abundantly into one canal, diminishes proportionately in the others."

* * *

Gracefully exchanging greetings and smiles to that brilliant audience of Salzburg Festival, deep in my heart I was a pathetic figure. For I knew too much, far too much, for one who is no entity. For an artist at heart—as I certainly am if I am anything at all—it is a small tragedy to be unable to create and to have instead only a seat in the first row of any opera house of both hemispheres. This suffering of mine was still augmented by the sad realization of how powerfully commercialism reigns over the shrine of Art nowadays while I must sit on the paying side of the ramp helpless to contribute a fresh spark…

* * *

If I suffered more acutely this time in Salzburg, it was because my suffering was without embellishment. Previously I had been swimming almost joyfully in the deep misery which—as it had seemed to me—made of me a superior being and ennobled my character a great deal.

Although not a Russian, I had nevertheless been contaminated by the defects of their qualities from living near them. I must have caught the capacity of immeasurable suffering and the deeper I felt its clutches, the deeper was my inner beauty. I certainly felt superior to those pygmies around me who were unable to bear their sorrow with grace. My only consolation was to feel that I am a martyr —perhaps even unconsciously seeking the martyrdom—and to imagine that among millions I am the one chosen for the privilege of suffering… What pride to be able to show swollen-lidded eyes as proof of willingly uncontrolled tears—what self-indulgent satisfaction!

To think that I once made fun of the Russian friend who said to me: "I enjoyed last night extremely. I went to the movies and during the whole performance I cried, I cried…!"

Now I understand more clearly my blind adoration for Duse, who actually enjoyed being unhappy and never wanted to profane her love for d'Annunzio by giving a smile to the world. Sad until her death, she imagined she would live and die in perfect beauty!

* * *

The healthy American atmosphere slowly but surely cured me of my self-inflicted craving for suffering.

Later, deep studies confirmed in my mind what a young undegenerated race—nearer to its foundations—instinctively knew about the force in the Positive and about the demolition in the Negative. Much later, I also came to the realization that real beauty cannot have birth in destruction but can elevate our soul to its highest limits only through joy. Generous Nature is extremely fecund but as soon as unlawful conditions arise she produces no more.

* * *

But back to Salzburg—Salzburg revisited.

Only now can I realize how happy I was years ago when singing here. Singing—that meant doing, striving with no time left to ponder the heart's aching. Rehearsing all day long, never left alone to analyze my mental problem and not only singing but also creating for I myself staged Massenet's beautiful "Manon" at its first performance at Salzburg.

While now it is the end… I know I cannot sing even though I continued my studies until the hour for my train to Salzburg and even here I came hoping to be able to work with Bruno Walther…

* * *

Last night, particularly low in spirits—demoralized by the heat which is the only outside element that I cannot yet control—I felt the emptiness of my soul especially strongly. To feel sad is natural to me but while I was studying many hours daily I had less time to analyze the state of my mind in such an acute way as now, here, during the vacation inflicted upon myself, having nothing to occupy my thoughts while bygone memories crowd all my mind…

I certainly was not happy on my previous visits here—far from it… But the fact that I knew less, that I had hope ahead of me, the fact that I had the irresistible desire to change the morale of one or another person around me and was ready to make all sacrifices for its fulfillment, as well as the fact that I had always—should everything else fail—the possibility of a final exit via a magnificent suicide, all those elements together with courage and unburdened forces made my sad life quite bearable…

Now I no longer have the consolation of saving others. Now I know I should not even interfere with the Karma of other beings for—beyond making myself utterly miserable—I cannot achieve any good results, as we are unable to live the life of others. They must answer the call themselves. They must give a full account of their deeds themselves to Mother Nature.

Neither is there hope in front of me any longer and the multitude of speaking facts of the past render the outlook rather dark. And the last consideration—by no means an unimportant one—is the realization that I cannot now end at will this miserable existence of mine and go to nothingness as I previously thought I could, for no matter how big a part imagination or hallucination plays in all philosophies, in all religions—still all creeds, all dogmas condemn suicide. (Even *hara-kiri* cannot be called an exception, for it is dictated rather by a national feeling of honor than by a spiritual conception). And—what is more important—all religions prove that suicide is the end of our bodily existence only while our mental misery continues, at least for those who, like myself, believe in our individual survival.

I am sure that the major part of humanity—through respect for their various religions, through fear of Heaven's condemnation or simply for the sake of consolation—believes in the immortality of the soul. How can it be otherwise? No thinking being can admit that we die like a misused machine the moment our physical heart stops beating. The creative idea of this machine still exists and will exist eternally, creating other machines and repairing the broken ones, just as the doctors do when trying to cure such negative matter as sickness.

* * *

In spite of Mozart's divine music I cannot this time enjoy the Festival enough to forget my thoughts and forsake everything else, perhaps because I know more about singing now than I knew ten years ago and I have seen and heard so much that now I am capable of making comparisons. Nowadays the artists seem to be less perfect than during my first visit to Salzburg. Indeed I am unable to lose myself completely in the music when the singers because of age, fatness, inexperience or lack of inspiration cannot give their maximum, which is not enough in the domain of sublime Art.

If I did not grieve over my own inability to contribute something to the beauty of operatic music, I did however regret that I was never rich enough to give the world—as a promoter of Art—the nearest standard of possible perfection. Only those who have had personal connection with opera know the terrific cost of it. When Mr. McCormick subsidized the Opera in Chicago, the deficit of running it during those few short months was at least a half million dollars. In the year when Mary Garden was responsible for the destiny of that enterprise the deficit increased almost to a million, so I was informed by Harold, despite Mary Garden's managerial ability.

For so many years, day out, day in, seeing all over the world the best that one can lay eyes on, naturally I have developed a just appreciation of decor and costuming to a pretty high degree. Therefore I was able to note instantly the smallest error of deportment, lack of refinement, false attitude, the slightest gesture of vulgarity or anything out of keeping with the style of a given performance. With so many trumps in my hand it seemed to me that I should have been able to help a great deal in raising the aesthetic standard of audiences by showing them real beauty in all its perfect harmony.

* * *

Still if those sad days in Salzburg were bearable at all, it was due to the advancement in my spiritual development as already I had an inner feeling of almost rock-like poise only lately acquired through solitary meditation, constructive affirmation and concentration in self-contained calm.

With a happy smile, I would receive the many compliments about my *Dirndl* costume. With an equally happy smile, I declined all social functions and saw only a few musically-minded friends. And still with a smile, I went nightly to the performances to take possession of my first row seat, like any other uncreative person.

Adoring Mozart as I do, my essential reason for going to Salzburg was my hopeful desire to be able to study with Bruno Walther, this great exponent and interpreter of the Salzburg Master. With anxiety but also with a smile, I awaited a call in answer to my request that he would coach me in Mozart opera and *Lieder*. The answer that came when I had already left Salzburg was negative—naturally!

* * *

Toward the end of the week I could no longer stand the atmosphere of greeting all of New York in the lobby of the *Oesterreichischer* Hof in the mornings, seeing all of Paris during luncheon and then meeting on the street those one would have liked to avoid—an impossibility owing to the tiny size of the place. Exactly like an ocean crossing, it was how-do-you-do to the right and how-do-you-do to the left, empty conversations, useless questions, not always sincere compliments, snobbish criticism of last night's performance, sympathetic inquiries about my voice and so forth...

No, I could not stand it any longer or I would certainly go crazy... I ordered my sleeping accommodations to leave. But as happens always in my life when there is not the slightest streak of light and the situation is almost hopeless—out of the clear sky came beneficial food for hope and the badly needed strength for the continuation of life. I heard in a private audition some pupils of a certain French lady. One of them, in praising her teacher's method, asserted that even if she were awakened in the middle of the night she would now sing correctly as she had acquired absolute control over her voice.

Control! That is it! I am missing in control. One day I can sing well and the next—for no apparent reason—I cannot sing at all. No, I should not even say the next day, the same afternoon, during my second lesson, my voice would have gone as if something were disconnected in me.

Listening to those girls singing, my soul was again filled with healing hope. I knew right then that I *must* see that professor, I must judge for myself as I always do, I must try my chances once again before condemning myself to complete inertia, deadly stagnation and involuntary silence forever.

Upon learning that this teacher was then at her country place in the Pyrenees where her pupils were following her, I immediately sent a telegram asking Madame Gilly if she would have time to take work with me the following week.

That night at the *Festspiel* I had difficulty in keeping quiet. Inwardly my soul was singing, joyfully singing… And my lips during the performance silently duetted all three feminine parts of "Don Juan."

Contrary to my habit I even went out during the intermission, unable to stand inactivity any longer, craving to walk, to stretch my legs and to spend some of my newly accumulated energy.

At the buffet I met the charming Mrs. Cornelius Crane of Chicago, who was most happy to see me because as she explained she tried to contact me those past months, having found an extraordinary singing teacher, a feminine mystic, who was receiving messages from her Tibetan Master to get in touch with me in order to help my singing.

Patatras! Embarras de richesses! !

Until four o'clock of that memorable day I had been a living corpse. Now two windows were widely opened to my heart's desire, giving me the fresh possibilities of renewing the lease of my life's struggle, both worldly and spiritual.

The next morning I received a favorable answer from the French teacher and during luncheon Mrs. Crane telephoned to St. Moritz to her Frau Professor and got Madame L'Orsa's kind acceptance to teach me, as well as messages of love and blessing for me!

Between a seriously recommended but regular singing teacher whose method I could already appreciate and one known to me only through the enthusiastic and exalted recommendation of a charming but vocally yet inexperienced young lady, I did not hesitate a second. Instantaneously I chose the one with mystic inclinations. I chose Madame L'Orsa.

* * *

That same day I was on my way home, where I stayed only long enough to take back Madeleine, my friend who had been my guest in Salzburg, drop my maid, and change my luggage. Twenty-four hours later I found myself in a sleeper on the Simplon-Orient Express getting nearer and nearer to the realization of my life's purpose.

Next morning, at dawn, I looked through the window of my compartment. Switzerland! I was in Switzerland! Switzerland! The name alone, without even seeing the landscape was sufficient to awaken in me memories not yet outgrown.

Involuntarily the past revived in my heart. I pictured myself in Poland, where as a young girl I had always heard Switzerland glorified as the most romantic place in the whole of Europe, the country where the newly wedded went to combine the beauty of their inner feelings with the glorious vistas outside!

I had made acquaintance with that country—so justly renowned for its attractiveness, with its many mountains so particularly appealing to one who like myself comes from flat lands, with those panoramas whose beauty had been described at length in every successful novel at the end of the nineteenth century, with that country whose beneficial climate resurrected flickering life to legions. I had made acquaintance with that land designed for joy in an atmosphere of anxiety unbearable to my heart. For, when first I crossed those evergreen beautiful valleys, my eyes were blinded by unceasing streams of tears.

I gazed at those white-turbaned mountains for the first time when destiny sent me there as an extremely young bride to take my dying husband to the gloomy sanatorium of the justly reputed Davos, since the oldest professors of the St. Petersburg Medical Faculty with the longest beards I had ever seen had condemned my bridegroom of a few months to death from galloping consumption. I had questioned those authorities of health whether I could save his life by taking him to Switzerland, that Lourdes of physical ills about whose miraculous potency I had heard so much.

With a condescending smile, I had been told: "My dear child, he certainly will not stand the journey. He cannot stand it!"

Though a mere child—in Poland young girls are brought up without initiative and thinking of their own; they are supposed to lean on their mother's experiences in every need—I already was reasoning and insisted to know how long he could live if I stayed home. When I learned that it could only be a matter of a few days, I decided to take the chance.

Small wonder that the more beautiful the view unfolding from the window of the train before my eyes as it entered Switzerland, the more acute became the suffering of my deeply wounded young heart.

The months, the years spent in those indifferent mountains—when we suffer impotent Nature seems indifferent to us and her rich beauty reminds us even more of our inward poverty—imprinted my future life with heavy sadness, fear and anxiety of losing my beloved.

When we love in extreme youth, we cannot get any consolation from the outside world, for we do not share our feelings with any earthly condition. We have no other ambition than the foolish desire to become older, paradoxical as it sounds. We do not realize the responsibilities of our situation because our only qualification is being newly married. We do not as yet know the importance of our standing, even if we have any. We do not have the philosophical consolation of elderly people who comfort themselves with the thought that death is inevitable. Moreover we are not greatly interested in the outside world, being entirely and egotistically engrossed in the feelings which we alone seem to have discovered and which we imagine no one else has ever felt before us.

At that tragic moment of my entrance into life, I felt I was not only losing my husband but also my own life, which seemed utterly futile to me without him. It also meant that I should lose my life not through the spectacular suicide I had always dreamed of—dying in a white satin gown *à la* Juliet, choked by the scent of a million tuberoses, in a death suitable to my romantic nature because it would mean Beauty in the absolute, Poetry in the highest, eternal Romance—but it meant dying vulgarly because the beloved had disappeared, dying a miserable death through the victory of crass matter, the victory of Ugliness. How horrible!

Such a state of mind makes one feel unjust toward surroundings, towards everything that is visible, everything that is touchable. Needless to say, no Freudian psychoanalytical theory is necessary to explain logically that the beauty of Switzerland, far from impressing me with joy, gave me rather a feeling of nightmare that has haunted me ever since.

* * *

Time, beneficial time, the best doctor even for the deepest sorrow, could probably have helped to erase, at least partially, in spite of the depths of my nature, the painful record written on the extremely sensitive solar plexus of my being, had it not been that many years later Fate should again choose Switzerland as the setting for further painful happenings. This time the situation was still more tragic as my heart automatically recognized the old feeling of anxiety, thus immediately putting my mind in a morbid state and my soul in a desperate mood of sorrow.

* * *

At the time of my first visit to Switzerland I thought that extreme youth and lack of experience makes us indefensible in the face of misery. Now I realize that the feeling of a great injustice helps us to bear the burdens that have been put upon us. Later in life when our hearts are more mature and our reasoning capacities developed fully, when we analyze more carefully—even though not always able to understand—when we know ever so much more but find no consolation in our knowledge, we are condemned to more suffering because the years of experience have added value to our mind and along with that we gain the ability to feel, suffer and agonize almost indefinitely. Given these conditions and added to them my exceptional capacity for constantly turning the knife in my heart, one can easily understand my not having a great love for that tourists' paradise—Switzerland!

* * *

During the second period of my acquaintance with that country, French *Suisse* that time, I was forced to leave my beloved Galluis—the only place in which I feel at home and less unhappy—in order to spend a day in Switzerland. Usually I arrived by five o'clock several mornings each week at the final station from where—not to lose time waiting for the funicular—I would climb the sharp mountain in a car. The sanatorium was situated, as those sanatoriums usually are, on the highest point of the mountain. In winter I often had to wait hours for the chauffeur to come back with a sleigh, as an automobile marooned in the deep snow would slip backwards.

When finally I arrived, it was only to witness from the next room the terrific operation of Dr. de Reynier introducing a dynamo into the affected throat of my teacher, Walther Straram. Anxiously, oh, so anxiously, I would await the result of each operation, realizing that the patient might choke to death any moment. With all the force in me I tried to kill that atrocious thought which constantly crept into my mind. All in vain, for the tanks of oxygen before my eyes, prepared for an emergency, reminded me of the imminent danger.

Completely broken in spirit and body from such unhealthy emotions I would take my train the same afternoon to return to my duties at the Théâtre des Champs-Elysées, sometimes only to be obliged to repeat the same exhausting experience the next day or the day after, when Dr. de Reynier would inform me by a long distance call from Leysin that the next day's cauterization might be fatal, especially if the patient were not inspired by my presence as he had been until then. Yes, Mr. Straram did not want to take care of his health. He preferred to die, to die rather than not breathe the same air that I breathed. For the sake of music I succeeded in prolonging his life with those dreadful operations.

* * *

Such a long explanation of my dislike—luckily enough my heart never knew any hate—for beautiful Switzerland is only to show the why and wherefore of such comprehensible antipathy.

The constructive moral behind those experiences had far deeper significance. In spite of the terrific price I paid, I can now realize only the blessings in those opportunities given me to develop my soul.

Ever-generous Nature, while sending me many hard trials, at the same time gave me much fundamental richness. I was fortunate, for instance, in never being able to remember any wrong done to me. I always did what, at the time, I thought I ought to do. But if things turned out to be wrong I did not burden myself with reproaches, neither did I regret my sad experiences. No, regrets never diminished my vitality.

I have received much from my Creator, even if life has given me little happiness in the general conception of the word. I was given much of the substance with which human possibilities could not have endowed me. If I was able to give much in return, it was because each time I thought it was the *only* time in my life. Consequently I made a superhuman effort to hold on, just as a race-horse will make a supreme effort to cross the finishing post victorious even though it fall dead on the spot from too much strain.

Although hidden and unknown to me then, some tremendous power in me was so strong that after each gigantic effort I recuperated instantly and was thus ready for each new great experience with its new great suffering.

Despite having seen much injustice in this world, I have been able to forget all the miseries and to forgive all conscious or unconscious enemies because revenge and bitterness have never touched my soul. Peacefully and happily I am now reaping the immense benefits therefrom.

By not failing, by not losing my courage, I added to the accomplishment of my Karma, being the best friend and the truest judge of my conscience and living together with myself on the best of terms.

I am deeply sorry for those who often made me suffer brutally, especially for those who are departed, departed in ugliness and fear, with dissatisfaction in their souls. I am sorry for those who are alive but unable to find inner contentment and to feel the serenity that brings happiness. For there is no happiness outside our heart, just as there is no permanent success built on a shaky foundation and no glory without peace of soul.

* * *

While approaching St. Moritz I was happy to realize the complete absence of superstition in my mind when, in the dining car at breakfast, without the slightest feeling of antagonism or preconceived antipathy I remembered all the other times my eyes had viewed the same landscape.

I was only seventeen when first I saw St. Moritz in its August glory. The most interesting individuals of that time from all over the world were at the Palace Hotel to enjoy the privileges their standing, titles and money accorded them.

Magnificently gowned women… Very romantic men… Even those of no great personality were attractive, for they had not yet lost their courteous manners and were full of adoration for womanhood. They were capable of waiting patiently a whole year long just to cast a glance at the worshiped lady of their destiny during that season. They found greater happiness in a single dance with her than the young man of today finds in spending the whole summer touring in his Hispano with his sweetheart.

It was the pre-war epoch when each person belonged to his class, unlike today when there are so many *déclassées* that they form a society of their own and are called cosmopolitan circle. Then society actually meant something. It was a time when a person's private life was not exposed to the front page of every newspaper, when decency was *de rigour* and not an exception, when every man took his hat off—(and not only in the elevator—!) when speaking to a lady on any occasion. And when I say a *lady*, I mean every woman who wanted to be a lady. It was the time when in French circles one would ask: "How is Madame votre mère?" Not like the young people of today who ask for one's father, "How's your old man?" Does that have a pleasant sound to the ear?

It was in that courteous time that I had my first contact with the English people of exquisite manners. I was even greatly embarrassed when two young girls of almost my own age curtsied to me when greeting me because I was a married woman! I felt the great importance of my new status in the social world.

There were many brilliant people world-known but unknown to me! Twenty-four hours later, I knew the *curriculum vitae* of those outstanding Palace *habitués*. To my unspoiled, ingenuous eye the hotel itself seemed the summit of luxury.

That elderly round-bearded gentleman was the Grand-Duke of Leuchtenberg... This statuesque lady, the celebrated beauty Madame Xantho, to whom the Russian Monseigneur was extremely devoted... Over there, the extraordinary creature famous for her ugliness was the "beautiful" Marchesa Casati ! This tall Frenchman dancing in torn shoes was Baron Maurice de Rothschild.

I could not, however, make up my mind as to who the tall, handsome, smartly but eccentrically dressed girl, in vivid colors such as only the *cocottes* dared wear—who could she be? Apparently she was unmarried, but when she played tennis with men she was accompanied neither by her mother nor by a chaperone. If I had not seen her with women known to be *comme il faut*, I would have placed her without hesitation among the *femmes légères* but then she could not have mingled with the Palace Hotel assembly—in those days of individuality one could not have dreamed of calling even such an amalgamated reunion as that a "crowd." That striking woman attracted my beauty-loving eye so much and aroused my curiosity to such degree that I finally inquired who the red-hatted, purple-gowned lady was and to what class of society she belonged and whether she was married or single.

"*Celle-là? Oh! C'est une amèricaine!*"- was the laconic and supposedly self-explanatory answer.

I understood. That statement evidently covered all points. Obviously in America a woman could dress individually and eccentrically even if she belonged to society without necessarily being thought an actress, which was then considered to be the criterion of frivolity. I also came to understand that in America it was permissible for young girls to go out with men who were not of their family unescorted by a *dame de compagnie*. I felt that their unconsciously natural behavior, which would have irrevocably ruined the reputation of a Polish girl, presented only an irresistible attraction, as those beautiful and frank girls were not governed by our European traditions and consequently were blameless.

* * *

My first visit to St. Moritz had been cut short. I had gone there from Davos where I had been living winter and summer in a sanatorium for tuberculosis in order to keep my husband company. I was the only healthy person in the place, for even the doctors, nurses and servants had weak lungs.

My bridegroom had consented to remain three years in that health resort only if I agreed to stay beside him, selfishly announcing that otherwise he preferred to die immediately at home rather than be buried alive for three long years alone.

The doctors accepted my presence on condition that I follow exactly the same routine as the patients did, in order not to create a demoralizing example to those unfortunate victims.

I submitted to all the rules. For instance, I went out only during the hours permitted to all and I ate much and frequently like the patients. It was somewhat like the way the piglets are gorged before Easter in Poland or the turkeys in America before Thanksgiving Day! Years ago, contrary to the present theory, the medical staff ordered the tubercular to eat a lot and eat often. There were never less than eighteen courses each meal. The order was to eat very slowly. No one was ever in a hurry to go back to his prison cell anyhow, as the dining room was the only diversion for those lucky enough to be allowed to leave their beds. Besides they were supposed to chew their food thoroughly and there was plenty of time for that as people never rush in Switzerland anyhow, the service being rather turtle-like.

For my quick and healthy temperament those meals were an almost unbearable function. To hold my patience in rein and shorten the boredom by fooling time away, I would fold the *Speisekarte* after each course. Sometimes, oh, rarely, it was a wonderful surprise to have the potatoes served together with the meat! That made two lines out of my menu at the same time! Hurrah! And what a relief when I could make the last fold in the menu for the coffee—if coffee was allowed!

Those were the only joys I had the first year of my married life! But those petty events distracted my attention from anguished thoughts about illness, for the routine was: "How is the temperature this morning?... Not very good?... Perhaps it will be better by noon... Let us hope that in the evening it will decrease in order that the night may be calm and the temperature lower in the morning... If it holds five days in succession, the patient will be allowed to make his *Liegekur* on the porch a few hours."

It is impossible to describe my anxiety while awaiting the results of Friday's weighing, the day of doctor's examination. I was not permitted to accompany Arcadie to the consultation room. In a far from enviable state of mind I would tramp up and down my room in uncontrollable fear, wringing my hands, clenching my teeth, imagining I heard the sound of his steps which I could not have heard anyhow because he and the nurse wore rubber slippers.

After what seemed to me an eternity he would arrive... How I endeavored to spy the truth in his face! How I scrutinized the nurse's eyes, afraid he would hide the truth from me if his weight had gone down again. And what relief, what a hopeful outlook if he gained fifty grammes that week! Already we would begin to make plans which, at best, could only materialize in three years' time.

It was like La Fontaine's fable of "Pierrette et le Pot au Lait" when the peasant girl on her way to market dreams that by selling the milk carried in the jug on her head she will get rich by successively buying eggs for hatching, then selling the chickens to buy a calf and so forth. She sees herself already mistress of a farm and full of joy at the idea she jumps... The milk jug smashes to the ground and all Pierrette's dreams disappear!

As a rule men have great difficulty in adapting themselves to the state of illness. My handsome Arcadie was no exception at all to this rule. On the contrary. Spoilt by his family, spoilt by women, having that irresistible *charme slave*, being young, brilliant, until then nothing in his life had stopped him from doing as he pleased. Naturally, the nursing-home routine seemed to him a dreadful prison where no smoking or drinking was allowed. Where were the days of yesteryear when luncheon was accompanied by one or two bottles of champagne?

Now he was forced to lie in bed for months and months without reading, without even a light after the doctor's nightly visit. My room was next to his, but I was not permitted to see him at will, only at certain hours. As I have already recounted, I was obliged to lead the same life as he did. For me also there was early extinction of the lights and early sleep with the doors wide open onto the porch. In that breath-paralyzing cold I was covered with feather quilts three stories high like the old Russian ballet.

It was not easy to fall asleep. The reminiscence of the day passed in anguish and the animal-like fright for tomorrow did not induce sweet dreams. In those moments before sleep I would review all the atrocity of the bygone day and my sleep was heavy with apprehension.

It was half a brutal reality, half a nightmare, in a state between consciousness and lethargy when for hours I seemed to feel something falling on my bed and around my bed... It seemed as if it were raining...

Yes, it must be rain... No, it is too big for rain, it must be hail... Enormous hailstones... One has fallen on my neck. Oh, it hurts!

What a night! I turned on the other side and tried to fall asleep again but soon the nightmare continued its torment.

Hailstones are falling again and again, more and more often. A big one falls on my forehead. I press the sore place and find a small stone in my hand. A stone?

No... I am not asleep! Now I am quite awake in the night! I open my eyes wide. In the blue-black darkness I see nothing, I only feel the pebble in the palm of my hand. Ah, if only I could turn on the light!

I approach Arcadie's door... I put my ear to the keyhole to make sure nothing abnormal is happening there... Silence... Absolute silence... He sleeps. Good!

Nothing else matters now... Brr, how cold the floor is to my bare feet... How freezing the iron on the door lock! Oh, quickly back under my feather beds... My warmed place is already icy without my body to fill it... I shall have to wait for my warmth to reheat the bed. I roll myself up in a ball like a pussy cat. Such cold steam issues from my mouth that I scarcely dare to breathe!

Three minutes longer, only three minutes and I will be warm again... I wait patiently...

What is that? Something falls on my bed... I am sure... There it is again... I put my hand out to try to find the place where I felt the feathers go down. I have it! A stone... Again a stone... Many more are coming now... one after the other... some are falling on the floor with a loud thwack as they hit the uncarpeted wooden parquet...

My eyes begin to get accustomed to the darkness. It is clearer already... I can soon see that the stones come through the porch door. I jump up and go to the door... the stones fly round me... they are being thrown from below. I cross the snowy porch and bend over the icy balustrade... A dark night... Nothing is visible...

Suddenly, I hear a murmur... I strain my ears... Now I can see human shadows on the white carpet of snow. There is no moon, not even any stars to cause a reflection... I am sure this time... it cannot be a hallucination... I hear my name! It seems to rise from a depth of a thousand miles... I cannot be mistaken, for I hear it again and more loudly this time, or perhaps my ears are getting accustomed to the stillness.

Now I hear my husband's voice calling clearly, unmistakably:

"Andzia! Andzia! Open the front door!"

The three shadows below are moving. Now I see Arcadie pantomiming in ballet manner to show me the front door with his left hand while his right gestured to make me understand that I should turn the key in the lock...

My stupefaction was so great that I did not move, I did not feel the frost through the sole protection of my nightgown, I did not even sense the crisp snow under my bare feet. I was quite paralyzed—my mind refused to understand. Was I still in a dream?

Suddenly forgetting myself, my heart realized in a flash that my beloved was standing in the cold snow, in mortal danger to himself. That idea took possession of all my mental and physical capacities. From that second, like a hunted animal, I did everything by instinct—or was it feminine intuition? I ran out of my room, still clad only in my nightgown, found the unlighted staircase, ran down two flights in the dark to the front door. I am sure a mouse could not have made less noise!

I had some difficulty in opening the two doors, the key of the first one turned round and round without any resistance. Finally I realized that the door was not locked and that the key was only there as an accessory.

When, at last I unlocked the second door, the three shadows were already waiting behind it. To make sure that this time the key had worked I opened the door an inch. Fresh snow fell all over me. Satisfied then that Arcadie could enter, that he was safe, I ran back to my bed.

I do not recollect what became of me then. I only remember that the next day I did not get up. No! I did not catch cold. I did not get pneumonia, but something happened deep in my heart and soul. I could not grasp the situation. Had I not been such a strong character I suppose I would have lost my mind that night. I was dumbfounded with shock.

Vaguely I saw Arcadie kneeling at the side of my bed, his tears falling on my hand which he pressed to his face. Was it the next day or many days later? I did not know…

Only his confession slowly brought me back to reason and life…

I shivered and the blood almost stopped in my veins when I learned that often after the nurse's last visit, when everybody slept, he dressed, called on two newly made friends, tuberculars like himself whose weak personality he easily dominated, and leaving the door unlocked went with them to the *Kurhaus* where they drank champagne, smoked cigarettes to their heart's content, breathed the stuffy casino air, played poker and around five o'clock in the morning came back and found their way in through the door they had left unlocked…

Somehow, on the memorable night of the pebbles falling on my bed, they had found that door locked. They could not get in. They knew perfectly well they would be forced to leave immediately if the Chief Doctor of the sanatorium discovered their escapade…

No! My husband's generosity would not permit him to bring such punishment on his companions for his audacity, so he chose that ingenious solution to crush my heart.

He swore on his love for me he would die that instant if I did not forgive him. I was helpless… I could not complain to the doctors or he would no longer be allowed to stay in the sanatorium. I wanted to leave him.

He took out his revolver…
I stayed.

* * *

Months later he did it again. Again he cried. Again he swore on oath. Again I forgave. Again I stayed. Only I gave him my word of honor that if he repeated it once more, I positively would leave him.

Again he did it. And now I knew I had to leave. I could not stay or he would never believe my word any more. I must go! But where? Where? No matter where I went my misery would follow me…

The nearest place I knew of was St. Moritz. I left or rather my body left Davos that afternoon. I was crushed, annihilated, broken more by our parting than by the reason for the separation.

When I arrived at the Palace Hotel in St. Moritz that afternoon, entirely overwhelmed by excessive emotion and in the gloomiest of spirits, I could not even find the necessary energy to open my suitcase. Still in my traveling coat I threw myself on the bed and lay there for hours dry-eyed. I suffered rather from not being able to suffer any more, not being able to feel or move…

A knock sounded. I could hardly say *"Herein"* when the door opened and in stepped Arcadie. As a lioness protects her offspring, the first thought that flashed through my mind was that the climate at St. Moritz was dangerous to his health.

Like a culprit I begged his forgiveness for leaving him alone at Davos. I accepted all his conditions provided he would go back to the sanatorium. But he was—or pretended to be—too tired to travel back that same day without immediate aggravation to his case. Anyhow, there were no more trains that evening. He had to stay over-night… Tomorrow he would leave obediently. Yes but tonight I should let him go down to dinner to see the dance… It would not hurt him,

on the contrary, it would do him lots of good to lead a free life far away from his jail just once again. He would not drink at dinner… The smoky atmosphere of the restaurant would not hurt him. We would take a small table at the side of the ballroom. He promised to go to bed at ten o'clock.
. . . It would make him so happy if I consented to his plan!

Naturally I consented. How could I refuse him anything? The quarrel was forgotten. Love has such healing power…

Arcadie did not leave the next day, for he confessed that the head physician had sent him away from the sanatorium as a black sheep who was contaminating the other inmates in the fold.

That was my first visit to St. Moritz!

MANY, MANY YEARS later I again visited Switzerland.

Working day after day, Christmas, Easter, summer and winter, Sundays as well as week days, the whole year round, I took a day off only when with vocal cords exhausted from overwork the laryngologist forbade me to sing and not even then until the doctor warned that if I disobeyed I might be unable to sing for weeks, months or maybe ever again. The fear of such a possibility made me meek. If I took a week off twice or thrice in fourteen years, it was always because a bad throat precluded the possibility of singing or because my teacher was unable to give me lessons. The last occasion occurred once in February when I had ten days to myself.

Ten days! With some friends, I went for the winter sports to—St. Moritz.

I hardly recognized the place under its white gown of snow. The pre-war atmosphere had also disappeared. One heard only English spoken. Could that ugly barracks be the luxurious Palace Hotel where I had stayed before? (Now I prefer the tiniest room in my home to all the magnificent palaces in the world.) But I was enchanted by the sleigh. Its bells charmed my ears.

I was carefree as a lark. I had come for ten days but already by the end of the second day of jumping in the snow in my ski-costume my cheeks got rosy and my friends were flabbergasted to see such a quick change, which I suppose must have come from a relaxed mind.

What a pity it got dark after four o'clock. But then the pastries were so good at Hanselmann's!

An after-dinner philosophical conversation with Charlie Chaplin easily compensated for the shortness of the day. And I had as a flirt the handsomest man Great Britain has produced! He was so very handsome! And his mentality did not overtire him at all! Wonderful—there was no possibility of getting into a discussion with him. We skated together.

He skated badly but his skating suit was so becoming to him!

Oh, those open air luncheons at the Corviglia Ski-Club way up on the top of the mountains where the proximity of the sky and the entire world below made me forget all the intrigue of the petty social gossip, how invigorating they were! What if the Bourbon Prince was the guest of a rich *parvenue*; if the Duchess of Alba switched her affection from the beautiful Russian girl to the very angular English lady; if there were two rival clans at the Palace to one of which the Baroness Gourgaud, American born Eva Gebhart, belonged—what did it matter to me, when during every meal two thousand feet nearer the Cosmic World I could take off one by one my fur coat, my gloves, the heavy sweater, the scarf, light sweater and finally joyfully present myself clad only in a sleeveless pullover to the rays of the sun, only to end up by having my arms covered with napkins to protect them from being burned by the too-strong rays!

Life was *beautiful!* Could it have been only forty-eight hours before that I had been in Paris slaving in my studio, where for twelve years I had been cut off from a glimpse of the sun by a high house opposite my window? I felt that it must have been a century since I had last been in the snow and also a century since I had been in St. Moritz. It seemed to me that I had arrived so awfully long ago and that my responsibilities were so far, far away.

My thoughts ran on until I began to wonder whether I did not take my singing too seriously and why—life was *so* beautiful! The moon shone divinely through the open window, its light increasing the whiteness of the snow.

What a pity I cannot look at the moon any longer… I feel so sleepy and with such heavenly fatigue… My bed is so comfortable… so *gemütlich*! No, I cannot read the newspapers, I am too drowsy… My eyes refuse to stay open… I will read tomorrow morning what happened in Paris yesterday. I… I… Ahaaaaa

* * *

My third day in St. Moritz! And more beautiful if possible than the previous ones…

My only fear is that Gloria Swanson will give birth to her child here in this inn where the food is so primitive, so good. Oh, those frankfurters—and that coffee!

Patatras, ca y est! La Gloria rises and before she actually moves her stomach protrudes to such an extent that it seems to take the first step. Probably she is going to her carriage to borrow the horses' hay to lay the little Swanson in like an infant Jesus… Not at all, she only fetches her vanity case from the sleigh to powder her nose! Ouf, I am relieved…

How beautiful the English King's cousin, Lady Louis Mountbatten, looks! How beautiful and how British! I wonder if her pearl earrings are genuine? They are enormous! If they are real, they must be very heavy, unbearably heavy. I know by experience how a weight pulls on the lobe of the ear. If they are hollow inside, they must be light and they are so becoming! But can it be that an heiress such as Miss Ashley could wear imitations?

Yes, they are not real. Jacques Cartier, of the London Cartiers—who has a villa at St. Moritz—so informs me. I am so glad for the sake of the English beauty's ears and also because on my return to Paris I will order imitations, too, for traveling purposes.

That night was a gala night. My countrywoman was giving a dinner for thirty. I was to be seated next to Charlie Chaplin. Good! And my English flirt would be opposite me. Good! That way I could see his handsome face and enjoy speaking to Charlie.

That night I had proposed to do something I had not done since my first year in America. I had promised to dance with the Britishier! Why not? Life *is* so beautiful! My black Chantilly gown so becoming!

The telephone rang…

I was ready to descend...

"What? Switzerland calling? But from where? Leysin...? Yes, Madame Walska speaking... Yes, Dr. de Reynier... Yes, Doctor, an urgent, maybe fatal operation...? Tomorrow morning...? Never mind how, I will be there, Doctor!"

I took off my lace gown. Half an hour later I caught the last train...

That was my second visit to St. Moritz.

* * *

No, I am not superstitious, only weak people are. The train stops. Where are we? St. Moritz? Already?

I can see the waving hands of Mrs. Crane and her handsome brother. Charming people! She is so genuinely happy at giving me the chance of my life, the chance of making me forget those teachers who, with wonderful sincerity, tell their pupils: "I am giving you lessons only because I need your money!"

Mrs. Crane is so delighted to bring me into the atmosphere of real Art and into the vibration of a great soul...

On the way to the chalet, while waiting for my hostess to finish some shopping, Mr. Parker, the brother, told me he was curious to find out my opinion of Madame L'Orsa, in whose personality he was disappointed because she did too much talking for a teacher and whose character he could not admire on account of her exaggerated love of—filthy lucre.

Unless the young man was completely mistaken—and I did not feel he was—my opinion of Madame L'Orsa was already formed. For experience had taught me that one cannot learn to sing on theory, on explanations, unless immediate application follows. I also knew that anyone with an extreme interest in money must have entirely the wrong conception of occult teaching. Consequently the Masters of Tibet could *not* have directed me to her!!

As we neared their home I learned that Madame L'Orsa

did not live in her own chalet. Having had a legal quarrel with a neighbor, the poorest kind of peasant, and furious at having lost it—she had decided never again to live in her own house, preferring rather to rent one elsewhere.

Before we reached Silsbasiglia I was certain I had followed only my instinct and not divine intuition! My human mind, only too anxious to have something to cling to, caught at that straw...

In the afternoon I met the fighting lady, took a half-hour lesson for an enormous price and did not change my opinion.

I left by the first express for Galluis...

That was my third visit to St. Moritz! Oh, but Hanselmann's pastries were still very good and my new philosophy could do such wonders!

BACK AT GALLUIS, I no sooner changed my luggage again than I was off in my old Rolls for another experience. How many I had had, only to meet inward disaster which gradually diminished my hopes! Each time my enthusiasm—constantly frozen—was becoming less and less able to revivify and could hardly sustain such great demands.

Tired of traveling, tired of wandering, tired of changing trains or asking the road to the next city, especially tired of hoping against hope, of expectations that were always doomed to disappointment—nevertheless I went to the south of France on my new search, this time however in a mood of complete apathy.

Slowly but surely my enthusiasm became rather anaemic. My hope was veiled more and more every day. This time I almost wanted to be disillusioned in order to cease forever my chimeric hunt for the Unattainable. But I could not have lived a single day in tranquility if I had left anything undone in my search either for the spiritual truth or for the realization of my life's work—my singing. Consequently, without the slightest hesitation and almost sooner than was normally possible, I desired to get out of my mind this new hope, especially as that summer when in despair seeing no light, making no improvement, I made my plans after the Salzburg Festival to fly to India. I wanted to ascertain myself if my destiny did not lie there, especially since Paul Brunton had urged me to see his Master as soon as possible assuring me the Maharishee would only remain on this planet two years longer.[18] He insisted that I should not lose the opportunity of seeing if the great Sage could not raise my vibrations to the highest degree and thus push me toward the right path. Until that summer, however, I had been unwilling to make such a journey in the spirit of getting something. Also my heart, afraid of losing at least one month of singing

---

18 Thank God, Brunton was a false prophet!

lessons, wanted to know in advance what I could get from the contemplation of a saint that would be more valuable to me than my advancement in singing. Intuitively I knew that by going to India in the spirit of expectation with my heart in my studio, I would be unworthy of divine help.

* * *

I was never able to stand uncertainty. Energetic people like myself need immediate action and never give power to hesitation. I wanted to verify immediately the real value of Madame Gilly, this new voice builder, especially as this time her name did not convey much to my imagination. My unsuccessful visit to St. Moritz had taken away my last particle of hope, this omnipotent substance that makes us forget everything past by rejuvenating our forces and enabling us to begin over as if reborn—to start again as pure as angels.

My final experience—for that period at least—was undertaken almost mechanically. I was as spiritless and without any joyous expectations as if going to a notary to sign a necessary paper. It has to be done, that is all.

Even the actual trip to Eauze was not easy or smooth. Radiator trouble caused the car to be stalled for four hours in the middle of the road under a terrific sun without a single tree in the vicinity to use for shelter. Later on the chauffeur took a wrong turn and went two hundred kilometers out of his way. Just like all chauffeurs, he was sure he knew the roads and would not have thought of asking for directions…

We arrived very late in that small town. Naturally the impression was not a favorable one. In the hotel the hostess told me my room was the best of all. Her father and her grandmother, mind you, had lived there!!

Alas! Those ancestors never knew the existence of any elemental hygienic necessity. To make up for the lack of it they hung up an enlarged snapshot of the present owner taken when, as a little girl, she had just made her first communion. It was the size of the entire wall. I was most certainly unappreciative for—in spite of the portrait—I missed my bath after eighteen hours of dusty traveling.

It reminds me of another bath-incident when years ago on a concert tour I arrived in a small town and asked for a bath. The astonished manager repeated the word several times, each time with a different intonation: "Bath? Bath…! Let me think… Bath, oh! Bath! Yes, how stupid of me… Bath… Naturally I know. Certainly we have one. Yes, in the hospital… They use it in severe cases of typhoid fever…"

* * *

But I was not yet at the end of my discomfort, for once in bed with the dust from seven hundred kilometers on me, I had to listen to the loudspeaker across the street, the Friday moving picture performance which boomed until late in the night. Naturally I would have to arrive on a Friday! When your heart is in a negative mood, everything conspires to give it satisfaction…

The next morning upon discovery that I had to wait until five o'clock in the afternoon in order to be allowed to present myself to the fair eyes of Madame Gilly, I made a decision not to stay in that town in that hotel over night but to go back to Galluis immediately after my trial lesson. I preferred to drive all night—all my life if necessary—anything rather than spend a second night in the heavy atmosphere of that provincial place, anything rather than to be bitten again by those funny little things I could not even call mosquitoes in the risk of insulting a comparatively noble insect who gives fair warning of its approach with the bravery of Alexander the Great who shouted to the enemy: "I am coming to fight you, defend yourselves!" But the tiny army of those gnome flies was more cunning than grand. They were so miserably small that when I inadvertently squashed one and looked for the corpus delicti, nothing but a bit of dust remained on my fingers, for they did not even draw enough blood to be visible. I imagined that they enjoyed hurting for the pure sadistic pleasure of it. And it made me feel that if I could possibly love my wonderful Galluis still more it would be because in the many years I have been there and in spite of a small pond, I have never made the acquaintance of a single mosquito.

The fact that my mind was so absorbed with thoughts of insects only proves how hopeless and uninspired I was by the prospective meeting with the new teacher. To me the fact that I was complaining about the lack of comfort had a significant meaning, for usually I can easily accommodate myself to anything, nothing or everything quite naturally, even to the point of being able to ignore the proverbial fly in the soup…

* * *

At five o'clock I shook hands with Madame Gilly. We drank tea. Afterwards I sang. Finally she gave me the first indications of her method. In amazement I recognized my abstract thoughts about singing materializing in her theories—I actually saw the reflection of my intuition in her explanations. I knew… I recognized the hand of Destiny…

* * *

I took calmly the new situation facing me. I took calmly my finding what I had been seeking for twenty years, seeking unconsciously—unless it was the automatic gesture of seeking and for conscience's sake—who knows?—lately even awaiting the opportunity to find a flamboyant indication that all the efforts of those long years were based on a wrong or imaginary foundation. I had been waiting to find out that the whole world was perhaps right to think that I was not meant to be a singer. I was waiting for some concrete indication, begging my soul to give me proof that I was wrong, that I had taken the wrong path, that I had played the wrong cards. I wanted the freedom to dispose of my destiny, to be given some other way to express myself—

if it were not too late—to be given an opportunity to free myself of that self-imposed obligation in order to be able to travel, to visit India's sages, Tibet's lamas, Egypt's pyramids, China's old civilization and birthplace of Confucius, California's philosophers, Mexico's excavations, Rios de Janeiro's port, not to mention all the music and drama festivals, inspiring exhibitions, Faith Congresses, fantastic jubilees of Hindu potentates, Seville's Holy Week celebration, Oberammergau's "Passion," scientific and literary lectures and so many other places and things full of interest and educational value. Those were the things I could enjoy fully and use to develop and enlarge my outlook, if my heart had been free from the slavery of a morning and evening lesson, if I had had time. My potentialities and possibilities for appreciation were unlimited.

I did not feel exuberantly happy when I realized that the focal point of my thoughts, my so greatly desired goal was almost visible to me and now within my reach. I felt that what my heart craved for and was no longer awaiting had actually materialized in the abstract—a thing most difficult to attain.

I ought to have recognized that that memorable Saturday meeting with Madame Gilly was the most important day of my life. Instead, I only felt surprised. I knew I was happy but I did not feel it. I did not feel the happiness running through my veins, for happiness—like all real things—is calm. Therefore I did not recognize it at once. My astonishment was too great to understand that Destiny was granting the long-awaited desire of my heart! And the realization of this tremendous gift came so naturally, so simply and so unexpectedly after so many cruel trials that my mind could not grasp its full significance.

For many months I did not dare to consider my future, stupefied as I was by the new reality of the fact that fundamentally I had won. WON! I had already won for the most difficult conquest is one won in our mind. Trained severely by incessant handicaps worthy of a Hercules' shoulders, my courage had to be gigantic, as a fortitude of lesser quality could not have stood those continual burdens. Now my soul, unaccustomed to receiving, did not know how to react and feel blessed. Even under the best conditions nothing came easily to me. Everything I got—and I got much—I obtained when it was already too late, when I had outgrown the desire for it or most often when I realized that it was not worth the price paid. Looking back now, I can see that although I seemed to be the loser, I was actually the winner, for the real benefit comes from the effort we put into any of our enterprises.

My human mind was first to grasp the latest development of my inner life, but my heart did not know how to respond to nature's generosity. What a curious sensation it was not to have the sword of Damocles over my head any longer! The acknowledgment of that extraordinary event filled my entire being during the first two weeks of my lessons while at Eauze, which I loved—including mosquitoes.

Feeling that blissful peace both mentally and physically, I did not envisage at all what it could mean to the future of my spiritual life for already then I inhabited a plane where time had no existence. I would probably not have realized what then seemed to me my curious indifference instead of exalted enthusiasm if, back in Paris and studying with Madame Gilly's daughter, as Madame Gilly was remaining longer at her summer home, while singing Beethoven's "*Ich liebe dich*" I had not understood for the first time since the beginning of all my studies what immeasurable happiness one can get by materializing out of one's mind tones only dreamt about and only heard in space as the echo of their existence in infinity until that time... Tones that materialized to the sense of hearing but actually dematerialized by melting into one cosmic vibration...

Not handicapped by technique that day, my soul was momentarily free from its bodily imprisonment and it let my spirit sing through me without the rebellious matter but by communicating directly with illimitable space...

A tremendous effort was necessary to control my humble desire to kneel and pray. I could not do so in the presence of my teacher...

When the door was closed behind me, I could not take another step—the feeling of immense non-earthly existence so paralyzed all my physical functions.

I could only repeat: "Oh God! Oh God!" and had only just enough presence of mind to remember that my teacher expected to leave immediately after my departure. Not wishing her to find me where she had left me, I went to seek the absolute and now indispensable privacy of my car. But how unusual! My car was not there, and I was not able to concentrate my thoughts on the next step to take. I missed the car. That was all!

In that state of beatitude I did not belong to the environment of the street... I felt I must go elsewhere... Like an infant or a stranger, I was hopeless on the sidewalk with such a vision of unearthly happiness in my eyes that I had tremendous difficulty in keeping them open. When we are happy, we close our eyes because the blissful feeling coming from inside us is all that matters, exterior things have no value.

I could not understand what had happened to my chauffeur. What time was it? How long had I been upstairs? How could time measure any part of the eternity of bliss?

I put my music case down in the middle of the sidewalk in front of me and waited, unable to do anything else... I saw a radio shop next door. I went in. I asked the time but my voice disobeyed me... People looked at me curiously... Again I struggled to repeat my question. I heard funny words coming out of my mouth... I heard them as if from a great way off, as if that voice did not belong to me.

Someone told me the time. I thanked him, but my words sounded so unnameable, so distant, that he certainly must have thought me ungracious indeed.

Again I found myself in the street…

A quarter past four! How could that be? I told my chauffeur to be here at a quarter past four and he is always ahead of the time set by as much as fifteen minutes… But everything was quite vague to my usually precise mind, entirely contrary to my habitual quicksilver way of thinking. All I sensed was that I could not trust my dimmed human judgment. Unable to make a decision, I continued to stand in front of the house with an empty brain as all my vital and positive forces had gone to my heart…

How long was I there? I do not recall… Finally I saw the car at a distance. I even had difficulty in recognizing my old Rolls… However, once seated inside it I began to pray. I prayed silently, without words, without destination, without dedication. I know now that the greatest prayer there is is the glorious feeling of happiness—the greatest homage to its Creator… the fulfillment of His desires… the sharing of His feelings… the unity with the Divine Sensation… Divine Substance…

I proceeded to my next appointment at my modiste's. During the whole hour of trying on the newest hats, I graciously accepted all flatteries and all obvious compliments. I saw myself in the mirror—deeply beautiful with the reflection of the glorious inner sunshine. Any hat seemed suitable to the perfection that was in me that day. I could wear none of them later…

With a feeling of immense goodness, I gave those girls the complete satisfaction of thinking that my beauty was due entirely to their creation, that those hats put the translucent light in the blue of my eyes and illuminated the softness around my mouth. In return I allowed them to attribute my highly augmented coloring for the most part to the fresh air of country life and driving in an open car!

I smiled wholeheartedly, smiled at what had always previously been an unbearably irritating *vendeuse* vocabulary. Truly if they had put the ugliest stewpan of a hat on my head—a sacrilege to my sense of beauty under ordinary circumstances—they would not have been able to disturb the glorified peace, the mighty sublimity of my inner being.

I do not recall how I arrived home. A devoted friend, my new disciple, as she insisted on calling herself, met me with the exclamation: "You look eighteen, darling!" Being superstitious, she gave me a four-leaf clover found at the exact hour when she knew I was singing. I later discovered it was not a clover but an ordinary shamrock of which our garden is full. Evidently as long as she thought it was a rare clover, it did not make any difference! I took the tiny leaf and put it aside preciously as I always do, for we should take great care never to laugh sarcastically or even faintly smile at what we think is a foolish idea or an erroneous interpretation of some people's religion. Instead, only when the occasion arises, may we demonstrate that any superstition counteracts faith in God, in the Essential. Often people say: "God will help me" and in the same breath they touch wood without thinking that by doing such a thing they are showing their distrust in God. It is like the girl who surprised a friend by her superstitiousness and when the latter asked her if she were, she answered: "Oh no, my dear, I am not superstitious because it brings bad luck!"

No! Superstition is useless, even at its best. When Polycrates, afraid that he was having too much luck, decided to throw a highly treasured ring into the sea, he found it again the next day at luncheon—inside his fish!

Nowadays scientists are increasingly occupied with vibrations. In these days of radio,[19] of whose powers we are still ignorant, we cannot call everything just blind superstition, for we can no longer ignore the fact that the power of a word or a thought is tremendous. If we think hard enough that a frog's leg will bring us luck, it certainly will. It is not

---

19 It has been noted in England that certain plants have lost their aroma since radio has become so widespread.

the leg itself however but the faith we put in it that works the miracle. Still the frog's leg brought good luck to human progress when used in the experiments which Galvani made and which were instrumental in the discovery of electricity.

The further the goal, the higher one must aim.
— FERDINAND DE LESSEPS

The fact of finding in Madame Gilly's method the revelation of my inner abstract ideas did not make all my miseries disappear instantly. By all means, no! Still more disheartening and bitter disappointments, even some doubts, treacherously awaited me around the corner.

But from that decisive moment of my life I kept going forward continually, even if obliged to climb extremely sharp mountain peaks. Hard work, severe trials, even dramatically gloomy moments were quite bearable now that I could see their constructive value. The fact that I had found myself, that I knew I was right, that I was assured the work of my life was singing and that it was my mission to express myself through my voice—all that put heavenly wings to my formerly earth-bound being and, no matter how discouraging some moments were, I never again started downwards in my inspirational line.

I did not always feel so highly elevated or so wholeheartedly happy. Sometimes my inspiration was lower and my blissful state was less demonstrable. But never, never in recent years have I fallen below my acquired equilibrium. I have never gone back below the line to sorrow, tears and despair. I have never felt sad since! I have never again felt thoroughly miserable. Never! And I never shall! *For now I know!*

Now I think, feel and act on and from that higher plane where the negative has no existence, where misery and suffering are powerless, where everything is comprehensible and therefore forgivable and forgettable, where there is the actual image of God's Justice, Wisdom, Law, Goodness and not the humanly distorted and fallible idea of Him.

Yes, finding my true spiritual path—which I was all those

years unconsciously nourishing, nursing—I was not yet at the gate of deliverance which neighbors on Heaven and the doors of Shambalah were still hermetically closed and far from me. Fortunately Wisdom generally allows us not to perceive our future in order that we may not become discouraged and lose our strength but can still firmly advance and persevere. Even with the feeling of Eden in me, there was no thornless road before me nor a quick one—contrary to my imagination, for I had thought that after conquering Evil in the abstract, there could be no obstacle in my path.

I even began to wonder and ponder when, a few months later, the actual improvement I had expected did not come. I began asking myself why it should take longer to enslave matter than to enter the Kingdom of Limitless Comprehension? Why in Madame Gilly's studio, for instance, young girls with little knowledge and practically no experience taking only a half-hour lesson a day—often skipping even some of those—were impudently advancing further in a year than I did? I, the legendary worker, pointed out as the exemplary student who never missed a lesson, the phenomenon who after singing four hours a day was best at the end of that time and could sing better still if allowed to continue longer...

Now I know that Destiny (Karma) is not only the Hindu word for something unproved to our conception, something abstractive, the comprehension of which is only accorded to a few sages, something that ancient philosophy speaks about only when explaining certain justifications for our present miseries. Besides, Karma is also the actual paying here below for our lack of knowledge.

Man-made law presumes that no one is supposed to be ignorant of the law. The same thing is true of Divine Law, for, having thought, felt and done wrongly for many scores of years, I have to pay for it now. Even if I *know* that it is easy to go to Pittsburgh, I still have to know when to leave the house, when to take the taxi, what time the train leaves and from what station and so forth…

During my studies with my new teacher those three years—not the three months I had expected to be all I would need in the belief that gods do not need any time, that Idea cannot be timed, that Infinite cannot be late—I had to pay to undo and forget all I had practiced in previous years. Only after that period did the sun begin to pierce the cloudy mist of this or that technique. And even then its light was rare and timid, appearing only at very long intervals to give a glimpse of *what* it could be when it *would be*—*if* it ever would be… That foresight, however, was enough to give encouragement, to tempt, enrich, overwhelm and enhance my work to the utmost.

Sometimes Destiny—perceiving that I was on the wrong track, on the track originating from human deduction and consequently based on the wrong foundation—in order to make me advance in the right direction, would generously take away the control over my voice for weeks.

There were also times when I almost seemed to be at my goal, when I progressed so far that I felt I might only need a matter of three months or so to reach the desired heights to which my life had been dedicated. At just such a moment it would happen that during a certain lesson I would sing so much better than my most daring expectation, producing such a glorious sound or two that the standard of my perfection rose and I was no longer satisfied with yesterday's conception of pure tone. And again I kept striving to better myself in order to touch that heaven which I was only allowed to glimpse at rare intervals because I was not yet sufficiently deserving. But in those furtive moments I walked on clouds, on a level with Perfect Harmony, Heavenly Music and Divine Rhythm.

I would be sleepless at night from the paradise-like feeling in me, but the spirit did not need rest and my body was so exalted and light that I did not feel its burden. The next day's lesson, however, would awaken me from my flight to the Kingdom of Sublime Sound, for my tone stubbornly would remain in my throat and all divine assistance seemed to have disappeared and deserted me…

What a greatness if you are able to understand fully Destiny's process of helping you and can therefore take all that is given to you only as incentive to strive higher and higher! No hardship is then unbearable. Fullhearted gratefulness and tremendous joy fill your being, leaving no room however small for complaint. What unspeakable joy! The humble tears of thankfulness fill your soul…

"Goodness! I thank Thee for all Thy bounty!"

But before achieving that moment of resignation, of absolute faith in the belief "Thy will be done," I had to strive patiently, to strive heroically, in order to make a step towards the perfection. Unceasingly I had to tear every one of my notes away from engrossing matter. How I fought that rebellious enemy during hours and hours! But the stubborn vowels had to be conquered! After winning one terrific battle, the fruits of which enabled me to give freedom to the vowels *I* or *E*, I still had to persevere to free *O* from its prison and return to the most difficult, a simple *A*. It was a merciless battle. It was a dreadful fight in which with bulldog-like tenacity I would not give up until I had conquered by inhuman effort the blood-soaked ground. Step by step I went and I would go on until all peripheries of my mind would surrender, until Pure Spirit solely would reign.

The ideal of existence is the realization of youth's dream at a ripe age.

— GOETHE

IN MY ASSOCIATION with many different mystically minded persons more than once I was told—in answer to my wondering about the strange difficulty I encountered in my vocal study—of a possibility of being able to heal through my voice. Suffering, and with reason, from an inferiority complex rather than from too much self-assurance, with the world-wide mocking reputation of the sweetness of my voice, with a nickname of "Phantom of the Opera" and with such newspaper reports as "No amount of McCormick's millions could force the people to hear his wife sing"—I certainly ignored the ironical prediction that I, of all people, should be able to heal with my voice, famous for its non-existence and lack of purity.

Once I also was told by an elderly American philosopher-astronomer that all over the world there were a few souls preparing to unite Heaven and Earth, so to speak, through the medium of their voices (which after all is not such a miracle since the advent of radio—the greatest miracle of all!) and that probably I was one of the select; but in order to become a worthy instrument for such an elevated mission I would have to suffer to purify my soul—hence my cruel difficulties.

I received all such predictions with extreme skepticism. When however the revelation of my life and its meaning came to me, I began to understand why the mystics paid attention to my voice. When I say *mystic*, I want to emphasize the fact that a mystic is not—in my comprehension and contrary to general belief—a fortune-teller, a psychic medium who gives you the illusion of speaking with your departed beloved ones, or a person associated with ghosts, spooks or any other unhealthy low manifestation. In a word, a mystic is not a man upon whom you cannot rely because he is "in the moon"—to say the least…

For years I myself did not differentiate between the above-mentioned freaks of nature and a real mystic. That very lack of true knowledge made my life miserable, for I was reduced to cruel disappointments and to such an extent that sometimes I even doubted the existence of God. All that thanks to a hundred morally weak often unbalanced minds and if not unbalanced at least shamefully commercializing human credulity!

No! A mystic is the opposite of a "man in the moon" because he implicitly obeys a great Universal Law. The Law that is in the making of the world, the Law of wonderful perfection, of absolute precision, of divine co-ordination, the Law that governs the Universe, that makes the sun rise each morning and predicts the moon's eclipse scores of years in advance, timing it precisely to the second, the Law that gives life and youth to all nature in the Spring and in the Autumn makes the birds choose the same day to migrate to warmer climates.

That is the Law which a mystic obeys. So do we all, but the average person takes it for granted that day comes after night, summer after winter, while a mystic consciously realizes the spiritual process of it and applies that Law to his everyday living.

Obeying that great Law—still unconsciously so—I imagined in the beginning at least that if ever I should be blessed with the God-given privilege of helping my fellow man, it would not be through a generally known form of healing, such as the relieving of pain through the touch—but rather by raising the consciousness of the masses to a higher degree through the medium of my voice and not in any unnatural psychic way but only in the comprehensible manner by which I myself so often received a great inspiration which helped me fight my path to the great altitude.

We hardly can go forward without an uplifting example to inspire us. When still quite ignorant and without any realization about the grandeur of life, even in my early youth I could feel deeply beauty, nobility of soul, heroism and expression of every art. When I saw the great Duse, when I listened to Toscanini's masterly interpretation of Beethoven's grandiose symphonies, when I was transported by "Parsifal" to the higher spheres, when Mozart's music put so much joy into my heart, when certain voices—especially those heard during summer festivals in cathedrals as in Salsburg and Lucerne—had lost their individual identity and melted into one with my vibrations, then my spirit rose as if my soul had departed my body and, enlightened, dissolved into one with the Infinite. For hours after such experiences I could scarcely regain possession of my senses and could hardly walk as far as my waiting car; my voice would desert me[20] and even ten years later I could feel that same inspiration and be a better person because of reviving those elevated instants. For it would make me see instantaneously the pettiness and unimportance of the fact that the new butler had radical ideas or that the piano tuner could only come the following week. My soul could rise immediately above those details that a few seconds before had threatened to poison the peace of the day and which, if repeated often enough, could ruin my whole life or ultimately induce a gangrene which could no longer be helped by great inspiration.

Yes I was skeptical. Still I had fervently prayed that over-generous Destiny might grace me with the power to inspire others and raise their vibrations above the humanly fallible sphere of thinking, feeling and doing, just as I was inspired and healed myself.

Yes, I was skeptical. Still what happened later made me think there was perhaps something in the prediction of

---

20 Gentlemen of the press would cleverly report that it is a well known and not occasional fact.

my healing power in a direct way, though I was entirely unaware of it, even much astonished when, on putting my hand on a sore spot, the afflicted person most surprisingly exclaimed: "Oh, my pain is gone! Entirely gone!"

Naturally I thought it was coincidence. I also took it for granted that it was coincidence when once or twice over the long distance telephone the sound of my voice instantly stopped a terrific headache in the other person. But when my prayers miraculously restored the sight to an eye which had been blind for five years, I began to wonder if my skepticism was entirely justified and if I should pay more attention to those predictions about having healing power...

I thought that if such were actually to be my fate, I would work still harder on my spiritual development in the knowledge of what a heaven would open before me! If it were God's will, what a blessing would be mine!

From that moment on I was much more careful with myself. I began to pay more attention to my health. In the past when flying in private planes I had ignored warnings of bad weather. Now I would not even allow my chauffeur to speed. I considered that perhaps a precious possession had been put in my trust for which one day I might be called to account.

Oh, no! I could not take a chance now. Life is too dear to me now. I have so much to do yet. I have scarcely started and I must now take care of my physical body that previously I ignored and despised as being vulgar matter. It must last till my work is over, it must be beautiful in order to give birth to Beauty, it must be full of inspiration in order to attract inspiration, as like attracts like.

* * *

If I do not attain success—as people understand it—in my chosen field of singing or if Manly Hall's predictions were right—and I do not doubt the stars but the fallible human interpretation of them—I would still not be a failure according to my conception of Life. If we are at one with the Cosmic World, we cannot fail, for the great Universe cannot fail, only its inhabitants are fallible. The sky has never fallen on top of our heads, only poorly constructed airplanes piloted by aviators with humanly fallible mentalities. If I should be unable to express myself through my voice, it would only mean that my mission lies elsewhere and my search in the field of singing was only a part of the process of preparing my soul for something bigger.

"Thy will be done. For only things coming through Thee can give me peace, the only lasting bliss…"

My vocal future—which no longer causes me any anxiety since I live no more in yesterday's sorrows or tomorrow's hopes but in today's beneficial present—that future will show if a writer in, I think it was "Town Topics," was prophetic when he said: "If there are any so foolish as to think that because of several rebuffs by critical audiences Mme. Walska will be deterred from pursuing her musical career, they show very conclusively that they are decidedly unfamiliar with the caliber of the lady's courage. Besides, is it not recorded in musical annals that the celebrated Jenny Lind was once hissed off the stage? And did not the Swedish Nightingale become one of the greatest divas of her time? Such is the truth and with such a precedent what may not Mme. Walska expect?"

Often friends were surprised that I was unwilling to do lesser things in the musical field, such as musical comedy, where my personality would show off to advantage and no one would expect operatic singing quality. Or they advised me to go on the concert platform wearing my wonderful costumes and marvelous jewels with a repertoire of old songs no longer heard nowadays and thus avoid unfavorable comparison with so-called real singers. Some wanted me to give my own operas and take some small parts in them. But those who begged me to sing at home for a few friends, friends who sincerely liked me, understood me and would therefore be indulgent, *those* exasperated me most!!

Understand me? Oh no they never could! They did not even guess what a great dream lived in me and what a glorious urge possessed me! They could not even imagine that if all the doors of all the operas in the world were wide open to me, I would not take advantage of it if I felt that I could not do it up to my standard of singing. I could not face any public if I was unworthy to sing for that great Army of Peace—the Salvation Army, for the public hospitals, for the inmates of Sing Sing, especially for lifers—because to them must be given only the nearest to perfection in order that pure tones may make them realize their soul's existence and the eternal freedom of their soul. Although in prison cells, they could work in their retirement for the liberation of their timeless minds; they could achieve more than they might in the unreal and so-called free world. If my singing could succeed in awakening such souls to the great reality, I would indeed then have done something inspiring.

It would certainly be much easier to give pleasure to those who seek only pleasure, as the majority of the opera audiences do—while those miserable bed-ridden or cell-locked souls need much more. They need the uplifting message through which Light might be brought to their Inner Beings. The greatest fulfillment any soul may desire is to help his fellow man in realizing Divinity in him, for we can advance only by passing to others what was already unfolded to us. It does not make any difference through what channel that knowledge is given as long as we can be instrumental in making another soul recognize the Reality. That is bliss, supreme bliss!!

> *He who seriously wants to reach the goal runs little risk of missing the right road; the conscience usually speaks fairly distinctly to whoever wishes to listen to it.*
>
> — VINET

BEFORE I ATTAINED the stable realization that all knowledge is in us—"Ask and ye shall receive"—when I would find myself in doubt, I feverishly wished that I might be in America in order to question that great soul, L. In moments of extreme depression, when blind faith deserted my mind, I would write to him begging for guidance. The actual answer, however, always came from my inner being during the process of writing to him or while awaiting his word of enlightenment. Moreover each time after sending such a letter I felt appeased for never could I hold back anything from one who possessed all my innermost thoughts. I could feel released and happy only when in complete communion with that soul…

When my letter was on its way, new hope immediately sprang up to chase away in part the blackness in me as I began to wonder when I might expect an answer. And yet my heart knew that L. taught me chiefly by making me solve my problems for myself, sure that I could do it. I would put the letter on the boat-train twenty-four hours before the sailing of the "Normandie" and immediately I would begin to calculate: five days to cross the ocean… one or two days from New York to Chicago… his answer leaving Chicago three days later… a week later in the morning mail at Galluis could bring me his illuminating message…

Still I was not at all disappointed when that much awaited letter did not come on the first possible day. A week later however the thoughts culminated in their maximum, and I felt L.'s presence so acutely that I craved to cable him a few words just to get in contact with his vibrations. But I did not dare monopolize too much of his valuable time with my persistent correspondence.

After tremendous expectation followed by a phase of apathetic indifference I began to feel *detachment,* an entirely new sensation to my exuberant nature. But in it I found myself much more at peace than in my normal state for I always suffered from over-intensity. The expectation of his answer became less vital. Already I could receive my American mail without experiencing a pang in the heart at not perceiving the familiar long envelope.

Since I was continuing my vocal studies with Madame Gilly, the greater part of my depression came from my inability to forsake those lessons as yet and be able to go to the States where I always felt I was breathing the same air that was in my lungs and whose natural vibration responded directly to my own vibration. I suffered from my inability to be in New York, because there I could easily fly to Chicago or telephone to L. asking him about some questions burning my soul. I also was sad missing all musical manifestations of the winter season as well as my study with that wonderful musician, Frank LaForge. So many operas and concerts went by without me! As I read American newspapers in France two weeks later it caused me sadness to think that yesterday Lotte Lehmann sang or that Marion Anderson was scheduled for the following week, that Bagby's Morning Musicales had started, that Elizabeth Schuman was to interpret some Strauss songs, that Flagstad was opening the Metropolitan Opera season, that Lily Pons would sing Rosina in "Barbiere di Seviglia" there for the first time, that "Fidelio" and "Rosenkavalier" were scheduled for the following month and, above all, that Toscanini was starting his broadcasts. Such an array of great artists and I not there to hear them! And I could not be there because of my daily ferocious battle with matter!

Sure that I would be able to control my rebellious muscles and master my voice, I kept expecting to go to my adopted country from one month to the next, postponing my sailing from September to Christmas, then to Easter, then again to September, November, surely by New Years and so on for three very long years.

* * *

Writing to L. about the problems of my soul helped me feel less keenly the division of my spiritual substance from him whom I considered my soul's guide and in the days that followed to feel less acutely the lack of America's vivifying *Prana* and purity of heart of which great possession that young country is unaware. I knew that between our souls there could be no separation and therefore there was no need to feel the distance and yet when I did not receive from L. an answer for months and months or even years, as happened later, still I could not refrain from cabling him from time to time a full-moon greeting. Oh, without expecting an answer! Besides—and on several occasions—I communicated with him directly without any wireless. Often it would happen that, while I was writing and questioning him about some form of Truth, most strangely I received his answer dated the same day I was writing him. Also many times I would merely be thinking how would he advise me to react on such or such problem when instantly I had his mental instructions as if I had just questioned him audibly and then there was the answer.

Without letters I knew, too, that during those white full-moon nights our spirit met around my friendly moon. I had only to turn off the electric light and instantly I was flooded by the rays of the lunar sun and could feel the presence of L.'s great soul more easily than if he had been in the room in the flesh as such a visit would have meant an earthly reality with its petty conventions. However, I did not indulge much in such reveries, strong in the knowledge that my salvation lay in concrete work. Returning from Paris daily after six, dead tired from the great effort I had expended during four hours of singing, I would close my eyes and try to recuperate my exhausted mental forces by being one with the Infinite, a feeling which I could not manage to achieve with open eyes while sending a smile to the moon. I also would never have enough time to write, read and study if I looked through the open window as much as I would have loved to do at those radiant rays on the green grass below my room.

Working all day—and my day now starts at six in the morning—I am fresh to the last moment, not conscious even of bodily demands for rest. But at seven, when the last phrase is sung and the door closes behind me, I immediately begin to feel the terrific weight that has resulted from standing still during all those hours while undergoing severe mental tension. My feet hardly carry me to the car and so blank is my mind that not a single thought can enter it. An hour later, arriving at Galluis mentally more in equilibrium but often scarcely able to get out of the car unaided—staggering like a drunkard—I find myself in my room *At Last*! I fall on the bed like a rag. Twenty minutes later my coffee almost restores me to my normal vitality.

Then comes the best part of my day. I am happy, quite undisturbed, for I have warned my household that unless the house is on fire neither maid, secretary or housekeeper may enter my room on any pretext whatsoever. Over the air comes Mozart's "Don Juan." My inspiration runs high... Through the open windows there is no more noise from the early-to-bed village... In November there are no more nightly reunions of colorless butterflies around the lamp over my head... Sometimes an ugly bat enters my room by misadventure and knocks its repulsive body against the ceiling, blinded by the lights, until I turn them off to give the flying mouse a chance to find its way out into the obscurity that is its kingdom.

Great, great beneficial silence... I hear the noise of my pencil touching the paper. My soul is conscious of an immense infinity encircling me.

What stillness! The slightest vibration, the tiniest evidence of life is perceivable, almost visible. The minutest touch at the window pane sounds like the impact of a tremendous force and almost shocks the stillness of my ears... It must be a radio parasite... Here it comes again, that tiny beating against the same window... Now I sense it under the right pane of glass. I look straight at the spot whence the imperceptible knocking seems to come. Nothing! I thought so. Back to my writing...

But there it starts again, much stronger this time. There cannot be a mistake. I sit up in bed... I look intently at the glass... Distinctly I hear the tapping like an S.O.S., like a Wall Street ticker, like a Morse signal. Still I see nothing.

Oh, yes, now I do... A poor bird is trying to come in, beating desperately against the glass to find the warmth of the artificial sun within my room. I want to let it in, but as the window-sill is covered with a radio, books and manuscripts, while I was taking them away my bird has disappeared...

The image of bygone years in Westhampton flashed through my mind of the time Dr. Fraenkel tried to catch a baby bird still unable to fly without its mama's assistance. Until that day Dr. Fraenkel had only known of nature's expression from Maeterlinck's "Life of the Bees," Jean Fabre's "Life of the Insects" and other similar books. Although near sixty, that was his first actual contact with our tinier brotherhood. Almost by a professional second nature he could not see one of God's creatures in distress without trying to help. Being Nature's child, as Dr. Fraenkel called me, I advised him to leave the bird alone, knowing that human presence would only prevent the mother from joining her baby. I further explained to the great man that the little bird was not the only one ever to take his first step unaided in this big world. No use! Dr. Fraenkel could not follow my advice. He must help the little one. As he got nearer and nearer to the bird, it hopped farther and farther away... And so the game continued till they neared the garden's edge. The Doctor was now quite sure he would catch the orphan, as there seemed no further place for it to jump from him.

The last bush... Slowly... slowly... silently he stretches his hand towards the frightened and poorly feathered sparrow now leaning against the wooden enclosure separating it from the road. A last movement and the Doctor closes his hand on—emptiness as the bird in panic jumps over the fence and tremblingly finds itself in the street... A car approaches... The bird hops still farther from his enemy, Dr. Fraenkel, and into the path of the car... The car passes... The bird lies dead...

For years afterward, Dr. Fraenkel would tell that story to prove his belief that one should not interfere with God's work.

Like a motion-picture flashback, that scene came to my memory. I started to think what I could have done to help the bird outside my window even if I had caught it. The beating of its heart would only have put anxiety into mine. It would certainly have tried to hide under my bed or fly away through one of the two other open windows. It was gone now, anyhow! The books, radio and manuscripts went back into their places. But for days the little incident made a strong impression on me.

I could not help thinking that a soul in distress had knocked against my window and I had not let it in. It was simply an unbearable thought. After all, I would not have needed to catch it. But not to have opened the window, not to have answered a desperate call, how could I have done it? How could I have been guilty of such disharmony? My reason tried to exonerate me by recalling Dr. Fraenkel's case and the fact that there were nests right over the window from which the baby bird probably had jumped to answer the attraction of the illusionary heat, not differentiating between electric light and sunshine. And then seeing its mistake it probably got back safely into the nest again.

The next day I looked under my window... I found nothing... And yet my heart was oppressed. Two days later, when I again heard the familiar noise, I jumped to open the window so quickly that I broke an old Venetian crystal *bénitier* hanging on the wall. In a second the books were on the floor, on the bed, everywhere and while holding my radio with one hand I opened wide the other half of the window. Too late... The bird was gone... Gone forever that time... It never came back. But because I was able to open the window the second time, I felt better.

Still that tiny incident made my soul heavier. I felt alone in the world... I particularly felt a gap in my communion with L.'s spirit, the only pure spirit I knew at that time. My being, lonely in this big universe, felt that my soul at the moment of my death, cutting the silver thread that unites me with my body, would experience the same feeling although probably to a greater degree and then in its immensity it would be bearable. But now... But here... Still in this world, if not of it, I had difficulty in breathing freely. I knew that something had happened to me, that something had happened to my inner being, as though I was passing through some endless labyrinth into the light... Yes, into the light...

But what had happened to me? And what had happened to L.? I no longer felt in touch with his vibration. Oh, by the way, that reminds me that I never heard from him... Two months of silence... My thoughts began to wonder if he was not ill. He spoke about taking some treatments... But how could I imagine such a great spirit being ill? Impossible! How could I entertain such a negative thought even for a second only?

Vainly I tried to chase this idea from my mind... Soon it became a certitude. He must be ill! And unable to control my impression I cabled him: "Please, please let me know how you are?"

I will have the answer tomorrow...

But already the next day I knew there would be no answer. With that certainty in my heart, I still kept asking several times a day if there were not a cable for me. It was rather a mechanical question. I did not even listen to the answer. I knew...

A greater and greater emptiness filled my soul... I was dazed. The day he should have received my anxious cable I could not get hold of myself at midday meditation. My face was bathed in tears... It was impossible to concentrate. I tried to pronounce the usually calming and quieting words... The sounds stuck in my throat. I looked at the picture of his Lord but instead of the usual inspiration shining from it, it only heightened the poisonous idea that it was just a photographic portrait, meaningless now, since I could not feel any connection with L. Everything that was in the picture was the vibration of *his* soul, *his* years of devotion that had left a divinely loving imprint on the pasteboard... Now I knew he was gone, gone forever from this planet... How could it be possible?

No, he could not have left me when at last I had found him after such a long life of searching for Truth, for Spiritual Knowledge, when at long last I had discovered—and thanks to him—the reason for my Being. My inner life—only two months old—and already shattered? Impossible!

I made superhuman efforts to change the thread of my thoughts, but persistently they came back. I asked myself why I felt so sure. Why this certitude? Perhaps he had merely gone on a silent retreat as he had done the summer before when, in order to help his sick friend, he went to California without saying in advance that he would be in absolute silence for many, many months. About that fact I only learned casually and later, much later...

Certainly he had done the same thing again... Yes but without letting me know? That seemed impossible! Impossible! Why impossible? He knows—I told him so—that now, thanks to him, I had found myself and this time forever.

I tried to persuade myself that he had left for Chicago probably, for Pittsburgh or some other city in God's service. Certainly… But the bird in distress at my window? But the feeling of disconnection with his spirit? No, he is no more… And I suffered so much because I had been unable to go to America nearer to his healing vibration. And now he is no more… The ways of God are strange indeed! What will become of me? I cannot see clearly, I am too dazed… It is so unexpected…

A radio transmission of Moussorgsky's music only fixed more deeply in my heart the fatalistic Slavic assurance that he no longer is…

Before me rose the vision of the Dutch woman crying that day we left Chicago when the train started to move and we could no longer see L., but his parting words kept ringing in my ears:

"The French say 'Partir c'est mourir un peu!' "

"Why do you cry, dear?" I asked my companion.

"I cannot but think I never will see him again. Blessed heart, soon he will no more be here!"

At that time I had protested her pessimistic prediction. Now it was different… Still I kept saying to myself that he could not leave me, that he *must* stay, we *must* collaborate, he must answer and explain and enlighten my remaining doubts. He *must*! Then, too, the realization came over me that I had not seen him since my soul truly recognized him. He could not go. He could not leave me lest I should again feel as I had in the destructive period of my life! Like the bird at Westhampton, I could not yet fly by myself. My keen intelligence would handicap my flight to the stratosphere. My already highly developed intellectuality and mental erudition would burn up my soul, inch by inch. *I must see him if only once more!* Those were the very words he had used when insisting on visiting me in New York…

I felt I must have him elucidate so many obscure questions which had crowded into my mind and were filtering down into my heart. He *must* explain to me why he wore glasses. He *must* tell me if his silence saved his friend. He *must* tell me why he had remained in the priesthood until three years ago. He *must* offer me the opportunity of doing something, not for him but through him, thanks to him. He *must* give me a chance to be useful. He had opened such enormous vistas to my eyes that I wanted more. I wanted the fulfillment of those fugitive visions. I wanted stability, fixity, the rock-like feeling of KNOWING!!!

He could not be taken from me now, for now it was not for myself that I wanted him. For myself I was quite satisfied with the idea that such a soul existed. But I must see him forthwith. I must see him once more on this earth! Only once more and then God's will be done!

* * *

In my inner agony I was unable to detach myself from those presentiments while my imagination kept building, building. It galloped away with me and overran my reason…

During those deadly days my moments of revolt were exasperating but the hour came one night when submissively I said: "Thy will be done about L., O God, Thine and not mine. Thy will… Thy… Yes, if it is Thy will that I should never see him again, even if he is alive, if it is Thy will that I should already stand on my own feet, if for this reason Thou sendest me this trial—I accept it. Thy will be done… Like everything else, I accept. I will no longer suffer at staying here and working and will count the months no more until I go back to America… I pray only for more serenity, for more peace, peace, peace… I pray for the peace of my soul…"

* * *

Why, O Mighty Goodness, are you sending me Baba at this moment? Is it a coincidence? Is it on purpose as everything else Thou doest? I never felt great holiness about Baba. Everyone, except those few hysterical women followers of his, has made fun of him.

O God, Thy will be done… I only pray to Thee, O Almighty, to give me inspiration and to charge my heart with purity, thus enabling me to recognize Divine quality in Baba if such be the case. Allow me to forget what I read about him. Allow me to forget all I know of him from his entourage. Allow that my judgment may not be prejudiced by my knowledge of Baba in the past. Why, oh why is he coming to me now? How strange… How very strange when this morning I received a telephone call asking me to give overnight hospitality to Baba and his nine disciples! Meher Baba… Baba about whom I had mocked Norina Matchabelli. Baba at Galluis? How strange that this Holy of Holies, this second Christ, should be corning to me, who never believed in him! Traveling from India to stay in the West less than ten days, why should he spend one night and half a day of his time in France to sanctify Galluis with his presence?

Is this Thy Will, O Infinite? And why now? Now when there is such emptiness in my heart? *Is* this Thy Will? I will ask Baba—he knows everything, he himself says so—I will ask Baba if L. is alive… Yes, I have prepared several questions to ask. The most vital will be about L. Moreover I can verify if the Omniscient One tells me right when I learn definitively, what has become of L. If it coincides with Baba's words then I can believe more easily the answers to my other questions. Perhaps the same day that Baba comes I may receive an answer to my call for help, for inspiration, and it will fill my heart with the ability to judge rightly. In one of his most recent letters—for no apparent reason whatsoever—L. wrote: "Powers in themselves, per se, are no evidence of high spiritual attainment…" Did he have Baba in mind? Was he again instructing me in advance of the actual event?

* * *

In those days of uncertainty about L. something strange also happened to my voice. I felt as if the sensation of cold had slipped in. I was still sure that nothing could stop the ascendant line of my singing, for I had felt the Divine Presence around me since the previous August. Was it through L.'s help? But for the past week and for the first time since I had found my new vocal teacher, I sang mechanically, I sang—as many others do—by habit, by that technical knowledge that I already possessed and only through the physical organs. Madame Gilly thought I had tired my muscles by using them too much, too constantly…

Before this period of depression, I had felt that L.'s soul and mine were in constant communication. From America he had heard me in Europe singing Beethoven's "*Ich liebe dich.*" And I had known what he was writing to me when the letter was still on the ocean.

Surely he is no longer among the bodily living beings, for why do I not feel his soul near mine and why this emptiness? Why? But if he is no more, why is his spirit not near me, even nearer than before? Must we be separated because he no longer has a body? Why? It cannot be that with the last living breath everything is finished…

* * *

No, I did not ask Baba about L… Why? I do not know… Perhaps I did not want to profane L's name… Or was I afraid I would have proof of Baba's being more of a hallucination than the omniscient being that his faithful disciples claimed him to be? Maybe I prefer not to know now…

"Thy will be done!"

* * *

I took Baba to the station, too sick at heart to see, to understand, to feel rightly. I returned only at midnight. The first time I had been out so late for the last ten months—the first time since I met with L.'s soul, the first time since he gave me the lotus ruby glass with a seven-day candle which had been burning since on the mantelpiece in front of his Lord's picture, framed on both sides by flowers. I never switched on the light in my room without first looking at the picture lighted by the red flame from the candle-holder. But that night for the first time the light was out… It was dark, cold, tragic… It was the first night I could not see His picture… I had no more candles… One cannot get them in Europe… I had hoped so much to be able to leave for America in October. …When I discovered I was not yet ready to go I had cabled New York for a big reserve. … They were already at the customs but the weekend and Armistice Day had prevented their clearance. How gloomy! Still this darkness corresponded fully with my heart's darkness… Thy will be done about my voice… I will await without revolt the day I am ready to go to New York… Thy will be done in everything…

* * *

That night I sent the following cable to L.'s secretary, "Anxious about L.'s health, please cable news," already in a spirit of resignation, in a spirit of "Thy will be done!"

When I awoke the next morning, the depression of the previous night was deeply engraved on my mind but I was fatalistically resigned. I only regretted that I must spend the whole day in my room Armistice Day… No going to Paris… No lessons… Rain, rain…

"No, there is no mail!"

Why had I asked?

* * *

An hour later…

Some letters arrive and the long envelope which bears L.'s handwriting… !

Is it I whose heart does not move? From whence comes

this apathy or this strength? Was the bow bent too much? Had it broken?

I did not open the letter… What could he write? Detached from earthly bounds now, nothing of a material kind could matter any more. Last night I had buried him and with him my own human desire to be happy the way I thought I ought to be happy. I had buried the idea that I must get help from outside. Last night I lost my individuality and became one with the universal Intelligence. I was only tired… so tired.

What a pity it was Armistice Day! Feeling like an automaton I would have preferred to busy myself by working out the whole day like any other day. I wanted to forget and not stay all day with the smallest part of myself…

"Thou weepest?"
"Oh no, it is but my eyes!"

* * *

He who is not master of himself is no one's master.
— P.J. STAHL

I FIRST CAME across Baba's name when reading Paul Brunton's "A Search in Secret India," where Baba was described in a rather questionable way. Later, Rom Landau, in his "God Is My Adventure," drew such a mocking picture of this new Messiah in an ironic interview with one of Baba's most ardent devotees, Princess Norina Matchabelli, that it only confirmed my first unfavorable impression.

The Princess's husband, creator of the famous Matchabelli perfumes, confidentially told me that Baba had taken his beloved wife away from him… Her blind devotion to the mystic had become proverbial among their many friends and nothing could make her see the unworthiness of that self-styled redeemer.

Prince George sadly confessed that Norina was the only

woman he loved and that she would remain forever *the* Woman of his whole life even though they were separated or divorced. He further informed me that in order to spare her faith and in justice to himself he had agreed to see Baba when the latter came to New York. However, he had been unable to change his previously formed opinion of him, though he had not the heart to tell the truth to Norina.

I saw the beautiful Princess for the first time when she played in the New York production of Max Reinhardt's "Miracle." Predestination? The author of that mystical play, Karl Volmöller, was Norina's first husband. She created the part of the Madonna when it had been given in Europe before the war. Curiously enough, more than twenty years later I, too, acted in the same "Miracle" at its revival.

I made the personal acquaintance of Maria Carmi, Norina's *nom de guerre*, at Mrs. Henry Loomis's where I greatly admired her statuesque beauty and her well-known white Hindu turban. We shook hands casually, little suspecting then that our paths would cross later in such a vital field.

In 1935 Princess Norina visited me in Paris and from that moment I took a liking to her. Who would not? She was so natural and so undivided. Her limitless adoration of Baba was tragically touching. She considered him the reincarnated Christ and could not even imagine that everyone around her was not of the same opinion. We, her friends, who liked her immensely and would not have hurt her for the world, we never dared shake the illusion of this entirely living-in-a-fantasy child. However, even if we had tried to shake her hallucination, it would have been to no avail, for she would not see it. Moreover, she took our affection for her as our belief in Baba's holiness.

I never met Baba but those who were allowed to present themselves before the eyes of the new Redeemer did not generally have a holy impression of him. But one spiritually-minded lady informed me that she had never seen such deep love in anyone as she had witnessed in Baba's eyes.

One serious-minded occult student roped a chair in his sanctuary with the inscription: "Here Baba was seated."

* * *

When I was leaving New York in April 1936, Norina in her surprise dramatically asked me: "Leaving? But what if Baba comes here directly from India?"

Upon my assuring her that I must go, she told me quite seriously that she would cable me to return immediately when she received news of Baba's coming.

Her certainty that I could do nothing else but return instantly was so childish that I did not even try to dissuade her from believing it was a possibility. It would have been no use beyond hurting her sweet heart, for she could never understand why everyone did not feel towards Baba as she did. Furthermore, even if she had been hurt, she would not have felt unhappy, for to suffer for Baba's cause was already a joy.

And one day at the end of October, Norina cabled that Baba was arriving in London where he would see me between the sixth and eleventh of November. I decided to go for a weekend, taking the ferry between Paris and London in order to lose none of my lessons. Our *bella* would certainly never have understood how I could possibly miss the opportunity she was giving me of contemplating the New Prophet.

I had arranged my plans accordingly when our Princess cabled a change of plans. Baba would see me in Paris instead, at the house of our mutual friend.

Much better! I would not have to travel.

A few hours later, however, a third cable arrived asking if I could accommodate nine people in case, just in case Baba wanted to stay at Galluis over night.

Patatras! November! The small house was closed and the Chateau dressed for the winter. We also had had some trouble with the heating. What work! And what a nuisance to have all that disturbance for a single night, especially when there was no assurance that it might not be all in vain. But how could one refuse Norina anything?

Also, deep in my heart I was thinking: "How strange! How very strange that Baba should come to me!"

Again doubts filled my mind, less vital however than in previous similar cases, for I knew now they were only passing moods. It is of capital importance to know that those moods are only passing… Still, if you have a toothache and you know it will soon be over, your suffering is just as unbearable in the meantime. The mere idea that it will soon be over does not diminish its momentary intensity, alas!

Nevertheless, uncertainty about Baba's real value disturbed my serenity and broke the lately established equilibrium of my soul. It also disturbed my singing. I wanted so much to be just towards Baba and just towards myself. I sincerely desired to be unprejudiced by all the uncomplimentary criticism I had heard of him. I did not want to fall into my usual tendency of exaggeration and look at Baba blindly through rose-colored glasses of an enslaved devotion such as his entourage had for their Master.

During that night and morning of Baba's stay at Gallu-is, I played the part of Baba's submissive disciple so well that the prophet himself as well as his apostles, took it for granted that Baba had accomplished his usual miracle of *Veni, vidi, vici.*

Owing to Baba's extreme restlessness—more than curious for a mystic—and to the fact that as hostess I had much of the actual work to do to make fourteen people comfortable during their overnight stay, I could not register my thoughts and I did not allow my feelings to interfere with the *Hausfrau* work. I was busy every second, running from the kitchen to Baba's disciples, from the garage to the housekeeper who complained that our cook had lost her head—*et pour cause!*—while my secretary in the meantime was suspended on the telephone for the Master's orders.

With this rush, nervousness, lack of serenity, I could not help having the clear impression that Baba was an exceptionally capricious prima donna and his disciples were playing the part of the typical enslaved accompanist, secretary and maids, while Norina Matchabelli acted the role of the Italian impresario—and what a beautiful impresario! All were extremely excited and scared to death of displeasing Baba, I am almost tempted to say—their mistress. They waited at his door—like a dog sitting on the floor, on the stairs—in order to respond more quickly at his call. And when a call came, they rushed in so quickly in military style that I trembled for any of my antiques that might be in their way.

Hardly had they started breakfast than, with a half-consumed piece of toast in their mouths, they rushed to answer their Master. The *brioches* actually had to be warmed six times before they got a chance to finish their coffee. The luncheon hour was changed eight times, the first order having been for one o'clock. But we ate at half-past eleven and for this reason the food was scarcely up to Galluis standards, for my chef could not possibly have prepared this complicated vegetarian menu with her usual finesse at an hour's notice, the last change of time having come through just after eleven o'clock. And the cause of all this trouble was that Baba wanted to go to the movies to see his favorite entertainment—a gay musical comedy picturing the life of Florenz Ziegfeld.

I was told that Baba naturally goes to such places only to help, as people are much more likely to be relaxed in the dark thus enabling the Master to assist them more efficiently.

Accustomed to the tyranny of opera stars, in this atmosphere of excitement nothing was new to me while Baba's long hair still increased the illusion of his being a spoilt soprano and the silence—he had not spoken for the past eleven years—reminded me of a great diva saving her voice before the performance. Old Battistini kept to his room in silence for two days before singing and when he happened to be stopping at the same hotel in St. Petersburg, he would send me a short letter every few hours.

After a thousand and one useless complications we took possession of our boxes at a second rate moving-picture theatre, bringing with us a restless and unstable atmosphere, for some were late, some went away, some had to come back and ask for their tickets, some came only at the end after doing errands for Baba…

When seated at last and for the first time in twenty-four hours, only then did I realize how painfully tight my nerves were. I consoled myself with the thought that in another three and a half hours I would be delivered from those performers, I beg your pardon, from—Baba's saintly presence!

The first film was all about bandits and there was so much shooting in it that I finally got a terrific headache. Further playing of the comedy was a great hardship to me, especially when I learned that Baba had changed his plans again, for the umpteenth time since the night before, and was not leaving until ten o'clock, an hour at which I had naïvely hoped to be long since in bed.

When I finally got to my room I stayed there for three long days to recuperate from that hectic, unhealthy, under-the-knout holy life.

The day after their departure, when my headache had died away, the souvenir flashed through my mind of Dr. Fraenkel's words when the then Margaret Mills (now Princess Murat) confessed being so much in love with Jimmy McVicker that she could not live without him and therefore she must divorce Ogden Mills. While saying this she complained of a terrible headache. Thereupon Dr. Fraenkel remarked:

"But if your love is so great, how is it that it cannot even cure your headache?"

The wizard was right—her love soon cooled off.

Like Dr. Fraenkel, I thought that God's presence, God's love in our heart and in our home should bring peace and serenity and not fear, panic, the feeling of hurry or physical diseases. Had I not seen Baba, I would not have lost my spiritual, mental and physical forces for several days…

But even under those circumstances, I did not wish to judge, especially as Baba's kindness to me was great. Contrary to his custom, Baba felt happy and harmonious at Galluis, a rare honor I was told, as His Saintliness rarely expressed such satisfaction. I felt particularly confused when he told me that my already beautiful soul would become under his guidance a precious jewel… Magnanimously he also promised to help my singing by telling me that if I looked at his picture before starting my lesson I would sing divinely.

"I will help you," he added.

I-will-help-you was his *Leitmotif*, his Open-Sesame to each person who asked advice.

As the height of his favor he also invited me to visit him in India, a rarissime privilege indeed, as some had been waiting in vain for years for permission to join his colony at Nasik.

Driving in the car and at the movies he constantly made me sit next to him… So much kindness and my heart could not appreciate it all, could not appreciate it enough!

I did feel small but I could not help it. I did not have my usual spontaneity. Even the next day when I was wiring to Marseille my thanks for his benevolent visit, I actually had to force myself to do it because Norina had suggested it to me. I did it as one does an obligatory conventionality and not at all with the indispensable *élan* of my usually over-generous nature.

I felt even worse when I got his very kind, if unexpected answer and still more guilty when Norina sent me a beautiful cable from London. So many, many thanks, so many blessings from all sides… Decidedly they wanted to choke me with undeserved kindness. I felt so sorry, so humiliated at being incapable of giving them in response my full heart, only a small part of my human mind instead…

* * *

When I recovered from that strange visit and its consequences, I started my normal life of action and went back to singing. It happened to be full moon Friday the thirteenth, my favorite day. The moon is my faithful friend, my inspirer; and whenever the full moon comes I am certain that a Great Soul—that of L.—sends me his highest vibrations. That day of full moon, oh, miracle, I jumped over all technicalities, overlooked what had been insurmountable difficulties till then, forgot all about not yet having adjusted my muscles to the new way of singing and sang beautifully. In the studio, behind the doors, everybody gasped with surprise. A musician who happened to be there told Madame Gilly: "Here is the greatest advertisement for your teaching!" An American student would not believe it was Walska who thus sang "Tannhäuser," while another pupil became quite unhappy at not having made the same rapid progress although having worked longer than I with Madame Gilly.

During the second lesson that afternoon, my seemingly phenomenal improvement was still more accentuated. For the first time in more than twenty years of my singing I was not handicapped by the slightest obstacle and met no resistance whatsoever.

That ease of singing took such fast possession of my being that I could not help smiling arrogantly at those great singers who always had some more or less weak spots while nothing darkened or veiled the mystery of that great Art to me that day.

It all came to me so suddenly that I had no time to think of the reactional consequences I might have from that memorial event. I only vaguely sensed that this miracle had happened not to me but to my soul and that the soul can not be dazed or surprised since it has none of the passing human qualifications of expressing itself while my physical being modestly acknowledged having no part in that glorious festival. I only remember deciding to sing from then on some new music... Those airs I had worked on so hard up to that time seemed to me too easy to sing any more... Yes, the next day I would start Donna Anna's great aria from "Don Juan," the *bête noire* of all singers.

But how funny... How strange that this great improvement should come so suddenly... Strange it should come after Baba had said he would help me! Was it because my voice was rested? My recuperation after Baba's visit had lasted five days and—as usual at such moments—my muscles were utterly relaxed. The minimum of four hours' daily singing all year round possibly tightens the muscles and tires the mind to a degree that might tremendously handicap improvement...

Why this smallness? Why not render unto Caesar that which is Caesar's? After all, it was a fact that I sang as I had never sung before. And it had actually happened after Baba blessed me and assured me of his help. Why cheapen my soul by preferring the calculations and hypotheses of my human mind?

Again I forced my heart to send a radio to Baba's boat. "Sang as never before," I wrote. The answer came immediately and more blessings with it. All that happiness and bliss had come from Baba, whom my heart did not choose to accept blindly as a perfect Master and of whom I thought rather unfavorably, pitying Norina for putting her heart, her life and her fortune at his feet!

Oh, yes—Norina. Here is a letter from her. She announces her return from London tomorrow and asks me to luncheon. She also writes that Baba has accorded me a new privilege—he is going to allow me to contribute five hundred pounds for the publication of his biography. The editor would agree to its publication on condition that I buy two thousand five hundred copies in advance, three hundred of which I must distribute gratuitously in Europe and the remainder in India.

Oh! I am *so* great!! I cannot help admiring myself for not feeling any ugly movement of my soul after reading the generous message. The smile on my lips was more childish than bitter.

Baba had said: "Her soul is a jewel…"

Jewel?

> *Life has worth only as long as one can take a step forward, enlarge one's horizon, augment oneself.*
>
> — EDGAR QUINET

WHEN I WENT to America in the winter of 1935 my heart was sure—as much as one can be sure about the four-dimensional sphere as judged by the human mind—that I had been put on this earth for some purpose greater and bigger than the usual conception of big and great achievements. I also realized that I was passing through the verification period of my learning, as I called it. Deep in my heart and without any doubts I sensed God's finger on me. I began to look into my past and I saw consistency even in my misery.

I summed up and totaled all my affections since my very early girlhood. Even then my heart had known the full meaning of loneliness. I was compelled to see that fate had decreed I should never be repaid with the same quality of feelings that I gave and that I gave without reciprocity of value in spite of the amount of unselfish love and patient consideration. No matter how much unrestricted devotion I gave in Kundry's service, I could not overcome those difficulties sent by Destiny. I began to understand that it was for a purpose which I was not yet permitted to know.

I could not help but see that unmistakably each time I loved profoundly, automatically misery became my faithful companion. And it was great misery, for I discovered—and always too late—either that the beloved was very poor in his feelings, humiliated by receiving more than he was capable of giving (and no man is heroic enough to stand such a situation) or his jealousy and vanity were stronger than his apparent affection.

Evidently some incomprehensible forces did not want me to settle down with a comfortable feeling of having achieved my goal and reached the desirable shore designated by my human mind. As Guizot said: "Time renders greater that which it does not kill."

Once satisfied in my heart, perhaps I would not have hesitated to abandon the chimeric dream about singing—for singing never gave me any joy—in favor of self-contented happiness with a beloved one. Obviously that was not Destiny's great design for me. Perhaps if I had been anxious about a husband and children's love, I would not have sought further or higher…

Meanwhile, as an absolute idealist, I awaited what could never materialize, as I now know that one cannot find happiness in other people's affection nor can one find peace outside oneself. I am not speaking about the small half of our personality but about our oneness with the Universal Heart.

Nevertheless, my inexperienced youth kept calling for happiness, calling for love, for which I prepared myself almost religiously in the purity and richness of my exalted nature. Still my call was never answered. While enjoying the reputation of a practical, cold-minded woman and doing everything to reinforce that opinion until it was apparently brilliantly deserved—I collected treasures of unbounded beauty deeply and secretly in my soul, always waiting for a Prince Charming to conquer that wealth and—braving death, ugliness, mediocrity, hypocrisy—to deliver his Princess, who awaited him as Brünnehilde awaited Siegfried.

* * *

After years and years, endless, endless years of waiting and hoping, I jumped to the other extreme. Suddenly I waited no more. I realized that no longer was I going consciously forward to fight for my soul's welfare. From that moment on I consoled myself with this fantastic philosophy: "If He is *bound* to come, He will and I shall know that He is the chosen one only if He comes as sunshine, without suffering, without misery, without doubts… But I will *not* wait for Him any longer… Let Him cross my path if *He* so desires, if it is essential to Him…"

After taking that decision, each time I saw ugliness in a man's eyes my heart prompted me that it could not be He—this one hurts me already by his gaze.

Though my mind waited no longer and no longer wanted anyone, curiously enough I still felt rather happy for the first time. Soon I was so happy that I could not imagine any but this independent happiness, happiness in and through loneliness… Soon the thought of losing that self-provided source of blissful feeling took such strong possession of me that anything else was almost unbearable and was certainly unthinkable.

And yet, like an obsession, I would sometimes picture myself sliding to the floor in front of a man whose figure was indefinite, whose features were changeable—depending on who was giving me the momentary illusion of being the Man of my Destiny at that time—and with closed eyes I would put my burning face on his knees to rest in eternity during one second…

Yes, I know I have yet to go through that phase in order to get free and liberate myself from the feeling of this dependence, from this craving to take final leave, from seeking the happiness that no person can give me, nothing but my inner limitless possibilities and infinite richness…

I also know I shall not do it… I know I would not do it… Moreover I know that if I used my will power I would be prevented from doing it anyhow, as I was so many times before… My beautiful guiding spirit would not allow me such human weakness, the divine part of me would not allow me to obscure my soul with an earthly expression of my personality through a regretful impetus…

Once, I remember, I was to leave for a weekend in the mountains where a fascinating but earthbound man waited for me, waited passionately—too passionately… As it was during holiday season there were no sleepers to be had on the trains either going or coming back. I insisted. I was promised the first accommodations to be returned would be mine. Late Friday I got them. But Saturday I awoke with a terrific fever such as I had not had in twenty years—nowadays I am never ill. A Mongolian doctor-friend thought I was bound to bed for two weeks at best. I laughed at him… I assured him I would be leaving in the evening. He retorted that even if I wanted to I could not. Again I laughed but in the afternoon I left my bed, took two steps and fell—I was so weak. Traveling was out of the question. By Sunday I was still worse. I felt as sick as any person can be who believes in illness and who admits the negative. My Mongolian physician advised me to wire home my inability to leave my room for three weeks at least…

Monday morning I awoke completely well, just as though I had had nothing wrong with me at all. Yes, I was well, for it was then too late to go to the mountains—and I did not need divine protection any longer…

Another time a diplomat who was very interesting but lacking in high vibrations was to telephone for confirmation that I would see him that evening. After much hesitation I decided to give him a positive answer… However, he never phoned, for while taking his bath he had been gassed and only miraculously awakened too late to communicate with me…

I could mention many, many similar cases.

I know… I know… Yet, in moments of extreme fatigue, when my forces are diminishing, I am calling, calling for the long-desired moment…

For years I fought the better side of my nature, the divine one. I fought it with all the will in my power—which was great—fought the battle against myself. Now, since I have finally and definitively recognized the providential Hand over me, I never interfere with its guidance, never complain if things do not go exactly as I think they ought to… I do what my intuition directs me to do, knowing that if anything is wrong I must have interpreted the idea solely with my human comprehension. Since I acquired such understanding, nothing is, nothing can be, wrong any more. I am just as happy when things go against my wishes as when they fulfill thoroughly my desires.

To furnish one's heart with pure and elevated tastes, is to build oneself places of refuge.

— ERNEST LEGOUVÉ

NOW COMPLETELY MISTRESS of my action, desire and movement, slave only to one wild cat—who did not like to be fed by anyone but myself and who, whenever he saw me putting on a hat, hid himself under my bed, so sad that I was leaving him—still if at this period of my life I did not further develop my inner soul, it was because my whole effort was concentrated in and around my singing. But as soon as I could steal an hour from this self-imposed duty, I ran to hear any lecture on metaphysical subjects that happened to be announced. I also took advantage of Sundays when my Catholic teacher of that period did not think it proper to teach. It was on one such occasion that I saw *le beau théatre* at Dornach and naturally I went to the Swiss Oberammergau particularly joyful, knowing that the *Goethaneum* was connected with the teaching of Ancient Wisdom and created by that great German mystic, Rudolf Steiner.

A long time would have passed before that visit—I was so anxious not to miss a single lesson—had it not been for some charming friends interested in art and mysticism who proposed my joining them for the weekend in order to see a Sunday afternoon performance.

Bless them for this inspiration. For, in Steiner's *Ashram* my soul found prolific nourishment and a wide field for creative, up-building thought.

What a new experience for me to see gathered in one place so many people from all over the world, united only by their soul's wish for development, so many *real* people, people with different characters, different social standing, different education, but all animated by one mutual desire, the desire for knowledge, spiritual knowledge, the only source of all wisdom, of all truth!

As Dornach had no hotel I was privileged to board with Dr. and Mrs. Grossheintz, the actual builders of Dornach, who, after Steiner's death, together with his widow and the Swiss poet Albert Steffen were considered the spiritual heirs of that Initiate.

Although I spent only ten hours with the inhabitants of this unique village, I felt we had known each other a long time. There was no mundane atmosphere whatsoever. One felt no embarrassment in finding words when meeting new people. The special characteristics of those seeker-workers who are practically anonymous (even the programme does not mention the actors' names) are quite visible even to a materialistically inclined eye. They have an utter lack of egoism. Without vanity, they have developed individuality to the detriment of personality, which they willingly and knowingly sacrificed as a sign of inferiority—a fact especially difficult for post-war Americans, great lovers of personality, to understand...

I am sure any casual visitor such as myself, independently of the state of his or her mental development, must have felt the atmosphere of absolute willingness to help and help for the pure joy of it.

The vibration of this natural life led by Steiner's followers left an extremely beneficial effect on my heart. I had the soothing feeling of being bathed in my own element. I felt peaceful in my Mind!

I do not intend to speak here about the Dornach Master, about Rudolf Steiner's doctrines. I can only try to register, like a human barometer, the atmosphere of one who, though no longer visible to the mortal eye, was the creator of those vibrations that bring us nearer to God's Island where everything is Peace and Beauty. It was something like the impression I got from Cosima Wagner who, although extremely aged when I saw her and no longer taking an active part in the *Festspiel*, was the spiritual pivot around which the whole of Bayreuth's musical life seemed to center.

I will always remember my first visit to Wagner's shrine. Around one o'clock, seated outside the primitive restaurant with its traditional *Wurstchen*, beer and paper napkins, lunching with Wagner's son Siegfried and his handsome English wife Winifred (now Hitler's friend), I felt suddenly that something had happened, that something was positively different in the air. As though transformed, the people rose, reverently took off their hats and waited silently, forgetting about their *Delikatessen* (proving that if they were satisfied with the coarseness of their favorite food it was because they did not attach much importance to its quality and merely fed their bodies to satisfy natural demands). I could not understand what it was all about. I stood too, as the others did, examining the transfigured expressions of their faces, until I heard applause and cries of "Hurrah" in the distance. Only then, following the direction of other people's eyes, did I perceive coming towards us an old-fashioned carriage, in which sat Cosima Wagner, dressed in black and carrying an open lace umbrella *à la Empress Eugénie*. Amid thunderous cries of *Hoch!* her carriage made the tour around the *Festspielhaus* and disappeared.

She was then already too old and too weak to be present at the performances but until her death, by thus appearing in her carriage, this glorious daughter of a glorious father —Franz Liszt— helped keep the audience from all over the world in that elevated ecstatic state which accompanied Wagner's creations during his life and after his passing to immortality.

The lack of any such inspirational element accounts for the atmosphere at Salzburg being rather more social and gossipy than sublimely elevating.

At Dornach, likewise, I felt to the utmost the inspiration of its great creator. When those gifted, if humble, seekers of cosmic laws found out that I was there just for the day, they generously—in spite of its being Sunday—opened the doors of their individual laboratories and studios. Mrs. Grossheintz was good enough to explain, with actual evidence in hand, much of the hidden Truth in Steiner's teaching, such as the influence of the eclipse of the sun and the planets on the different minerals of the earth.

Before my wonder-stricken eyes they demonstrated all the prolific store of products of that coordinated, already widespread colony, created in unison from the different branches of art and the research for human, animal, vegetable and mineral betterment.

The village without hotels with over two thousand inhabitants is not a tourist haven. There are no butchers—a paradise to me who am not much of a meat appreciator, preferring my garden vegetables and fruits—no cafes selling any spirits. Only *The* Spirit was felt in the air...

Following Rudolf Steiner's instructions, they are learning to tear from ignorance new to their understanding the old laws of Nature that govern this Kingdom of Mystery, working always and solely with the reverent idea of their departed Master, in an ecstatic vision of his actual presence among them or within their living memory, to deeply enlighten them.

Dornach's whole life is concentrated only around its Creator. Each artist and artisan finds his own reward in the thought that Rudolf Steiner would have approved of their effort to advance according to his doctrine and without ever taking any personal credit. Some severe critics well acquainted with Steiner's teachings might even reproach certain of his followers with being *plus royaliste quo le Roi*.

My short visit to Dornach uplifted to the highest degree my spirit and my singing. Spirit through association with real people; singing because the Steiner Theatre made the actors speak outside the lips in a special manner. Therefore I invited one of those instructors to come to Galluis and for weeks I struggled to put vowel and consonant outside my mouth.

Two years later I went further into the art of vocal perfection with another of Steiner's disciples, who herself amplified her master's theory in order to apply it as well to singing.

If one had the angelic patience—and I had—to persevere in the tedious method, the tone had a sound of perfect purity and the physical organs were powerless to interfere. But it was indeed difficult work, extremely difficult work. One needed extraordinary courage to hum the inaudible tones for hours and hours and that endless ABC after having spent already many years singing all great arias!! It was practically a torture to go back to kindergarten!!

* * *

Another moment of almost stolen inspiration was when I visited Salzburg again in 1937…

Yes, again Salzburg. But what a difference between Salzburg today and the Salzburg of a year ago when everything seemed gloomy, dark and hopeless! Certainty reigns in me now, whereas doubts were invading my broken spirit then. Knowledge, an unmistakable knowledge, has smoothed out all the problems that then appeared insurmountable.

And yet today… ? Is it a headache? Is it the *Erinnerung* of past mental experiences that left their destructive vibrations in this city, in this hotel? Or is it still necessary for me to climb higher mountains before entirely possessing the sun? Is it the reaction of so many months of strenuous work under extremely hard circumstances, owing to the rather difficult character of one of my teachers whose vibrations differ completely from my own? I do not know… But today I am actually depressed and cannot rise above such elements as heat and human stupidity which, according to Renan, is the only thing that makes us comprehend the idea of the infinite. Alexander Dumas said almost the same thing: "Human genius has its limitations but never human stupidity."

In that heavy state of mind I went to hear *"Die Zauberflöte"* and only at that night's performance, although having heard it hundreds of times before, did I fully grasp the significance of its great Mystery. I understood that I, too, was passing along that wonderful if hard road of Initiation...

My depression disappeared instantaneously. I felt blissfully happy and humbly grateful to my Creator for having allowed me to arrive at this most precious realization of my soul...

> *To be free is to have possession of oneself.*
> — LACORDAIRE

I WAS FORTUNATE that even in the last period of my struggle, in spite of some shocks and some quickly passing doubts—perhaps thanks to them—my soul never again registered negatively. And those momentary backslidings did not even make any impression on the emotional side of my nature but rather my understanding grew stronger and stronger each day. Outwardly those shortcomings were not visible at all, for people feeling my potential calm, sensing my daily growing serenity, seeing only the positive, the good and the wonderful coming to me, often asked how I got such power and such control, what was my secret and which philosophy was I applying, which religion I followed or even what domain of science did I practice in…

It was difficult to answer those questions in one word, for although I was born Catholic, I do not follow any specific religion. I am a Christian in the real interpretation of the word, while my philosophy is a mosaic of all philosophies.

* * *

> *Morals were not formed all at once, they were formed by all the small victories won by man over the brute within him.*
> —F. BUISSON

I HAVE STUDIED western and eastern philosophies for over twenty years. And even while I rejected some of the doctrines, something always was left from each of them in my inner depth and that kaleidoscope of many visions mirrored the reflections in my soul.

I am certain that had I not read so much and in the end so well—automatically one chooses only the best spiritual food—I would not yet be on the upward road to Understanding. But perhaps that is only my personal experience, since each individual finds a different way to the realization of his being. I progressed so gradually towards that inner stability, going ahead extremely slowly and tortuously—thanks to my critical mind and profound admiration for poisonous intellect—that I myself hardly noticed the transitory period and was quite unaware of it at first when I found myself in the position of a constructive teacher rather than in that of the unbalanced sentimental and destructive seeker I had been all through my life.

The transfiguration was such a slow process that I was not even conscious of the fact that friends were asking my advice. I answered them simply as I felt, giving what I already knew, at first rather repeating other people's ideas.

But even before this serene stability filled my mind, already I had distinctly sensed that in the most trying cases I was certain of advancing, even if the progress were imperceptible to my conscious knowledge and my human comprehension.

My life was all the more eventful although otherwise seemingly monotonous. In spite of the apparent lack of variety something was going on inside me all the time, my inner thought was in action every second and my feelings like lightning were perpetually registering the slightest inner movement. My continuously effervescent mental cells expanded ceaselessly for there were a thousand worlds in my inner world while I was still doing discouraging and mechanical work!

The feeling of going definitely forward was not even perceptible to my consciousness, which was awakened only to the few facts my human comprehension could grasp. I was still consciously making a complete division between external manifestation and inner dreaming, unable as yet to melt them together and dream continuously with wide open eyes.

I did not make a subdivision between my marked personality which I owed to my physical appearance and my individuality which, like all true manifestations, was complete, powerful and perfect even though not yet discovered comprehensively and thoroughly by my senses.

Sometimes I could judge my progress by comparison with my environment, when I again saw those friends who had remained, morally speaking, where I had left them years and years ago. I could hardly understand how it had been possible for me to have spent so much time with them, we had so little in common.

Somehow it reminds me of a story from my childhood and the time when at school we held a beauty competition between ourselves at the age of ten or eleven. From the twelve girls in my class I was awarded eleventh prize. Thinking the decision quite just, I did not mind the physical disgrace in the least. But years later when I went back to that city to introduce my husband to my family, I saw six or eight of the girls who had been judged as beauty number one, two and so forth. They were definitely ugly creatures. Mentally I protested then and dismissed the taste of my ex-colleagues. However, I was curious to see number twelve, for according to the inverted standard of judging, she ought to have been more beautiful than number eleven, which was I. It seemed that she had committed that dreadful sin of marrying below her class and so I was told: "Oh, her? You know we do not see her any more…"

The memory of that decision about my looks had made such a lasting impression, nevertheless, that when I married and went to St. Petersburg, only to be unexpectedly chosen as the example of typical Slavic beauty by the court painters and, at the command of the Dowager Empress Maria, asked to sit for a portrait which was designated to hang at the Hermitage Museum, I was simply dizzy with surprise and could not understand how that could happen![21]

---

21 Bolshevism spread before that picture was permanently placed in the

* * *

"Emotions, interestingly enough, seem to short-circuit the battery so that the discharge practically disappears. This confirms everyday experience that it is difficult to think when emotionally upset and that emotional people are not noted for straight thinking." Those words might have been written expressly for me.

Fortunately the blessed time came when I understood quite clearly that my worst enemy was what, till then, I had taken to be the greatness of my nature—my excessive emotion, which had developed only the destructive and not the creative side of me and had enabled me to feel anything or everything immeasurably. From the moment of that discovery dates my comprehension of the real nature of all things. I was saved! I was I, unchangeable and stable... And soon, one after another, the veils fell away from my adopted personality and the real *I* emerged to the surface.

In a moment of perfect meditation in deep silence I was allowed to realize that excessive emotion, "an unlimited activity whatever its nature, ends up by bankruptcy," is a disturbance, a mental and physical disturbance, rather than the great idol I made of it. People with great unbalanced emotional capacity are lacking in general equilibrium. Consequently they cannot express through the successful building of their minds and are also unable to help others if the necessity arises. They never feel the real peace in their inner being without which their souls cannot achieve anything worthwhile.

* * *

Sometimes I know it is rather difficult to understand what I mean when for instance I say that *nothing* can touch me *now*. Time and time again when I have tried to explain my idea my friends have been invariably appalled, accused me

---

museum, so I cabled the painter money, which he needed badly by then, and now my portrait has hung in my New York home for years.

of having no heart and of being purely and solely egotistic. Unable yet to put the right idea into the right words, I was misinterpreted. The examples I gave only helped the misunderstanding. It does not mean that I have no heart when someone has died and I then, instead of crying and disbelieving in God, have recognized that it was that person's destiny and have consoled myself with the knowledge of "Thy Will be done—Thou knowest best!" At such times I prayed only that I might have more light in my mind and more love in my heart so as to see clearly what that Will was and not confuse It with a human interpretation of God's motives that might be more accommodating to my welfare.

* * *

I have been better able to recognize Nature's desire since I realized that the negative side of our thoughts, feelings and emotions such as depression, judgment, irritability, criticism and condemnation are profoundly devastating to our inner life because they sow deadly poisons with each breath we take in. That perception was a tremendous help to my advancement because it produced a definite metamorphosis of my mind, even if I needed years to put it into practice. But once done I achieved the greatest treasure one can possess—stability in peace!

Taking Seneca's thought that anger is a short madness, I deduced and verified in myself that each dissatisfaction with others instantly and inevitably turned against me, disturbing the vibrations of the perfect balance in my inner being for days at a time. All I did or felt in that state of unbalance was consequently untrue, unjust and unreal, for it was not I who thought, felt or did thus and so. It was my unbridled emotion—a mild case of folly but, as Jean Cocteau puts it, "The speed of a runaway horse does not count."

If a man kills in a drunken state, he may be acquitted and receives the benefit of extenuating circumstances under the excuse that he is not entirely responsible for his act. One could adopt the same attitude towards killings committed in a state of extreme jealousy, when the verdict declares the assassin of unsound mind.

For a long time I kept constantly changing maids. A personal maid is a very important element in one's daily life as she is the first person one sees upon awakening. Therefore if she brings the wrong vibration with her appearance and we are not strong enough to counteract it, our whole day is out of harmony. For years I looked for a maid with the quality of rhythmic vibration necessary to my sensitive aura where sincerity and truthfulness were more important than a knowledge of good sewing, excellent cleaning or perfect packing. For a decade I could not find a desirable maid and meanwhile I accumulated much disappointment in my heart, for each time I discovered that a girl had lied, I felt utterly miserable and could scarcely look her in the eyes, I was so ashamed for the ugliness of her nature. As my timidity did not permit me to send her away I would spend a long time waiting for her to depart of her own accord. Then a new maid would come and go. I took it for granted that, with the luck against me, I would continue to wait years and years for a perfect maid, a perfect secretary or a perfect housekeeper, being quite miserable in the meantime. And miserable I was until finally it became clear to me that I should not give in to my environment but should be able to control myself so as not to be disturbed by inevitable circumstances and inharmonious surroundings, just as I knew I could, if it were necessary, accommodate myself to any discomfort or ugliness—such as living in a noisy, hermetically closed hotel room—without the slightest complaint and almost without seeing the actual condition, feeling naturally like any insensitive person who never craved the open and beauty in all its perfection.

When I succeeded in conquering this dreadful enemy, my inner balance disturber, only then did I finally find peace and—incidentally—a good maid. Moreover, I am sure now that those not-too-good servants and especially irritating secretaries were sent to me by my generous Destiny for the purpose of developing my inner forces, just as all my vocal handicaps and visible injustices in connection with my singing were created in order that I might not be satisfied with the popular mediocrity and that the craving for the Sublime might be awakened within me.

* * *

But Rome was not built in a day. In spite of the recent acquisition of that serene feeling, times and times doubts still swept over me and my intelligence still needed some positive proofs of being on the right path. Fortunately I was able to give the Doubting Thomas in me a few examples of what might be called miracles. For six years I had been obliged to wear glasses, unable even to sign my own name on a check without the aid of those artificial eyes. Muscular and other semi-metaphysical treatments had been totally unsuccessful. The best eye specialists had assured me I could not be helped; on the contrary each year I would have to use stronger and stronger lenses as the tissues of my eyes each year would become older and older. But one day my inner voice said to me:

"Stop wearing those glasses!"

It was the same voice that had spoken in many other cases before, to which I did not dare to listen for fear of being fooled. As false humility teaches us, I thought it pretentious and conceited to consider that I might know something deep within me. But, somehow, that time I understood and obeyed. And since then I have never touched my once necessary and therefore friendly helpers. I do not even know where they are though I had so many of them. The Cartier platinum inlaid-with-diamond *face-à-main* which I had for evening wear has long since been presented to a friend as a Christmas present…

When still very young in my search for Truth I imagined

that Spirit, that God was a kind of wizard who, in Santa Claus fashion, ran from place to place generously distributing his favors, gracing a few, chosen ones while avoiding the multitude. And I suffered pathetically, crying: "Where, oh where is justice? Where is God?"

I cried because the Spirit ignored my frenzied call sent out in oceans of tears. Suicide seemed the only possible solution to me, since I felt unable to adapt myself to life in a world where God was not, for I reasoned that if He existed He would not permit the child to be taken away from this poor mother, for instance, or He would not allow my sweet pussy to catch and devour with greatest of pleasure the colorful butterflies. If God existed, He would not stand for collective killing, for the war; he would punish the offender and would protect the weak.

So I no longer thought of God as an archaic all-powerful, white-bearded patriarch who braves the laws of gravitation by suspending Himself in the clouds, nevertheless I still personified His Spirit in some form, abstract but still a form. And I prayed to Him to manifest Himself by healing, protecting, saving and especially by administering justice and punishing the villain.

Injustice always made my mental life unbearable until I fully understood the law of Karma (reward or punishment for our abiding or not abiding by the law in past incarnations) and until one Wise Man, to whom I had confessed that the existence of injustice in this world veiled the luminous vision of God from me, said this to me:

"Justice is good but generosity, forgiveness are of nobler quality!"

The burden fell from my soul. From that moment on injustice troubled me no more. I understood…

The next barrier in the way of the much desired peace of mind—that most valuable possession—was execrable Matter, my worst enemy. But finally Grace enlightened my mind by allowing me to comprehend that Matter is only the materialization of the Spirit and that Nature—so highly elevated in my mind—is Matter.

Vivekananda says that "All the varied forms of cosmic energy such as matter, thought, force, etc., are the manifestations of this Cosmic Intelligence." And, as Inayat Khan preaches: ". . . all that lives in matter is spirit."[22]

And so Matter was no longer the stumbling block in my way forward. And, when my disdain for Matter had disappeared then also came the understanding and readjustment about the money question. The shame for an income procured by commerce, such as perfume or cosmetics vanished and my heart was filled with gratitude and love for those inanimate objects that procure us comfort or necessary luxuries.

During my traveling, if ever I saw in the field a Harvester International machine I always sent to it a feeling of love or with my finger a tiny kiss. In the country where I was born, McCormick's name is certainly better known than the name of the president, Poland being essentially an agricultural country and an aristocrat, a farmer, a peasant looks upon those machines as a benediction sent to him by God.

When I went back to Poland for the first time after I was Mrs. McCormick, my compatriots could not believe that such a great name could be associated with one individual person, especially when this person was just a Pole as themselves and when, on top of that, she is a woman.

And when I moved to my chateau near Versailles Mr. McCormick, sweet as only he can be, on learning that I own a farm, had a charming idea for my birthday, to send me all the machines that Harvester International produces. At six in the morning, to my great surprise, when I looked through the window my eyes were greeted by a whole regiment of

---

[22] Theos Bernard in "Heaven Lies Within Us" adds on this subject that: "There is no differentiation between mind and matter, mind being merely the product of highly organized matter partaking of the qualities of both spirit and matter."

robot-soldiers standing there on exhibition and put there during the night that I might be surprised.

For many days after, all my neighbours, the simple field laborers as well as the rich farmers, were coming to look at those machines with the same admiration that the women would look at an exhibition of rare jewelry. I was even advised to give a public demonstration and charge an entrance fee for the benefit of some local charity. Such a devotion can be easily explained by the fact that after all those inanimate machines are producing the essential food to millions and millions throughout the world.

In this quasi-religious atmosphere, it was easy for me to catch the spark, the feeling of which not only changed my almost disrespectful disdain for the income from commerce but filled my heart with gratitude towards those silent, obedient servants of humanity.

After that day my whole conception was spiritualized. If ever in the future I should think to enter again the perfume or cosmetic business it would be with that feeling of love for the spiritualized matter, and not solely with the idea of making money, as in my first venture, even though I wanted that money for the sake of Art. Now it would be with the thought of creating and of being proud of it instead of being ashamed.

In my youth Poland occupied by Russia was intentionally separating herself from the business part, run by Russians. The country had its existence entirely on what this God-given "good earth" could produce, never mingling with city commerce, exercised only by the professionals with whom one would not associate in a social way. When I came to Paris—the French democracy—during the pre-war winter and was invited to a dinner given in honor of the Diaghilev's Russian Ballet which, with Nijinski, Pavlova and Krzesinska, now the wife of the Grand Duke André, was just then making a furore—I found myself seated next to Mr. Doucet, great art connoisseur. His collection was known all over the world but to me his name then was familiar only as a very smart Parisian dressmaker. My surprise was great to learn that a man can do women's gowns but the discovery that I had dined with a dressmaker assumed the proportion of a shock!! It wounded profoundly my Polish honor!!!

Hardly had I recovered from this infliction upon my superiority when, arriving for the first time in America during the New Year festivities, friends insisted that I should join them in a big party given by some wealthy people whose name was no different to me from Jones or Smith—I did not know even then about any Jones or Smith—I was very reluctant in accepting this invitation and with old-fashioned provincialism said: "I do not know those people! I was not introduced to them! I did not get a personal invitation… They did not call on me…" So before weakening entirely, I carefully was enquiring about their standing, and laughingly, I was assured that they were all right, only I should not mention… shoes in their presence!!!

We entered the Fifth Avenue private house and instantaneously I found myself waltzing with the host who met us at the ballroom door. I was telling myself how rich and grandiose was everything there, when just in that moment the high heel, studded with stars, flew away from my slipper. My charming partner most naturally and gaily caught it and restored it to my dancing slipper.

Seeing this scene my friends had a good laugh on me, for then only they explained the mystery of the silence about the shoes—our host was Mr. Hannan, from Hannan Shoes and knowing my ridiculous attitude of separating the classes and parting society from commerce, they did not wish to tell me beforehand where we were going, lest I would refuse to join them.

.

> *What an amount of time is saved by him who pays no attention to what his neighbor says, does or thinks, but only to what he himself is doing, with the object of rendering his actions sound and just.*
>
> — MARCUS AURELIUS

I made a great and final accession to the peaceful state of mind when I understood consciously—unconsciously I had already sensed it for years—that uselessly wasting energy on empty chatter, superfluous repetitions, unimportant statements, low vibrating gossip, uninstructive plays consumes our vital forces and diverts our creative thoughts and extra strength away from their proper channels.

After reaching that wonderful realization I slowly but surely stopped leading a so-called social life. I am sure that it is a permanent decision for I did not come to it under an emotional impulse in a moment of exaltation but gradually and thoughtfully I prepared for my final retreat.

At first I took only the evenings for myself and, on rare occasions when I was forced to accept a dinner invitation, I did so on condition that I be excused for leaving before eleven, using then as a pretext the necessity of my presence at the Théâtre des Champs-Élysées, not wishing to divulge the real reason for my early retirement. Boni de Castellane, already afflicted with his fatal illness and under orders to be in bed before eleven, if he was present at the same dinner, would make me the sign agreed upon in advance. We would meet at the cloakroom, and I would take him home, as his meager fortune after his fastidious life while married to the Gould fortune did not allow him to have his own car.

By going to bed early I was able to awaken early and live at one with nature, undisturbed by earthly vibrations, as humanity was still asleep.

That dual life lasted for years until the day when I arrived from America and was faced with ten invitations a day during the great Parisian spring season. In order to meet that problem I made the only decision that could get me out of such a delicate situation. I decided not to accept a single card, as I had to accept all and return all the courtesies or none, for the cosmopolitan society in Paris consisted of the same few hundred people one met at the embassies, ministries and other prominent houses of international renown.

From that moment dates my actual life, my real life, life of development of my inner self and the work of my Divine Art, each automatically dependent on the other, for the higher my realization of Infinite Possibility becomes, the more elevated is my singing. Previously I had naïvely put singing in the leading place in my life until I understood that it was only a materialized result of inner advancement. The ardent desire for those two developments soon became the only criterion for my living. Everything else had to pivot around the indomitable decision of my great purpose.

Slowly, with the will of one who knows her goal and whom nothing can keep from attaining it fully, I eliminated everything that could have diminished my vital force and disturbed the peaceful vibrations indispensable to my mighty achievement.

I began to live on the principle that "He who wants to usefully employ his life should always act as if he were to live for long years and regulate himself as if he were to die shortly."

No more brilliant musical functions at the Rue de Lübeck, where even during the gala luncheons an orchestra had played and where many artists like Conchita Superria had made their Paris debuts. It was known that my receptions were always musicals where marvelous artistes as Pasquier Trio, great Quatuor, or other outstanding talent appeared. The brilliant audience of *tout Paris* was always gathered to listen, to appreciate and to *lancer* if necessary the exceptional but still unknown star.

Sometimes I was badly caught by a protégé, either of some government or of a charitable friend, who forced upon me the future Kreisler, Paderewski, Caruso or Chaliapine who only needed such a musically frequented *salon* as mine in order that he may come into his own.

Particularly insistent was my Berlin manager, the well known Louisa Wolf, who during the whole winter begged me so much to give an opportunity to some poor devil of a pianist that finally, for the sake of peace, I consented. This time—having had previous unfortunate experiences—I decided to be cautious. Therefore while inviting the critics, who by the way in France are almost all the composers, I asked them to come this time just for my own sake, as I could not guarantee them the musical value of the new guest artist.

Challenged, they all arrived: Maurice Ravel, Andre Messager, Arthur Honegger, Roger Ducasse, Florent Schmitt, Paul Ducas, Darius Milhaud, Claude Delvaincour, Emil Vuillermoz, Louis Auber and many others. Obliged to remain seated in the first row to entertain my royal guest, Infanta Eulalia of Spain, I begged my musical friends to stay at the door of the music room. Thus easily they might escape to the *buffet* if the artist was not satisfactory.

The young, poetic looking pianist started to play. He was… Wladimir Horowitz who only a few months later got 25,000 francs to play half an hour in private musicales. My friends, the critics, still are sure that I played a practical joke on them.

* * *

No more original entertainment at the Théâtre des Champs-Élysées…

No more champêtre galas at Galluis with sylphide dancing on the lawn by the Duncan girls and with the guests signalled at the gate by a hunting-horn and then met by a different orchestra in each corner of the park: Russian in honor of the Grand Duchess Helen, Auvergnat in honor of the Minister of Aviation, Laurent Eynac, and son...

No more lamb with rice *à la grec* in honor of the father of the Duchess of Kent, Prince Nicholas of Greece. No more of that extra fine bird, *riabthik*—found only in Russia and Finland—generously filled with the best caviar brought specially by Air Mail from Romania, that found such favor with that genius in decorative architecture,[23] Tony Montgomery, that he wanted to congratulate the chef, who by the way had been a colonel in the Czar's Hussar regiment and who was frightfully shocked when my American friend said: "Your caviared *chicken* was a masterpiece!"

Adieu to the beauty of a dining-room table where each plate, fork and glass represented several-century-old workmanship of exquisite wonder. The champagne glass from which the Polish Ambassador drank was a 17th century goblet engraved with the Polish eagle; the Grand Duke Alexander of Russia quenched his thirst from a glass bearing the portrait of Catherine the Great; the lips of the Infanta Eulalia of Spain touched the glass made for Louis XV after the design by Bérain; the Minister of Czecho-Slovakia held a tumbler made centuries ago in Bohemia; while the wife of the Chinese Ambassador, the exquisite Mrs. Wellington Koo, could appreciate the *bleu de chine* finger bowl in front of her, in which the water was perfumed with an enormous gardenia brought from London that morning.

Adieu, the luscious meals *à la russe* when lunch started in the small chateau with *hors d'oeuvres* and when an hour later the major-domo announced: "*Leurs Altesses Impériles et Royales sont servis!*" much to their surprised consternation as they had thought the thirty different hot and cold dishes served with vodka were the luncheon itself.

---

23 He transformed my 200-year old stable at Galluis into a most enchanting guest house and added other lovely touches to the chateau and park with the most infallible taste.

Adieu to the pleasure of seeing the delight of my feminine friends during the distribution of presents massed high on Sicilian carts and distributed by the Duncan Girls in Greek tunics.

Adieu, Thanksgiving festivities with everything that Earth-Nature provides from celery and tomatoes to pomegranates and figs as a table decoration and the hostess herself dressed to correspond with the golden autumn leaves of the center-piece in a striking Chanel creation of heavy gold tissue.

Adieu to the Easter table bearing suckling pigs, Russian, English, and Prague hams artistically dressed in white sugar. Adieu, lamb, colorful pastries, the gigantic chocolate egg decorated with a huge ribbon and almost touching the ceiling, which was later the delight of the village children. Adieu, the beautifully painted paper eggs with a surprise inside that gave everyone so much pleasure to open.

But adieu also to all that artificiality when the unimportant takes proportion of almost "to be or not to be," as for instance those complicated protocolar placings at dinners or galas at the Théâtre des Champs-Élysées when for three best seats you have four equally important persons to seat and when a mistake is easy to make even when following the directions of the protocolary. Once I recall, when still quite inexperienced, I had two Grand Dukes to place. Naturally, and without hesitation I put the uncle, Grand Duke Alexander, at my right and the nephew, Grand Duke Boris, on my left. I was very surprised when the uncle turned to his nephew and with respect excused himself for taking his place. Later I learned that age has nothing to do with precedence, which is controlled by the hierarchic position in relation to the throne.

* * *

Adieu brilliant but superficial life… Occasionally I saw a few intimate friends and only those who were interested in the line of my vital conception, unless it was those who needed my assistance, although I only received them on Sunday afternoons, unwilling to sacrifice to anyone any moment I could give to my studies.

And my puritan life, as a friend wrongly called it, went on to such an extent that it became humorous. Once while lunching at the Ritz in London I told a friend that I knew he did not drink. He contradicted me so strongly that, in my surprise, I reminded him that he had always refused any wine at Galluis.

"Yes," was his answer. "But at Galluis, in order to please you, I was told that I should decline even the after-luncheon cup of black coffee, so indispensable to a Frenchman!"

I never tasted any alcohol in my whole life. Its smell alone would prevent me from touching it. But there is plenty of wine at Galluis, even if we do not have whiskey and are uninitiated in the art of making a cocktail. For those few friends who wanted to follow my path, I gave orders—to avoid unnecessary temptation—not to serve any wine before asking first if they drank wine or whether they might not prefer cider made from our own apples, knowing well that the French cannot eat if they do not have their habitual digestive glass of wine. Even the three-year-old girl of my gardener takes some red wine diluted with water during her meals and what is funnier yet, she drinks that vinegar-tasting beverage with great pleasure.

If I am against alcohol, it is by all means not puritanism. Far from it, for I am an absolute believer in free will and consider puritan ideas as cruel, enslaving and heartless, because puritanism condemns everything without any differentiation...

I am merely anti-spirits, because I am aware that alcohol, like any artificial stimulant, is the strongest medium in keeping us further from Reality, from Mother Nature. For being natural is the only condition capable of rendering us happy and happiness is what we all want—the so-called unattainable happiness that is actually unattainable only to the ignorant but is quite within the reach of those who have enough persistence to wish for it hard enough and accept the way in which it manifests itself. Only in the way by which Destiny wants to make us happy can we be stably happy; and that is the happiness to be desired rather than in the way our ignorant and conceited ego wants us to be.

Wine can sometimes give the illusion of well-being. Some weak people can stand neither their trials nor their sorrows without that doubtful nectar. But the fact that they feel worse the next morning and are physically ill in addition proves that it is not a real remedy but only a momentary relief. If one understands the Universal Law, there cannot be any more unsolved problems nor can there be helpless misery in that person's life. Even physical suffering has but little power unless its origins are purely Karmic.

* * *

Happiness lies within us…

I wish everyone could have the same certitude in their heart that I now have in mine. I wish everybody knew as I do now that their happiness lies in themselves, exclusively within themselves and quite independently of outside circumstances; and that no power, riches or lack of them can change their inner peace.

For what is power? Man with power is born a man tied and bound. And with power, automatically comes also the vibration of jealousy and envy from the opposition, not to speak of the hate that one then sees more easily in the eyes of those who unsuccessfully still covet that power.

We never hear of a happy man in power. Certainly no king, no dictator could say that he found his heart's desire while envied so much by the whole world. One certainly could not call the great Napoleon's life a happy life. On the contrary! And, if the Duchess of Windsor is mystically inclined—as I have good reason to suppose from several well-informed sources—it is small wonder that Edward VIII saw, when he abdicated, the unreality of power and his inability to help his country by serving in the present materialistically-minded world. He stepped out, visualizing his mission elsewhere, no doubt, desiring to express himself perhaps by the self-development without which one cannot rule others. Perhaps he wanted to become master of himself before mastering his subjects, as this is the only mastery and the only Power that counts.

For what is wealth? If money could buy health, emperors and fabulously wealthy Hindu potentates would live forever. Alas! they are as subject to maladies as any factory worker, probably even more because the laborer is not acquainted with the indigestible *pâté de foie gras* and other expensive foods that are poisonous to our systems. As a consolation to them, statistics show that rich people die younger than the poor.

> *O Fortune! Thy power is destroyed if we are wise: it is our weaknesses that thou owest thy divinity.*
>
> — JUVENAL

I was so happy in my solitude that I could hardly understand those who do not voluntarily aspire to emerge from the prison doors of convention. Ah, if those who struggle for social recognition—and there are legions of them—could total their endless humiliation, their constant disappointment and the force they waste in the hope of getting where it is not easy for them to get and if at the same time they could realize how little they get out of it, certainly and without hesitation they would stop idolizing the false gods. For at best those social climbers get only pitiful misery in return for their chimeric struggle. What pangs of the heart, what sacrifice to their dignity in return for a much coveted invitation!! And once there in the so desired false paradise, what endurance, what hesitation and fear as to the doubtful reception to be met with! Without the slightest benefit to their well-being, only when home they feel relief again. Why not save one's self all such useless misery?

If only those women—it is mostly women, for men are too selfish and not heroic enough to endure such tortures—could understand how lucky they are not to be of the social class, if they could realize how privileged they are at being born free without carrying the burden of family, set, tradition, with the responsibility for their station, honor and class! A case in point might be when a society girl marries a man much below her rank. She does so because unconsciously—she desires by that act to liberate herself from the ties imposed by her birth, while people in general, not seeing the psychology behind such an act, merely call it a scandal.

* * *

Women themselves are responsible if Cholly Knickerbocker becomes the arbiter of their social standing. Being well born himself, he admits openly that "being in society today is nothing more than a state of mind."

Their fear of being quoted by Walter Winchell made him the knout of those politicians whose consciences are not quite clear but his power would be null and void if many other "Mr. Smiths went to Washington." Cholly Knickerbocker and Walter Winchell pursue their vocation as every individual does and therefore the fault lies with those whose whole life depends on the casual mention of their name in the gossip columns.

As for myself, when I was still very ignorant of real values in this world, I disliked Will Rogers very much because while chewing his gum and playing with his rope he would say: "It is almost ten days since we last heard anything about Ganna… I don't know if she has married or divorced again…" He never suspected how unhappy he made me and how I became afraid to go to the theatre lest he or someone else would again say something about me. Poor Will Rogers! I was told he was a wonderful man… When I read about his tragic death, I sent the vibrations of peace to his soul and begged his forgiveness for my negative thoughts.

* * *

How many women envy those who are considered by them lucky enough to be presented at the Buckingham Palace! Envy what? Do they envy the extreme nervousness or the unbearable fright that manifests itself sometimes months before the presentation so that by the time she is actually curtsying before their Majesties her knees shake making her awkward looking? And what for? It all amounts to having afterwards a photograph in the presentation gown. Is that worth while? Is the price not too big, especially as those presentations have become commercialized, nowadays? Are not the débutantes on the threshhold of their coming of age—after long and perfectly good acquaintance with night clubs—selling themselves to the press and to the photographers?

Fortunately when Joseph P. Kennedy went to London as American Ambassador he changed and almost abolished that ruinous tradition, for it was an open secret that a poor girl had no chance to curtsy before the British Majesties since convention had it that she must establish herself in London for at least six months and be sponsored by a dignified duchess, who presumably gave parties and balls for her, the expense of which the débutante was to defray...

When I married Alec Cochran, who was well known in England, where he had his hunting place, his yacht—which in 1914 he presented to His Majesty's government together with his own services—an American born marchioness of Huntly was greatly surprised that I was furnishing a house in Paris instead of London as she wanted me to establish my headquarters on the Thames in preparation for my spring assault on the Court of England!!

And it is useless to pretend that speaking with the crowned heads of this world is ever a pleasure.

When I was presented at the Polish Embassy to Queen Elizabeth of Belgium who flew to Paris to attend the Polish festival organized at the Théâtre des Champs-Elysées, that that musical sovereign was gracious enough to wish to speak first to me and embarrassed me immensely by praising my efforts on the altar of music in a way that showed she was *au courant* with everything I had done musically speaking since I took possession of that beautiful theatre. My uneasiness was great for I was not allowed to interrupt even for my modesty's sake. Finally, no longer able to bear it and in order to stop her eulogistic monologue, I said boldly:

"Madame will excuse me... I know the protocol... I should not speak unbidden, still I wish to say something. May I?"

"Do please, by all means!" said Queen Elizabeth.

"I only wanted to say that I, too, studied with Ysaye, your Majesty's teacher…"

And what vibrations of jealousy that royal distinction raised around me! And what hypocrisy in the court circle when the Belgian Ambassador, Gaiffier d'Hestroy, who had never paid much attention to me before, instantly had himself presented to me by Madame Herriot, wife of the President of the Chamber of Deputies, and then crudely and not very diplomatically told me how he had been my ardent admirer for *so long*—all that to demonstrate his friendship for one who had been singled out by his Queen!

* * *

Speaking of royal and state receptions reminds me of the time I went to Rome for an audience with Mussolini and was told not to be disappointed if he only received me two or three minutes, as lately that was his established length of time for an interview even to important ambassadors he granted only a maximum of fifteen minutes. I hesitated whether or not to leave the Palazzo Chigi then and there without seeing Il Duce, for I realized that in such a short time one cannot get any conception of the real value of a man—and that was my motive in coming to Rome—since it would take that long to merely go through the banalities of making acquaintanceship. However, I did not leave and ultimately stayed with His Excellency forty-six minutes, much to the surprise of the reporters and photographers waiting for me outside.

In those early days of Mussolini's reign stories often appeared in the press about Duce's fear of being assassinated. There was also much condemnation of his suppression of newspapers, magazine or books not favorable to fascism. In France especially he had a very hostile press.

When I left Paris to visit Il Duce, my compartment was full of newspapers and magazines which mercilessly criticized this self-styled Napoleon. One cunning friend even brought to the station a book by Bedel—if my memory serves me right—that had just appeared and which directly attacked the Mussolini regime.

I was warned that I should throw all anti-fascist literature out of the window, as it would all be confiscated at the Italian frontier and perhaps I would not even be allowed to enter the glorious country of Dante.

I went to sleep early, knowing that I would be awakened in the middle of the night by the customs officers. However, I slept perfectly all through the night and in the morning suspected that we were terribly late until I discovered that we were almost at Rome.

No one asked me for my passport. No one even glanced at my luggage, and at the Grand Hotel where I stopped, the anti-fascist Paris newspaper *L'Oeuvre* was delivered to me promptly during the week of my stay there.

Certainly I could tell anti-Mussolinists in America and Paris that they were too quick to judge without verifying the actual situation.

I could also tell of their erroneous opinion about Mussolini's fear of assassination, for when I went that afternoon to Palazzo Chigi for my audience, I could not find, in the whole unguarded, unprotected building a single person from whom to enquire the whereabouts of such an important place as the office of the chief executive. I vainly passed two or three inner courts. The entire place was completely deserted. At a loss what to do, I was already turning towards my car when I finally saw an old, unofficial and stupid-looking man, who on my question, "Dove é il capo del governo ?" indicated in an amateurish way a door in a dark corner. I saw a large, deserted, mysterious-looking stairway and went up… No one on the first floor… A heavy antique door looked as though it had not been opened for centuries… I went higher up… Again a deserted place, again silence… I touched an enormous door… it opened. I faced a long corridor at the end of which, O joy! a man was sitting. But I already doubted his reality. Perhaps it was one of the armored figures of the castle! Repeating my question, "Where can I see the chief of the government?" in an undisciplined manner, almost nonchalantly he pointed to a door, beyond which the Minister of the Press personally brought me directly before Mussolini's piercing eyes.

Realizing that my name and my doings always attracted first page attention, the orders evidently had been to let me enjoy complete freedom in order to offset the rumors of the censored atmosphere that the supposed-to-be free people of Italy were enjoying. A few months later when passing through Rome during the Christmas holidays, I wished to pay Benito Mussolini an unexpected visit, and I was almost arrested just for my attempt to approach Palazzo Venezia. When I did come near it, two husky men jumped on the step of my car to prevent me from putting my feet on the ground in Il Duce's vicinity.

One of the amusing incidents which occurred to me while on this visit to Baron Fassini, a friend with a great personality, was this. During the dinner there were interminable waits between the courses. I expressed the fear that we would be late for the theatre, and begged my host to hurry the service. I was much surprised to learn why faster service was impossible. Baron Fassini—the owner of the beautiful old house where we were dining—himself occupied the ground floor with the only kitchen on the premises, but rented the two other floors of his palazzo. One to Mussolini, then rising dictator, another, if I am not mistaken, to the president of the Senate, Tittoni. But as those apartments were without a kitchen, meals were cooked in the Baron's kitchen. That evening, when delays seemed interminable, Mussolini was having his dinner at the same time. As my friend did not want to take the responsibility for Il Duce's life, every course that went upstairs was first given to a dog, and if within half an hour the dog did not become ill or die, then the food was sent to the Chief of the government!!!

* * *

I can also remember now when I was in St. Petersburg at a very young age, I was taught to kiss the hand of the Dowager Empress Marie at the charity bazaar arranged by the Grand Duchess Vladimir. It was expected that Her Majesty would thank us, the saleswomen, for our participation in that beneficial work. Night after night I spent sleepless hours worrying about how I could manage to kiss that hand without raising or lowering it as I made my deep, deep curtsey…

* * *

While I am at this kind of souvenirs I might as well tell how Marechal Lyautey, builder of the French Empire, very authoritatively insisted on presenting me to the Sultan of Morocco, then present at the Paris Colonial Exhibition. The aged soldier did not hear well and like all those afflicted with that calamity never wanted to admit it. He escorted me before the Moroccan Majesty who was seated, according to Mussulman custom, on a low cushion almost on a level with the floor. The Maréchal, thinking he was whispering, said very loudly in my ear: "Curtsey very deeply!" He did not realize that since the Sultan gave me his hand from such a low position it was totally impossible for me to bend low, unless some future Mr. Einstein will again change the laws of gravity.

No! To be presented to a sovereign is not exactly a sinecure, even when one does not seek that honor—and how much less so if one tries to do the impossible to achieve what has become his or her heart's desire!

> *The weak try to make themselves to be loved; the strong are content to be worthy of love.*
> — EMERSON
>
> *The weak take a deep interest in men and the strong in things.*
> — BONALD

THE DAY must come—or the end of the world, the second sinking of Atlantis—when we will no longer need man-made law and its unrightful justice, the justice that from all evidence is a complete failure for it does not better mankind. The Chinese philosopher Lao-tze rightly said, "The more laws there are in a country, the more numerous the crimes."

It is centuries since the conception of our present standardizing system of justice which, unlike the wisdom of Solomon, is applied indiscriminately to each individual case—and it is long enough to clearly demonstrate that this system cannot diminish crime, efface low instincts or cure insanity.

Man will never create anything that will be able to change man. The Great Intelligence, Cosmic Will, Mother Nature will win in the end. Everybody has more or less been subjected to the experience that to sign a paper nowadays is often the equivalent of automatically getting into trouble, if not even risking loss of possessions. I personally experienced it at great cost when a manager of the Théâtre des Champs-Élysées, gambling with the theatre's capital, lost several million francs without having even the satisfaction of putting him in jail, for, as president of the theatre, once a year I had to sign a very thick book of which I did not know the contents; and the law is that once your signature is given you have no right to protest.

Another time I let myself be persuaded that with the

name of Ganna Walska I could make millions *à la Coty* if I invested in the perfume business. At that time I needed those millions, for I had taken possession of the Théâtre des Champs-Élysées and I knew that in order to make it a Temple of Music for International Festivals and make it enduring I would need a fortune much larger than my comfortable (or even call it luxurious) income. The idea of going into business was antagonistic to every fibre of my being, but I thought I had no right to consider my dislike when music was at stake. I invested. Instead of making millions I lost them along with my faith in written law and its defenders...

People in general are quite aware that the law of today is an absolute failure, a dead matter, a negative protection incapable of doing creative and constructive work. The best proof of that statement is the sentencing of innocent people to hard labor and other wicked punishments, when often the actual criminals are discovered years afterwards, sometimes too late, unfortunately.

Humanity eagerly awaits a new form of justice, a justice of man towards man. They realize that only goodness would be able to bring us sincere and constructive repentance capable of building from an outcast a great soul—a Jean Valjean.

One frosty winter's night long after ten o'clock, my maid inadvertently opened the door to a coat-less ex-convict who admitted quite simply that he had only lately left Sing Sing, that he had tried unsuccessfully to find work, was hungry, cold and ready to do anything however desperate. I gave him some money to go out and eat something warm, sleep in a heated place and return the next morning when I would have a warm coat for him. He did. While he was looking for work I helped him a little bit. When he found he could get a job at the port of Baltimore, I got him a ticket to reach there. He thanked me with tears and later wrote me on a Christmas card that he was quite happy. Perhaps his entire life would have been different if I had sent him away that night.

A young English society girl, Miss Deirdre, did wonderful work by helping those miserable beings whose uncontrolled emotions or bad instincts had pushed them towards crime. She had a farm where she gave work to those ex-convicts who had just left prison and whom nobody dared employ. Thus she provided them with a decent means of existence while giving them a chance to recover their human dignity.

Only Understanding and Trust in possibility that is Infinite can save those who fall deeper and deeper into the abyss of wrong-doing if blamed or punished. Only mutual help can bring us nearer to the desirable goal—to our betterment and consequently to peace within us.

* * *

Nowadays man-made law is not considered sacred. We are informed that when we are put under oath we must tell the truth; otherwise punishment awaits us. But we do not feel the proper respect for the law which should be considered almost holy and should inspire the same respect as the national anthem. On the contrary, how often people who have just signed a contract automatically feel free of their obligation or even immediately go so far as to seek a means through their lawyers of evading the issues of the contract! Not so the people who seal a bargain by shaking hands—they would not perjure their parole for all the world. One does not need to resort to deep psychology to understand the clear fact that if a person seeks the protection of the law in a contract, it means he has no trust in his fellowman; whereas the individual who voluntarily contracts some moral obligation would never consider breaking the trust put in him. Just take a look at the underworld to see how that can work. Unable to have the protection of the law, being lawless themselves, they never betray their colleagues, knowing that they would pay with death for the treachery.

* * *

Before the blissful age of real self-government is reached, the world, during this present transitory period, needs rather more leaders like Salazar, the Portuguese dictator,[24] than a political brain or military genius even of Napoleonic grandeur. For only a spiritually powerful man can bring about the absolute impossibility of war, the idea of which should not even flash through our minds. Only when people put fraternity higher than patriotism, that feeling would cease; for, as Béranger said: "When one crosses bayonets, ideas can no longer get through."

Only Lohengrin's spiritual force could change the heart of man, which is certainly harder to accomplish than just changing a regime or a man at the head of a government.

To preach goodness one must be good. Therefore only a good man, actually good and knowing Infinite Goodness and not the humanly fallible conception of goodness, could himself realize and demonstrate to humanity that only Goodness, Goodness of heart can stop killing. Not the man with the mistaken idea of goodness, like the Englishman who brutally beat a cat to death for catching birds. I prefer my favorite story about a little boy who during Good Will Week was asked what charitable act *he* performed. He happily answered: "I gave my canary to my cat!"

Killing is killing, whether it be killing humans or animals. Whether it be in self-defense or killing an animal in hunting, it is still killing. As long as we nourish ourselves with such

---

24 As much as I can judge from what I have heard about him and what I personally witnessed of the atmosphere in that country when I stopped over night at Lisbon when about to board the American Clipper. For at the hotel there was no safe large enough to hold my enormous jewel case which was worth a fortune and they merely proposed that I leave it some place in the lobby saying: "No one will touch it—we sometimes have millions of dollars worth of jewels just left on the window sill…" And it was the truth, for my limited fifty pounds weight (allowed on the clipper) of emeralds, diamonds, rubies and pearls were safely on the window sill open to the street when I returned late that night.

perishable substance as the flesh of animals, we poison ourselves with the fear that the condemned creature had at the moment of agonizing death—for death is agonizing in spite of all the modern ways that have been evolved of presenting death on a silver platter. Not to mention the fact that vegetarians or those who cannot afford meat are much more healthy.

If the man who is electrocuted does not suffer from the pains actually inflicted by the electrocution—and they do not come back to confirm that statement—their mental horror of the Unknown is far greater than the physical suffering would be. Besides dumb animals have senses more developed than we have and can see beyond our eyes. For instance a dog is able to see a ghost and can sense death before it actually comes. And in some countries they have laws which cause stray dogs or cats to be killed within twenty-four hours if they are not claimed—simply because they are unable to tell their master's name and address!

There cannot be such a thing as humanitarian killing. Any living thing that dies an unnatural death at the hands of man dies in fright whether it be the beef, pork or lamb that is to grace the dinner table; the animal and bird hunted for sport or killed for its fur and its hide, or caught for its feathers; or the fish pulled from the streams and the sea just for mere pleasure. The vibrations of those creatures poisoned with fright do not end with their death but continue their venomous effect in those who eat them.

It is up to the government to enforce the law of not killing if the old routine is so strong in us that we cannot purify ourselves and free our souls from the worst sin: "Thou shalt not kill." It is up to the government also to forbid bull-fights and cock-fights if there remains so much of the cave man in the human composition.

Only spiritually powerful man can change the consciousness of the human comprehension of law. For this he must rebuild, recreate himself first, before undertaking to lead humanity as only then he will be able to help his fellow man. This is not an Utopia, nor is my idea merely the result of the exaltation of my fervent soul. I am not a fanatic. On the contrary, I arrived at my present philosophy by the hardest way and not at all by walking in a dreamland. If by brute force, one man can change the geographic face of the Old World and become absolute lord over millions and millions, surely greater power can be found in a man who can spiritually unite all mankind—for the power of Good being eternal is stronger than any contemporaneous or circumstantial power. Did not a single man—Jesus-leave the greatest impression of all men, an impression which has lasted twenty centuries despite His short stay on earth? And before him, Buddha...?

"He who masters education can change the face of the world," Leibnitz said. How much more then can the man achieve who will make that education spiritual as well as intellectual?

Like attracts like. Therefore only a good man may expect to be followed by the masses without distinction of race, creed or political belief. But in order to lead he must set the living example of true justice and must not govern the world according to the dead written law that has proved its impotency to help humanity. Above all he must encourage the feeling of brotherly love—the only sure way to enable all people to solve all problems.

However, until the blessed day comes when people will be guided by their conscience, we are in absolute need of some new laws. One of the first of those laws to be created must forbid killing defenseless creatures, especially hunting for pleasure, destroying for sport. This law will be much more for the sake of a hunter than for his victims.

The law must be enforced until fathers who greatly cherish their children will understand in their hearts that they may be killing the mother animal whose children may thus be orphaned. The law must stand until men realize within themselves what their feelings would be if the same thing happened to their own families and until they are able to understand that by killing they harm first and foremost themselves by darkening their souls. People capable of killing things without even having the excuse of self-protection or hungry necessity cannot expect to avoid fratricidal wars, abominable crimes or the tragic insanity that is so dangerously frequent today. Dr. Carrel's *Man The Unknown* would startle any average person with its statistics on present day insanity.

How can peace be expected to reign between nations when their leaders visiting each other to discuss the possibilities of friendly relationships start their sacred missions with hunting or shooting parties and gloriously exhibit their trophies to the public eye through the press, instead of opening such a mission with contemplative church silence or with hearing Inspirational Music such as "Parsifal"? Full of vibrations of satisfied vanity from the enormous quantity of God's creatures they have assassinated, they take up the gigantic task of discussing the destiny of nations and the lives of millions of living beings!

And, oh, irony, St. Hubert is the patron saint of huntsmen and on his nameday the clergy celebrate masses and bless the pack of hounds that is going out to wound, kill and leave young lives vainly awaiting the return of their mothers…

* * *

And who will have the great privilege of stopping the torturing of animals for the sole reason of beautifying ladies' backs? A few decades ago the killing of chinchillas —from which came the most expensive and consequently most commercially desirable furs—was forbidden in South America. It was done, if I am not mistaken, to preserve the species which was in danger of disappearing. No matter what motives were behind the law, it proved that such a thing can be done and has been done. The same thing should be done with other animals killed or tortured for their furs. And just as those *belles* who had accustomed themselves to those soft greyish-blue capes, scarves and muffs of chinchilla became accustomed to going without them, the same habit would be developed and applied with regard to every other fur-coated animal tortured in abominable horrors and killed in excruciating agony in order to enrich a fur dealer or to give depressing vibrations to whoever wears them. Not to speak of the follies some women commit in order to get their mink, ermine or silver fox coat. People cannot even imagine with what atrocious cruelty the trapping of wild animals for their fur is carried out! ! !

America by forbidding the importation of paradise and aigrette feathers cruelly plucked from live birds already has taken a tremendous step towards liberating herself from barbarism. Will she continue to set the precious example to the Old World, too old to free itself from aged traditions? Individuals are rarely capable of tearing themselves away from deeply rooted habits established by their ancestors and inherent within themselves. Humanity needs nothing less than the example of a Parsifal to change the unconscious killer into the divine man within himself.

* * *

In countries like the United States where prostitution is not tolerated by the law, morality is of a comparatively higher standard. Anti-moralists would protest that it is useless to go against nature and yet they forget that we do not let small children play with matches, we oppose babies' desires to swallow everything in sight such as pins and needles and we put bars on the windows of the mentally weak. Just as parents try to develop the conscience of their children, so grown-ups must be educated by a collective intelligence—the Law—to help them withstand temptation.

If all lights were out by midnight, if night life were to disappear, if dancing halls and cabarets were closed at an earlier hour of the evening, people would be obliged to accustom themselves to lead a normal life. If the Creator of the world sent us the darkness of night, He meant that we should rest during that time just as the birds, animals, flowers and other creations of God do. We cannot prolong the day with impunity or escape the punishment of trespassing upon divinely established laws.

If women did not see fur coats in shop windows, they would not be tempted to own them. Then even those who already realized how the skins came into the shop would no longer say to themselves as I myself so often have: "Yes, I know I should not do it. But those poor animals are killed anyhow... If I do not buy this coat, someone else will..."

Skeptics may easily mock and say that according to my way of thinking all one has to do to become good and go directly to Heaven is not to give one's wife a mink coat for Christmas, not to have a steak for luncheon and not to go to the nearest woods the first day of hunting season to shoot partridge. Yes, it sounds childish if put that way. Yet it is a fact that if no one, not a single soul, had the heart to kill a squirrel, a lamb, a grouse, or any other animal—people would be able to govern themselves and the prisons of today would tomorrow become the barracks of those wonderful samaritans of the peaceful army, the Salvation Army—the greatest humanitarian institution in existence in our time—to shelter those *Heimatlos* who are not so much in need of a piece of bread as they are of the friendly word that goes with it.

The human heart that is both unwilling and absolutely incapable of killing a rabbit certainly could not consider killing a human being. I do not mention even the duels, outlawed and rarer each day.

Humanity must understand that for no reason whatsoever can it take a life, any life, even the life of a fly if it is not absolutely necessary. If this long-sought blessed peace must come and stay, this understanding must be in the heart and not in the mind. Once a student of mine—we are always student of some and pupil of others—young in the search of the Truth, saw that I was bothered by some black bugs which had flown through the open window attracted by the electric light. Wishing to rid me of them and keeping in mind my rules about no killing, she took them from my room in a napkin. When I warned her not to hold the napkin tight as it might smother them, I was assured by her that they were being held quite loosely. But the next morning, to my horror, I saw the bugs all drowned in my bathtub! And she thought she did not kill! No, merely drowned them!!

Life, the great mystery, the great possession, is the most precious treasure of the universe. It is the universe, because life is movement and through motion the universe comes to existence.

Individual life is given to us to make a whole, to make a part of a whole, thus being indispensable, indispensable to the whole and indispensable to us as it is our only way to evolve. Therefore, by shortening our life or that of others, we commit unspeakable sins against the fundamental law. That is why suicide is such a terrific crime against ourselves and our Karma must be very bad if we can not overcome the desire to kill what is the greatest in us. For as the proverb says: "Where there is life there is always hope…"

I find no good without burden in this world…
Is it better that in our garden there be thorns
so that there may be roses or not to have roses so
that there may be no thorns?

— ST. FRANCIS OF SALES

WHILE I WAS waiting for the soul of my soul, waiting in vain, tragically lonesome in a seemingly happy life, somewhere in England a man was seeking the woman of his dreams. During his youth he passionately adored his mother and her death broke his spirit and his health. Only his life's work saved him from the worst…

Like myself he joyfully dedicated his life to study. From the age of twelve as long as his mother lived, he desired nothing more than to experiment with electricity, unless it was sheltering homeless cats or protecting nests of carefree birds whose song and habits he knew better than any ornithologist. Sensing his affection for them, the cats in the streets would approach him in full confidence and when he left on a trip to the States, one of his toms committed suicide.

Once I had the same experience in my own household, therefore I know that the notion that cats are not attached to people is entirely unjust.

* * *

When we met at the Authors Club in London that afternoon, he did not say: "Here you are at last… I have waited for you so long…" No, the conversation between the four of us in the party was rather superficial. Several times I overheard him telling Gita that I was most charming, as if he were speaking of any unimportant person in *his life,* saying it as one does when he honestly cannot say anything better, anything more or anything less…

(It reminded me of the cases when I was introduced to

Americans who had formed their opinion of me in advance from the many foolish newspaper stories that had been circulated around me. With joyous sincerity they would look me straight in the eyes and often say with frank surprise: "But you *are* charming!" *Merci!*)

Only when he escorted us to the car, instead of the traditional: "It has been a great pleasure," he said:

"God bless you!"

I rather liked that and under the spell of those words and the deep look in his eye—he only had one—I suggested to Gita that she invite him to come with us the next day to hear "Palléas and Mélisande," which was being given at Covent Garden during the Coronation and for which I had lent my scenery from the Théâtre des Champs Elysées.

He accepted eagerly the chance to see me again. However, I was not able to get an extra seat next to ours in the first row and could only get one six tiers farther back.

We arrived at the opera very early, as I usually do. He was already there awaiting us. The theatre was still empty, so temporarily we chatted at our seats.

When the conductor took his place and the lights dwindled, he left to look for his seat. Something urged me to let him stay with us. But already he was up and logic told me that it was better for him to go before the orchestra started. No one yet had claimed the seat next to ours but I knew it would be taken since no amount of thoughtfulness on the part of the management had been able to secure the extra seat for me.

During the first act the chair next to me remained empty. I thought it a shame for someone to miss the three first scenes of Debussy's masterpiece! Still I should not judge so rapidly for traffic during the Coronation was very heavy and the buses were on strike… Probably the holder of the seat had come just as the curtain rose and not wanting to disturb anyone he was even then standing at the door, waiting for the intermission to find his place…

No one came during the first *entr'acte*. No one ever came… My guest returned and remained between us the whole evening… The Opera House was sold out, not an empty seat anywhere, not an unoccupied chair in the boxes—yet the place next to mine was vacant… Was it Destiny? I began to wonder.

But is it possible *now*… ? No, it is too late… ! I do not *wait* any longer… I do not *need* any longer… I do not *want* any longer…

* * *

Is it possible that the progress of civilization cheated me of a great moment, that the vital desire to gain time could annihilate the essence of our inner life? Could it be that science, to which he had been a faithful soldier and on the altar of which he had given the sight of one eye—"On est toujours puni par où l'on a peché"—that science changed the substance of his soul into self-accommodating clay? For it was over the long distance telephone for convenience sake and in the unmysterious bright light of the day that he told me he loved me.

And how strange that he followed that confession by saying: "You believe in my sincerity, do you?"

It was even stranger when he insisted until I assured him that I believed him. But that was not the point. In the back of my mind I kept wondering why this question, as generally sincere people do not mention the fact of their sincerity… The only justification I could think of for his telling the Lady of his Destiny over the telephone, "I love you," was that he was so full of love he could not control his feelings or wait any longer. But, to ask whether I believed him—strange, very strange…

"Will phone you again later in the evening," was his closing remark.

No, he did not ask: "May I?"

* * *

He telephoned. He told me his sister was dying... Cancer... But I thought his friends had told me that he had been working on an invention to conquer that terrible malady. Was it not yet perfected?

She could live a week longer... He was going to her the next day...

"Good-night, darling!" very depressed he said finally.

How I disliked that familiarity and "darling" coming from an Englishman shocked my sense of rhythm and beauty even more.

I put down the receiver... I felt free again... I felt relieved... My heart became light. I was no longer in doubt—I knew he could not be the man I had been seeking. Generously I let my brain have a feast and how that human mind took advantage of this opportunity! (I never mind if my servants ridicule me, as long as I cannot hear them.)

What an extraordinary man! He knows the precise day his sister will pass away, still he does not feel his beloved woman is fading from his life...

He did not mention anything more about his coming. ... Naturally... His sister is dying... She will live one week... The greatest physician cannot predict for certain the death of a sick person... But, a loving brother's heart has more intuition... Yes, that was it! And he has used all the intuition a man is capable of to predict the exact number of days his sister will stay with him in this incarnation... He was left too poor to feel that I am already far, far away...

* * *

What does the coming into my life of this man mean anyhow? Especially since he has come at a point when I no longer expect a personal expression of love. Can it be a temptation? I have none. Is it a trial—a trial to see how much I can stand without losing the spirituality I have acquired, without descending to the lowest regions? Or is it to be a stepping-stone to as yet unattainable summits? I wonder...

* * *

Can it be that such expressions of love as marriage are still necessary to my further development or does that depend solely on the strength of my soul? Must I succumb to earthly conditions in order to deliver myself conclusively from the illusion that we live on this planet? Must I be as little as a *wife* in order to become bigger? And why? Is it essential?

Would I have enough purity to convince his heart of what mine is? Would it be right of me to ask him to go against his conception of Nature?

After all, if *this* world exists—and he and I are here—is it not Nature that perpetuates itself through us? And if so, why would it be unnatural or anti-spiritual? I wonder. . . . Still I feel as if I were going backwards... I feel diminished... I wonder...

* * *

He said his heart had recognized me at once and only his reason was fighting him... But I could not seem to get in touch with his heart. All I could see was his fight—his fight with himself, with his friends, with imaginative enemies, with the government, with collaborators, with his biographer, with the climate and now with me...

No one escaped his scorn but those who admired him blindly. His lips pronounced words of love and hate in the same breath. The word hate never left his mouth...

* * *

He was always suing someone for calumny. He always defended his good name through the offices of his solicitor. The anonymous letters which he received made him desperate and he was never satisfied until he had succeeded in jailing their authors, in spite of the knowledge that they were more unbalanced than they were wicked...

Everything about him was negative. He looked older than his age. He seemed haggard. Quite blind in one eye, his other, saw but little. His hands trembled so he could hardly lift his glass of vermouth to his lips from which a cigarette eternally dangled. His hair was untidy because of the black elastic eye-patch which squeezed his head mercilessly and gave him atrocious headaches for years. His forehead was irregularly shaven because of his poor eye but why he shaved it I never understood. Some accident... A silver plate under the skin...? I never knew... But his photos in the English "Who's Who," taken in his youth show his hair growing rather low on his forehead, while with it shaven he looks like a thinker—somewhat like certain portraits of Goethe.

He considered himself a victim of his epoch, victim of jealousy, envy, injustice and treachery. But most of all the victim of Great Britain's lack of appreciation—forgetting that a prophet is not without honor save in his own country. He had given everything to his country: his health, his sight and his fortune. He, the celebrated inventor of the Death Ray, according to the press, was ready to save humanity from wars, cancer and other dreadful maladies but the government was not willing to collaborate with him.

Fortunately, private individuals with more foresight and clearer vision believed in him and finally promised they would put a private yacht at his disposal so that he could demonstrate his submarine invention—his fond child which he had nursed for seventeen long years—for which he had been promised any amount of money he desired and a title!

If only he could hold out two more months! But his health was very poor and it was feared he might have a nervous breakdown at any moment which could have been fatal to him with his defective heart aggravated by the sleepless nights since he fell in love with me.

His only happy moments were when reading about

himself in the newspapers, although he knew the articles only appeared because he himself gave out the material for them. He certainly enjoyed the fact that the press never mentioned him without calling him the author of the Death Ray. It gave him real pleasure to read how important *he* was and how unappreciative the government was of his genius. Furthermore, since our meeting he wanted to impress me with the greatness he carried in him. His love for publicity was so strong that somehow the reporters and photographers always knew when I arrived at Croydon or when I lunched with him,

I was informed that he could not visit me in France as his government was afraid he would be killed abroad by the enemies who had reason to wish that his invention never see the light of day. In London he was not allowed to take two steps without being escorted for the sake of protection by a Major in the Intelligence Service.

His jealousy was immeasurable. He was especially jealous of those in his profession, always believing that Branly, Marconi and others took his ideas as well as the credit for them. Thinking it must be of vital interest to him, I would always read him any article that appeared in French and American magazines I happened to see about inventions that were in his line, since he could not read with his one bad eye. But the idea that someone else could achieve where he failed upset him to such an extent that even two or three days afterwards he would still be in such low spirits that I stopped giving him information concerning his vital work. He was also jealous of anybody who approached me, man or woman. When I pointed out to him that this characteristic was rather small and unworthy of such a big man, he became so depressed and sad and worn looking that I was afraid he would not survive the night in those low spirits. So I forgave him, tried to forget his shortcoming and see in him only the poor human wreckage with divine possibilities. Under those conditions, however, I craved to leave

London. But he spent the night sitting in the car in front of my hotel and sent his bodyguard as a messenger to warn me that if I left London he would collapse, he would die.

Genius is like a child. Like a child he could not live if I were not there to bid him a smiling goodnight. I stayed…

* * *

When his nerves got the best of him, when sleepless nights and constant headaches almost drove him crazy, I was asked unofficially by the government and certain English patriots if I would give him some hope, as it was feared that my indifference might kill him before his invention for detecting submarines and defending London against bombardment through rocket shooting could reach the hands of the War Ministry. I gave some hope…

But one day he confessed he could work no longer—and he must work for humanity, mind you—if I would not consent to marry him.

Marry? I had never thought of it!! Not for anything in the world would I marry again. Never ! ! I was so happy with my newly acquired liberty and had adjusted myself to it so quickly that marriage now would seem to me like a prison.

With contorted face, blind eyes, shaking hands and trembling feet, he would ask me hourly whether I thought I could ever marry him, begging me to give him a hope if only for the later future.

I mumbled something about never considering marriage again…

* * *

In the meantime, under the pretext that I needed an investment that would bring me enormous and quick return I begged him to allow me to help him financially to carry on to a finish his work those last two months. Why did I beg? Because I did not know that he would have taken my help anyhow and gladly, since he believed it was a duty and even a privilege for anyone to help a genius who was trying to save humanity!

* * *

The August day approached when the final experiment was to take place thanks to the member of Parliament who put his yacht at Grindell-Matthews' disposal.

Too arrogant to those close in his environment, not sufficiently broadminded to understand others, quick to condemn people, always judging everybody from his heights and suspecting everyone of bad motives, he naturally was friendless though some men still believed in his inventions and had helped him to a greater or lesser degree. Those patrons now begged me to pretend I would marry Grindell so that he might have a free mind to give his best to this universally important discovery that would rid the world of fratricidal wars.

I knew it would be unfair to pretend I would marry him and then let him down, once he achieved his long desired goal, because ever since falling in love with me he had lost what little balance he had had previously when, at least, he could work free-heartedly.

Lengthily and profoundly I pondered where my duty lay. My preference clearly was for personal freedom. But the clouds were heavy over Europe at that time and several British submarines had been attacked anonymously, so to speak, in Spanish waters. Had I the right to selfish consideration? What to do? I could not turn to L., as he never wanted to advise me on the subject of any of my personal problems, probably thinking that by then I could fly on my own. And then I did not even know how to reach him. He might be in California, in a silent retreat with no contact with the world at all.

In those doubtful days I happened to visit Rom Landau, the Polish writer living in England whose mystical books had interested me and led me to think that after great disappointment he himself had become an adept of detachment. I mentioned to him therefore that I might be obliged to marry against my desire…

"Why?" was his answer, "Why not? Selfish comfort? Do you consider yourself spiritually above the multitude?" Yes, he was right. Selfishness… Comfort…

I gave hope…

* * *

He failed in his experiments, blaming naturally everyone and everything including the water at the Isle of Wight. I gave him all the encouragement I could, quoting examples of all the great geniuses who failed at first. Yes, I encouraged him but it reminds me that once when he was present at my singing lesson he told me afterward that some of my notes were sweet but most of them sounded—as he said it: "terrrrrible!"

Winter approached. So new experiments were out of the question until the following spring. Our great man was still more broken—not in spirit though, for nothing could diminish his self-assurance, he did not know even the meaning of the word humility—and nearer to a nervous breakdown than ever before, while the pain in his eye maddened him with constant suffering. An operation was absolutely necessary on the eye in which he had partial sight in order at least to save it.

* * *

I prayed… I prayed, prayed in my way, by trying to tune with the Positive where sickness has no power and while singing each pure tone I succeeded in producing I was sending to the Infinite as a divine messenger to beg for the restoration of sight to a man needed by humanity. And once during the Salzburg Festival hearing Mozart's Mass in the pious atmosphere of the Cathedral when I was able to reach the higher sphere—I raised his eyes with me to bathe them in the Universal Light...

* * *

The operation was performed and quite miraculously he recovered his sight in—in both eyes! Even his surgeon could hardly believe such a possibility had existed, much less been realized. How humbly grateful to God I was! My soul was saturated with joy!

Such a grace! I must consider it as a divine privilege to save this man for God's work! I hesitated no more... I decided to marry him...

* * *

Thereafter I put all the force in me at his service, the service of humanity—God's divine service. I always sensed that the fortune in my possession was put by Destiny at my disposal in order that I may be able to help a great cause. Now I fervently hoped that I was chosen to be instrumental in saving the world from the calamities of wars, for the War Minister, then Duff Cooper, announced that with those two inventions, on which Grindell was working, in hand he would proclaim their existence to the world and distribute them to friendly countries so that no enemy would be *Don quixotic* enough to invite suicide. Later Sir Kingsley Wood, the Air Minister, in the *Evening Standard* of October 24th, 1938, said: "One of the greatest benefits could come of some effective means of defeating the bomber machine. I do not despair that this will come, and I know that today many are engaged upon that work..."

* * *

Our great genius also assured me that, with the help of my voice and his color inventions, cancer and other deadly shadows could be removed from this earth.

And already I built a special laboratory at Galluis for the purpose of furthering those researches...

How reverently I received this mission in my heart! What great care I took of the man who was chosen for such an elevated purpose! Ineffable peace bathed my soul! I was only sorry I could not breathe for him to save the work of his weak heart! And how I desired to become purer and purer so that the Divine Inspiration might be manifesting itself through his and my minds! How carefully I tried to change his scientist's skepticism into belief in God's Infinite possibility! And how gratefully humble I felt when finally he realized that everything true comes only through God! And what a joy it was when he agreed to carry the symbol of Divine Mind that governs our doings, a triangle on the gold chain which I begged him to wear as an admission that Universal Intelligence is above human brain...

* * *

Galluis—already an earthly paradise with its wonderful rosary, green lawns, fantastic grotto, Goya's fountain, curious grotesques, extraordinary forms of fruit trees- Galluis With the greatest known collection of Spanish, Portuguese and Dutch tiles united in one place, with a unique assemblage of coral and crystal, with primitive Italian mirrors and great quantity of *velour de Gênes*, in one word—Galluis, which until then had been an Eden here below, was to become a celestial haven which High Inspiration had chosen for its dwelling—there where wild, hungry and sick cats together with pheasants and hares that escaped the huntsman's gun found refuge, this Galluis was to hear now such heavenly sounds as its birds had never created and to see colors never before seen by ordinary human eyes—and those sounds and color combinations would annihilate any dreadful disease...

* * *

Lover of nature as Grindell was, Galluis was an ideal place

for his convalescence. I myself tenderly love the trees and the majestic murmur of their family—the forest! Considering them as living things, I never pass by without liberating those silent companions from their broken branches, being positive that, wounded, they suffer as we do.

My gardener never could understand such a queer idea. Therefore I was very happy when I found that Grindell shared with me this peculiarity. Being tall, skillful and with experience that he gained on the Welsh mountain where he had built his laboratory, he freed hundreds of Galluis trees from the heavy weight, thus bringing many again to life so that I no longer had the feeling of walking on a battle field. He begged to spare only the mistletoe, as the druids had some superstition about cutting and separating it from trees; the horticulturists of today on the contrary consider mistletoe as a parasite that lives on the vitality of the trees and that it should be taken away.

He also was a great benefactor to all birds, lovingly protecting their nests. He knew each call of every different bird on the property. Every egg and all the habits of our feathered friends were familiar to him.

Now he was in good health, not the smallest detail escaped his eyes—he could even drive a car if he so desired—his hands trembled but little, he looked fifteen years younger and he could work under the best possible conditions without any worry about financial problems. Here and at his laboratory in the mountains of Wales everything was provided for him. He had everything that a favorable atmosphere could provide in order to create and give himself to inspirational work.

That state lasted a few short months and then he got jealous again, jealous of God who gave him all that. Not acquainted with humility, he thought that anything coming from God diminished his own merits and then, too, he considered that, after all, God was so far away and quite unproved, while you could read in "Who's Who" what he himself had done…

In his opinion the only thing that counted was *time*. He must have his success now when there was so much talk of war and when the Admiralty would be more generous with him. He deduced he would then become Lord of something-or-other. Already he was calling me Lady Grindell and was unable to grasp why I was not thrilled at the idea of wearing a title. He just could not comprehend that one can outgrow the desire for all human distinctions and was quite puzzled that during my eventful life, having had the opportunity to become the wife of a Grand Duke of Russia, of an Archduke of Austria, of an Infante of Spain, of an ambassador representing a great country, of a prime minister in a very important European capital or one of the wives of a picturesque Hindu potentate—I refused those honors.

He thought that it was all right for a woman to talk about God but such a personality as his got everything from his own brain. And in a moment of uncontrolled rage—which was his dominating characteristic—again and again he would throw away the symbolic chain I had given him. Symbolic for me, for only then I understood that his small soul could not fulfill the Divine Mission of saving humanity from the wars…

GALLUIS
SUMMER 1939

WINTER 1940
NEW YORK

To carry out great deeds one should live as if one were never going to die.

— VAUVENARGUES

RE-READING THESE memoirs this winter, I had great difficulty in keeping myself from tearing them to pieces, especially the description of the last few years of my wanderings through that mysterious mental labyrinth when so many contradictions confused my judgment and obscured my vision. If I did not give in to that destructive desire, it was only on account of my wish to demonstrate to my readers the fact that the Light comes to us progressively and that we must accustom our vision step by step to its full greatness.

If I have confessed so much unhappiness in these reminiscences—and I have only put down the most minute part of my suffering as it would require volumes to tell of all the trials I experienced—it was for the sake of emphasizing my present happy state of mind to show how I came to this great possession and in the ardent hope that my example would encourage some in their evolution. And it was to describe what a long and thorny road I was designed to travel before arriving at my present comprehension, which is great. For, in spite of the terrifying world's tragedy and happenings which only yesterday were unthinkable, unbelievable to our mental conception, I can witness human self-destruction with Hopeful Serenity and Absolute Faith in Ultimate Goodness because I know that each living creature, being a possessor of that Goodness, will—by the simple method of desiring it sufficiently—finally be brought to the only unchangeable reality… to God!

* * *

Some people are born happy or at least have what we call happiness... Their lives are eventless or empty of tragic atmosphere... Evidently there is no necessity for them to suffer in this incarnation... Obviously they are not strong enough to be blessed with such an elevated privilege...

To those my cruel experiences may seem useless. They may consider this message of mine merely as a more or less entertaining autobiography—a purpose certainly far from my mind. Even if I know that my real motives may be misunderstood by many who will only see the skeleton of the words instead of the soul behind them, still if I have opened my heart in spite of my great reserve, it has only been with the thought that through doing so I have accomplished what I believed was my duty, and with the sincere hope that my narrative may be useful to some seekers of Truth, especially those who like myself are lucky enough to pay *right here, this time* and not *mañana* the toll for their soul's elevation!

* * *

It is said that happy people, like happy nations, have no history and—no shirts, to quote the story I heard so often in my childhood. The fable was that in bygone days a Wizard informed his King, who was dangerously ill, that only by wearing the shirt which had belonged to a happy man could he be cured. Thousands went searching for the lucky man who would be the savior of their Monarch. . . Thousands came back empty-handed... Neither within the kingdom nor outside its limits could a happy man be found... More thousands rushed this time in new directions. Still they returned with no better results. One day, a much disheartened messenger was surprised to see a very poor, vermin-ridden man singing away joyfully. "Why do you sing—you, there, hungry and infested as you are?"

"I sing because I am happy!" was the answer.

"Happy? In such misery? How could you be happy?"
"Just happy! Happy!" said the smiling man.
"Happy? Then give me your shirt to save our King!" "My shirt? I have no shirt…"

* * *

It was almost easy at the time to write about those events in my life that materialized in tragedy and beset me with trials. But now with peace impregnating my inner being where nothing is changeable, where everything is stable, I find it a quasi-impossible task to put such a rock-like state of immense tranquility into a few misleading, poorly written, badly read words. Now, when everything is clear, my past blindness seems to me to have been almost a voluntary obstinacy…

It is still more difficult for me to explain that process which enabled me to obtain the comprehensive wisdom of feeling that in spite of all outside appearances even the most miserable life is the greatest gift we are receiving and that death can frighten only the ignorant.

Recently a man after killing his estranged wife explained the motive by saying to his children: "I killed your mother because she did not deserve to live." I do not suppose he actually understood the great meaning of his words —"not deserve to live." Yes, one must deserve to live, his only chance for evolution.

Once we are given to understand the great Universal Law, then so-called death only takes on the aspect of a transfiguration, much as the end seems to come to a rose-bush when it has fulfilled its mission of blooming and loses the glorious garment visible to the human eye until the following summer.

* * *

Where previously doubts paralyzed my activities, where distorted judgment handicapped my progress, where autocratic intolerance in search for Perfection *built the wall between me and simple understanding,* where emotion entirely blinded my vision—now Certainty reigns in full! What seemed to be obscure only a few years ago has become clear now, for the readjustment came and with the recognition of a Free Will in every one of us, it mattered little or not at all whether it was through this or that technique, or which spiritual teaching was correct in leading to the right comprehension of God! The great knowledge of the infallible Law nullified all negative feeling. All destructive thought and condemnation, blame and criticism had no more existence in me.

The profound feeling of Love, Love for all, Love for even the stones that pave the streets and keep us from walking in the mud, exiled forever circumstantial love, the love which depends on reciprocity, the love which demands dividends—selfish love!

I am grateful now to Providence for those experiences in the past which easily confused my mind in its spiritual search. They enabled me to learn that each individual, each teacher of any Truth with whom I came in contact—no matter to what extent they were intellectual or commercial—was doing *some good*, in fact great good at times. Even spiritualists who suppose to give you the messages from your dear departed ones do good because those consolation-seekers, even though they may be unaware of it, are admitting the immortality of the soul[25] —the foundation of our spiritual future life.

Any typical witch-like, mustachioed old woman with the traditionally indispensable fattish cat who predicts a shining present resembling a diamond, a letter with the prospects of money or the freedom of your sweetheart through the death

---

25 Which brings to mind the story about the professor who did not believe in the immortality of the soul and then proceeded to tell his students that when he died he would communicate to them the proof of its nonexistence.

of his wife before July—*is* doing good —not through those unhealthy predictions but because the person getting them becomes a seeker and seeking is good, no matter where and how! Seeking opens the door and each time that door opens it opens on a higher conception. Yes, *seeking!* Everything but satisfaction, anything but inertia! Seeking is *Life*, while apathy is *stagnation*.

The French provincial druggist, Coué, who first taught self-suggestion in Europe by repeating: "Every day in every way I am getting better and better" did mountains of good. At least as long as the millions of this spiritual-psychological pioneer's followers repeated those simple words, destructive thoughts could not enter their minds.

* * *

Summing up my past experiences I must be eternally grateful to those who badly hurt my sensitive soul in the past. I should be grateful, for instance, to Dr. Mills and also to Mr. Rawson for initiating me in meditation which made the foundation of my future inner stability, even if the fruits did not ripen until a quarter of a century later and not in a way I expected or had been promised.

Those twenty dollar horoscopes were useful too, for they proved to my rather skeptical mind the existence of some great if unknown power, unknown to our humanly interpretive intelligence but unfolded to the infinite soul in us!

Instead of the quick condemnation after one unfortunate case that I had indulged in during my youth, I know now the full value of such a gift as Mary Baker Eddy bestowed on the masses in giving them Christian Science!

Instead of criticizing, condemning, finding fault with all of those small or big teachers who try—often in spite of themselves as when pursuing their selfish ends—to elevate our souls, each in their individual spiritual progression, we should accept with *open heart* everything they are capable of giving, everything we are able to receive! We should steel our minds that are only too ready to judge. Soon we would search out only those masters who have evolved—if only partly—higher than ourselves, leaving the teachers of yesterday to those who, like ourselves, were more ignorant than we were twenty-four hours ago.

* * *

No indeed, I am even grateful to Edith Rockefeller McCormick for so cruelly interfering with my career, for I see now that she was only instrumental in my spiritual welfare. I am sorry that I am repaying her with ingratitude by mentioning her selfish motives on these pages. But to help others efficiently I must tell them the whole truth; otherwise their hearts might sense insincerity and not be benefited...

Now I just smile when I think how desperately I felt because Dr. Cannon was not slender and wore white spats. ... Now I judge no longer by external appearances. I might say even better: I judge no more! Nor do I wonder any more as I did about Dr. Cannon's real being. Now I realize that an individual who takes to the teaching of metaphysics is a human being just like anybody else, with defects and weaknesses as you and I. Instead of discouragements now I find always an inspiration in meeting those who aspire to learn something about their inner being and who try to make acquaintance with God.

Now I do not doubt God's existence because Manly Hall was married, contrary to what I *thought* were the philosophical ideas he preached.

Now I reason calmly that spiritual teachers must also eat and therefore charge for their instruction how to enter Heaven. Alas, their Karma does not yet allow them to divide with others without remuneration the knowledge they already acquired.

Now it is not a question of death and life because Meher Baba desired to be glorified through a eulogistic biography. I am exceedingly happy that while I was not impressed particularly with this Parsee master, still I did not hasten to judge, thus leaving the door open into future development. This fact taught me once more that each of us has a different medium to the evolution of our souls as the case of Princess Matchabelli demonstrated to perfection. Through the association with Baba she enabled her real nature to dominate over her human ego, she comprehended the real value in this world, she had the courage to discard all material burdens and to fill all her soul only with love for her Master. She is the only person in my *entourage* who actually applies and lives the teaching and who from intellectual perishable knowledge made a living growth for herself and an inspiring example to others.

Now I acknowledge and respect the right of Free Will for each being to dispose of his own fate! As the Vicomte de Bonald said: "God leaves man to do wrong in order to credit him with right doing."

Now I do not feel crushed by limited human comprehension! The meaning of my whole life is based on Understanding.

No more need to criticize even if it is only in the abstract, as in my case… So, there is no blame in my heart for Paul Brunton upon learning that he considers suing his Maharishee, whom he introduced to the Western World through his books.

Yes, Paul Brunton is suing the Wise Man of India, his Master, the Eastern Saint, for whose high vibrations I yearned so intensely, and the same Maharishee who gave him such a prominent place in the bookshop windows all over the world.

Maharishee is being sued by his most devoted disciple—and *I* remain calm and peaceful! A few years ago I would have been able to think of nothing but suicide upon learning of such a soul-shaking monstrosity! Now I am calm. Now not only do I not criticize Brunton but on the contrary my heart is immensely grateful to him for having been instrumental at a critical period in pushing me towards that higher path…

Now there is no desire to be swallowed by an earthquake because L.—that unwilling teacher of mine, not by what he taught me but by his being—again four years later for no evident reason made an appointment with me and again changed his mind, mysteriously disappeared and since then would not even acknowledge my Christ's and Buddha's birthday greetings!

I met this strange behavior with an immense calm that time… I did not even seek or wish to know the reason of his mysterious conduct, understanding that he has his own Karma to deal with and that thought must be sacred to me. Perhaps I was more sorry for him than anything else, sorry that his instability might handicap the spiritual advancement of his great soul, the advancement which he desired so ardently and to which I wished to contribute even at the cost of my own development, a thing I would not have done for any other living being until then.

Now I also can see perfectly well that my slow progress in singing was due to the fact that I was not ready for this great mission, as well as that it was not the destiny of many of my teachers to be instrumental in bringing me nearer to the sun.

THE YOUTHFUL ROMANCE I spoke of in the beginning of these memoirs put in me the seed of a future seeker of perfection in singing…

Necessity arising from the first World War forced me to persist in the continuation of my studies…

The sincere desire to become worthy of Dr. Fraenkel's opinion of my character (Goethe said: "If you desire that a person possess certain qualities, attribute to him Publicly those qualities.") was what inspired me to strive for some usefulness in this world and my voice was the only medium I then had at my disposal…

The following years of long work was a case of almost unconscious revenge: "Aha, you all think I have no voice! You will see! I will show you! !"

Fortunately vanity has never been a dominating trait of my character; thus the feeling of getting even with the whole world disappeared little by little and with it vanished the fight for the self-satisfying wish of appreciation, while the desire to be a so-called professional singer became transformed, first into something hardly explicable to my then veiled comprehension, then into the conscious hope of being granted the divine privilege of serving humanity—and finally into the absolute certainty that no matter what the final outcome of my vocal studies might be, the fact that I strove for betterment, for perfection, would develop my character and bring me nearer to God!

From then on the wound in my heart which had been constantly opened during all those years miraculously closed itself and healed. Yes, this so easily bleeding wound was healed, healed because comprehension heals everything!

From that time I stopped living in the future, stopped trying to make beautiful plans agreeable to my ego. I also realized then that singing—or any other work such as cleaning shoes, pruning trees or managing a Wall Street office—has only importance for the spirit which goes into the work and not at all by reason of the work itself. It is the process of doing that develops our souls and not what we do.

Since that date I do not dictate to my desires. My desire becomes Divine Will and I no longer suffer if those selfish yearnings are not identical with Destiny's wishes! I continue my vocal studies patiently as before but I do so entirely in the abstract, as if I were never destined to sing. Now I even do this hopeless work with joy!

I do not count months and days… I do not anticipate a point when I shall be ready to sing… Moreover, I am immune to the ironical attitude of the press when it mentions my name and never misses an opportunity to picture me as a great aspirant of picturesque but totally unsuccessful prima-donnaship!

I am also indifferent now to the sympathy of friends, while for what seemed like an eternity in my life, the mere mention of anything about my voice by anyone sent a cool shower down my spine…

And I merely laughed when Maestro Toscanini, planning to give "Pelléas" during the Paris World's Fair, persistently asked me if I did not know of any *good* Mélisande. That was after I had sung Mélisande myself and, according to those who worked the score with the composer himself, was considered *the* Mélisande. At this great musical occasion Madame Claude Debussy sent me an autographed picture of her husband—that mystical genius who for years now had been in a better world where his cancer-ridden body no longer drove him crazy. Considering herself the heiress of that most spiritual musician since Mozart she wanted to emphasize the fact that my interpretation of his masterpiece would have been fully approved by *Claude de France*.

(That performance of "Pelléas and Mélisande" at the Théâtre des Champs-Élysées was a great musical event of

Paris. It was directed and produced by Walther Straram in the mediaeval style. The scenery and lighting created a wonderful atmosphere and gave great inspiration to the performing artists. Sir Thomas Beecham asked me to lend those artistic settings to Covent Garden for their performance of "Pelléas" during the brilliant Coronation season. Sitting in the orchestra, I could enjoy the beauty of it better at a distance than when I had been on the stage taking part in it!

On that memorable night my friends took that opportunity to express with flowers their appreciation for the good music heard in our theatre. As a result of their thoughtfulness, the Mélisande death scene was transformed into a gorgeous garden, for around the bed—where a few seconds before I had mystically released my soul—were more than a hundred and seventy floral pieces, mostly gigantic baskets. I could not keep the malicious thought from my mind that I was being given a first class funeral! But only I could understand the irony of it, as I knew the flowers were sent to me as a hostess, a patron of the arts, a friend and not at all as an artiste.)

* * *

Yes, my wound healed so well that where previously I would have felt unbearable suffering, it only seemed funny to me when, for instance, Frank LaForge—with whom I had studied daily but whom I had not seen in the three years I was living in Europe—never even inquired about my voice when we met again in Paris evidently thinking that one does not speak about a rope in the house of a hangman. The war had interrupted my study in France and sent me back *via* clipper to New York, where during a whole hour I sang for Mr. LaForge from "Traviata" to "Oberon," passing through "Louise," "Lohengrin," "Aida," "Otello" and some other of the most difficult arias in musical literature for a dramatic, lyric and coloratura soprano. I actually *was* singing all those versatile operas—while three years ago I could not go through one page without being stopped or stopping myself (mostly stopping myself) in despair, saying or thinking, "I can not... I can not!"—hardly realizing then that it probably was not meant for me to go ahead vocally before developing further spiritually. But at that moment I sang for Mr. LaForge every feminine part of all Mozart's operas, Beethoven's "Fidelio," everything, anything! And yet he never interrupted me, never complimented me even for the sake of encouragement! When I had finished the last note of *"Dich teuere Halle"* he just casually asked:

"When do you want to come again?"

Laughingly, I said "Good-bye," merely remarking to myself that my extraordinary (as I thought) improvement had so impressed this wonderful musician that he had lost his powers of speech and with it his customary kindness! Still, I had a feeling that deep in his heart he believed in me! Even though he was afraid people would know I was working with him and my full name never was mentioned in his appointment book, only the initials G. W.—George Washington!

* * *

Still slowly but surely I began to see that the tide was rather coming towards me as if in reward for the spirit that would not give up, perhaps also because instead of buying my operatic success I just studied years and years longer after each of my unsuccessful debuts in every capital of the great world and instead of wishing immediate but mediocre success, I searched for a method that could give me permanent knowledge. While looking for that method I progressively developed the urge for betterment, little satisfied with the now generally accepted standard of achievement. That search for perfection made me discover in turn that the Sublime can not be imprisoned in a humanly conceived method because Truth can not be anything but free—consequently the voice can not be placed here or there, it can not be placed anywhere. Therefore I made it my task to find a way which would allow me to forget the wrongly learned teaching, especially to forget the *wrong thinking* and discover the way to entirely reeducate my mind, if the mind *is* fundamental and first to consider.

I felt perfectly sure that I was on the right track mentally but I was the only one who thought so. Everybody, everything gave me a thousand denials to disprove my new ideas, calling them pure folly. I was told and retold that the greatest teachers of the past and present generation had their wonderful methods, that even Jenny Lind before becoming the world's nightingale could not sing until Garcia "rightly" placed her voice, that Caruso, Sembrich, every great singer had wonderful "production." And who was I to turn my back on those already century-proved results? An eternal débutante, belle, rich, amateurish, operatic joke of the country, an easy *Witz* for the sensation-seeking columnist, a voiceless dilettante whom even the Mayor of Nice as reported in the paper had considered banning her singing when her engagement was announced on the Riviera, a foolish woman who was supposed to have desired to buy for a million dollars the tonsils of a musical comedy star, Vivienne Segal!

But Faith is the greatest conqueror! There is no greater urge than desire for knowledge once it has been awakened. Nothing! For it is the only Power, driving Power, irresistible Power!

Therefore I continued my patient search, in the meantime "methoding" many hours daily—thus praying to God and the devil simultaneously—until I could endure the terrific and hopeless hardship no more and, after almost a quarter of a century, at last I decided to give up. But in that desperate moment I met Madame Gilly who, even though she spoke the theoretic and conventional language of a singing teacher, taught the same thing that my mind conceived about *the liberating of the voice from any placement whatsoever!*

Without conscious knowledge and as far as the professional expression of a regular vocal instructor allowed her, that charming woman (widow of Dinh Gilly, the great baritone in Caruso's golden days) felt the Truth, even if she called it an old Italian method, which was a handicap for me as I was obliged to translate her technical vocabulary into the abstract where words are needless, where human comprehension is meaningless... And since—in spite of the mental exhaustion of a double work—for the first time I began to go forward and acquire something each month even if my advancement was slow, oh, very slow! "In sorrow thou shalt bring forth..." So I did. In spite of it, however, my star was brighter and brighter each day and nothing could have dimmed my hopeful outlook, nothing could have broken my indomitable, my undaunted spirit, that spirit possessed so strongly by souls born on Polish soil!

Nothing could discourage my attempt to reach my goal, even the knowledge that the farther I might go, the farther out of my reach the goal might be! When I was a child, I would walk miles and miles in the country to see the place where the sky touches the ground. While each step forward kept me at the same distance so that I was unable to fulfill my desire, each time I would decide to come again some other day to look into the spot where the red sun fell into the field. So it was later with my singing. Undiscouraged, often it was I who had to encourage my pessimistic teacher, promising to sing better the next day, trying to close my ears when she cried out with all her heart: "Oh! If only you had come to me twenty years ago! With your timbre you would have been the greatest singer of the century and I— the greatest vocal instructor!"

No! I did not want to hear my condemnation! I could not admit is was too late... I was even unable to tell her that in the essence of perfection there is no time, that God can not be late, that Infinite Spirit has no limitation, that Idea is timeless and available to whoever sufficiently desires to get it.[26] She would not have understood… She could not follow me and comprehend this simple truth that no one can lose the voice, that the singing voice is the same voice as the speaking one which we do not lose when getting older but which lasts as long as life is in us. And if we can not sing as well after fifty, it is only because we replaced the God-given law with one that can endure only a certain time, like anything that is made by human conception or by hands. While our body is getting older, we are losing some of our vitality. But the voice—not imprisoned in our physical body—can not get old or stop to vibrate.

Air is always young, energy is always fresh, electricity is always undiminished, no matter how much used. Why should it be different with the singing voice? Life is manifesting itself in everything perpetually. Waves on the radio are never exhausted or sleepy and it is not the waves in the radio that often are faulty but the defective instrument that prevents us from receiving those waves correctly.

The same sun shines for all, the same law applies to all its applicants. We have heard, however, so often that at about fifty singers begin to lose their voices that we consider it extraordinary when a person still can sing at seventy as was the case with Battistini. In Paris I often heard at the Opéra Comique Lucien Fougère still singing beautifully when he

---

26 There is the story of the Holy Man in India, who on his way to Heaven passed by the caves of the wise hermits as they sat in contemplative meditation, nourished year in and year out only by tree roots and berries or an occasional bowl of rice. Upon learning that he was going to visit God they asked him to make some inquiries for them. While some wanted to know the quickest way to get to Nirvana, the last one merely wanted to know whether he was serving God in the right way.

On his way back the Holy Man again passed by the hermits. He brought them answers to their queries, telling one it would take many hundred ages to reach Nirvana and others that they would need many thousand lives to become like Buddha and then as he was telling the last man that his way of serving God was good but that he would have to continue it for many centuries more, with joy the saintly man burst out: "Is that all?"

And in that moment he was with God in Heaven.

was more than eighty years old; if his voice had not the vigor of a young man, it was not the fault of his voice but the fault of his instrument—his body was less robust but the voice, the breath, the life was always the same.

No! I actually did not hear hers or other people's paralyzing destructive words... I was deaf, deaf and blind but blind and deaf *à la* Helen Keller, whose spirit sees and hears surer than her eyes and ears! I was blind to everything that blocked my clear vision! Deaf, blind and so often completely mute! When working more than ever to be one with the Spirit of Music, just last winter during the intermission of "Figaro," having seen my lips moving to the delicious Mozart melody, a friend candidly asked me: "Do you not miss singing, you who studied so much for years?"

Yes, mute, too...

Nothing could daunt my Faith, while generous Destiny sometimes rewarded me in her mystical way for such strong belief as mine, for instance by sending me a message from India—that stronghold of God conception and in my imagination then the country where geographically God preferred to dwell—directing me to study *less* but to remember *more*...

Remember?... What great inspiration to learn that I am just *continuing* this life expression. I am a continuation! I am part of a Great All! And what a sure indication that singing was my mission in spite of the press—in spite of this changeable world, only the contemporary world!

To remember? Yes, I see... The rare moments when I was capable of uttering perfect tones were the moments of total absence of my senses! Once at Galluis, as an example, while singing "Traviata" with the door open into the garden, I saw a stranger at the threshold to my great astonishment, for strict orders had been given that no one should ever be allowed to disturb me during my lessons... It even happened that when the aunt of Alfonso XIII, then reigning King of Spain, paid me an unexpected visit she was told:

"Madame Walska cannot be disturbed while she is singing!" Grande Dame that she was, she understood and only asked permission to visit my beloved rosary... I also remember that the theatre being built for the Paris World Fair of 1937 was never opened until a month after the closing of the Fair. This created a desperate situation for the Fair had contractual obligations to provide a hall that season for exhibitors from almost every nation. To help out in that hopeless situation I presented the Fair for its duration with the Thèâtre des Champs-Élysées, an ideal frame and in the immediate vicinity of the exhibition grounds. During the *pourparlers*, the French White House sent an urgent letter to my country place which I only received the next day—as my household was so afraid to disobey my request that nothing disturb my work that even the presidential car bearing the tricolored cockade failed to impress them. Almost the same thing happened when Madame Pierre Laval, wife of the then Prime Minister, called my office at the Thèâtre des Champs-Élysées to find out my private telephone number—only to be flatly refused owing to the strict orders I had left.

That afternoon mentioned above, the unwelcome visitor happened to be a druggist. My teacher had ordered some medicine and, as it was Sunday, the druggist had brought it himself to accommodate me, entering the chateau through the village gate and directing his steps towards the sound of my voice. When he left, I resumed my singing but my mind was still quite occupied with thoughts of the unexpected interrupter whose kindness touched me greatly. Suddenly I saw a look of astonishment on the face of my teacher... I was then holding the highest note I could take at that period and one with which I had been struggling bitterly when interrupted so inadvertently. I did not understand her surprise, for the note sounded beautiful to me and I held it quite easily... When I finished the aria, *mia maestra* informed me that I was singing not the note I thought but a note three tones higher than the one which a few minutes before I had so hopelessly tried to liberate from the clutches of my throat...

And again, when studying during the forced vacation at the Lido, one day Madame Alda wished me to work on a new piece. I had never studied that melody before and naturally had not the music with me, so I went to Venice and got a copy. I sang it daily... And daily I would make a musical mistake in the same place! Madame Alda was furious... I could not understand my difficulty because as a rule I was very quick to grasp an idea and most attentive to all remarks but that time I just could not seem to follow the written notes... When I returned home and looked at my score of "Don Giovanni," I discovered that the Italian edition had a misprint! Intuitively I had been singing the right note...

Yes, to remember...

I DO NOT KNOW how long I would have struggled against the better part of myself and how much I would have allowed myself to be handicapped by my entourage of great but human intelligence—strong intellect—if Destiny had not sent me back during the second war in my life to Inspirational America!

When I arrived that October I was mentally lost for a while as I usually am when I am not working on my voice… I had not expected to see New York again until I was ready to sing. But alas! I was far from being prepared to herald the Divine Tone, for in those last months in Europe I had worked even less than usual, first because my teacher took her vacation and then because the mobilization came… There could not be any singing… My chauffeur had gone… Gasoline was restricted and my Rolls drank plenty!

If I had not returned to the States before during those last few years, it was on account of my desire to continue my life-long studies and because my recent teachers had not wished to follow me to this country as previous instructors had. But now, since it was impossible for me to work any longer I was able—without reproaching myself with satisfying selfish preferences—to return to this promised land of prophets! To this Mecca of equality where everyone is American regardless of his land of origin, race, trade, professing sect or creed, as John Latouche emphasized in "Ballad for Americans."

* * *

America, the haven for all souls inspired for freedom, where even during the war conscientious objectors have something to say, where anyone, young or old, no matter what his background or purpose, is immediately assimilated.

America—the only place in the world where a foreigner within the first generation after immigration and sometimes even within the space of a few years becomes a typical citizen, a typical American.

America—the Ark of Uncle Sam! For just as Noah took a specimen of every kind of life with him into the ark, so America took and takes any and every kind of man and welds them together into the American soil.

America, whose Statue of Liberty for the first time is now taking on its full meaning, not because that monument must now be a great symbol to so many seekers of refuge but because this country, even before the conception of that statue, was a land settled by refugees impelled here by their desire for the higher, for the freer!

America—where the only restriction is our own limited expansion of consciousness.

America—the protecting Citadel of the High Ideal against materialistic concepts of happiness. For, contrary to somehow erroneously evolved European opinion that people in the States are rather materialistic—because of some tourists who most certainly do not typify Americans—the real Americans *are* idealists, the American of wealth constantly spends his money on building schools, universities, hospitals and other public institutions. Those very millionaires who give their fortunes to their native towns make their money as though it was a sport rather than for any selfish motive. Such millionaires ride in subways, live in one room of an unfashionable hotel and in many instances they do not take personal advantage of their wealth but their thoughts are constantly occupied with the idea of endowing some great cultural or philanthropic development and giving the best that money can buy to their fellow citizens.

America—where real houses are not meant to be skyscrapers but eternal habitations of peace within ourselves!

America—where the worth of work lies not in its fruit but in the resulting expansion of the consciousness—where people work because the very doing of it betters and ennobles them and because by raising their individual standard of living they raise the standards of the country as a whole. The entire spirit of work in America is typified in the motto: "Through the individual to the whole!"

America—where material improvements, modern conveniences and mechanical luxuries are permitted to develop not as pleasure and dissipation or for the mere luxury itself but because as they quicken work and are time-savers of every kind they make more of that most precious thing: Time—time in which the individual can develop himself and his inner being. Development depends upon yourself here and now. Therefore a man must work not just for his rent or his livelihood but that the tangible progress may give him more time to find himself!

America—the predestined haven for refugees seeking a higher spiritual order and not just the land of last resort where the refugees of today come because it is the only place they can go. It is true that the founders of this country were themselves refugees. But as they participated in the events of the growth of the land, those men of high vision deserved the glorious title of American Citizen. They were guided by men of mystery and were directed by a Divine Force that, to the ignorant, almost took on the proportions of miracles. Those pioneers were the inspiration that made of these shores a land where free souls ardently desired to come and be in communion with those already privileged to play host to them!

For what is America? And where is it? It is not a reality. It is only a place where reality can manifest itself and when that privilege is granted to each human heart, no matter what his race, color or creed—that is America.

America—which perhaps gives nothing but certainly offers everything. For, although we may not be born equal, at least we are born with equal potentiality and so can attain anything. This is the country which offers all spiritual things to everyone, the country where people are more aware of the necessity of achieving them. Because from the solace of liberty, from the inspiration of freedom of expression and from the ecstasy of fulfillment comes the enrichment of our being!

America—not only the gatekeeper of the betterment of our souls but also the new stronghold of culture and Art! There was a time when Americans believed that only things European in the sphere of music, literature and all branches of art, as well as in higher education at the universities, were better. For a long time America had many examples of the best in the arts and sciences but only enough to serve as an inspiration and an example that let its citizens go to Europe for further studies. Ever since the first World War the infiltration of foreign teachers and artists into the United States has been steadily increasing, until today there is no need to study painting in France, science in Germany or singing in Italy. The great masterpieces have been bought by Americans and can be seen now in museums all over the country, as well as in private collections. The gigantic musicians of Toscanini's caliber have come here where they found wider audiences and unrestricted expression. The Einsteins and Russells prepare the future Thomas Edisons in American universities. While Franz Werfel, Thomas Mann and Lion Feuchtwanger, unmenaced by police, can continue to endow us with their enlightening writings.

The situation is now completely reversed—it is Europe that must come here for learning, for inspiration! Europe must come here now for everything—even for the great couturiers. Until 1914 Paris was the undisputed center of the dressmaking world but due to the necessities arising from the war and also due to the development of sports for women, Chanel changed all that by annihilating individual elegance and making all women dress alike, in uniform, so to speak. The United States, however, being a nation of many different origins in the midst of its great unity, developed much more variety in dress and now, owing to the present European situation, has easily become the leader of styles.

Personally, I would far rather get a dress in the United States than a famous Paris model for I might never see another gown like my Yankee one, while there might be tens of copies of the fashionable Parisian model at luncheon at the Ritz.

The present war is forcing the United States to make those materials and ornaments that formerly were imported from France and England and, as always, when America does anything it does better than others, if for no other reason than that it manufactures in such great quantity. And now that Americans have had a taste of their own fabrics, the chances are that they will not be willing to pay enormous duty for the garments from Europe; still it is wise to remember that *"Nul n'est prophète dans son pays"* unless the boundaries between all nations finally are demolished to form a brotherhood.

This so-called *new* world, America, has become *the World*, the safe deposit for all the best from the Old World, the new dwelling place of old civilization, the birthplace of a future spiritual empire, the root of Awakened Consciousness! For, while in the Old World intellectuality reigns in full, America looks to the soul to give it inspiration or to open something up. The fresh soul of America is not ashamed to seek—and he who seeks the betterment of his soul can not fail.

But as every medal has two sides, so this search for something higher is the reason why fraud can exist so flagrantly here. Any Oriental putting on a turban can proclaim himself a mystic because he knows that the American people are seeking anything that will enlighten their inner life. And as we are enjoying freedom to worship in this country so anybody can found a new religion and have followers, no matter how absurd the principles of it may be—because people are feverishly looking for new expressions of God, new cults.

* * *

Only those who have lived away from the States for a while can appreciate the high awakening of the soul in this country! The majority of Americans, making a part of it and being of it, can not see the implication, can not sufficiently feel the tremendous spirituality which surrounds them—as the trees stop us from seeing the forest. They can not *fully* comprehend the great privilege of being a citizen of the United States.

I became an American citizen automatically through marriage during the first war. It was just a matter of formality and I did not think much about it until two years later when returning from Havana. On the boat, when we had to present our passports, United States citizens were shown to one side—aliens to the other. In that moment, standing in line, something happened to my soul. Purifying tears joyfully filled my throat and the memory of my first communion with the Holy Host came over my heart. I received the baptism of this country and in the midst of the rushing crowd I mentally knelt to say my thanks!

Perhaps not all Americans realize that this country of the Future has been guided step by step by some Force, that its founders came just at the moment they should, that it is historic fact and not the flight of a pseudo-mystic's fancy that a mystery man always appeared at the darkest moment in the construction of this nation to guide its builders. Professor C. E. Norton of Harvard University has written: "Not only were the founders of the United States Government masons, *but they received aid from a secret and august body existing in the East, which helped them to establish this country for a peculiar and particular purpose known only to the initiated four."*

To the people with intuition it is quite evident that America was meant to be *the* Future World, otherwise it would be hard to comprehend the accepted record that a stranger, a so-called professor, a totally unknown individual with a foreign accent, a mystery man—could dictate and be listened to by George Washington, Lafayette and Benjamin Franklin in that grave moment of the birth of the Constitution of the American nation. It would be incomprehensible otherwise that the Colonial flag of 1775 could have been designed after the pattern proposed by just an "unknown," that the voice of an outsider saying "God has given America to be Free" could have united belligerent parties into a complete union. Such a man *must* have been sent by some superior force, if his advice was listened to with respect and obeyed.

Yes, everything points to the fact that America was always heavenly protected. She was guided when the emblem of the Eagle was made equal-headed, symbolizing the nation's impartiality and union—one supreme crown —the Soul, the United States!

Also, the use of the number 13 in connection with the founding of this country appears too purposeful to be just a mere coincidence.

The Great Seal of the United States appears to be a glorified symbol of this mysterious Number 13!

To enumerate these we find on the obverse side:

13 stripes on the heraldic field, composed of six red and seven white: (According to ancient color symbolism red stood for the 'Blood of the Christ', the White being the Light of Purity of the perfected Soul.)
13 leaves and 13 olives of the olive branch held in the right claw of the Eagle.
13 arrows held in the left claw of the Eagle.
13 stars composing the design of the interlaced triangles in the sphere of clouds above the Eagle's head.
13 letters in the National Motto E PLURIBUS UNUM.

While on the reverse side there are

13 letters in ANNUIT COEPTIS. And

13 tiers to the Pyramid whose Capstone is the Spiritual all-Seeing Eye, which in Eastern terms alludes to the thirteen initiatory steps which lead to the Source of Illumination.

The Declaration of Independence was signed by fifty-eight representatives—the 5 + 8 = 13.

There were thirteen fateful years between the Declaration and the beginning of Government under the Constitution.

The Mace used in the House of Representatives is composed of twelve rods held together by a thirteenth!

Everywhere our research and analysis lead to the same inevitable conclusion that this country was founded by men of the 'Force which dispenses the Essence of Life'.

Still it is difficult to say so with utter conviction when living in New York, where it is impossible not to hear the ticker of Wall Street which has become the bible of the new generation and the pulse of the great majority; where every second the radio brings us details of wars, gangsters, misery and hopelessness; and where every inventor is trying to beat his competitor in perfecting more and more deadly weapons to annihilate men, women and children in the space of a few hours.

Yes, America is certainly the scene where the great Spiritual Renaissance will take place but where can we see the first indications clearly? Does it manifest itself in the big cities? How is it possible with the Broadways, the Wall Streets and the materialistic conceptions of so many New Yorkers, Chicagoans and other city dwellers...?

Naturally American has its handicaps, as has everything that grows. One of these is the fact that people here do not fully appreciate the tremendous richness they possess, the inner and unworldly richness. It is time for America to overcome its inferiority complex and to rejoice in the very unsophistication that has made it look with awe towards Europe (and the Social Register). It is time to realize that

America *is* the leader because her soul is the greatest value in the universe!

Another handicap in the development of the United States is the fact that the nation is spoiled by not having had to suffer these last generations. Satiated with the contentment which this land generously procures for them, Americans know not the suffocation of yearning, they do not realize that suffering is the true measuring rod of nature. For those who have not suffered have not lived. Everything here is made too easy for the individual, and while some use the leisure so created to devote to spiritual life, many become almost ruined by all the modern conveniences and time-saving devices. Having things made too easy, they do not go through the growth that comes from suffering. In the big cities here you cannot even have God-given natural weather such as the lovely winter snow fallen in the night, because it is removed from the streets by eight o'clock in the morning to allow business men to drive downtown more conveniently. Americans do not know how to use all their resources because of the easy path that is prepared for them and they forget that without adversity one cannot advance. "Necessity is the mother of invention." They take for granted the material progress that Destiny has so generously sent them, instead of using the resulting advantages only for their development.[27]

Certainly an individual cannot reach his ultimate and deserved development in misery. He must be happy, and in order that he may be happy God sent all the improvements to this country so that its citizens would find that happiness in order to progress. Still those who have not suffered have not progressed and those who have suffered have learned to find happiness in the spiritual growth of their soul. Living

---

27 The fact that Americans always think of the easy way out reminds me of an incident that happened when I saw a Russian play in which the wife, unable to solve her marital unhappiness, committed suicide. An American in our party said he found the play quite incomprehensible, as the woman could so easily have solved her problem by getting a divorce.

on this planet is not a reality but merely a passing moment in time and space allotted us for our growth.

Man is born into bondage and given a life in which to find his way out. The liberation of a soul is possible only in a land where all beings can live in harmony with one another and where the only dictator is man's own imagination. It rules as does Nature, never speaking, never ordering—but ever guiding and encouraging! It offers to all the rewards of joyous living!

Life's only rule is to live and let live. Its principle is that by which the trees of the forest achieve their gigantic size as they aspire for more air and light, the flowers of the garden scent the paths with their desire to reveal their glory, the birds of the air soar into the fathomless blue to herald the coming dawn, the beasts of the field spend their time in peaceful complacency, and Man releases the perfume of his soul through Art and Science! *That is why America is the land where Man will build a civilization from which will come the greatest Spiritual Renaissance the world has ever known!!!*

For the second time in my life leaving Europe for America during a fratricidal war—all wars are fratricide— I felt free again and more than ever before I breathed easier. The new way of freedom became quite an experience! Divided from war-torn Europe only by a twenty-six hour ocean flight, I was still living in that censored atmosphere and it surprised me not to be asked every second to show my passport or my permit to walk on the street, to drive a car, to be on the train, to leave a city or to enter a village. I was especially surprised that my telephone conversations were not cut because I spoke English…

Yes, I was finally breathing the air of America—so necessary to my lungs—the air that enabled me to unite easier with the Infinite!

Without a teacher, however, I was vocally lost. Not taking lessons twice a day and for the first time in a quarter of a century having my mornings and afternoons free, I almost did not know what to do with my time. Instead of rushing to the studio as I was so accustomed to doing, I found myself slowly wandering through Central Park without special destination and surprised to realize that such a thing had never happened to me since I first came to the States almost twenty-five years ago.

I tried to sing alone but being accustomed to work always under a teacher's supervision I was afraid I could not correct myself in the right way. Having depended so long on those supposed to know more than myself, I had easily developed an inferiority complex, even though I believed in my voice. At that moment I was paying for that privilege of having had as many lessons as I could physically take without breaking my vocal cords. I was also afraid that if I started to sing alone and sang badly I would again lose confidence in my voice. It was then that I understood why surgeons can not operate on their own children!

A few weeks later, however, my Angel-Spirit came to my rescue as it had so many other times before, choosing almost a stranger to force upon me a book on mental singing. There are so many books on singing I could hardly be expected to read them—it is impossible to get instruction from the written word anyhow—but in appreciation of Juliet Rublee's kindness in sending me the book I turned the first page and my eyes were arrested by these prefatory words: "Music is in the Mind." That same night I read Alice Lawrence's "Lessons for Everyone to Sing" and I hardly could wait for the next morning to telephone the author and ask for an immediate appointment.

From then on, like an inexperienced beginner, I was daily learning how to think of music first and only give the words secondary place until the two should automatically become one.

Another vocal instructor sometime later disagreed entirely with this form of idea, disagreed in "theory," however, because while I was following Mrs. Lawrence's way to "visualize" first the music and not telling it to her, she called this *her* way and self-sufficiently would say: "Now it *is* right!" Six months later from a clear sky when I was wrong she was even correcting me as Mrs. Lawrence might have only using instead different words: "Do not pinch the vowel." It was *exactly* the same thing!!!

That incident—one of thousands—again proves that singing is fourth-dimensional and can not be used as an established method but solely depends on the individual development of a student as well as of a teacher.

Fortunately in this period of my study I knew well enough *The* Law that if a new vocal dictator told me to sing in my shoe or bracelet I would do just as well taking only one second of my time to translate his deceptive vocabulary into fundamental knowledge that I was lucky already to possess.

And *à la fin de fin* not a single teacher taught me anything but each one helped me to discover the Truth that is in me. Knowing that Destiny does not play favorites—instead of praying fervently, meditating for the special occasion or leaving everything to "Thy will be done"—I tried, as much as my Karma allowed me, to feel rightly and act accordingly and this way my prayers were always answered. The better my thoughts the sooner and more automatically I saw the benefit—the more and more constant feeling of peace in my heart.

* * *

And again I began the work right at the start, just as I had done more than twenty years ago. Again I was working on my A-B-C's, this time without discouragement, however, although without hope either, for hope is only an auxiliary to doubt and one who *knows* does not hope any more—one just knows!! I worked patiently with the patience of those who do not idolize Time and its nonexisting power! I worked with the granite-like knowledge of governing those world laws.

If any uninitiated person had happened to be present during those lessons he could never have perceived any possible outcome of that long mumbling and those hours of quasi-inaudible repetition of i-a-i-a or da-de-do-du… Passive—unless it may be called active to try to the utmost not to help Nature take her rightful course—I was fastened to my chair to such a motionless extent that I sometimes had to struggle painfully against the overwhelming desire to sleep that derived from the complete inertia of my over-relaxed mind. To brighten the task—as if that were possible—I repeated over and over hundreds of times, "How calm and cool," when all the while through the open windows came the terrifying noise of Broadway on a torrid June day. Another exercise, "I long for rest," was more close to my feelings but the continuous repetition of that phrase only served to bring up the memory of my language studies and the reading of such inspiring highly intellectual sentences as: "My brother has a black eye but my cat caught a mouse."

However, if I could endure such mediaeval torture, it was possible only because, as never before, I was spiritually myself during those lessons. I had no need to interpret the teacher's words into a meaning comprehensible to my mind. Mrs. Lawrence spoke my language. My own words echoed in her mouth: "Join outside the ocean of music! Express the divine melody and *not* the human words! Make an effort only *not* to make any effort! Liberate your voice from the body! Let go completely inside! It is *not* a place—it is a sound! Forget about breath, think only of music!"

And only then I understood what that great singer of the last generation, Victor Maurel, meant when years ago in answer to an anxious query of mine about breathing he said: "Leave your breath alone! I never bothered about it!"

* * *

During the first few months of that mechanical and uninspiring work I was still calculating—although I did it without obscuring my soul with impatience or with the mildest revolt—approximately when I would be ready to apply my newly acquired knowledge to actual singing. By March, when the musical season was approaching its end, it was difficult to keep my inspiration high, for I realized that at best I must wait until the following winter to manifest myself. Tiny doubts began to creep into my heart, my mind wandered and the thought of Manly Hall's perhaps-prophetic words that I should be unable to express myself through the voice helped to diminish my courage.

But just then I read the music critic Pitts Sanborn's article on the occasion of Tetrazzini's death, the one in which he spoke about her famous *legato*. May God bless you, Pitts Sanborn!—because the desire for that *legato* again sent my spirit up and from that instant on and forever I annihilated from my mind that dreadful enemy—Time! I became totally indifferent to the beginning and ending of seasons. I said good-bye forever to the illusionary, tyrannic master of the calendar—the day, month, year! And, if by spring I again got an inferiority complex about my voice, it was only because during the past winter of mumbling timid exercises, with only an occasional lullaby but with no singing of any powerful bracing music as I had done for years, I had not heard my own voice for so long that for the first time in my pursuit of a goal I thought, along with the whole world, that perhaps I had no voice and could never sing…

* * *

That summer, unable to return to my country place in France on account of the war, I took the opportunity to visit California, hitherto unknown to me, without any special reason in mind—or so I thought then, little realizing what Destiny had in store for me. Perhaps I went there to change the atmosphere as I feared to deepen the dark conditions connected with my voice. Perhaps I feared that one day, maybe very soon, I would have to find an answer to the question that kept coming up in my mind: . "What next?" And I could not yet answer that question in an entirely satisfactory way. I could not yet face my tomorrow unless singing held the most predominating place. I was not quite ready for that greatest step of my life—the step into the abstract…

* * *

From the highest mountain peak of Hollywood, I looked out over the most limitless and, at night, most fantastic view one could ever set eyes upon when Los Angeles lay at my feet. In the sunshine of daytime Nature herself seemed to invite me to pour out the vibrations of my voice far into the open space that stretched before me… Alas too late! I had lost confidence in the sound of my voice from not having used it the whole winter. I could not overcome my lately acquired timidity… Pretending excessive physical tiredness, I begged my teacher to give me a few days' rest in order that I might gather the necessary force to continue my habitual Calvary…

* * *

In the meantime, an extraordinary thing happened to me.

That last winter, a young man—who taught me much about Forgotten Teachings—an old soul dwelling in a young Arizona boy, who already had time in the flower of his youth to gather much knowledge in India and Tibet, informed me that in the East there are still those who have voices developed according to the Great Law and who can by their sounds not only heal any physical illnesses but can even transfer spiritual knowledge to the truth-seeking soul deserving of such illumination.

Deep in my heart I considered such information as a *great, great* gift Destiny had bestowed upon me. Not reacting visibly, my informer could hardly have guessed how reverently my soul received that message. I certainly considered that discovery as an indication that I had a still greater goal towards which to strive in my life's pursuit! I also understood that before going to India to look for that new *guru* (teacher), I must first develop further my own being. I must grow to be worthy of attaining that hidden knowledge. Therefore I desired to conquer primarily the condition which would enable me to master my voice to its highest degree, for by then I had learned that the voice is the breath and the Breath is the Spirit! I must spiritualize the voice for that highly divine purpose!

How? I did not know… I did not even question myself. But on that day of ultimate discouragement when my voice refused to commune even with the spacious California breath of air, at luncheon time and almost casually—if anything can be casual in the great scheme of things—the same California-born prodigy who had brought the purest pearl to my string of knowledge remarked: "Do you remember I was telling you some time ago about certain vocal studies still practiced in India, though very rarely. I just learned that the Western possessor of this rare knowledge is hidden somewhere around these mountains… It is a very strange old woman who is unwilling to communicate with the outside world… Only a friend of my friend's friend from the desert may, perhaps, be able to discover her whereabouts and try to get in touch with this rare phenomenon… But the question would be to persuade her to see a new face!"

However, everything worked like magic! A mysterious man, whom neither I nor that strange woman ever knew, went and authoritatively said to her: "Come with me! Someone needs you!"

Like a lamb the tigerish woman followed him obediently. He brought her to my threshold, rang the bell, left her there and disappeared. To this day I have never seen him or known his name…

Casting my eyes over the extraordinary appearance of that tiny masculine woman, I was rewarded at that moment for never having judged souls by their outside frame! Certainly I was helped by grace from Heaven because, in that instant on seeing that peculiar personality, doubts did not enter my heart, doubts that such a person could have any knowledge to impart. Her face was wrinkled like the woman in "Lost Horizon" after she left Shangri-La, her speech was broken English—she was Danish—but she could not speak any languages. Her rebellious hair was matched only by her total disregard for her clothing. She looked a hundred years old but had not a single white hair and could run as nimbly as an athletic girl, while her grasp when she shook my hand was as powerful as the iron hand of Commandatore in "Don Juan." But the richness of her Spirit blinded you to such an extent that those outside appearances were totally unimportant except as they made us feel our own smallness and our destructive capacity to see the ugliness of forms...

That most curious, mannish female, who without any reason screamed furiously that no one could buy her, that no one could stop her from telling the truth—Queen or no Queen!—expressed herself about our meeting in this way, as she told me afterwards: "I am grateful to my Heavenly Father for the privilege to contact that Voice, to contact that Spirit... I was waiting for such a moment the whole of my life, waiting to deposit in her God-given knowledge..."

Since the day I was allowed to meet this teacher of the essence of life based on the Universal Law, I have been pouring out my tones and hammering my breath day and night, yelling—as I irreverently put it to tease myself—to such an extent that in my New York house even my neighbors protested by knocking violently on the wall to stop the noise.

This work has nothing to do directly with singing but it revitalizes your whole being and builds the foundation for everything, a foundation that enables you to approach God in everything...

Independently of the final result of this work and indifferent to what application it may lead to, in spite of the fact that these last months I have not sung at all or even been near the piano—still I have found again the full confidence in my voice and what was of greater importance: I registered the feeling of the tremendous Power within me together with 'the comprehension that the divine voice in us should not be lowered to any mechanical instrument.

If only singers, while studying, could sometimes stay away from the piano and not be slavishly dependent on its already imitative tone, certainly and soon they would recognize the great superiority of their natural resources. We, women, particularly can not easily speak the words on the breath as that great vocalist John Charles Thomas does so wonderfully. We *sing* too much...

* * *

Before contacting the great spirit of Thor Neilsen, in my daily association with various vocal teachers I often admired their patience and sometimes even their love of teaching which was almost beyond my comprehension. I personally thought I could never have endured such torture as they underwent. But after only six months of my study with Mrs. Lawrence, I had begun to change my attitude to such an extent that at times I suspected even Dame Nature of wishing to prepare me reverently for the high priestly mission of unfolding such Truth to ardent seekers. The highly moral character of Mrs. Lawrence transformed into God-given Grace what until then I had only regarded as a profession that brought in a comfortable income.

However, after collaborating with Miss Neilsen, I came to understand that eventually I would be called sooner or later to initiate those whose soul strives to express itself through the channel of the voice and probably I would be guided to share my knowledge with those who are handicapped by undeveloped physical conditions in reaching the bigger illumination and whose Karma has already allowed them to advance further. However, as I have mentioned above, I do not plan any more about my future life expression and its mission. I leave Destiny to direct my steps…

Until that winter of 1940, I imagined that every new experience, new teacher—vocal or spiritual—was to be the final one. But as I advanced in the task temporarily designed for me while partly acquiring that knowledge—first in the abstract and then in real form—then and there came a higher teaching, a higher comprehension of the Law and so on *ad infinitum*… Until my vision finally allowed me to perceive that this progressive unfolding would never stop but would go on forever from year to year, from this life to the next… I then opened myself to anything or to nothing that may come and an avalanche of most extraordinary events rushed through me, each one bringing higher and better knowledge, knowledge of myself, knowledge in myself.

Instead of feeling discouraged, however, as I would inevitably have done before, I found it to be a natural phenomenon, being of All and not merely a part of it, no longer living in specific time. That realization certainly filled me with a serenity which my poor erroneous words are incapable of describing.

* * *

In this culminating year of finding myself on the right trail, I also most naturally was more ready and better prepared for the next step to learn, to meet the next teacher. For it is said that whenever a student is ready, the Master will appear! And that Master was the American boy I have mentioned above. He unfolded to my soul so much the Real Knowledge of Divine Law that I have stored up in my inner being enough food to digest and assimilate for the rest of this earthly life, that richness I was blessed to receive from this fortunate possessor of great undying Truth. Thanks to him, the concept of the Spiritual Law that governs us—simple in its greatness—now lies so clearly in my mental and godly being that already I can pass on those gems of purest water to those who, unlike myself, have not yet been privileged to realize some parcel of Truth... .

My feeling is immeasurable when I acknowledge most humbly my devotional gratitude for the greatest of life's expression: to unfold God to others, even if only in a microscopic way!

* * *

Now all my mental life is unveiled before me most clearly. Now I can easily see how I changed first from an incredulous youngster into a Slavic type of negative fatalist and from that somnolent state of mind I became, in later years, the slave of Destiny, slave of the Will of God, which, at best, could only be interpreted with the comprehension of the changeable (because mortal) mind and by this again fall an easy victim to the previous exaggeration. I became actually serene, wise and peaceful only when neither noisy spook nor even a wonderful guiding spirit played the slightest part in my life. I learned to follow my intuition implicitly. I found that it was always true unless confused by my human thought… But even if my intellect prevented me from receiving the direct Light, I was no longer affected through it… I was neither affected nor impatient for I was no longer striving for a specific advancement. For me, now, every action, every thought, every experience, every feeling, wrong or right, was an advancement, for at the bottom of my heart there was only the conscious desire to grow! Hence each moment of my life became an advancement! For we advance till the Soul dwells within our body… When it leaves our personality, we interrupt our betterment during the sleep that follows, till the next earthly journey.

It is easy, therefore, to see how important our body should be to us. Unable to make progress unless it be on this plane, we must take extraordinary care to prolong our existence here as long as possible in order to learn more, to develop more, to grow more and more…

When the right comprehension illuminates our heart, then the care of our body is necessary, providing that the guiding motive in us is not small or selfish. It is right, however, if our Inner Intelligence instructs us that our physical being must take a preponderant place.

In early youth—not knowing any better and doing only as others around me did—I accepted illness as a common misfortune. Then for many years I rejected its powers as I rejected all other negative conditions… Perhaps I was just hiding my head in the sand… Still it was good to shut the door of my soul to anti-natural law because during that time my mind could not dwell on anything unpositive and in that way, very slowly but surely, I could not even conceive of the idea that sickness could touch me and I treated any physical shortcomings in me by ignoring their existence—and it worked perfectly!

But it was only last winter—oh, how rich that winter was to me!—that I learned and understood, again thanks to my youthful teacher, for the first time the actual value of our physical body, the dwelling place of our spiritual being! *Mens sana in corpore sano.*

Only then I clearly comprehended that there can not be spiritual advancement without a young and healthy body, that even the slightest ailment handicaps our ascension, that age and finally premature death cut the only medium through which we can develop.

Indeed my fortune was great in allowing me then to learn how to master my body instead of becoming a slave and a victim of it.

AT THE SAME PERIOD and always from the same source, sent by Destiny, I clearly comprehended woman's moral standing in this world. I say therefore: Women! It is time for you to realize what an elevated mission you hold in your privileged position of being born women!

Wake up, women! Take your rightful places! Acknowledge the Godly message in your soul and raise the conscience of humanity! Wake up and realize what glory lies in womanhood! What grace, what divine grace to be destined to bring Inspiration to Mankind! What bliss to be designed as a messenger of the Highest Ideals! What sublimeness to possess an altar in our hearts where man can deposit his great potentiality!

Those women who so earnestly desire equal rights are unaware of the fact that they strive for less than generous Fate has already bestowed upon them. For centuries man has striven to put woman on the highest pedestal possible. Therefore he has unconsciously resisted giving her an equal place in the ugly surroundings of an office with low vibrations and that solely because he has wished her to enjoy the greatest of all positions—her own!

To man, woman is not only sweetheart, wife and mother—she is the Ideal, the image of God, the symbol of sublime Love, man's Eternal Dream!

No matter how earthbound he might be, the man was never born who did not carry in his heart the feeling of adoration for woman—that feeling he is so eager to express! It is the woman who is to blame if she can not bring to the surface those great overwhelming feelings in a man's heart. There is no man who would not wish to ascend as high as a woman would allow him and the more cynical he seems, the greater the dreams that hold his heart!

There is not a man who prefers the physical expression of love to the sublime feeling of the godly nectar that is living in him and if Don Juan constantly changed the object of his attention it was only because he could not deposit the beauty of great emotional power in the soul of one woman. Hence he sought the illusion in many, many different arms hoping that quantity might at least replace the Divine quality that was lacking.

Man has never wished to degrade us. It is we who provoke him when through total ignorance we flatter his low instincts instead of acknowledging the God in him. Man never desires to possess us—he is born an idealist—it is we who evoke such desires by our vanity and as proof of our irresistibility!

If Eve had not offered temptation to the first man in the form of an apple—he would not have lost the godly feeling towards her and man would idolize woman to this day!

And, certainly there is no sacrifice man would not joyfully perform for his all-beloved, if only that woman would keep her heart in Purity!

Woman! Give man a chance and he will bring you a bit of heaven "and all these things shall be added unto you," even in the form of such earthly possessions as a mink coat or a few carats of diamond, if such is your wish…

The rich feeling of intuition enables woman to perceive the greatness of man's heart. Therefore, oh sisters, allow man—full of Divine Potentiality—to put us next to the Deity! to put us back in the place whence we so foolishly insist on descending only to diminish ourselves!

See, O blind woman if you need any proof, see how man adores his mother because by her unselfish love she permits him to be himself, to be as he is—the Spirit of God!

Women! Take your place—that place designed by God! Not behind the earthly throne through intrigue, chance, opportunity or physical beauty but behind the Spiritual Throne through your inherited Divine rights!

Recognize, O women, the power that lies in your birth, the only power that can change the heart of a man and thus abolish war! For if man were full of sublime feeling founded in divine companionship, he would no longer seek the false illusion of imaginary power!

Opinion prevails that if women were in power because they are mothers, they could abolish wars. Not exactly! But if women in every home would realize that man builds a shrine in her heart and if she would keep that shrine pure and glorious, he could not feel anything but peace!

Look around you, women! Scrutinize your heart! Remember history! Read again and you will see in all literature that since his conscious existence man has lived with only one purpose: to find a woman upon whom he can bestow Love and Adoration in order that he may grow and feel godlike!

> *When you will have stopped dreaming of happiness, you will have found it.*
> — SECRETAN

TOTALLY ABSORBED IN my work as I always was, it is little wonder that I could never find time to visit California. It has been my life-long practice never to travel for the sole sake of travel—travel for pleasure, for seeing places. There had always been a purpose for anything I did. Following the fundamental law of life, I have always endeavored to conduct accordingly all the activities of my existence. I always directed everything I did towards my one goal of fulfilling my destiny through my voice. This has been the basis for all my decisions with regard to all my human relations, to my study as well as to all my travels. This accounts for the fact that I never had enough time to visit India, Egypt or China, in spite of my great desire. Every minute has been budgeted towards my single aim. For this reason the famous California boosters failed to influence me, until now.

Intuitively, however, I knew that the day would come when I would go to that Golden State. I felt positive that one time or another I should live there… Live and perhaps even finish my earthly existence there… Somehow I had the feeling that I belonged there even if, strangely enough, I was not in a hurry to get there, for I never anticipated or planned my going to the Coast. I simply knew that there was something for me in those parts when the time for my going there should mature by itself. I also knew that it was not for me to decide where I was to go. My role was only to persevere in my present self-imposed discipline and go where and when the Fates might direct my steps.

* * *

Now that day of ripening has come as I had expected and it happened so naturally that I was robbed of the expected thrill of "going to California."

During all those years, I had stayed with each teacher until my need for them faded away, as the needs of childhood are lost in the blossoming of maturity. Now it happened that my newly discovered teacher planned to spend her summer in Los Angeles. So when it came time for her to leave there was nothing left for me to do but follow her. It was not as though I were going to visit California but as usual I was just going where my study might continue.

Once there, with that excessive curiosity of my mind, it was only natural that I should take advantage of the opportunity and make myself acquainted with that Vacation Land of America, as I had heard glamorous Hollywood called. I expected to find myself amid the sophisticated atmosphere of a great artificial life but in its stead I found that the people in this Babylon—including the cinema stars that wish to shine longer in the bright constellation—were more concerned with living life than anything else. Therefore I found California a most suitable place for one whose sole desire was to work.

As fate would have it, through a friend, I found myself located for the summer on top of the world, with the fairyland of man beneath me. The small studio house which I occupied was typical of that new world where everyone lives with Nature, throwing aside all the shackles of tradition.

So, in this America, I finally found a place where people live, actually live without collective rushing, without precipitating themselves towards the grave, where they are—selfishly, you might almost say—preoccupied solely with their own living, regardless of wars, economic depressions or earthquakes. A place where I often saw people reading yesterday's papers most naturally, not being enslaved by that tyrannic master—Time. And if they were one or two hours late for an appointment, it was indeed quite a normal thing to expect, for California grew up along the stretch of shoreline of a great body of water with considerable distance between settlements, a fact which contributed to the annihilation of space and time—an element so essential to our growth. Those same distances likewise prevent Californians from frequent or public reunions, thus throwing individuals on their own resources to find themselves.

It is still more amazing how little one hears out there of business—that inevitable topic in the New York world—for the only business they really profess there is the business of living. It is also amazing how much time they have to spare! If you stop your car to ask a person the best road to a place, in the kindness of his heart the individual might be quite willing to drive you from Los Angeles to San Francisco, just to accommodate you.

Nature, herself coquettishly conspires in pressing you to her bosom by offering herself in the form of those sun-kissed vegetables and fruits. Even the speaking voices ring with a human note in that sunny land—and, as a curious phenomenon, the people are decidedly more interested in your being than in your pocket. In those transplanted souls from all over the world certainly something sings from their innermost depths. They seem to be in tune with the vital flow of life. There is something true about them. Their voices are not trained but their hearts *are* true. This I learned from innumerable experiences with newsboys, service station attendants, traffic cops, the idle wanderer and hotel maids as well as people from the other walks of life.

* * *

Here again is the gateway to the East, where are to be found the hidden treasures of knowledge that will in time be uncovered to lead man to greater heights on his path of evolution. One need not be in California long before he feels his soul beginning to stir. The air is magnetized... the consciousness awakens… the soul *must* speak. To those who do not understand the workings of the Greater Laws, it may seem mysterious in the same way that it is difficult to explain the record of the spiritual attainments of those ancient races that once lived in Egypt, India, Tibet and Greece. How did they attain such strength of spirit that it is impossible for us today to fathom their thoughts? It is fundamental that if you will provide the soil, the flower will bloom. So it is with the heart of man. Once the environment is found, the soul will release its perfume in all the creative channels of civilization.

Here is the seed of the new world which is the future America. It is the nourishment of the coming epoch. What is seen today is nothing but the adolescence of the coming spiritual rebirth of the world. The endless oddities and fading fads which are so prevalent here are only precursors of the coming "Golden Age." The freedom that people enjoy here heralds this as the land where the spiritual leader of the coming era would be born.

* * *

In my celestial hermitage among the clouds overlooking the most spectacular array of jewels my eyes have yet seen, I began to fill my very being with the vital substance of this charged air. It is this very atmosphere that accounts for the pilgrimage of millions of searching souls to California, for the hum of the new industries, for the inspirations of the screen, for the construction of the world's largest telescope and for the world renowned symphonies under the stars at the Hollywood Bowl.

It is this atmosphere that accounts for such fantastic feats as reclaiming the sun-baked wastelands to nourish our nation by bringing a river of water hundreds of miles across a blazing tract of desert. Also, it is here that we find an inexhaustible supply of fuel. Here is the center of the new industry that is giving "wings" to democracy. And this is merely a quick passing-in-review of a few of the high spots in this land that is so much nearer to God.

Analyzing the California atmosphere, one wonders if such apparent unappreciation of time and such *lèse-majesté* against well-established common and social rules has not some meaning after all. Perhaps even some deep meaning...

Could it be that those inhabitants of the Golden West are right in feeling and acting differently from their fellowmen in the East? Could it be that they know how to live better than their countrymen of Park Avenue or Wall Street? Could it be that they are not altogether wrong if they listen on the radio more about religion and health than about war and politics? Could it be possible that those foolishly naïve people who engage themselves in seeking the Truth at various more or less sincere centers are, after all, better off than the sophisticates of the great metropolises who while away their hours in night clubs?

But is it not self-evident that America cannot be judged by the business population of New York and similar big cities where the paramount struggle of man's daily life seems to be for material progress in life, even though deeply hidden in every one of them is the spark of spirituality?

If the creative artists, the profound philosophers, the writers and the scientists and above all the deep Truth Seekers are choosing California as the place where their inspiration runs high, would it not be reasonable to think that it must be due to some condition, perhaps atmospheric, of that vast land, of that burning desert near the Pacific Ocean, of those valleys and that exhilarating air in those high mountains?

Is it not plausible to believe that something is attracting the mystical world—and all true artists are mystics, are avatars—to that part of the United States? Is it not credible to reason that this part of the United States is predestined to become a spiritual capital of the future American Empire—the Vatican of all Spiritual Truth seekers?

* * *

It is a short year since my first and almost unwilling visit to California. Only a year? Indeed great things are timeless, for during that period, so short but fertilized by many centuries, in this California wonderland—where God's creations flourish overnight—Truth of the Divine Law, old as are the worlds, had crossed the Himalayas, for the ways of God are impenetrable! crossed the Pacific, annihilated space and time and come to life again by depositing the Living Knowledge in predestined Santa Barbara's "Tibetland" where the mystery of our being is to be unfolded to all Truth seekers.

The Spaceless, Timeless, Invisible Government has deposited through the medium of its Adept the Infinite Truth with its symbols—as in Shangri-La—and thus consecrated profane dwellings into a sacred Grail with its fantastic gardens where blooms the Divine Lotus, planted by unknown hands, and where the Powers-to-be built on the neighboring mountain heights the Penthouse of the Gods!

For—there is always room at the top!!!

NEW YORK—1941

THE END

Epilog

One Story Ends and Another Begins

At the encouragement of Theos Bernard, Ganna Walska's future sixth and last husband, she purchased the 37-acre Cuesta Linda estate in Santa Barbara in 1941, intending to use it as a retreat for Tibetan monks, and renamed it "Tibetland." The Tibetan monks never appeared, and sometime later, after divorcing Bernard, Madame Walska changed the name of her estate to "Lotusland" in honor of the sacred Indian lotus growing in one of the ponds on the property.

She then began her transformation from well-known socialite to legendary garden designer. Most of her energy and resources were poured into creating a botanic garden of rare plants using her natural artistic talents to create a fantasy world of exquisite beauty. To accomplish this she worked with a number of talented landscape architects and designers, including Lockwood de Forest, Jr., Ralph T. Stevens, William Paylen, Oswald Da Ros, and Charles Glass.

Madame Walska herself was a designer and loved to mass single species of plants together. She wanted the best, the biggest, and the most unusual plants available and was often willing to pay any price to get them. So determined was she to finish the work she had begun that in the 1970s she auctioned off some of her jewelry in order to finance her final creation—the cycad garden. Up until the last few years of her life, she was the feisty, intractable "head gardener" of Lotusland.

Ganna Walska died on March 2, 1984, at Lotusland, leaving her garden and her estate to what today is a public charity, Ganna Walska Lotusland. She created the performance of a lifetime and a magnificent lasting legacy - a legendary and world-class botanic garden called Lotusland.